THE NINTH CENTURY

1. Picture on the reliquary case of the cross made for Hugo of Tours

The Ninth Century
and the Holy Grail

W.J. Stein

TEMPLE LODGE

Translated by Irene Groves and revised by John M. Wood

Temple Lodge Publishing
Hillside House, The Square
Forest Row, RH18 5ES

www.templelodge.com

First published in English 1988
Second edition (under the title *The Ninth Century, World History in the Light of the Holy Grail*) 1991
This edition 2001
Reprinted 2009

Originally published in German under the title *Weltgeschichte im Lichte des Heiligen Gral. Das Neunte Jahrhundert* by Orient-Occident Verlag, Stuttgart and more recently by J. Ch. Mellinger Verlag, Stuttgart

© Temple Lodge Publishing 1991

The moral right of the translator has been asserted under the Copyright, Designs and Patents Act, 1988

All rights reserved. No part of this publication may be reproduced, stored in a retrieval system, or transmitted, in any form or by any means, electronic, mechanical, photocopying or otherwise, without the prior permission of the publishers

A catalogue record for this book is available from the British Library

ISBN 978 1 906999 04 9

Cover by Andrew Morgan
Typeset by DP Photosetting, Aylesbury, Bucks.
Printed and bound in Great Britain by Cpod, Trowbridge, Wiltshire

*To my brother Dr Friedrich Stein
who fell in the First World War
on 22 March 1915 at Prezemysl
on the day of the surrender of the
fortress by blowing up the arsenal.*

The following words were dedicated
to him by Rudolf Steiner:

> During his life his thoughts
> Were turned towards the spirit,
> So may he find in death
> The life of spirit.

---

*With him are
the thoughts of his loved ones.*

Contents

List of illustrations   x

Introduction by John Matthews   xi

Preface   1

1. **Rudolf Steiner's Visit to the Eleventh Class**   5

    Here is related how the underlying conception of this study was indicated by Rudolf Steiner on the occasion of a visit to the Waldorf School, and the method suitable for continuing the Grail-tradition.

2. **The Rise of the Grail Experiences in the Eighth and Ninth Centuries**   9

    This chapter includes (a) A passage from the *History of the Holy Grail*. (b) Narration of the *Translatio Sanguinis Domini* of Reichenau. (c) The Molsheimer Legend of Knight Hugo, who received from Louis the Pious the rose-coloured blood of the first outpouring of the blood of Jesus. (d) In Charlemagne's surroundings we find a circle of men whom the Saga mentions as receiving the blood reliquaries of the Saviour. They cultivated a German folk-Christianity. (e) As Charlemagne sealed the alliance with Roman Christianity, a new esoteric Christian stream independent of Rome became necessary. (f) This continues the impulses of Ulfilas and is through destiny connected with the esoteric Christianity of Dionysius the Areopagite.

3. **Flore and Blancheflur**   67

    This saga is an expression of a quest directed towards the Orient, *two generations before Charlemagne*, which prepared the Rosicrucian *Grail*-Christianity.

4. **Orient and Occident** 78

   Here is shown that the history of the Grail is the history of the wisdom that draws from Heaven to Earth which, in progressing from *East to West*, fills itself inwardly with Christ-Love. What threatened to be lost in Persia—the union of the Persian Christ-prophesy with the life of wisdom engendered in Greece—Charibert of Laon saved—preserving it until the time when humanity is permitted to receive it.

5. **Wolfram von Eschenbach's** *Parzival* 91

   As a way of man's inner development, as instruction for building up an organ for perceiving the working of destiny, and as a presentation of events of the Ninth Century.

6. **Pope Nicholas I and the Eighth Oecumenical Council of 869** 271

   A presentation of the struggle of the Spirit of Truth with the Spirit of Untruth. Grail-impulse and Klingsor-stream.

7. **The Grail Lineage** 281

   Here is shown that the Christ Impulse must be experienced ever anew. In the Ninth Century a family relationship was the Christ-bearer. In our time the Folk-Souls are preparing to bear the Christ.

Afterword 293

Appendix I **From the Collected Works of St Gregory the Great** 294

   The legend of Pater Nonnosus (a complement to the Waldo-Legend)

Appendix II **Introduction and Preface to the Book of Jashar** 297
   (A contribution towards the source material of Wolfram von Eschenbach)

Appendix III **St Lawrence and the Grail Tradition** 303
   of St Juan de la Peña in Spain (an indication)

Appendix IV **The Chronology of Wolfram's** *Parzival* 306

Appendix V **Text and Facsimile of two letters by Her Excellency Eliza von Moltke-Huitfelt.** 308

Notes	312
Select Bibliography	334
Index	335

Genealogical Tables, Two Surveys:
    (a) Individuals connected with the Grail-saga.
    (b) Relationships of individuals in Wolfram's *Parzival*.
	361

List of Illustrations

1	Picture on reliquary case of the cross made for Hugo of Tours
2	Portrait of Einhard, biographer of Charlemagne
3, 4	Paintings from the walls of Richenau-Mittelzell church
5	The castle of Hugo of Tours
6	Front of cross made for Hugo of Tours
7	Back of cross made for Hugo of Tours
8	Explanation of pictures on back of cross
9	Empire cross from the Imperial Treasure House
10	Picture from the Altar of the Cemetery Chapel in St Nabor
11	Picture from the Cross-Altar of St George's Church in Molsheim, Alsace
12	Ruins of Niedermünster Church; the St Nicholas Chapel and the Hochburg on Odilienberg
13	The four stages of man's inner development
14	Portrait of Empress Richardis and Charles the Fat
15	Entrance to Andlau Church
16	Details of carvings round the door of Andlau Church
17, 18	The 'Head of Lazarus'
19	Chapel of the Sacred Blood in Bruges
20	The Relic from the Chapel of the Sacred Blood in Bruges
21, 22	The Imperial Lance, Imperial Treasure House in Vienna
23	The Imagination which arises when one becomes free of the body
24	Stone Sculpture on Andlau Church
25	The Eleventh Key from the Twelve Keys of Basil Valentine
26, 27	The Rosicrucian-Alchemical Path of Knowledge
28, 29	Portrait of Pope Nicholas I
30, 31, 32	Duke Eticho and his daughter St Odilie
33	The bell from Arlesheim Church
34	Facsimile of letter from Eliza von Moltke, 26.11.27
35	Facsimile of letter from Eliza von Moltke, 27.12.27
36	The Cup in Valencia Cathedral, Spain
37	Facsimile of letter from Eliza von Moltke, 10.12.27
38	Facsimile of letter from Eliza von Moltke, 3.12.27

Introduction

The book which you hold in your hands has taken sixty years to reach print in English (although it was translated in the 1950s it remained in typescript in the Rudolf Steiner Library). Previously it has been known only through the writings of the late Trevor Ravenscroft, who met the author in 1945 and subsequently wrote about his work in two books, *The Spear of Destiny* (Spearman, 1972) and *The Cup of Destiny* (Rider, 1981). Both these books failed to give an accurate account of Walter Stein's work, and indeed misquoted it in several places. The theory of the Carolingian and Merovingian parallels with the Grail material, first advanced here by Stein, has been substantially extended in recent times, yet the present book and its author have remained in shadow—though there can be little doubt that *The Ninth Century* constitutes one of the most valuable and original works on the Grail yet to appear in any language.

Walter Johannes Stein was born in Vienna on 6 February, 1891.* He was educated at Schottengymnasium, a school run by Benedictine monks, and at Vienna University, where he studied Mathematics, Physics, and the History of Philosophy and Psychology. He seemed set upon a career as a philosopher or a scientist; until one day he picked up a volume by Rudolf Steiner, the founder of Anthroposophy. It was *Occult Science: An Outline* (1909) and it changed Walter Stein's life forever.

For the next two months he read everything he could by Steiner—a not inconsiderable feat considering the latter's huge output. Then on 19 January, 1913, Stein attended a lecture in Vienna on 'The Supersensible Worlds and the Nature of the Human Soul'. During question-time afterwards, his every thought seemed to be picked up and answered by Steiner, to whom he afterwards spoke, asking to become his pupil. Steiner told him to read Berkeley and Locke and to write a thesis avoiding the mutually opposing directions of either. From this moment Walter Stein was Rudolf Steiner's pupil, and continued to support the work of Anthroposophy until his death.

The 1914–18 war followed, in which Stein served in an artillery unit.

---

* I am indebted to Charles Lawrie and Bernard Nesfield-Cookson for all biographical information on Stein. See also my *Household of the Grail* (Aquarian Press, 1990), which contains the chapter 'Dr. Stone: Walter Stein & the Grail' by Charles Lawrie.

Under heavy bombardment, anticipating death at any moment, he seemed to see Steiner, assuring him that his time had not yet come. He survived, completing his thesis in 1917 and receiving a doctorate from Vienna University.

After the war he joined the first Waldorf School, founded on Anthroposophical principles. Though his knowledge lay in the field of the sciences he was given responsibility for history and literature. Somehow Steiner had recognised that his pupil's real strength lay in this area, and he was to be proved correct when in 1928 Stein finally published the earliest version of his book on the Grail in ninth century history.

In 1924 Stein had the first of a series of profound religious visions, culminating in a recognition of his own past lives. Looking backwards at these lead him into the period of the ninth century and he began his long study of the period and its links with the mystical subject of the Grail.

Rudolf Steiner died in 1925, leaving others to continue his work. Walter Stein began lecturing to the Anthroposophical Summer School, delivering as many as 300 lectures a year. He became increasingly absorbed in matters of world economy. In 1924 he came to the attention of Daniel Nicol Dunlop, who was organising a 'World Power Conference'. Dunlop invited Stein to assist him in the work of preparing and publishing the conclusions of the conference, and having agreed to take up the post Stein moved to England in 1933, where he was to remain almost permanently until his death in 1957.

It is clear that Stein saw the problems of economics as a type of Grail Question. Traditionally, that question is: Whom does the Grail serve? The answer, however phrased, is generally given as: Those who serve the Grail. To Stein the whole earth was a Grail and its resources were there for those who served it by their proper division throughout the world. Any possibility of such an event was crushed forever by the advent of the Second World War.

Stein's part in the great conflagration of 1939–45 has been much written about and considerably dramatised. It has been claimed that he met Adolf Hitler, in dramatic circumstances, in 1902.* Stein himself declared that he had first heard Hitler's distinctive voice at a meeting he attended in Berlin in 1932. There is no evidence at all that he ever spoke personally to the future Führer.

It has also been said that he was invited to England to advise Winston Churchill in the question of Hitler's occult practices. This is only partially true. We have seen that Stein actually came to Britain at the invitation of Daniel Dunlop. The truth of the matter seems to be that he was consulted as someone knowledgeable about the particular aspects of esotericism then rife within the Nazi party, particularly in the figures of Hitler himself (whom some have identified as a type of Klingsor) and Heinrich Himmler, the head

---

* Trevor Ravenscroft, *The Spear of Destiny* Neville Spearman, 1972.

of the SS. The latter was definitely interested in the Grail, sending a team under the command of the historian Otto Rahn, to the ancient Cathar citadel at Montségur, where it was believed the actual vessel was hidden.

Stein's approach to the Grail was wholly different. For him it was not any physical vessel that made the subject unique, but the deeply spiritual reality which transcended all such objects. His book, the book you are about to read, took the form of a commentary on what many believe to be the most important of all the many versions of the Grail story—the *Parsifal* of Wolfram von Eschenbach, written sometime about 1220.* Within this work Stein found close correlatives to actual historic personages from the ninth century, and in particular from the Carolingian and Merovingian dynasties.

We are more used to hearing of the Grail as part of the traditions surrounding King Arthur. Stein saw in the deeds and accomplishments of Charlemagne a reoccurrence of the patterns found within the Arthurian myths, and was able to identify many of the characters in Wolfram's poem with figures from the Carolingian court. He read, in the account of the twelfth century *Livre du St Graal* of the hermit who received the story of the vessel in AD 750; and in the account of the Holy Blood of Reichenau, how certain sacred relics, including an onyx cup containing the blood of Christ, were brought to the monastery of that name by its Abbot, Waldo. Delving deeper, he found Wolfram's description of the book from which he had taken his source for *Parsifal*, written by one Kyot of Provence from the teachings of the oriental Flegetanis, who wrote of the mysteries of the starry Grail. From these he began to perceive a new synthesis of material, drawn from Persian, Manichean, and other esoteric sources, which permeated the entire matter of the Grail.†

But Stein was not concerned only with sources. He states quite clearly the reasons for writing his book:

> 'The preoccupation of the Grail-Saga with the problems of Kyot, who interprets the starry script and the signs of the times—now however for the nations—is literally a burning, present-day problem. What the present can gain by a spiritual interpretation of history, this is what we wish to show: for no other reason would we engage in research into the history of the Grail.'

For Stein the starry book of Kyot-Flegetanis was a book of bloodlines, of a lineage descending from the ultimate foundation of creation—in fact, the Family of the Grail. Wolfram wrote of this at length, and of the way in which it was set in motion:

---

* A recent translation is by A.T. Hatto, Penguin Books, 1980.

† See my *Elements of the Grail Tradition* Element Books, 1990, for more about the oriental influences on the Grail myth.

'Thus the Grail Its Maidens giveth,
   in the day, and the sight of man,
But it sendeth Its knights in the silence,
   and their children It claims again,
To the host of the Grail are they counted,
   Grail servants they all shall be.'

Thus, whether hidden or revealed, the Family of the Grail enters the world and does the work of the vessel therein. This lineage has continued to percolate through history to the present time. Now it is made up of all the men and women who daily set out on their own search for the Grail, who have no need to explain themselves beyond the words of two medieval knights who visited the ruined castle of the Grail and when they returned, changed, could only say: 'Go Where we went, and you will know why.'*

Walter Stein had certainly journeyed to that castle many times, and always he returned with fresh insights and revelations into the great mystery. His book is not always easy reading—he makes demands upon his readership which twentieth century education seldom meets—but the rewards for persevering are great. A fresh understanding of the relevance of the Grail to our own time, a teaching of the ways in which we may begin to heal the Wasteland of modern life. As Stein himself puts it:

'The Grail race has the mission of expanding to cosmolitan proportions all that belongs to the narrow group, of enlarging separate interests to world interest. In our times this mission lies no longer within the family group. How the present day faces this impulse will only become clear as through our consideration of the ensuing centuries, we step by step draw nearer to the problem.'

John Matthews

---

* cf. *Perlesvaus*. Translated as *The High Book of the Holy Grail* by N. Bryant. D.S. Brewer, 1978.

Preface

Recent investigations have yielded such excellent introductory results—necessary for an historical grasp of the Grail narrative—that only a new point of view can justify further elaboration of this theme. The writer owes this new point of view to his teacher, Dr Rudolf Steiner.

The writer is a teacher at the Independent Waldorf School in Stuttgart, which was founded by Emil Molt in 1919 and, since its foundation, directed by Rudolf Steiner, who was responsible for its curriculum. This was established upon an anthroposophical knowledge of man, that is to say, a knowledge of the developing or 'becoming' human being, gained by a supersensible process. This supersensible knowledge enables the later stages of development to be already recognised in the earlier, and finds in the later appearances the metamorphoses of what was present originally as something purely germinal. Thus, the result of such knowledge, which is the true extension of Goethe's doctrine of metamorphosis, is to reveal not merely the 'product', but that which is in a state of becoming—the living, the self-unfolding.

It is the task of the teacher of history and literature, as of every other teacher in the Waldorf School, to know what may be appropriately imparted at any given age. The curriculum, in its distribution of subject matter, forms the basis of such knowledge. It lays down no laws, but expresses the needs of child nature and human nature at any given age. The pupil of the eleventh class, aged from sixteen to seventeen years, requires different matter from the pupil of the tenth class, aged from fifteen to sixteen years. In the tenth class, the Song of the Nibelungs is studied, the poem of Gudrun and Oriental history to 338 BC, the date of the Battle of Chaeronia. The syllabus for this class ends with the appearance of the young Alexander upon the stage of history. The whole course of literature and history in this class leads the children to realise that the gods once guided the destinies of mankind, but they descended to earth and became human personalities. Brunhilde, who in the Northern representation is still a divine Valkyrie, appears in the Song of the Nibelungs as an earthly woman. The god Baldur appears in human form as Siegfried; the god Hödur as Hagen; the conflict of the gods in the 'Götterdämmerung', becomes the battle of the Nibelungs with the Huns.

When Oriental and Greek history are added to the study of this literature, the picture is thereby completed. Out of the misty realms in which gods and men associated with one another man descends to earth and becomes a personality. The fifteen to sixteen-year-old needs to feel himself established upon the earth as a self-conscious human being. He likes hearing these events described in his history and literature lessons, for they show him in the evolution of humanity what he, as an individual, is going through in accordance with his own age in life. The growing boys and girls become thoroughly healthy when everything that is being presented to them during this period is brought into connection with the earth. The difference between the shepherd tribes of India, clinging for so long to their nomadic habits, and the Persians, who turned early to agriculture, is shown to have sprung from climatic conditions and the nature of the soil. Babylon is described in its connection with the clay upon which it stands, and the expression 'Egypt is the gift of the Nile' becomes easy to understand. Even the religion of these people is studied from the point of view of the influences coming from the climate and the earth. The fact that nomadic and shepherd tribes cultivate moon religions (for instance the 'Soma' cult of the Indians) is shown to be a law, and similarly that agricultural peoples worship the Sun, as in the legend of King Djemjdid, to whom Ormuzd gave the golden dagger, the plough, with which to pierce the earth. It cannot be said that such studies are prosaic; they are indeed only one of many approaches, for the next school year introduces the opposite method, which in its turn must not be called fantastic, for it corresponds to the very nature of man himself. The adolescent youth at the age of fifteen or sixteen needs the firm sense of the earth. Between sixteen and seventeen, however, he must reconquer the world of the stars, but now as one who stands established upon the earth. If this possibility is taken away from him, he is delivered over to all the suffering that comes from the forces of an ungoverned physical nature. Those alone fall a prey to greed or passion who cannot in innocent purity rise above the bodily nature to the world of the stars. The subject matter of the eleventh class provides for this need. We take the legend of 'Poor Henry', speaking of the power of pure love to restore health; we tell how the suffering Amfortas is healed by the pure fool Parzival, even though Parzival comes laden with guilt and must point for point expiate this guilt, until he finally achieves the Grail.

Concurrently there is placed before the pupil the history of human intelligence from Aristotle to the present time, wherein is shown how, in the later development of mankind, the intellect has severed itself from love, yet true knowledge comes only with loving comprehension of the known. (This is contained in the word 'philosophy', which unites Wisdom and Love.) Naturally, this does not come before the pupil as an idea, but is given by means of historical and literary examples. Parzival is the hero who comes to knowledge through pity. The pupil realises that sympathy must be found again through knowledge; that love and pity may be felt for everything in the whole world. In this way the growing youth becomes free from his body. He becomes a citizen of the wide universe, so that he may learn—as Herder says—to feel the earth as a 'star among stars'.

We have indicated here something of the whole circle of ideas and feelings which induced the author to take up the study of the narrative of the Holy Grail. The book is not intended to be pedagogical in the narrower sense, but the author believes it is his duty, side by side with the actual daily work of teaching and its more immediate educative values, to provide the material for instruction. That is what this book sets out to do.

All the important ideas which will be found in it emanate either directly from Dr Steiner himself, or have been gained by further research based upon them, in harmony with his intentions. Not that the work has not been done independently. Experience has taught us that Dr Steiner's ideas have life in them, which has not yet been exhausted in all that he was able himself to bring to fruition. The world of his ideas will never be contained in any book, for it is inexhaustible. There can be no completed work, for his Thought is *Life*, striding onward from resurrection to resurrection—a Spirit Being, showering light. We can become independent and creative when with sacred ardour we grasp the unspoken and unprinted products of Rudolf Steiner's spirit.

Walter Johannes Stein
Stuttgart
Easter 1928

1
Rudolf Steiner's Visit to the Eleventh Class

The days when Rudolf Steiner visited our school were red letter days for teachers and children alike. As he came up the steps in his black coat, his eyes beaming with love and kindliness, the children would run to meet him, seizing his hands or at least his coat-tails. He would come across the court with the children jumping happily around him, but as he passed up to the staff room they hung back with shy respect. He generally arrived in the morning. Later, when the lessons began, he visited the different classes.

On 16 January 1923, he came to the eleventh class. We were reading Wolfram von Eschenbach's *Parzival*, and had just come to the following verse when he entered the room:

> The sword will withstand the first blow, at the next it will break in twain,
> An thou to these waters bring it, from their flow 'twill be whole again.
> Yet where at its source the streamlet flows forth from its rocky bed,
> Shalt thou seek those healing waters ere the sun stand high o'erhead.* (V: 477–480)

Dr Steiner listened to what we were saying about the sword of the Grail. His custom was to listen quietly to the talk between teacher and children. He sat at the desk, looked at the class and listened very seriously and attentively; then a bright light broke over his face, his eyes shone, he stood up, and continued the lesson himself. At such times he was always very animated. He asked questions, glancing round to see who was ready with an answer. There were always the most wonderful conversations between him and the children. On this occasion he said, '*Graal*, that comes from *gradalis*; that means "gradually", "by degrees". The way of Parzival is accomplished stage by stage, from dullness, through doubt, to *Saelde*.' He took the chalk, wrote the word *Saelde* on the blackboard and said, 'That is blessedness (seligkeit). The word *soul* (seele) is in it. *Saelde* is connected with soul.'

He then asked, 'In what period did all this, that Dr Stein has told you, really happen?' The children said, 'It was the Middle Ages.' 'Yes,' said Dr Steiner, 'but we can date it more exactly. In the description of Parzival's experiences we can see very well that the conditions of the eighth or ninth

---
* The quotations from Wolfram von Eschenbach's *Parzival* are based on Jessie L. Weston's translation (London, David Nutt, 1894).

centuries are being described. Those were times of bloodshed. Men were accustomed to live among bloodshed. And at that time, too, there were wild forests everywhere, and there men fought. They still shed blood in their sacrifices. From time to time shining forms of light clad in scintillating armour passed through the forest. When they came to inhabited places, the people met together and conferred with one another, and no longer went out to fight and plunder. These knight-errants, who appeared from time to time in their flashing armour, sought to establish, in this bloodthirsty age, an order that was based on bloodshed. The central body of these knights, who were scattered about everywhere, was formed by the Knights of King Arthur, or as we may also call them, the 'Knights of the Sword'. They had their centres in Northern France and in England. But there were other knights too at that time. Now think. If Arthur's Knights were Knights of the Sword, what sort of knights could the other knights have been?'

Dr Steiner then made the children guess, and helped them, until at last one of them said, 'The others were "Knights of the Word".'

'Yes, indeed,' said Dr Steiner, 'that is quite right. The others were really "Knights of the Word". The word is a sword too, but not an ordinary one. The word is a sword that proceeds out of man's mouth. Here you see this sword is mentioned.' Dr Steiner took the book from my hand and began to read, interspersing his reading with explanations.

> The sword will withstand the first blow, at the next it will break in twain.

The Grail Sword breaks when it has grown old,' said Dr Steiner, 'therefore, that of which only the fragments have been handed down must be brought back to its source. What is old must be renewed at the living spiritual source. There the Grail Sword will become whole again.'

> An thou to these waters bring it, from their flow 'twill be whole again.
> Yet where at its source the streamlet flows forth from its rocky bed,
> Shalt thou seek those healing waters ere the sun stands high o'erhead,
> [literally, 'ere yet the day has illumined it.']

As we read on further and talked of what we read, we came to speak of the wellspring, of the source. Wolfram describes it thus: 'Above the well was a globe and on this sat a dragon'. Dr Steiner said, 'The dragon that sits above the well from which the spring bubbles out, points to the savagery of the men of that time. Parzival must conquer this savagery, the savagery of the forces of the blood.'

When I saw that Dr Steiner was prepared to say still more, I brought forward a question that we had not been able to answer. I had previously drawn the children's attention to the fact that certain events in *Parzival* are described more than once, for example, Parzival's two meetings with

Jeschute, the wife of Duke Orilus; his meeting with Sigune or with Kondrie, and his coming twice to the Castle of the Grail. So I asked, 'Herr Doktor, we have not been able to explain why it is that in the *Parzival*, the same pictures are described twice over, but the second time they are better, purer, nobler.'

Dr Steiner then said, 'The *Parzival* pictures come twice over because the old is always experienced first, and then one finds that one cannot make use of it. It is then re-experienced as something new, renewed from its spiritual source, and only then can it be used. Besides this, all Grail pictures have not only an historical, but also a universally human meaning. For example, as a human being one must always return to the source, as does Parzival, who keeps his connection with the spiritual source intact, by sending the conquered Knights—after each deed of arms—as messengers to the woman who guards the spring.'

This then is what Dr Steiner told us. He indicated two things of special importance. First he gave the period in which the Parzival age must be placed, in the eighth and ninth centuries; then he indicated a method—and this is the second point of great importance—by which the Grail narrative can be continued, viz. the way to the source must be found. In a subsequent conversation, Dr Steiner showed me that I had understood him correctly: 'Yes, the Parzival age is the turn of the eighth and ninth centuries. The descriptions that are given show this very distinctly. The amount of blood that was shed is really a characteristic of the eighth and ninth centuries.'[1]

A Note to Dr Steiner's Interpretation of the Grail Sword

Chrétien de Troyes is the poet of the '*Conte del Graal*'. He 'began the Perceval, but Death overtook him and did not allow him to relate it to the end. Three other poets, whose names are known to us, took up the work in turn. The first was Gautier de Doulens, the second Manessier, and the third Gerbert. Gerbert is of special interest to us, for his part of the poem is interpolated between that of Gautier and that of Manessier. He branches off from certain adventures of Parzival's which start from the same point as in Manessier's continuation and also lead back again to the same point in the tale. It is the point where Parzival, after many difficulties and adventures, comes for the second time to the Castle of the Grail, and '*welded the good sword* (the Grail Sword) *together again*', seeking for the meaning of the Grail and the bleeding lance. The passage in which Gerbert's name is mentioned runs literally: 'Gerbert continued the work. God granted him strength and victory to eradicate all traces of evil, so that he could finish the poem of *Perceval*, as he was instructed by the book in which the material was inscribed. Gerbert, as it is told us, began where Parzival, at the cost of much effort and labour, welded the good sword together again, inquired after the Grail, and asked the meaning of the bleeding Lance'.

Thus we learn at which point of the narrative Gerbert made his interpolation. Manessier is mentioned at the end of the complete work: 'Whoever visits this land will see the tomb resting upon four golden pillars, as Manessier testifies, who brought this matter to an end in the name of the Countess Jeanne, Lady and Mistress in Flanders, the lady valiant, whom God hath richly endowed with understanding, bravery and goodness, with courtesy, beauty and candour, with generosity and with honour; and since I have heard tell so much of her good habits, I have ended this book in her name. In the name of her ancestor I began, and none other besides set hand to it or undertook to end it. Mistress, for your sake Manessier has taken such pains to come rightly to the end in accordance with the history. *And without doubt he began with the welding of the sword.* So much has he narrated concerning it, as may be found in Salisbury where King Arthur sat, according to the testimony and proof of history. All those who journey thither may still find it sealed in parchment.

In connection with these two passages,[2] W.L. Holland, in his work *Crestien von Troies* (Tübingen 1857), p. 214, remarks, 'It must strike the reader, as Lachmann has already noticed (*Wolfram von Eschenbach*, p. 21), that both Gerbert and Manessier, who both refer to a written source, claim to be the first to resume the interrupted poem and give the same point of departure for their own work, namely Perceval's visit to the "roi pecheor" where he joins the broken sword together.'

Dr Steiner's interpretation of the Grail Sword enables us to understand this. The broken sword is the poem existing only in fragments. *Each* of the continuators must therefore begin at the point where the Grail Sword—the poem—is welded together. He who would continue the narrative must come provided with the fragments of the sword, and must appear by night beside the rock that is unillumined by the sunlight of waking consciousness. Here at the Source of Inspiration, at the Well of Kunneware (as Wolfram von Eschenbach names the woman who guards the spring), the Spiritual Sword will again be made whole out of the fragments of lingering tradition.

2

The Rise of the Grail Experiences in the Eighth and Ninth Centuries

Rudolf Steiner has said that the Grail narrative was made exoteric about the year 1180. The different Grail stories did, as a matter of fact, first become generally known at this period; but they had already been present in the souls of men since the eighth or ninth century in forms which finally took the shape given to them by Chrétien de Troyes or Wolfram von Eschenbach.[1] For the present, a few indications will be given here from which it will be evident that the narrators of the Grail story knew that the Grail experiences actually dated from the eighth or ninth century. For instance, the so-called *Grand St Graal* or, as the book is entitled, *Lestoire del Saint Graal*, relates that in the year 717 after the Passion, that is in AD 750, in the night between Holy Thursday and Good Friday, a hermit living in the solitude of the Bloie Bretagne, and beset with doubt concerning the Trinity, experienced a vision. The Saviour brought him a book the size of a hand, in which the hermit read first his own genealogy, and then the history of the Holy Grail. We have here a witness to the fact that the fashioners of the Grail legend themselves point back to the eighth century. Such a reference is itself a historical fact, and there are other historical facts also which show distinctly that the experiences which we are considering must be sought for in the eighth or ninth centuries. It is obvious that we cannot expect to find any documentary evidence in the year 750, for at that time the Grail History did not exist in *book form*, but as *vision*; therefore, facts dating back to the year 750 cannot be come upon in any other way than through references made by subsequent writers. This is inherent in the matter itself. Just the most important documents relating to the period of Charlemagne, and which have to do with our investigations, belong to a later period. This too cannot be otherwise for the original esoteric impulse only gradually becomes accessible to all, and is at first concealed in what is handed on by word of mouth. There it is still entirely *living*. I emphasise this at this point so that those who demand contemporary documents may understand that their demand cannot be satisfied. Should we then demand the impossible?

Again, a later reference to the eighth century (in this case the turn of the eighth and ninth century) is the so-called *Translatio Sanguinis Domini* of Reichenau. This is a history of the conveying of the Blood of Christ to

Reichenau (Codex Augiensis LXXXIV folio 125/136). The Latin text is incompletely published by Mabillon and also by Pertz, but published in full by F.J. Mone in the first volume of his *Quellensammlung der badischen Landesgeschichte* (Collection of the Sources of the History of Baden), published by C. Macklot, Karlsruhe 1848. On pp. 67-77 of this document will be found the 36 chapters that remain of it. (The German translation was supplied to the author at his request by Joachim Schultz whom he now wishes to thank. The notes and formulation of the Latin verses are by the author.)

I give the legend in full and with a detailed commentary so that the reader may see that a stream of historical events, which has hitherto remained almost unnoticed, developed at Charlemagne's court during the eighth and ninth centuries, which had as its central figure the Abbot Waldo of Reichenau, described in the legend as a Seeker for the Grail. The historical material is indented so that the reader, if he will, may follow the main trend of the book without studying the sources in detail.

Of the Sacred Blood of Reichenau

> 1. Thou, whose body hung on the broad stem of the Cross, O Christ, hast taken upon Thyself all the guilt of the world. I entreat Thee, illumine my confused mind with the light of Heaven, and loosen the band of my stilled tongue. Be Thou the inspiration of my spirit, be my Guide, the Leader of my actions. What Thou hast given unto me, that I may begin it, O lead Thou it to its proper end. I sing Thy praise and call upon Thee in the Name of Thine own blood, that Thou, O white Lamb, hast poured from Thy tender body. Thou camest down to me from Bosra, in Thy garment of bright colours.[2] Thou art He who alone trod the winepress. The brutish peoples follow Thee alone. Full of love and humility, like a Lamb Thou hast suffered the torment of the Cross. O Jesus, Saviour, Thou hast risen as the Lord of Death with Thy mighty power. Come to my succour, my Redeemer. Thy Resurrection broke the bonds of death asunder, and brought with it the eternal joys of the longed for life.

These are the verses with which the narrator introduces his story. He refers to Isaiah LXIII, the same chapter, as we shall see, to which reference is made in the picture given of the Cross of Niedermünster, which Hugo of Tours brought here, and which contained the relic of the first blood-shedding of Jesus. To this reference he further adds words which show the serious mood with which he starts on his work.

> 2. As I am to begin to write about the precious blood of Our Lord Jesus Christ, through which the human race has been rescued from the power of the Arch-Enemy, I should like, O Father Nonnosus,[3] to entrust

myself to your prayers, for it is at thy request and that of the other brothers that I have taken upon me a burden all too heavy for my slender faculties. For never was it right to refuse anything demanded by pious men; for obedience is better than sacrifice, and you others must not withhold from me (so liable to slip) your help and furtherance. Thus then, I shall begin the task laid upon me, to which, it is true, I am not equal, but which yet I owe to my Saviour. For what can be more worthy and salutary than to spend time in His praises and ever again to mould His glory into thoughts and words as He redeemed us by His Passion and healed our wounds by His blood? And this, ages ago, was already foreshadowed by the picture of the Lamb. Just as it once set free the people of God, the flock, from the injury of the robber through the shedding of its blood, thus also we were saved from the invasion of the enemy by the true Lamb when the stream of His blood was flowing. Of this Lamb the Apostle says: 'As Christ our Pascal Lamb was sacrificed for us.'

At the same time, to glorify the Crucified, we must remember that memorable wood whereon hung the precious limbs of the Son of God, and call to mind the radiant lustre of the Holy Cross. For on this stem of life-forces rests our salvation, our redemption. And the effectiveness of the Cross, which brings peace, extends over the whole circle of the earth to the glory of the One who hung thereon. The word Cross is in Greek, *Oraupos* (Stauros), for the reason that through the same the universe was restored (restauratus). If we thus speak of Christ, we surely must not deny His dual nature, for by His human nature He is capable of suffering (passibilis), and co-equal to God the Father through His divinity. But thee too, thou poisonous death, I should not like to pass over, for as a righteous pious man, roused by thy exceptional badness, I should like to break forth and put thee to confusion, thou whose nature is shameful enough; thou who, conceived in guilt, springest from the seed of the serpent, but dost perish through pardoning tolerance when it prevails. Whilst thou hast defiled everything with shameful sloth, thy defilement has been expunged through the absolute purity of the stream of Christ's blood. Thou hast been threatened, thou faithless death, long ago with death by the prophetic mouth of the Divine World: O Mortality I shall be thy death (mors = death), I shall be the morsel (morsus) for thee below in the depths. Thou hast taken thy terrible name, mors, from the bite (morsus) into the apple that brings destruction. Thou, who wast victorious once by the Tree, hast also been vanquished by the Tree. Whilst thou didst attack the Author of Life, thou seest thyself pierced by the barbed hook of thy dreadful shamelessness, and by thy own so biting sting. Sighing, thou wilt lament that thou goest into perdition alone when all the dead in Christ arise to life. For with greedy bite thou hast thrown thyself, as an enemy, against the Divine. Death is swallowed up in victory; death, where is thy sting?. . .

3. At the time of the renowned Emperor Charlemagne, a certain man named Azan,[4] prefect of the town of Jerusalem, heard of the virtues, miraculous deeds and incomparable battles of Charles the Great, and the burning question rose in him as to how it might come to pass that he should be able actually to behold the countenance of this great man, to enjoy his quickening and refreshing talk and to make a bond of friendship with him. Therefore he sent messengers to Rome, opened up his desire to Pope Leo,[5] asking him at the same time whether perhaps, through his intercession, it might be possible to procure for him the pleasure of a meeting with the Emperor. He promised to present the Emperor with an incomparable treasure if only by God's will it might come to pass that they should meet and that Azan be thus allowed to behold the beloved features of the imperial countenance. So precious was the treasure that neither he himself, nor his ancestors, could have acquired a more precious one, and it was certain that never yet had anything similar been brought over the sea to the realm of the Franks. And thus it came about that Pope Leo with all haste sent messengers to the imperial palace in Aix-la-Chapelle, where the Emperor at that time happened to be, told him of the petition of the prefect Azan and entreated him to grant his request. The emperor, however, looked upon such a message as of no importance, declared it to be nothing, and further made no arrangements to start out and meet Azan. When the Pope heard that the Emperor had refused Azan's request, he was painfully affected by the news. Once again he sent other chosen messengers to the Emperor and is said to have communicated to him the following: 'If thou art he whom the whole world and the surrounding universe takes thee to be, the one who is celebrated as the most famous of all, then thou shouldest, since the whole connection of things surely points to it, give thy life, and on thine own feet wander and wander until thou hast acquired such a treasure.' Through such words the Emperor finally allowed himself to be moved, for is it not by divine power that he bears his sceptre? He then quickly mounted and started on his way to Rome.

4. Full of a joyful presentiment, the town prefect Azan also started out from the city of David, on his way to meet the Emperor. On his journey he bore with him the afore-mentioned precious treasure, and thus came as far as the island of Corsica. Here, however, he was forced to remain in consequence of a great loss of strength and could not continue the journey which he had begun with such endless longing. Therefore, he sent a message to Rome and explained the cause of his weakness, asking the Emperor not to refuse but to come to him on the island. He promised him the most noble treasure which outweighed all others in worth. The Emperor, however, feared the dangers of the sea. He had

2. Einhard, biographer of Charlemagne
   Max Buchner, in his work 'Einhard als Künstler' [Einhard as Artist] has shown that Einhard bequeathed to posterity his self-portrait on the bronze doors of St Denis in Paris, which he himself had made.

always been afraid of the flowing water.[6] He, therefore, summoned all his trusty counsellors and asked their advice as to which of them he should send to the island. As, however, he found none of the others prepared to undertake the journey, he himself decided upon one, viz. the priest Einhard,[7] for he considered him to be the most suitable for all his affairs and commissions. He, therefore, ordered him to hasten to the island. But even he was full of fear before the wide stretches of the sea, and we are told that he answered the Emperor as follows: 'You may send me on land to the furthest boundaries of the earth, even to the remotest peoples and I will faithfully obey thy behest. To embark, however, upon the waterways, so full of danger and so unsafe, before this I shudder.' When the King heard this he was greatly stirred as he knew not how to find a messenger since the others also excused themselves, pointing out the dangers of travelling on the seas. And thus three days passed.[8]

5. Among the nobles of the King, however, there were two, viz. Waldo and Hunfrid. Hunfrid at that time was in charge of the whole of Istria and Waldo was Abbot of the Monastery of Reichenau. Besides this the King had committed to the latter the bishopric of Pavia and also that of Basle. After the death of the former bishops, he was for the time being to turn his care and attention to these bishoprics until the business matters in hand should be settled. For Waldo was wise in virtue and was an intimate confidant of the King, so that the latter had chosen him as his confessor. Further on we shall have to refer to him again, but for the present we must continue our story.[9]

6. Finally at the end of the third day, when the sun in its course inclined towards setting and night was gaining upon the red hues of the sky, Waldo began, among other matters which he was discussing, to urge Hunfrid, with most penetrating words, that he should undertake to become the messenger for his lord, and to journey to the Town Prefect Azan on his island: 'Dost thou not see how perturbed our Master is because he cannot get his wish fulfilled? Azan could have led to its goal the journey laid upon him; our Master, however, on his side is not able to bring about the connection with Azan.' Hunfrid took ill these words of Waldo and said: 'What thou requirest of me that I should do, thou thyself wouldst not wish to undertake,' whereupon the former replied: 'If thou wilt go, I will surely accompany thee.' As Waldo thus insisted still more strongly, Hunfrid at last agreed and pledged himself to undertake the journey.

7. Rejoicing that Hunfrid had agreed and had given his promise, Waldo, after evensong, went to the King who had retired to his bedchamber, knocked at the door and was admitted. With comforting words he relieved the King's sad mind. 'O Master,' he said, 'thou hast

a man who is prepared to go and whom thou canst send.' And in so saying he gave news to the King of Hunfrid's pledge. Then spoke the King, 'God be thanked!' and said, 'Go thou again to thy friend and ye shall both come back to me at daybreak.' Whilst Waldo was conversing thus with the King, Hunfrid sent a message to Waldo saying that on reflection he did not think of undertaking the journey upon which they had decided. But Waldo said to the messenger, 'Oh! But how can he possibly refuse to start on the journey since I have already informed my royal master of his promise?' When Hunfrid heard this he saw that, forced by circumstances, he would have to decide upon the journey. Quite early in the morning when the rays of dawn were already colouring the sky and the stars were extinguished, they both went as commanded to the palace. The King held counsel with his princes and then sent Waldo and Hunfrid to the Town Prefect with presents of immeasurable value and much money which he had collected from all corners of the earth. The two now embarked, laden with numerous treasures and after a happy voyage reached the aforesaid island. There they found Azan himself bedridden and severely ill and they presented to him the great gifts which the Emperor had sent.[10]

8. Grant, O kind Saviour, the prayer of thine unworthy servant. By the torments of Thy Cross, by the sacred shedding of Thy blood, strengthen my spirit, loosen my tongue, that I may tell of the treasure that Corsica gave us and worthily praise it.

With due reverence Azan received the fulness of the gifts sent to him by the Emperor. He was very sad, however, that the Emperor whom he had awaited with unspeakable love, had not come himself, and amongst other things which were said on this subject, the following is reported to have been said by him to the messengers: 'Truly, I am weighed down by a grave illness and it has not been granted to me, unworthy as I am, by the divine spiritual powers personally to appear before him, for whom I have yearned so long that I might behold him, and that the joy of his longed for gaze and address might flood me. Ah, if only he had succeeded in coming to me; but by the fear of the sea he has allowed himself to be deterred as often before.'

9. These then are the worthy presents, of all the gifts of the world the most desired, and the sacred treasure lofty in its value beyond all preciousness, which were brought from the island of Corsica to the ruler Charles: a vessel (Ampulle) of onyx-stone filled with the blood of the Redeemer. Further, a small cross made of gold and precious stones which contained in its four arms the blood of Christ, and bore within its centre a splinter of the Cross of our Lord. This little cross Thou, O Kind Jesus, hast deigned to send to Thy people at Reichenau for their protection and comfort. To Thee O Christ be honour and praise. There

3. (i) Waldo of Reichenau receives the Blood of Christ from the dying guardian of the Relic
   (ii) Waldo of Reichenau and his friend Hunfrid hand Christ's Blood to Charles the Great
   (Paintings from the walls of Reichenau-Mittelzell church)

4. Charles the Great rewards Waldo and Hunfrid
(Painting from the walls of Reichenau-Mittelzell church)

were also presents in this treasure: the Crown of Thorns which encircled the beloved head of our Redeemer. Further one of the Nails which fastened to the Cross the delicate members of Christ, and also wood from the Cross of our Lord on which the precious members of our Lord hung. Further a stone from the grave consecrated by the healing forces of Christ's body, besides various spices and ointments and various other gifts. And with these the Emperor was festively presented.

10. With the wonderful gifts they had received, the messengers blissfully embarked again on their boat, and smoothly sailing—as we believe, in the safe keeping of the great treasure which they bore with them—they steered their course until they came to anchor at a spot which belonged to the convent of the blessed Anastasia and which is said to be in Sicily. There Hunfrid left Waldo behind to guard the holiness of the treasure with utmost reverence. He himself, however, hastened to the Emperor who sojourned at that time in the neighbourhood of the town of Ravenna awaiting his messenger, told him of the success of the mission which he, the Emperor, had conferred upon him and described in detail the incidents of the journey, and told him also of the results of the whole undertaking. Finally he informed the Emperor where he had left Waldo with the all-holiest treasure. Full of joy at this unspeakable token of grace, the Emperor, together with his nobles and all his hosts, without delay started out barefoot on his way. And thus they proceeded on their pilgrimage with naked feet along those five hundred miles from Ravenna to the afore-mentioned spot in Sicily and found displayed there the much spoken of treasure. In all humbleness the Emperor received it and bore it with him thence. That which he himself did further for this sacred treasure is that, being a zealous worshipper of God, he laid down a great part of the treasure in his chapel so that he might always have it there, and a certain part, however, he shared out and sent of it to other holy places.[11] It is, however, out of place here to describe this in all its details lest this my account be all too lengthy and the zealous reader become wearied. For have I not from the very beginning of this story pledged myself to describe in detail only the manner in which the redeeming blood of Christ, enclosed in the little cross, came in more recent times to the island of Reichenau?

11. Highest glory, honour and praise be to Thee O Christ,
    For Thou holdest the ruling sceptres of the uppermost spheres,
    That full of mercy towards the wide lands of our Earth
    Thou shouldest bestow just on our region such a comforting gift.

After all these things had been brought to a happy end and the imperial commission was accomplished by Waldo and Hunfrid with good success, the Emperor took counsel with his princes and conferred with them as to how he might reward his faithful messengers for their trouble and present them with fitting gifts. As all his counsellors agreed to such a plan, he is reported to have said to them somewhat as follows:[12] 'You alone have carried through our commission so efficiently, whereas no one else in my realm has been willing to venture on this so dangerous journey. Therefore, with all confidence, ask what you will of my possessions, and I will grant it to you without delay and proclaim the same to everybody.'

12. Then the Abbot Waldo made known his dearest wish and asked the Emperor for a privilege for his brothers in Reichenau. This he obtained on most favourable terms, so that he not only had the privilege granted to him but also much land and money besides, so that he was able to endow the Abbey with an excellent administration.

13. Moreover as regards the afore-mentioned places for the bishopric of Pavia and the Bishop's seat in the land of Basle, his request was granted by the Emperor. What he asked was to appoint to each place its own Bishop and further that the Emperor should shew himself as a true man of God by granting his full support to this independent administration.

14. The unique excellence of Waldo's virtues and the qualities of his character made it impossible that he should be passed over in silence.[13] After some time he also became the Rector of the Monastery of St Dionysius (i.e. of the Abbey of St Denys near Paris) the Martyr of Christ. The Emperor had selected him for this post because, on account of his devotion to God and his position as the most intimate confidant of the Emperor, he was found worthy of it. But here Waldo found the discipline of the monastic life was almost destroyed and the brethren more devoted to a worldly than to a spiritual life. Quickened by the mighty zeal of divine fire, he sought immediately by forceful means to coerce the renegades again into obedience to the rules of the Order. So much so that he even himself led armed soldiers, when he, as the tales do tell, penetrated into the Chapter and quelled the rising of those who obstinately resisted as it were in battle. Nevertheless he had, up to the last moment, trusting to the higher grace of God, taken care for their salvation by urging them to observe the rules of the Order which they had forsaken, not only by resorting to force after ceaseless warnings but through the prior example of gentle pleading. Thus out of degenerate brethren he made modest, zealous and obedient ones. O blessed man, whose memory will never be extinguished in this place, whose name will ever be praised so long as the earth continues its course.[14] For the brothers are said to have been devoted to him with so great a love and to have shown their dear Father such honour that when he forsook the

instrument of his body they had a light uninterruptedly burning on his grave both day and night. This is said to have been in an apse. Indeed, even in our days this custom is perpetually observed by the love of those devoted to his memory.[15]

15. Hunfrid, on the other hand, was already aged and less desirous of temporal gifts, and thus he is said to have brought his requests before the Emperor in the following way: 'O my Lord, I am already old and must think more of the future life and less it behoves me to trouble about worldly honours. Therefore, I seek from you nothing else as a reward than the little cross in which Christ's blood is contained. Do not refuse this gift, the request of thy humble servant.' When the Emperor heard this he was at first reluctant, yet as he wished to keep his royal promise as is befitting, he did not refuse to fulfil the request.

16. When Hunfrid had finally thus obtained the fulfilment of his wish and had received the desired treasure, he built a monastery in Schännis[16] (for he was at that time lord of Churrätien) to the praise of God, and to the honour of the cross and blood of Christ.[17] At the same time, both for the Emperor Charles and his own salvation, he handed over the holy cross to this place of God and had it worthily set up to be worshipped, and when in addition a number of sacred things had been placed there in safe keeping, he indefatigably had hymns sung in praise of these precious relics as long as he lived. But when he himself departed from this earthly life, his son Adalbert inherited this cross along with his father's other possessions.

17. Only to the honour of the blood of our Lord and this cross be it permitted to insert here the account of a memorable miracle which happened at that time as follows: When Adalbert had come into possession of his father's estate according to the rights of inheritance, as mentioned above, it happened that Ruodpert, a vassal of the Emperor Ludwig, by cunning flattery induced his master to make Churrätien over to him, and so it happened that Adalbert was driven away and Ruodpert seized his possessions.

Denuded of all that his father had bequeathed to him, and bereft, as it were, of all his belongings, Adalbert, now only in possession of the blood relic, fled to his brother who was then in possession of Istria. With his help he gathered a host of men and marched against Ruodpert who was just then in the town of Zizers.[18] Ruodpert wanted to flee as he was not in a position to fight. However, on arriving before the town, he was struck on the knee by a horse—we are told that it was a black horse which was being led by its bridle and kicked out—and he immediately fell from the horse he was riding. He was straightaway laid on a shield and since the work of death was quickly completed, he departed miserably from this present life. Certainly this occurred by the help of the divine blood and the splinter of the holy cross, which help—one cannot doubt it—was vouchsafed to Adalbert who, as was his wont, bore the little cross with him and thus gained the victory over his enemy. Adalbert, moved with pity, himself accompanied with his hosts the body on the bier and handed it over to the monastery of Lindau to be buried. Then he returned to his inheritance which he kept in possession to the day of his death, ruling over it with a strong hand.

18. After him, his son Udalrich received the paternal inheritance. He too guarded the treasure in a worthy way to the end of his days.

19. His daughter succeeded him, Emma by name, who as co-heiress of the paternal possessions guarded carefully the precious wood which had come down to her from her father and she, while still alive, handed it over to her son Udalrich.

20. At this time a certain Walther and his wife Swanahild (Schwanhilde)[19] felt in a wonderful way a burning desire to acquire the immeasurably precious treasure, for both were deeply devoted to the divine and busily occupied themselves in the praises of the divine world and the saints. Now it came to pass that Udalrich[19a] sought from Walther and Swanahild their daughter to wife, and obtained her as his spouse; they, however, the parents, took this opportunity of asking for the cross[20] and they obtained it from him. As soon as they had obtained it, they set it up in the chapel which they had built in their castle with due prayers and worship.

21. Upon this there straightway followed a sign from heaven which we can hardly pass over in silence. The mistress in her devotion to God wanted to hide the little cross entirely, lest some nobleman should perceive the precious ornament and desire it. Therefore, she hung it behind another cross in the same chapel. But on entering again she found it hanging in front. In a miraculous way it had changed its place. In the belief that one of her people had brought about the change and removed it from the back of the cross to the front, she scolded her servants about it severely and had the cross replaced in its former position. But, as soon as she returned, she found the little cross once more hanging in front. Then only she recognised the holy and miraculous deed and, if I am not mistaken, was strengthened in the belief that the Redeemer who shed His blood for the whole of humanity on no account wished that the health-giving force of the holy wood should be kept hidden, but that, on the contrary, He wished that this healing force should be revealed to His praise.

22. We believe further that we should not pass over a second miracle in silence. There was a state of hostility at this time between the Duke Burkhard of Swabia[21] and the above mentioned Walther. The Duke

had assembled a great host of men and besieged Walther's castle. As he was about to storm it and the men of the castle were filled with terror, the devout mistress stepped forth to meet the enemies raising the holy cross. In a loud voice she implored and begged them by the love of Almighty God and the sacredness of the day (it just happened to be Maundy Thursday) that they should desist from this gruesome fight and allow the inhabitants of the castle solemnly to keep this day in peaceful rest in common with all other Christians over the whole earth. They, however, having lost all fear of God, violently insisted on battle and threateningly declared they would on no account leave off before they had won the victory. Finally, one who was bolder than all the others climbed over the rocks to the summit full of hope that he could penetrate into the castle. Then a priest who belonged to the inhabitants of the castle struck the enemy by hurling a mighty stone against him so that he fell backwards with his shield, probably half dead. In truth he was a poor fool who should dare to resist so great a might raying forth from the cross. When those who were storming the castle saw what had happened they desisted from the fight, and fear calmed the strife. For who can doubt that Christ through His blood and His holy cross stood by and helped His people against the enemies? He who already in this sign triumphed over the old fiend and redeemed all mankind through the shedding of His blood.

23. After these things had been accomplished to the praise of God, the two kept the Cross of the Lord safely for a long time and firmly resolved to give it to no one else as long as they lived. After the end of their days, however, so they vowed, it was to be brought over to the island convent of the Blessed Virgin Mary. O how ignorant they were of the higher guidance and of that which was predetermined by this higher guidance as that which must happen.

24. Further my discourse shall continue to tell of the valuable treasure, how, in the end, it was brought to the lovely island of Reichenau. Grant me, O Son of God, grace and strength for this work.

Meanwhile, it happened that our mistress visited the monastery of Reichenau in order to pray there, and after that to make a pilgrimage from there to the most revered shrine Zurzach.[22] When on her way she had reached Muneheresdorf,[23] the last resting place before Reichenau, the Chaplain, who without his mistress's knowledge bore the little cross with him, asked her where he should lay it down. At this she was greatly astonished and reproached him, asking how he dared to take it with him without her orders.

Oh what thoughtlessness which was yet to serve for the salvation of many! Oh great miracle, always to be praised by the monks of the island! Must not one believe that Thou O Christ hast wanted to give a sign from heaven, and thus, through the good hap of it being called to mind, for the salvation of the monks of Reichenau and also for the people throughout the land, hast taken care that Thy Name be eternally honoured?

25. Therefore we sing unto Thee O Christ, exalting Thy glory,
   For Thou broughtest at costliest price of Thy blood to the brethren
   With glorious pledge a salvation and crowning.

Now when Swanahild came to the monastery, quite secretly bearing the little cross with her, she was reverently received. A suitable room was allotted to her and some brethren were appointed to serve her. Now when it was evening and the time approached when 'Phoebe from her nocturnal ship rays down her light unto earth', she had a lantern lit and placed before the little cross. Then the brethren sought to discover what kind of a sacred thing this could be. She, however, very much wished to conceal the true facts of the matter and explained that these were relics of Saints which she, for her salvation, was in the habit of always having with her whether at home or on journeys. Yea, so firmly had she resolved to keep secret from all the knowledge concerning this precious treasure, that she would not even reveal it to her brother Udalrich[24] who at that time was gate keeper of that monastery and must have been closer to her confidence than the others. When these, however, one after the other, urgently begged her that she should reveal to them the true circumstance, she allowed herself to be prevailed upon by their insistent request and revealed the secret so far concealed. Then the brethren rejoiced highly and began to put it to her that she should for this night set up this sacred jewel in a basilica. She, however, refused and would not agree that even for a moment the relic should be removed from her. But the brethren replied, 'It cannot be that any precious relic remains outside the church. It is far more seemly to bear it into the House of God, where in a more worthy way the service of honour is rendered, than if it remained in a profane place!'

Thus, as the brethren did not cease their begging and even her own vassals joined with them, she allowed herself to be persuaded, and gave at last her consent which she had previously refused. One especially of her vassals named Tougolf[25] was most insistent that she should grant their request. And, in truth for doing this, the fortunate man later on experienced a miraculous help, which I shall here pass over but shall describe in the right place. Full of joy, the brethren now carried the holy treasure with them and proceeded to the Church of the Blessed Virgin Mary, where they set it up with all reverence, after which they informed the rest of the brethren of the happy event.

26. When the brethren had heard all this, they began, full of unspeakable joy, at the first dawn of morning, 'When in her rosy

chariot Aurora soars up to the heavens'[26] to pour water into a vessel and to consecrate this water by immersing the little cross, in order at least to have health-bringing consecrated water for making the sign of the cross, in case the mistress should deny the miraculous gift itself to their request. For as yet they did not know how it would end. Through the enjoyment of this water certain sick ones felt themselves instantly healed. One of the brethren in particular who had been laid low with a long and weary illness was instantly made whole again, in a miraculous way, as he himself testified through the enjoyment of the health-giving water.

27. Then the brethren lifted up the cross in deepest humility and carried it barefoot in procession round the monastery, praying fervently that the blood of the Saviour might be bestowed upon them as a gift, and that this incomparable treasure should for their everlasting comfort and in accordance with the gracious will of Christ, not be removed again from the monastery. Thus, singing praises, they reached the Chapel of St Kilian.[27] There the mistress whom they had called thither, was awaiting them in prayer. Outside, however, the brethren threw themselves down on the ground in the form of a cross and sent five of the older monks to the mistress, among whom was her brother Udalrich whom they selected the more willingly for the purpose of conveying the message to his sister; for they thought that his words would doubtless carry more weight with her. These, therefore, entreated her, by the love of our Saviour who redeemed us by His cross and blood that she would after all present this little cross to the blessed Mother of God and Virgin Mary, so that it might shine forth in glory in the temple of God and remain there for the eternal salvation of *all*. They promised her to bring before Christ and His Holy Mother perpetual prayers and ceaseless worship, and to continue in this untiringly, as well as to do whatever they could for her in worldly obedience.

28. Swanahild, however, received this request with great reluctance. She reflected and in the end she is said to have spoken somewhat as follows: 'How can I decide in this matter without my husband? Without his consent and his advice I dare not fulfil your request. Besides, already long ago, I have vowed a sacred vow and firmly resolved never to let this precious jewel out of my hands as long as I live, or allow myself to be bereft of such comfort as long as I continue here in the body. But, after my death, this I have vowed, the little cross shall forthwith be given over to the Blessed Virgin Mary.' After these words, full of joy, she took to herself the little cross and departed. The community of brethren, however, she left behind in deepest grief.

29. Thou, however, O Jesus—praise to Thee—in Thy mildness and

gentleness hast turned again unto joy the souls who were turned so sadly, and hast changed grief into radiant rejoicing.

Now when Swanahild, on her journey to Zurzach, reached her inn in Erchingen[28] and all, after supper, being wearied went to bed, she too lay down to rest. And when already the greater part of the night was over, she was suddenly shaken with violent shudders of fever; sweat streamed over her body as though she were laved with hot water. Full of fear that death was approaching she called her people and told them of her painful complaint. Then Tougolf, of whom we have spoken above, hearing her lament, answered—and the rest agreed with him: 'We believe, O Mistress, that an illness has befallen thee because thou hast denied the request of the venerable brethren and has left behind so many servants of Christ in painful confusion.'

30. Then at last she clearly saw the reason for her illness and hurriedly ordered that the little cross should be taken down to the monastery. As, however, her people sought to excuse themselves because of the difficulties of a night journey and requested postponement until the morning, she said: 'I shall not live till morning, nor see the light of a new day, therefore hasten that ye need not share my suffering any longer than till tomorrow. Go, endeavour in all haste to fulfil the vow made in my need.' She felt herself in the grip of an intolerable oppression, and did not believe that she could escape the power of death if the carrying out of this matter were to be delayed a moment longer. As soon as, with firm and unshakeable consciousness, she had ordered what was to be done, she felt forthwith a wonderful and incredible relief and knew herself restored. Yea, she even herself accompanied her messengers who were carrying the little cross down to the monastery, as far as the outer gate—barefooted—not fearing the freshly fallen hoarfrost which covered the ground.

31. In the early twilight, when Titania's torch was chasing away the golden stars, the messengers reached the monastery. They laid down the precious treasure in the above mentioned chapel of St Kilian. And so it came to pass in a wonderful manner, that the cross, at the same hour in which it was taken away on the day before, arrived here again on the next day. The messengers, calling one of the brothers aside, conveyed to him the kind and friendly greetings of their mistress and showed him the cross so unexpectedly brought back. They described to him what had happened to their mistress on the way and explained how she, tormented by severe pain, sent back the sacred treasure, thus relating each of the events one after another.

32. The brother was at first astounded at the unhoped-for sequence of events. However as he considered these things he was filled with joy. At their request he fetched Udalrich without delay; to him they handed the

cross and he, full of impatience and joy, caused the news to be announced to all the brethren. These all felt comforted in their hearts and rejoiced deeply. Without delay they gathered together and proceeded barefoot to the chapel, and with the sign of triumph lifted on high they walked in procession round the monastery. They carried it into the temple of the pure Virgin Mary, with joy and praise. There all the monks of the island gathered in a circle, candles were lit everywhere in the church. With bells ringing and with fervent voices they began to sing 'Te deum laudamus'. When the singing was over Udalrich took up the health-giving holy cross, placed it on the altar of the eternal Virgin Mary, precisely in accordance with the wish of his sister, as conveyed to him by her messengers and in deep humility held it up before the praying brethren. Thus sadness was changed to joy. Then they decided that henceforth they, as well as their successors, would every year, as an everlasting custom, celebrate worthily and festively the day on which this precious sign had come to Reichenau. They designated the 7th of November of the 925th year of the Lord as the day on which the precious treasure came to the island. And in order that this transference be never forgotten, but for ever remembered, they had it recorded in their book of rules in which the other festivals of the saints were to be found.

33. But we may by no means pass over in silence a great miracle which happened on the very same day. Tougolf, whom we have mentioned before as a vassal of Swanahild, had a son who from birth onwards had been weak in the structure of his limbs. For ten or more years he had been lame and unable to walk along the ground with his feet. He lacked all firmness of limb for any kind of walking, and remained bedridden. Nevertheless on the very same day when the precious jewel came to the island, thenceforth to remain there, his bones and his weak limbs, by the grace of God, became strong and sound and the child received back his longed-for health. Who does not see the merit of Tougolf revealed in the healing of his son? Was he not, as mentioned, the most importunate with his mistress? He it was who laid it close to her heart on no account to deny the request of the servants of Christ, but to present the glorious jewel to the monastery.

When the father came home and beheld the greatness of the miracle which had been accomplished on his son, and moreover observed that the miracle had happened just on this very day, he, on coming to the monastery again a little later, announced this miraculous event, and all gave thanks to God and ascribed to the merits of the father the healing of the son.

34. How can I so praise Thy radiant splendour, O Blood,
    Which flowed from the body of the pure and holy Christ,

That everywhere in the world Thy nature should radiantly beam forth,
For Thy flowing Blood healed the misery of the world.

After the pilgrim in great awe had sent the little cross to the monastery, she continued her journey safe and well to Zurzach, a place which we have already mentioned. After she had completed her business there, although she should have returned by another route, she dared not—because of the terror already described—do otherwise than return to the monastery by the way she had come. Thus she came to the chapel of St Kilian, prayed there, and only then greeted the brethren who came up to her, relating to them the sequence of events in their proper order, as was reported above, telling them all that had happened to her on the way through her own guilt. Then bending her body, she prostrated herself on the ground, and confessed herself guilty of having acted wilfully against God and His Saint and also against the brethren whose importunate prayers she had so obstinately refused. When she had received absolution from them she asked to have the holy little cross shown to her. Full of reverence she took it into her hand and then handed it over to them forever, to be kept safely in a case in the House of God to the honour of the holy Virgin. Also she humbly requested the community of brethren to include her and her husband Walther in their holy prayers, and with her whole heart promised them henceforth her services and entire obedience. They agreed to her request and promised diligently to pray for both of them at all times. At this she was greatly rejoiced and made a vow that she, as an earnest servant of God, would send over to the House of God, in honour of the holy cross and Blood of Christ, whatever should be needed of oil, of tallow and other things for the upkeep of the lights. This vow she fulfilled humbly and faithfully year by year, entrusting the care of this holy service to her brother who was still in the bloom of youth. And, because he was always ready for further reverence and obedience to God, he willingly took over the duty put upon him by his sister, and with great diligence carried out all she had asked. That will be further elaborated later on.

35. When all these things were accomplished Swanahild finally commended herself to the divine spiritual world, to the health-giving cross and healing Blood of Christ and to all Saints, bade the brethren farewell and, departing with good wishes, returned home full of unspeakable joy. As she arrived home from her journey, Walther her husband at once enquired where the little cross was. When he learnt that she had not got it with her he became very angry and reproached her bitterly. She however spread before him in detail the whole sequence of events and related what she had encountered on the journey and how, under great terror and heavy oppression, she had handed over the little cross to the monks who had so urgently besought

it for their monastery. Finally she closed her story with the words: 'Truly I confess, had I not sent the worthy Sign in all reverence to the monastery, I, seized by the most violent pains, would have fallen a victim to death and never have seen the dawn of the following day.' As her husband heard these things he marvelled greatly. His anger changed to wonder and he was appeased. In the end he praised the divine powers for what had happened and offered thanks to the Lord and His Saints. When later he himself came to the monastery, he confirmed the donation with his wholehearted consent.

He commended himself then to the prayers of the monks and lifted up by their strong consolations, he departed full of joy.

36. Now that I have completed the narration of all these events we will continue concerning the above mentioned brother . . .

The legend here breaks off unfinished.

This legend concerning the conveying of the holy Blood to Reichenau shows clearly that the writer of the legend wishes to bring the idea of the Grail into connection with Charles the Great and his environment. Definite people are clearly referred to, and they are placed in a light in which the rest of the historical tradition is not placed. Persons who in Einhard's description do not appear clearly are here purposely placed in the foreground.

Further, although the Translatio Sanguinis was only written in A.D 950 it is, nevertheless, a valuable document. For it shows that already 150 years after the event a strong tradition existed of the presence of each of the two streams which we have here especially to bear in mind. One of these streams is the Latin, principally represented by Einhard; the other, which is represented by Waldo of Reichenau, fosters rather what is characteristically Germanic (see note 9 and p. 62 'Roman and Grail Christianity at the Carolingian Court'). Only one with the knowledge of these two currents could characterise these things just as the writer of the legend does. But the presence of these two currents is a fact that comes clearly into evidence within history but fails to appear clearly in the ordinary accounts of history. In no wise can the writer of the legend be looked upon as the originator of the tradition, but rather must be seen that after the lapse of 150 years he was still conscious of the contrast between the Latin and German currents.

We add to this Waldo legend a second one which we give to the reader because from it can be clearly seen that Waldo of Reichenau was not the only Grail-seeker at the court of Charles the Great. We learn to recognise a second seeker of the Grail in the Knight Hugo. Step by step the reader is made acquainted with the circle of friends who served the Grail in the environment of Charles the Great and Louis the Pious.

The Legend of Hugo the Knight

The following legend is drawn from an ancient manuscript which, according to Grandidier, dates from the year 1434 and belongs to the cycle of legends dealing with the journey of Charlemagne to the East. This document, therefore, came into existence much later than the Translatio Sanguinis. This late tradition with all its details can, however, be easily reduced to its original historical nucleus. For all that is narrated by the writer of the legend with great detail can be traced in the historical tradition if this is only studied with the help of the legend. From this point of view our second narrative is likewise an important document. The document of the year 1434 was unfortunately destroyed by fire in Strasbourg in 1870. But Grandidier still had the opportunity of seeing it and has given us an extract of it. In his *Histoire de l'église de Strasbourg*, 1776 he mentions on page 362 that this manuscript was copied by Mr. de Laboureur Prévot de St Pierre-le-Vieux in 1698 and that he, Grandidier, is in possession of a copy of this copy. Knowing at least this extract of Grandidier, we are able to see that the essential content of this manuscript has passed into the work of Pater Lyra which is still in existence both in Latin and in German. In its Latin edition this work bears the title of 'Historia de Antiqua Sancta Miraculosa Cruce, quae in Templo Societatis Jesu, Molshemii pro veneratione devote asservatur Collecta. In gratiam piae Congregationis subtitulo Agoniae Christi Salvatoris. Opera et labore Cujusdam Sacerdotis ex eadem societate. Anno MDCLXXI (1671), Molshemii. Permissu Superiorum Typis Episc. Arg. apud Jo. Henric. Straubhaar. Sumptibus Caspari Rösler Bibliop.' In the library of Strasbourg it bears the catalogue number: M 18160 and the German copy bears the title: 'Historia dess uhralt-heilig- und wunderthätigen Creutzes, welches in der Kirchen der Societät Jesu zu Molsheim auffgehalten und andächtig verehrt wird, erstlich in lateinischer Sprach von einem Priester gemelter Societät beschrieben, jetzo aber in das teutsch übersetzt, und zu einem Newen Jahr denen löblichen Bruderschafften, deren Herren Burgern und jungen Gesellen daselbsten verehrt. IM Jahr Der GebUrt ChrI JesU Unseres eIntzIgen ErLösers. Molsheim (1672)—No M 18161.

Both books are in the Strasbourg library. We publish [a translation of] the German text abbreviated only in a few passages:

(Ch. IV in the original German) Charles, grandson of Charles Martel[29] and son of Pippin, King of France, named 'the Great' by reason of his manifold and glorious deeds, had ruled for a span of 47 years in laudable manner, both the Roman Empire, towards the West, as well as France, and had spared no effort to promulgate and to defend the only true Catholic Religion. Like to the sun, far and wide he spread triumphantly the luminous rays of his name. This is recorded by the above mentioned written history book[30] which describes him by means of a few but none the less glorious titles of honour.

There lived at that time (so the record runs) a King in France who was great in might, honour, riches, courteous in manner, fortunate in his ruling, endowed with beautiful and virtuous children, and (which is the most important) ardently Catholic, and whole-heartedly devoted to the teaching of Christ... Now this King Charles was well renowned for his victories in Germany, Spain, France and Hungary (Pannonia) and he was an invincible warrior of the Christian Catholic Faith, a never ceasing enemy of paganism and idolatry (of which Saxony can give sufficient proof), a mainstay of the Apostolic chair, a heroic destroyer of heresies in the time of Popes Adrian and Leo, and an arch-uprooter of all vice and shame. It was his custom to tackle nothing that was of importance without the counsel and help of the most excellent, the wisest and the most experienced men. For military purposes he availed himself of the services of the brave, dauntless and well-proved heroes Gerald, Roland, Theodoric, Rudolf. His Royal court was ruled by Echardus and Volradus (Volrautus). The city and the municipal affairs were entrusted to Eschinobaldus (Erschinobaldus) and Eginardus. Aluinus (Alcuinus), Albinus and Clement helped the King in science and learning when matters of great import called for solution.

Likewise in this time (thus speaking in the words of an ancient chronicler) [*verba sunt in historici* in MS] there lived in the kingdom a mighty and wealthy knight, Hugo by name. He was wedded to a matron, pious and retiring, generous and impeccable both in word and deed, whose name was Aba (Hugo dictus habens uxorem nomine Abam timentem Dominum). Her liege and spouse was the gentlest of all men; of noble birth, mighty in all matters of the world, peace-loving at home, brave and daring in warfare, wealthy of estate, a patron of the poor, generous towards strangers, kindly and gracious towards his own people. He ranked first and foremost in the King's grace. None other's converse did the King like better, and none other's counsel sought he than Hugo's. He was—to put it briefly—the King's most confidential, chief and noblest, dearest servitor. Above all His Majesty felt assured that he was not only a constant lover of truth and justice, but also intelligent, prudent, of good intent and wholly imbued with honesty. Thus the prince is described by the simple-minded but candid writer,[31] who can be trusted all the more because he is in accord with Gebweiler in his life of St Odile.

The record runs, he says, that Hugo was born in the duchy of Burgundy, being of princely origin, and that he lived a sincere, earnest and devout life. He lived in marriage with the pious lady Aba, and he enjoyed high renown and favour at the court of Charles, King of France, by reason of his great virtue and justice. The King availed himself of Hugo's services in all the most important affairs, knowing full well that everything entrusted to his care would not be neglected or abandoned but that it would be brought to a successful end by means of his faithful and diligent care. His good repute with the King as well as with the people was such that it was commonly held that the welfare and prosperity of the entire realm were mostly to be attributed to Hugo's skill. Therefore, the wise King thought that both he as well as his realm could never fare better than when he availed himself of the services of a man who always had God before his eyes, who was a man according to God's own heart, who shone before all men with his good example, so pure of heart and God-loving that one could well trust his judgement and counsel. Nor was he ever disappointed if it be considered that as long as the King followed the advice of those wise men and accepted their judgement, fortune would abide firmly with him and his realm 'spread like unto a cedar'. But alas! as the loftiest trees are sometimes shaken by the most terrible storm, whereby the poet's words are confirmed (Turbarum speciosa domus fraudisque, maligna Aula est).

> Uproar, pursuit and fraud,
> Full oft they meet at court;
> Be loyal, just and above all wise,
> For envy can bring thy fall.

For this reason I will dwell with greater detail on the description of the thunderclap that burst so suddenly over Hugo's head: partly because our miraculous cross will again be made manifest in the jocund clouds of happiness after the sun has again fought its way; partly too, because it should be recognised how uncertain is the position of those who place too great a trust in the grace of high rulers.

Jealous Courtiers Plot how to bring about Hugo's Fall

The shadow is the disfavour of the body, but it is also the inalienable companion of virtue. With envious eyes it always watches the favour gained by chivalrous deeds and virtues. Socrates has said well, that for the ungodly nothing is harder to endure than the happiness of the pious. They are in truth of the spider's brood, sucking poison from the loveliest flowers. At the price of great harm Prince Hugo learnt the nature of these malevolent men, and a heavy toll he paid for the lesson. His princely virtues which had gained for him the love of so many filled his enemies with the gall of bitter hatred, and the poison of envy. Wherefore, so the story tells us, as men of piety cannot dwell side by side with those of evil mind, some of the envious courtiers began to plot how they could best upset Hugo's chariot of honour. In order to achieve this they deemed it right above all to make Hugo hateful in the eyes of the King and to deprive him of the King's favour—thus they talked among themselves. 'Unless Hugo be lifted out of the saddle of grace,' they said, 'he will never be caught in the meshes of misfortune. For he who is protected by the favour of the sceptre and crown[32] is far too safe; it is intolerable and altogether beyond endurance that Hugo should have the pre-eminence in all matters of state; as if we others were nothing and without avail, being the King's counsellors only in name.' Even if Hugo be the moon at court, still it is not right that he obliterate the stars. For after all—was there no victory gained, no matter happily settled, no difficulty of State solved before the arrival of Hugo? Can the well-being of King Charles rest on no other foundation than on Hugo? Is he alone the Atlas, so that none other can offer him support and assistance? No building stands firmly on one stone alone, no kingdom on the judgement of one official. To put too much trust in one man is the source of all royal decline; for his hand would at all times be too ready to reach out for the crown and have the sceptre in his power who had taken possession both of the King's as well as the people's heart. Nothing is more unreliable than the mob who so easily fly to arms and rebel against the appointed authorities whenever a mere semblance of new freedom appears, for a fresh yoke always seems less heavy than one to which they are accustomed. What? If the country were to be burdened by new taxes in view of approaching peril or any other emergency, would the people not then flock around Hugo like unto a sacred Jeroboam? What misfortune and disaster would then result from this? Surely it is necessary without hesitation or delay to consider how to eliminate from the court this Burgundian as a suspicious element before his power grows still greater. His dismissal from the royal Court will prove to be of great benefit for the latter, and bring peace. It must and shall be brought to the King's notice, that to love one, only one, is to hate the whole of one's country—and to lean on one too much is the last step before a fall. The cover must now be lifted from the pot, and Hugo's cunning, far-reaching and dangerous advice must be made known to the whole royal council.'

These and similar traps were laid by the hardened enemies of the innocent Hugo, by means of which he was ultimately drawn to his destruction and was robbed of all his honour and rank.

Hugo is Charged with having Insulted the Royal Majesty

Historical remark: Hugo of Tours and Matfrid of Orleans were sent as commanders of the Frankish troops to the Spanish Mark in the first half of the year 827. At the Frankish court the message had been received that Abderhaman II had sent an army under the command of his relative, Abu Marvan, which was supposed to have already arrived in Saragossa. Hugo and Matfrid proceeded too slowly, so that the Spanish Mark was entirely devastated. Why it happened that the two proceeded so slowly the documents do not tell us. It appears, however, that there was a sort of opposition between these two and Bernard of Barcelona, who was at that time in possession of the Spanish Mark. Bernard is the son of that William, with whom Wolfram von Eschenbach later dealt in his 'William of Orange'. Of Bernard the story goes that he exercised his magic on the Emperor Louis the Pious. It is to evil sorcery that Bernard was supposed to owe both his unlimited power as well as his all too strong influence with the Empress Judith. 'Dubium non est, sicut multis est notum, quod a quibusdam praestigiis atque diabolicis illusionibus ita mentes quorundam inficiantur proculis amatoriis, cibis, phylacteriis, ut in insaniam versi a plerisque judicentur dum proprias non sentiunt contumelias' (Mansi XIV, 595). In this connection it appears to be a remarkable fact that in the poem 'Der Wartburgkrieg', Wolfram von Eschenbach is called Herr Terramer. According to Clarus 'William Duke of Aquitaine, a mighty man of this world, a saint of the Church, a hero in legend and poetry', Münster, Theissig 1865, page 132, this Terramer is identical with the general Abderhaman.[33] In the 'Wartburgkrieg', however, the devil Nasion appears. He is sent by Klingsor to Wolfram in order to tempt him. Naso is, strange to say, the pseudonym for Bernard of Barcelona (p. 329, Ludwig der Fromme, Vol. I, Simson, *Jahrbücher der deutschen Geschichte*). Has the poet of the 'Wartburgkrieg', stimulated by the history of the 8th and 9th centuries, purposely mixed up these names? In the language of the 'Wartburgkrieg' the all-too-slow progress of the Grail-bearer Hugo and his friend, Matfrid, had been a trick played on the devil Naso (Bernard of Barcelona). This was the accusation brought against them:

(Chap. VI) When Hugo's antagonists had thus plotted to accuse him, deeming the situation to be sufficiently compromising, they thus accosted the King in a propitious moment:

'Invincible, great and mighty King, and gracious Sovereign! Inasmuch as it is manifest to the whole world, acknowledged by the enemies and joyously accepted by the subjects that your Majesty's wondrous mind, victorious arms, and prosperous and mild rulership are held in honour and high esteem, it is not needful for humble and faithful servants to recount this here any further, more especially as the above is clearly to be traced on the innumerable pillars of victory and triumph erected in the conquered countries and kingdoms. But just as the morning sun going forth in its glad radiance and manifesting its shining countenance to the world conjures a glad spectacle before the eyes of man and is received and greeted by all with exceeding great jubilation, whereas when it is sometimes covered with thick and dull clouds, breaking through to the earth, but dark and half obliterated, because other forces in the cosmic spheres thus determine it, so likewise when your Majesty is obscured by the slightest rebellion and the mists of insurrection, in the hearts of the subjects there will be stirred untimely displeasure and abhorrence towards the authorities appointed by God.

Now may Your Majesty graciously be appraised (however greatly to our sorrow) of the course which has brought the subject countries into so dangerous a condition that neither peace nor unity can truly and lastingly be any more maintained. It is necessary that the evil instigator who is perpetually present at court and enjoying great favour at the hands of Your Majesty be checked and put out of the way before Your Majesty's sceptre and crown, health and life, be still more exposed to danger and the restoration to safety be subsequently achieved with increased difficulty.

May Your Majesty graciously lend an ear to a summary relation of the character of the entire matter: Hugo, the Burgundian, on whom Your Majesty conferred such glorious benefactions, who had attained so many posts of honour, who was ever furthered and raised—he it is who is not only least intent on serving Your Majesty's honour, the kingdom's good, the people's welfare and prosperity, but, on the contrary, he it is who, with scorn and mockery and contempt and desire to bring about the downfall of the whole royal house daily incites the people by means of gifts, promises and flattery. Like a new Absalom he hopes to draw the people towards him so that ultimately one might everywhere hear the cry, 'Long live King Hugo of Burgundy.' By virtue of our loyalty and our duty, we have neither wished nor dared to conceal this imminent danger from Your Majesty. May it please Your Majesty to search in all houses, villages, boroughs and districts, whereupon you would learn to your amazement how the people are wholeheartedly attached to Hugo, whereas on the contrary, their attitude to the Crown is but cold.

Wherefore it is urgently needful that Your Majesty hasten to put your hand to the quenching of the bursting flame of dangerous insurrection and mutiny. What disaster might not be expected to arise out of the long smouldering hotbeds of insurrection if a cruelly ravaging flame were allowed to grow out of the slowly glimmering spark?

Thus it will be of greater profit and benefit to the entire realm that in forestalment of all evil and distress, a traitor and perjuror be punished according to his deserts rather than that the kingdom should be divided and the people troubled, wronged and harmed by the sudden outbreak of rebellion and (which is least to be tolerated) Your Majesty should be exposed to increased discomfort.

Inasmuch as we have never known Your Majesty other than ready to punish evil and to check all troublous persons according to their deserts, we would humbly beseech Your Majesty for the sake of the love of your throne, the prosperity of the royal house and the peace of the fatherland, to visit Hugo, as the offender of Your Royal Majesty, with a quick and well deserved punishment.'

Thus the innocent Hugo was accused before Charles[34] by those under whose tongue the serpent-poison of jealousy and the dragon-gall of envy lay hidden.

Of the Imprisonment of Hugo, Duke of Burgundy

(Chap. VII) This unexpected speech, so fraught with anger, impressed the King, and quite distracted him. As the tempestuous wind furrows the ocean and makes the waves tower ever higher so that the ship totters and rolls upwards and downwards, so too this invented fable had set the royal mind of Charles into unsteady and contradictory motion in a measure which would have worked havoc even with the strongest of spirits.

On the one hand the king was deeply moved by the fidelity and the constant candour of the above mentioned Duke. Nor could he forget his exceedingly wise counsel and judicious advice, his care and unceasing toil, the excellent service rendered to the whole kingdom, and the great benefit received thereby. Nor could he leave unconsidered the unimpeachable character of all the Duke's life and doings, as was witnessed by his great name and fame resounding throughout the country. The King needs had to confess that there was no room for punishment. When he was reminded of his subject's love and esteem for the accused Duke he was unable to perceive ought else but the true witness and proof of a great and uninterrupted loyalty. On the other hand the King deemed it to be true what Seneca says:

> In Praecipiti dubioque
> Excelsa loco stare Regis.
> Nunquam placidam sceptra quietem
> Certumque sui tenuisse diem.
> Aliam ex altis curam fatigare
> Et vexare animos.   (Seneca, Tragedies, 8)

Namely, that his royal highness was resting on a sandy, yea, perilous soil which made no rest safe, either for a year or for a day. In one word: anxiety upon anxiety and a never ceasing misery. Nor had he outgrown the deep wound[35] inflicted on his heart by Pippin, his royal but misguided prince, who had not only conspired against his father's crown and government but had also dared to plot against the King's blood and body, life and state, following the instigation of impious subjects and joining them in their evil scheming. By reason of his own kith and kin being found guilty of treason, Charles gave room to all the more jealous thoughts, doubts and suspicions concerning Hugo, and ever less to the memories of his past fidelities and his services.

Furthermore, the King's heart and mind were heavy, firstly because the accusers were of high rank; secondly because of the significance of the various witnesses and proofs; thirdly because he actually experienced manifold secret persecutions, discovered plots and disloyal gatherings, which had been of such a nature that the fire, long concealed in the King's heart, now burst forth with might. This flame suddenly and unexpectedly struck Hugo. By royal order a derisive sentence was passed on Hugo depriving him of honourable office and power as well as expelling him from court and from the company of princely persons.[35a] Under armed guard Hugo was to be led to a horrible dark dungeon, through public streets and places and accompanied by the jeering of the envious. He who was wrongly accused of high treason, was now to share the prison with men of low degree suffering their punishment for misdeed and crime. A sad spectacle indeed! Wherein Hugo, a great prince of noble birth and rich in virtue, honour and heroic deeds, his great name known far and wide, a lord amongst the nobles, was now nothing but a prisoner, an outcast, a scorn and mockery to the whole world. Even he who like a radiant star had previously illumined the whole royal court was expelled and banished, and with him too went sincerity, truth and loyalty, in order that fraud, jealousy and infidelity with all the other vices could spread and flourish the more.

This was a hard blow but it neither hurt nor injured Hugo. He did not lose courage nor was he afraid of this contrary wind, and the more so since he willingly obeyed the King's order and having humbly and reverently listened to the command, he bid goodnight to the court he had served for so many years. He advised his friends, princes and lords to bear with fortitude the misfortune which might befall any one of them (for all ill-luck and shame are nothing but the well-deserved reward of courtiers). For he will not be faint-hearted and despondent who is mindful of the fact that innocence, even when in danger, still does not sink when it trusts in God and founds its hope on his protection although all and everything should forsake it.

Of the Prayers which Duke Hugo said in the Dungeon during his Imprisonment

(Ch. VIII) Meantime the imprisoned Duke was guarded with increasing severity and slandered by evil tongues. Receiving no comfort from men, nor hoping for any even from his friends, but also not wishing to remain so bitterly alone, he now turned to God, in complete trust that he would find the open door of loving kindness with Him whom he had always feared and loved. Thereupon he knocked at this door by means of devout and earnest prayer and he committed all his troubles to the Supreme Judgement, and with due acknowledgement to the Saints, he took his conscience for his advocate, devotion for his witness, knowing full well that at this High Court all evil must shrink away, for justice itself can be called upon and it hearkens to the appeal.

Being in this sad plight the unhappy Duke wished for nothing else than that the motions of his heart should speak and bear witness to his innocence in this High Court. To this end were directed all the sighs coming from the depths of his being, and all the tears. Willingly would he have hidden all his inner pain but in order to give vent somewhat to his sorrow, he humbly addressed to God the following lament:

'Almighty God, searcher of hearts, behold Thy servant, here I stand before Thy divine eyes, as a poor iniquitous sinner, as a bloodthirsty man, as a traitor of the royal name, as a corrupter of the people; for with all this I am charged and for this reason I am in bonds and fetters and am guarded by all those around me until the day of my death. Thou, O Lord, knowest my thoughts, my most secret plans and all my purpose and Thou knowest likewise that my path has never deviated from Thy justice, nor have my feet ever abandoned Thy footsteps. As for me, I know myself to be innocent of all these doings, my conscience is silent and does not accuse me of any bloodthirstiness, besides which my mind has never been attracted or captured by such pursuits. To Thy divine justice I submit my whole condition. Thou, O divine Sun, irradiate all the innermost of my heart and search whether such misdeeds have ever been kept and hidden therein. Shouldst Thou—contrary to expectation—find me guilty then I shall be content, yea, I pray Thee and most humbly demand, that Thou might reveal this and make it manifest to all the world for my punishment. Should the rumour and accusations be untrue, as I sincerely believe, then I pray Thee for Thy divine help and fatherly assistance, that Thy fatherly hand may protect and save from the present distress the man whom hatred and envy have snatched from the heights and thrust into the depths. Forsaken by all men and having nothing but Thy help, O Lord, I pray Thee to loosen these bonds, to dissolve the alliance of the ungodly, through whose envy and falsehood I am innocently condemned to death, by violence and force in the face of all right and justice. I know, my Lord and my God, that justice is near to Thy heart, and therefore I cling to Thee in this storm, as to an immutable anchor and I strengthen my trust in Thee. Oh turn away and destroy the evil scheming of the unrighteous ones that they should not boast that Thou, my Lord and my God, my hope and my trust hast forsaken me and the righteous are mocked and scorned.'

Such were the sighs, the breathings, the prayer of the sorrowful imprisoned Hugo in which he spent, as history tells us, all the night while fettered and bound. When falling asleep faint and sore hearted he would go over and over in dreams the loyalty which pledged him to the royal court. The ingratitude of the world and the court would at times strike him with horror; then, terrified by the false and secretly laid snare, he would endeavour to disentangle himself from it in order forthwith to serve freely none other save God. Well could one have inferred how true that is which is written in the Song of Solomon (Chapter V): I sleep and my body and my senses are heavy with sleep but my heart and my thoughts are awake and are filled with hope that God will not forsake innocence.

How Duke Hugo was Condemned to Death

(Ch. IX) In the meantime, while the imprisoned Duke Hugo was endeavouring to vindicate his innocence before the countenance of the Supreme Judge and Court, the night passed silently and the bloody day of Hugo[36] drew nigh. At dawn he awoke; he, to whom the light was an unwelcome messenger of the forthcoming execution. 'It is,' thus he spake to himself, 'the time and the day, yea, the very hour, wherein I must be a spectacle unto the whole world and play my part. It is time for me now to prepare and array myself in a seemly manner. The plot of the play will be innocence; envy and rancour will provide the illustrations, the end of my life will form the conclusion of the whole tragedy. The grave that is to follow and the final rest alone comfort me, above all because the highest justice[37] holding the scales equal will not forsake me nor close its doors to me.' This was his only refuge, for he remembered well that the poor little boat floating without human help, without oar or rudder amidst the great and mighty billows, might easily sink and perish. As might well have happened if Almighty God had not turned the weather and broken the waves, the above named prince undoubtedly would have suffered shipwreck in his innocence.

The King hastened to make an end of this matter which was of so much importance to the whole kingdom. For this purpose he called the Counsel and the High Court of Justice, that the judgement concerning the Prince, accused—as they thought, rightly—might be pronounced. The matter was to be expedited with all the greater celerity in order that all persons who might possibly oppose the course of things and join the cause of the above-mentioned Prince might have meted out to them adequate punishment and that this be proclaimed. Therefore, in obedience to his royal Majesty, the princes and lords, the noblest of the country's servitors, the judges and councillors, appeared at court. The charge was laid by both parties, innocence was protected as far as possible, outrage was kept within bounds, the evidence brought forward was considered, witnesses called. Here, on the one hand, stands outrage (Frevel), on the other hand the obvious and inevitable danger to the entire royal name and race and the prosperity and well-being of the whole kingdom. To the good of the accused, however, are his innocence, his loyal service, his candour and the love and good name awarded him by his fellow men. But by reason of the royal mind having been previously supplied with false and deceitful chords, the song became a sad one and Hugo was found guilty and condemned. His royal Majesty thereupon confirmed the sentence, after which it was publicly read in the presence of the accusers and the accused as well as a great multitude of men. Duke Hugo, as a traitor to his country, a rebel and a perpetrator of outrage on His royal Majesty is to be given over to the executioners and to forfeit his life. But who could imagine that even with devout and pious kings innocence should be made to suffer? Who could have thought that the wrongdoings of so honoured a Prince should be accounted so great that they could not be atoned for by anything short of princely blood? To make a long story short: when the people heard that the life of this faithful, well-proven Prince was past reprieve and that his execution was being prepared, then the whole city came running together and folk without number gathered from all quarters, filling all the streets without and within in order to watch the sad farewell of the condemned Prince.

When great crowds of men from all boroughs and towns had assembled at the tragic spot where the innocent Duke of Burgundy was nevertheless sentenced to offer his head to the blow of the sword, and the drums were beaten, and the trumpets sounded their melancholy blast, lo, there came Duke Hugo, sorrowfully awaited by so many, dressed from head to foot in mourning. His eyes, gait and gesture stirred one to compassion. He went straight up to the place of his death, so that his blood be spilled for those who had thirsted for it—poured out fully, without stint, without fear. One might well have thought that here on this stage (schauplatz) he would proclaim and make known to the whole world, his innocence and lament his condemnation. But the miserable spectacle, the dire wrong and the violent suppression of justice had dumbfounded him and robbed him of speech. Nevertheless, the princely countenance and his eye so full of woe could not conceal the innermost thoughts of his heart, more specially that they were so directed as to give utterance to the heart's lament: 'Ah, where are my friends and my kinsmen? Where is the royal grace and favour? Oh my God, what is more inconsistent than the world! I have ever been the backbone of the country, the refuge and relief of all, a father to all the King's subjects. Which of them all now thinks of me? I am now shown up before all men as a traitor of the royal blood and race... Farewell, then, friends and kinsmen! Farewell then, to high honour and dignity! Farewell then, most gracious King and Lord! Here at the last I wish Your Majesty all the prosperity you could wish for yourself and to my foes all possible wellbeing now and for ever more. To Thee, O God of Heaven and earth, I give my life, received from Thy Almighty Being. To Thee I live and to Thee I die, to which this blood of mine, condemned to death, bears testimony. Blessed shall I deem myself when, following

Thine example, I shall appear before the throne of God in the robe made purple with mine own and not another's blood!'

How, and in What Manner Duke Hugo was Released from Death by the Special Help of God

(Ch. X) Here one might truly and justly say, 'Behold how the righteous man dies, and yet no man is stirred! The innocent man is taken away, and there is hardly one who takes it to heart! How blind are ambition and foolhardiness! Innocence is bowed down, envy and hatred are puffed up. Look down upon us, Oh Lord! Behold, Oh Lord, the wrong which my foes do unto me; Oh Lord, liberate me from all evil powers and let me not be overcome by the deceitful, flattering tongue!'

Meanwhile, Duke Hugo humbly submitting himself to his death, had put off his apparel and bared his neck, and with eyes bound and knees bent, giving himself up to God, he offered his head to the stroke of the sword—in complete and willing expectation of the blow just about to descend. But as the executioner approached from behind raising the sword and intending to strike, a sudden unexpected fear which he had never experienced before, seized him in such a manner that he turned round and round and asked in astonishment, 'What is this? What does this mean? Whose voice is it? Whence this command? Am I to put my sword back into its sheath? Shall I, covered with shame, at the risk of losing my life, withdraw from this spot without having accomplished the deed? But I know not what this is; I feel within me no strength, no force, no power. I shall protest to all those present that I can go no further, you can do with me as you choose, I can no more.' This aroused the wrath of the crowds—some of the men blaming the executioner for his hesitation; others suspecting a secret agreement between the two, some others, again, wondering about the Duke now suspended between life and death—and others again pursued other thoughts. In order that no discord or rebellion should spring up among the assembled crowd, the executioner was once more ordered by royal command to set about his work, with the remark that his own life would not be spared if he failed to fulfil his task. Neither good words nor threats availed against the hand of God, for this it was that held back the drawn sword and took away all strength from the executioner. Finally, when it was realised that all the cries of encouragement to the executioner were in vain and as, moreover, none could be found who would dare to strike the blow in view of the miracle consummated before all eyes, the King was seized by a sudden pallor. Fearing that he might become a laughing stock to his people and dreading that this might give rise to sedition and rebellion, the King was seized by a great wrath which he vented thus: 'Have I lived to see the day when even the least of my subjects refuses to submit obediently to my orders? What? Am I to suffer in my realm, at my court, in the midst of my most privy councillors, the presence of a convicted traitor plotting the downfall of me and my crown? I will not tolerate it, I will not endure it, Hugo must die even if I should have to stain my royal hand with his blood.' In this ardour he raises his arm, draws the sword, thus intending to express his wrath. But all is in vain; for in the very same moment the King's arm became rigid and immovable, the sinews hardened in such manner that the King was neither able to move his arm or his sword.[38] Perceiving this, His Majesty took counsel with himself, recovered his spirit and decided to try other means. And thus the King spake: 'Now, now I see how much I have erred, I acknowledge the just and mighty hand of the Most High, the Protector and the Refuge of the innocent. Come hither, my beloved Hugo, let me embrace you, thou whom God has protected from injustice. Come hither thou faithful honest hero; through thy prayer reconcile me with God, who is rightfully angry with me, and beseech Him that it may please His Omnipotence to restore to my arm its former strength.'

The cords and fetters by means of which Hugo was bound were then loosened and removed and he was set free. As soon as he raised his previously bound eyes and looked at the King the heart of the latter was so moved that His Majesty fell on his neck and implored Hugo's forgiveness for all the wrong he had inflicted on him and likewise he besought the Duke to bring healing to his arm. Hugo fell at the feet of his sovereign the King and is raised up by him in his turn. Each one mourns for the other; the King grieves for the obstinately inflicted insult and public wrong which was suffered by the innocent man; Hugo suffers at the sight of the impotence of the King's arm. And he continued thus to suffer until Almighty God stretched out His hand and healed the King's paralysed limb. Whereupon great joy and jubilation broke out throughout the whole court and spread throughout the whole city. This induced the King to make a new covenant with Hugo, offering him thereby not merely honour and rank but desiring to confer on him all royal grace.

Subsequently the author tells us he must confess that Eginardus does not communicate this story. But Einhard himself admits:

> that he did not give a complete account of Charlemagne's life. And this present story may be among the omitted ones, a story which otherwise does not deserve to be numbered among the other glorious deeds of the King. But it is none the less true, primarily because the Alsatian Chronicle lays special store by it in consequence of certain events that followed thereon which are clearly and beautifully recorded.

He then raises the question whether Hugo was rightly called the Duke of

'Burgundy' and whether he is the same one whom Regino mentions as a count of Turon and names as an ambassador of Charlemagne's to the East. He therefore quotes Regino of Prüm:

> Regino writes anno 811, that Haido, Bishop of Basle and Hugo of Turon[39] were sent as royal ambassadors (by Charlemagne) to Constantinople in order to confirm the peace treaty concluded with Emperor Nicephorus. And had nothing else occurred to mar the high dignity of this lord (Hugo of Turon), the purpose of the embassy and the royal favour bestowed on this lord, there would be ample reason to give credence to the account.

With these words Pater Lyra closes the first part of his narrative.

Historical note: Pater Lyra's supposition is correct. Hugo really is Charlemagne's ambassador to Constantinople in the year 811. But the legend made Charlemagne's embassy to Constantinople into a crusade of Charlemagne's to Constantinople. Here this strange legend finds its elucidation. The narrative of this legend can be compared with an old French text published in the *Altfranzösische Bibliothek* by Wendelin Foerster, Vol. 2 (Reisland) 1900: *The Journey of Charlemagne to Jerusalem and Constantinople*, published by E. Koschwitz, fourth edition. Here we are told how Charlemagne set out on a journey in order to visit King Hugo of Constantinople because Charlemagne's queen had declared that Hugo was worthier of the crown than Charlemagne. According to this tradition Hugo is depicted as being the thirteenth in a circle of twelve to whom Charlemagne with his twelve Paladins journeys. Hugo demands that Charlemagne and his twelve knights should actually perform what they had been bragging about—otherwise he means to decapitate them. With the aid of the relics the Paladins succeed in accomplishing the twelve hard tasks so far as is necessary for obtaining Hugo's pardon. The relics which Charlemagne receives are as follows: the arm of St Simeon, the blood of St Stephen the Martyr and the head of Lazarus. According to historical information, this head of Lazarus was brought from Constantinople to Andlau (at the foot of the Odilienberg) by the wife of Charles III, St Richardis.[40] This is a clear indication that the author of the legend of Charlemagne's crusade attributes to the latter what partly refers to Charles III. This tallies completely with the story depicting Charles III as a helpless man.

His wife Richardis too could certainly raise the question as to who was the greater and worthier of the crown: Charles III or Hugo of Tours. Everything is elucidated in the most satisfactory way if one only compares the dovetailed periods of the legend with the actual historical dates. The Empress who considers Hugo to be more worthy than Charles is Richardis. The legend of Charlemagne's crusade is nothing else than the Richardis legend in combination with the Saga of Charlemagne and his twelve

5. (i)   The castle of Hugo of Tours
   (ii) Plan of Tours with the place marked where Hugo's castle stood
   (From: 'Tableaux Chronologiques de l'Histoire de Touraine par Clarey-Martineau, Tours')

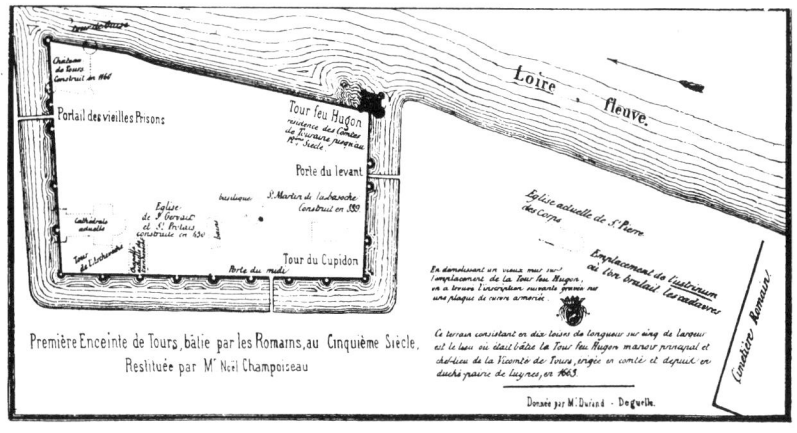

Paladins. Hugo's journey to Constantinople in 811 and Richardis's much later journey which resulted in the bringing of the head of Lazarus to Andlau have been mixed up. According to the record of the old French text Charlemagne brings back many relics: the chalice of Christ, the crown of thorns, the nail that pierced the feet of Christ, a silver dish adorned with gold and precious stones, the knife which Christ had held in His hand when He ate, as well as hair from the head and beard of St Peter. Furthermore he brought the milk[41] and the shirt of Mary. It is of interest that Peter Comestor in his Commentary on the Gospel (Historia scholastica) in the passage relating to the Naming and the Circumcision of the Christ, makes the following remark: 'It is recorded that the praeputium domini (i.e. the relic of the first shedding of the blood of Jesus) was brought by an angel to Charlemagne while he was "in templo domini".' Charlemagne is supposed to have taken the relic to Aix-la-Chapelle, whence Charles the Bald brought it to the Church of the Saviour near Carosium.

It is precisely this relic which ultimately reaches Hugo of Tours according to the Hugo legend as related by Pater Lyra, the narrative of which we interrupted by the present historical consideration. Peter Comestor says that, according to others, this relic was brought to Antwerp where it is an object of the greatest veneration. Grandidier, however, records op. cit.: The claim to the possession of this relic is made by a whole number of places, for instance, the Lateran Church in Rome, l'Abbaye de Charroux dans le Poitou, Coulomb près Nogent-le Roi, Hildesheim, Anvers dans le Pays-Bas, besides this a monastery in the diocese of Chalon (p. 362, Vol. I, Histoire de l'église de Strasbourg). It is clear that for our purpose these relics only come into consideration in as far as they show that there existed a current in which the ritual was especially linked to the *first* shedding of the blood, while others were connected with the subsequent sheddings of blood. The Grail legend, the legend of the blood of Christ, has many forms and there is a difference whether a given legend is connected with the blood at the Circumcision, or the blood shed during the Prayer in the Garden of Gethsemane, i.e. the bloody sweat,[42] or the shedding of blood during the Scourging, or during the Crucifixion, or at the Piercing with the lance when blood flowed mingled with water. Compare what is said by Jacobus de Voragine about the five kinds of the shedding of blood in the *Golden Legend* in the chapter dealing with the Circumcision of our Lord. For further information one should consult the comprehensive work of Franciscus Collius of Mediolanum, published in 1617 under the title: *De Sanguine Christi Libri Quinque*. This book deals in detail with the problem whether blood relics, as such, are possible, since Christ by His resurrection has caused the resurrection of His whole blood. Then follow further considerations about the whole attitude of Thomas Aquinas to this problem and about the various types of blood relics. A fair survey of this matter can be found in the interesting little book by A. Jox: *Die Reliquien des kostbaren Blutes unseres göttlichen Heilandes insbesondere die Reliquie des kostbaren Blutes zu Brügge in Flandern*, Luxembourg, Peter Brück, 1880. The appendix to this book contains a good description of the various sheddings of blood. In regard to the first shedding it is mentioned that the ritual for the fostering of the virtue of chastity is directly connected with it. At this point these considerations tally with the words of the Grail legend: 'Only is illicit love unto thee forbidden' (Book XV, lines 790-1). We find that it was with this relic more especially that Hugo of Tours was connected, and having noticed this, we turn once again to the continuation of our narrative.

In the second part of the story about Hugo the Knight, Pater Lyra, quoting the Alsatian Chronicle as his source, begins as follows:

(Ch. 1) Charlemagne had considered the matter more fully and had, above all, reminded himself of his servant's great loyalty, as well as the great services which Hugo the Duke had rendered to the people at large. Against this he weighed the shame, disgrace and insult that had brought danger to his body and life as well as loss of honour and all worldly possessions. Thereupon Charles perceived that it was only fair and just to wipe out this deed and cancel it and publicly to shower on him all royal favours. For this purpose he called all his councillors and courtiers and reminded them of the grievous error publicly committed in consequence of the false information, due to envy. Furthermore he reminded them of the outrage perpetrated without cause on the innocent Duke of Burgundy, as well as of the chastisement received at the hands of God and known to the whole world. 'For, of a certainty,' said Charles, 'he has suffered much thereby and has endured a great outrage which I am bound to make good as far as I may. What is your counsel? His innocence must be acknowledged by means of a royal favour proclaimed throughout the whole world.' Each and all agreed with one accord to this gracious intent, but refrained from suggesting to His Royal Majesty aim or measure, leaving the decision rather to His Majesty's discrimination.

Hereupon Hugo was called to court and was received with gracious look and heart, Charlemagne himself addressed him thus: 'Full well I know, my faithful Hugo, that thy heart cannot soon be healed after it has been so deeply wounded by the poisoned arrows of the evil tongue. Nevertheless, with great wonderment we have seen and recognised in all thy deeds thy great virtue and thine invincible courage in the endurance of all the insult, shame, mockery and injustice. Whereby thine enemies have been put to shame, thou, however, hast attained to an undying name for all time to come so that it becomes manifest what men are in the habit of saying: 'Misfortune has brought many a man more good than harm.' And as I feel myself guilty for having lent my ear to false speech and accusation, it is now my will and desire that thou choose of all high honour and dignity within my kingdom whatsoever may please thee.' Whereupon Hugo thanked His Majesty with all due reverence for this gracious and generous offer, adding likewise that he had never deserved so great a favour of His Majesty but that he held all his powers and possessions ready for service and prosperity of the Crown. Should this latter command his servant to accept the said gracious favour he would most humbly request that he be not hurried in his answer, requesting a few days grace so that he might conform to the King's order in a befitting manner.'

Historical note: The historical sources subsequently relate that in the dissentions between Lothair I and Louis the Pious, Hugo and Matfrid took the part of the former. This is quite comprehensible in view of the fact that Lothair's wife was Hugo's daughter. (It is too a correct feature of the legend of Charlemagne's crusade, that we are told of one of Charlemagne's Paladins having wooed Hugo's daughter. This Paladin, whom the legend names Oliver, is, as we perceive, Lothair the First.) There follow now the imprisonment of Louis in 833, Lothair's taking over the rulership, and the ultimate reinstatement of Louis in 834. Lothair, Hugo and Matfried had now to implore pardon on their knees from Louis the Pious. This pardon was granted, but Lothair was obliged to pledge for himself and his kinsmen that they would dwell henceforward in Italy and never leave that country without permission. This was confirmed by an oath, whereupon Louis the Pious granted them an amnesty as well as their lives (cf. p. 378, Böhmer, *Regesta Imperii*, 1 Karolinger 751–918, 2nd Ed. Innsbruck 1908).

There followed a regular emigration of the first men of the kingdom to Italy. In 843 Lothair received the Middle Kingdom, Charles the Bald came into possession of the West, whereas Louis the German retained the East. This was prepared by Lothair emigrating, as it were, into the southern continuation of the Middle Kingdom, Italy. The legend preserves silence in regard to these events, but records them in its own special way. It mentions Hugo's receiving of the relic of the first shedding of the Holy Blood, by means of which he was made into a bearer of the Grail impulse.[43]

Of Duke Hugo's Chosen Relic and Other Sacred Gifts

(Chap. II) The author tells us of a precious thing kept in a little silver casket which Charlemagne had received from the Patriarch Fortunatus in Jerusalem,[44] 'according to the testimony of what can be read in the life of St Hildulph in Chapter IV.'

In the year 799 this Patriarch sent a priest to the aforementioned king with the humble request that he should ask the grace and permission of Aaron, the then King of Persia, to free the Holy Sepulchre and to grant permission to the Christians dwelling in his land publicly to profess their faith; for the King of Persia held Charlemagne in great esteem and reverence on account of his named and great might being renowned far and wide. The above mentioned silver casket contained nothing less than the tiny fragments of a sacred skin left after the Circumcision of Our Lord and Saviour; a fragment of the Holy Cross and part of the raiment of the Holy Virgin Mary, as well as other sacred objects of which the ancient and previously quoted legend of the Holy Cross bears record.[45]

The author tells us also that these sacred objects are mentioned by Gebwiler, *Leben der hl. Ottilie*, und Wimphlingus in *Catologo Episcoporum Argentinens*, under *Conrado the 58th Bishop of Strasbourg*.[46] The transfer of relics from Jerusalem is also mentioned by Aimonius 1. 4. C. 89 *de gestis Franc. und Regino* under 799 in his chronicle.

'Inasmuch as Hugo remembered well that such a treasure existed and although he knew that it was held in high esteem by the King, he took no delight in anything else but in this precious and proven treasure'.

Hugo asks for this treasure.

'This I request and demand alone that your Royal Majesty may graciously grant and bestow on me the gifts sent over from Jerusalem among which are contained a portion of the Holy Blood of Our Saviour and Redeemer, a piece of the Holy Cross[47] and Blood shed for us and other relics, and above all because this alone will blot out and make good all the insult poured on me.' This request stirred the King's heart to its depth and he replied briefly: 'My dearest Hugo, thou demandest more than if thou hadst claimed my whole kingdom. Nevertheless, in order to fulfil my word I will command that thy request be granted even if it be through my loss. And what has been my comfort and joy shall thenceforth be thine.'

Of the Love and Veneration which Hugo and his Wife Bore for this Relic

(Chap. III, p. 91) Unspeakable was the joy and comfort which the Duke had in the possession of this priceless, yea, royal treasure. In beholding it all pain and memory of the previous storm entirely vanished, so much so that he deemed himself happy to have suffered and endured all that had opened and paved for him the way to the acquisition of so much grace. Now only one care was left and that was how to transport this treasure of great price to his own home, and thus bring joy to his family. Therefore, having greeted on his return his spouse and dear friends, he displayed with great joy his costly gifts and spake thus: 'These are the gifts which Charlemagne bestowed on his servant and comforted him. O precious Ark and holy Casket wherein lies hidden a very precious treasure that will henceforth bring riches to me and mine. Beloved wife and all my friends, rejoice with me and wish me happiness, forasmuch as I was lost and have now been found again. I was at the gate of death[48] and am happily set free from it. Behold,' he said, 'the document of my joy and prosperity! Behold these silent but world-convincing proofs of my innocence. I was cruelly accused by evil tongues before my most gracious Lord and King of having committed an outrage against his Majesty, and I was condemned to death. I had already bared my neck to the sword in undoubted expectation of the last blow, but in a manner transcending all hope the hand of God, that works marvels, saved me by great and glorious signs. Rejoice and thank ye the Lord. These gifts are requital of all the shame endured and wrongful mockery of my enemies.' On hearing these words Aba the Duchess greatly wondered, as well as all those of her kin. But after they had learnt in which manner their lord and master had been liberated from all that had threatened his life and blood they gave praise and glory to God and to the eternal triumph of heroic virtue and wished Duke Hugo and all his kith and kin happiness everlasting.

Meanwhile, the princely couple were anxiously intent on placing and keeping the venerated relic in a spot where due homage could be paid to it. Failing any other accommodation they apportioned a special place in their own house, adorning it with all manner of decoration, in order to seek therein comfort, devotion and eternal bliss. Nor did this fail to happen, for they were so much aglow with the love of God that they turned all their senses and thoughts from all that is earthly and directed them to the eternal, bequeathing and promising all to God as their sole and rightful heir, desiring in their hearts to know how they could best make and fulfil their vows to God. Whereupon they both knelt before the aforementioned relic and humbly implored God in His Almighty Power to make known to them His Divine Will.

Hugo orders a Costly Cross to be Made in which the Relic is to be Kept and Preserved

(Chap. IV, p. 95) The prayer had pierced through the cloud and was heard by God in such a manner that Hugo was inwardly illumined and urged to have a costly image of Our Lord hanging on a cross made in everlasting memory;[49] whereupon he ordered a large, well shaped cross to be made of oak wood.[50] It was to be six feet high, one foot wide, about two fingers deep, covered with silver leaf, without and within and adorned with repoussé-work in so masterly a way that next to the image of our Lord of the Cross the greatest Mysteries of His holy life could be

6. Front of cross made for Hugo of Tours
   (From: Silbermann, P.A., 'Beschreibung von Hohenburg oder dem St. Odilienberg', 1781)

7. Back of cross made for Hugo of Tours
   The relic of the first shedding of blood was enclosed within the central round capsule)
   (From: Silbermann, P.A., 'Beschreibung von Hohenburg oder dem St. Odilienberg',
   1781)

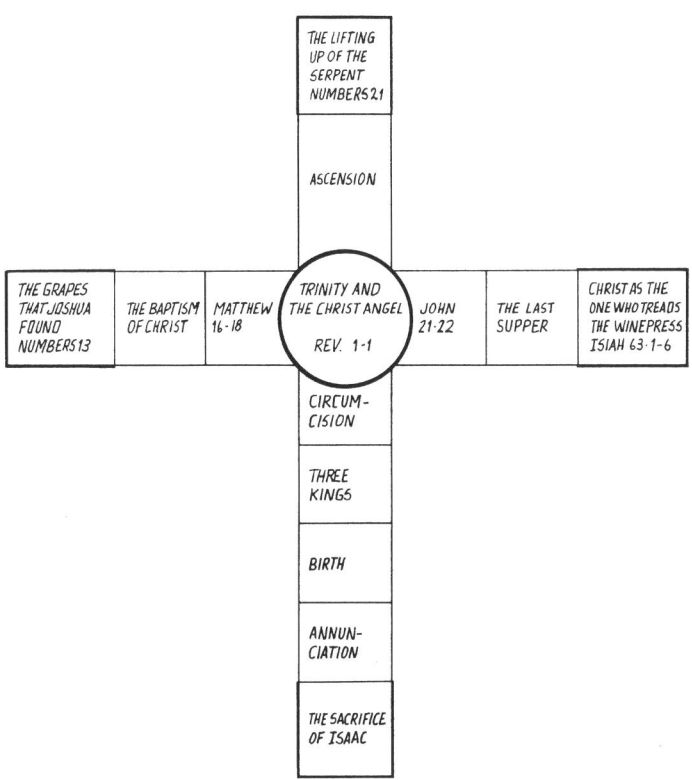

8. Explanation of pictures on back of cross
   from Matthew 16–18: 'Thou art Peter, and on this rock I shall build a community of human beings confessing the Christ-Impulse and it shall not be overcome even at the gate of death.'
   from John 21–22: 'If I will that he remain till I come again as living water, what is that to thee?'
   from Revelations 1–1: '. . . and sent this sign by His Angel to His servant John.'

9. The Empire cross from the Imperial Treasure House in Vienna, in which the 'Holy Lance' was incorporated
   (From: 'Die deutschen Reichskleinodien' [The Imperial Treasure of Germany] described by Julius Schlosser, Vienna)

perceived and learnt. At the four corners the symbols of the Evangelists were set in gold and adorned with precious jewels.[51] In the centre was Christ the Lord with outstretched arms, all gilded, [52] and in the sacred wounds, beautiful and luminous jewels; above the head a pelican opening its own breast in order to feed its young with its blood. On the back of the cross at the four corners were the following figures from the Old Testament: first, Abraham making ready to sacrifice his son Isaac to the Lord;[53] second, the mighty cluster of grapes, (Numb. XIII);[54] third, the divine Vintager, (Isaiah LXIII);[55] and finally, the figure of the brazen serpent suspended on a cross, the sight of which procured healing for those who had been bitten by the serpents, (Numb. XXI, 6).[56] In the centre of the cross was the raised figure of the Holy Trinity, in the act of taking counsel concerning the redemption of mankind, to the right the Son of God pointing to what is written in Ps. XL.[57] 'Then said I, Lo, I come; in the volume of the book it is written of me, I delight to do thy will, O my God; yea, thy law is within my heart.' Besides this there were various other beautiful reminiscences from the life of Christ, which it is not necessary to describe here, since they are better seen in the accompanying plate depicting the cross. But whose this figure may be on the right, with bowed knees and holding weapons, as if thereby protecting the Church—whether this points to St Peter, the true champion of the Church, or to Hugo himself, who was entirely surrendered to the Lord—this must be interpreted by each one according to his own lights.

After the work had thus been completed, Hugo put inside it the praeputium of the bloody circumcision of Our Lord; likewise a fragment from the true cross, and some of the holy Blood and several other precious relics, in order the better to preserve them. Aba, the princely spouse, meanwhile was no less busy. She collected various precious books of the Old and New Testament, as well as some others, all beautifully written and bound in gilt, adorned with precious stones, thus giving them over to God our Lord.[58]

The Lord was exceedingly well pleased with this work. But because these two princely persons did not know where it ought to be taken and delivered into the hands of God, they submitted it to God's care, in order that He might do with it according to His pleasure.

It is this treasure for which Hugo asks.

Historical note: Hugo experienced a strange destiny. He went to Italy, accompanying Lothair, together with the other nobles, 'on whom rested the valour, the strength and the wisdom of the country.' Here Lothair distributed gifts. Matfrid received the Veltlin possessions of St Denis (the monastery in which Waldo had once been Abbot). Hugo's daughter received St Salvatore in Brescia, Hugo's wife an estate in Lambro. But almost all who had emigrated with Lothair died simultaneously in 837 during a fever epidemic: Wala, Matfrid, Hugo, Lambert, Godfrey and his son Agimbert, Burgarit, Jesse and Bishop Elias. One only was saved: Richard (p. 166, Simson, Ludwig der Fromme, *Jahrbücher der deutschen Geschichte, 831-840*, Vol. II, 1876). 'The almost simultaneous death of all those who represented the bloom of the Frankish nobility, but who had abandoned their liege and ruler, could not fail to produce a strong impression. Louis the Pious was deeply stirred by the news. Beating his breast, with eyes filled with tears he implored God to grant peace to their souls (op.cit. p. 167).

The writer of the legend speaks of Hugo as the donor of the holy relic (it is the same which Charlemagne had received from an angel during his journey from Jerusalem to Constantinople),[59] that Louis the Pious had bestowed on him and which he now returned to Niedermünster, at the foot of the Odilienberg.

How the Sacred Cross was Laid on a Camel and How Divine Providence was Called Upon to Accompany it on its Way

(Chap. V). Hugo remembered with approval what the Philistines had used of old when they placed the Ark of God, acquired by their sword, on a vehicle drawn by two milch kine,[60] with the behest that it be brought to its destination without the help of man. Thereupon he too placed his trust in Divine Providence and commanded that this treasure, given over and devoted to God, should be laid on a camel, but with no driver or runner to accompany it, so that it might be led by God's grace and care. In order to protect the sacred Cross from storm, rain and any other emergency on the journey, the sacred Cross was enclosed in a chest and the books and writings were placed in another convenient box. Both were then fastened on either side of the camel, in undoubted hope and trust that it would convey the burden to that spot which should be most pleasing to God. But to secure news and to have some witness of the hoped for achievement, Hugo thought it fit to send five trusted knights, renowned for their rank and virtue, who were charged to follow the footsteps of the camel until they should reach the spot where the riderless animal chose to lay down its burden. After all preparations for the journey had been completed, Hugo and Aba, dwelling in their thoughts on all that had occurred, rejoiced and deemed themselves happy to have encountered so unusual a messenger. They wished the camel good luck on his journey, but above all, they gave thanks to the Lord for having been deemed worthy to keep so great a treasure so long, till it could be brought to the place which God had appointed as its final resting place. They also gave thanks for having been granted the illumination of His Supreme Wisdom for having been enabled to perceive and understand the Divine Will, through discovering a course of action which, as was fitting, demanded sacrifice and at the same time furthered the glory of His Holy Name.

To the messenger, ready to start, they spake: 'Thou who bearest these sacred things and to whose care we have entrusted them, take heed every step of the way in order that these treasures may not be dishonoured by a chance fall, nor suffer harm or damage of any sort. Go whither God and His dear angels lead and guide thee, without anything unforeseen befalling thee: go over hill and dale, through forest and heath, through towns, boroughs and villages and, by means of the bells attached to thy neck, ask where thy resting place may be, and where that heir is to be found to whom the sacred treasure laid on thee is to be given over.' Finally they spake: 'And you, accompanying witnesses, take care of this messenger, hasten not nor goad him on, let him not suffer hunger nor thirst, at our expense provide for all his needs. Go in the name of the Lord and diligently take note of all your paths, the towns and boroughs, so that you might give us an account of all your journey.'

Having received this farewell greeting the messenger bravely set out on its journey as if it had been given a special sign, and as if its path had been made smooth and even. It went over meadows and fields, climbed over hill and dale, penetrated through forest and heath, taking the direct road from Burgundy to France and straight to its capital, Paris, rousing all men everywhere by its bells, so that all people came to their windows in order to watch with wonder this strange procession and more especially to praise and glorify God for what He has so wondrously ordained. Far and wide the news had spread and it had been made known by the accompanying knights what was the purpose and end of the journey, and how sacred a treasure the camel bore— briefly, the whole story had been noised abroad. In consequence of which each and every man desired that such happiness might befall his own house and that the camel might lay down its burden with him. The citizens and inhabitants of the royal capital would have welcomed it if the camel had stayed with them for their protection, more especially because handsome buildings and churches were already there to receive the sacred treasure. But it was not the pleasure of God that this should come to pass, rather did the camel still continue the journey, nor could it be led astray or stopped.

How the Holy Cross Journeyed through Alsace and Arrived in St Nabor

(Chap. VI). Great crowds had gathered in all the streets and houses for the purpose of seeing the miracle of widespread fame. One man told the other and one man led the other in order to follow the messenger and

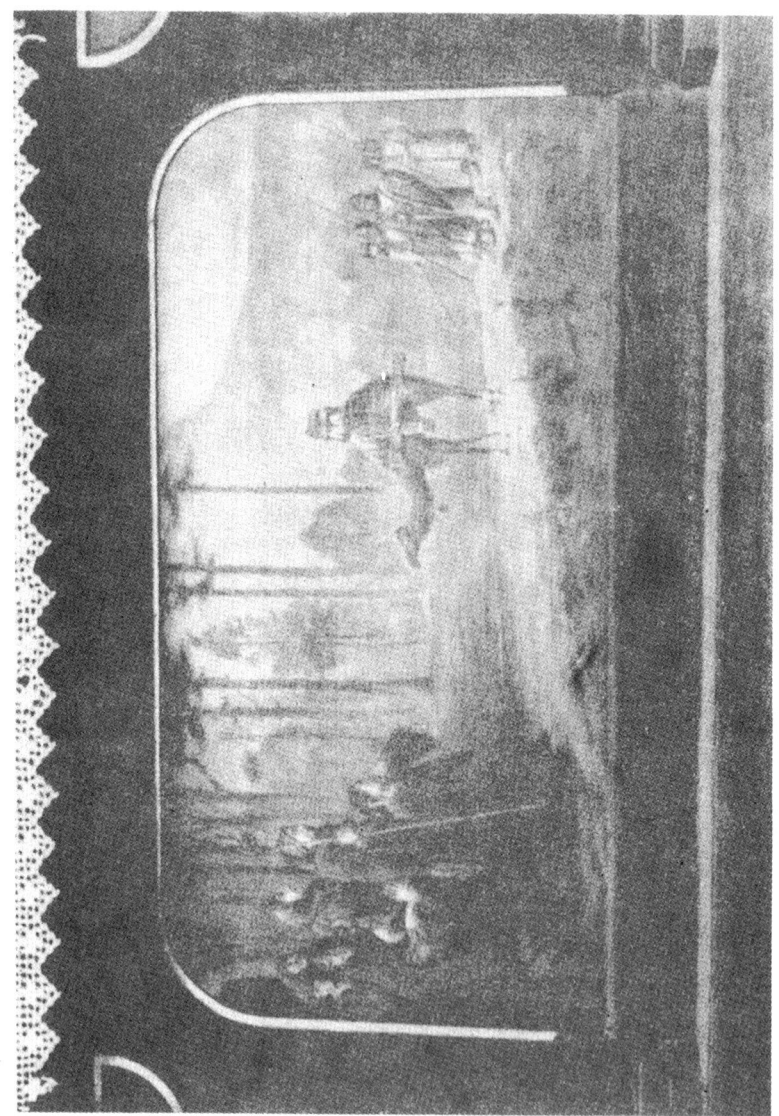

10. The arrival of Hugo's cross with the Blood-Relic in Niedermünster *(Picture from the Altar of the Cemetery Chapel in St Nabor)*

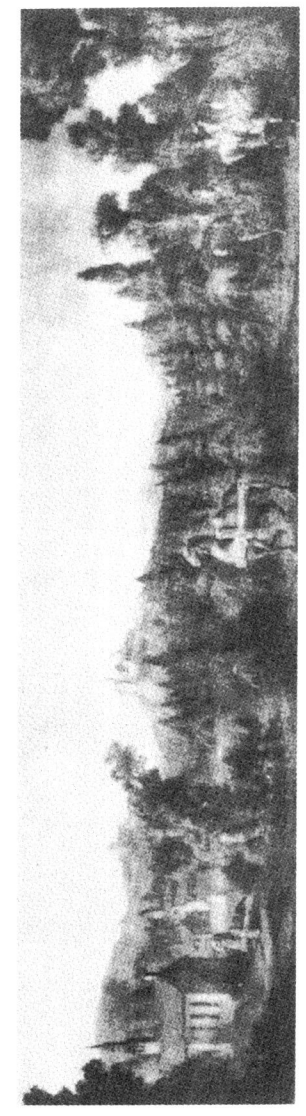

11. The Camel takes the Cross and the Blood-Relic to Niedermünster accompanied by the five Knights of St James
(Picture from the Cross-Altar of St George's Church in Molsheim, Alsace)

to learn where it would stop and bring good fortune. Thus a great crowd of young and old men and women followed the messenger. Meanwhile the camel had reached the Alsatian country and pursued its way through the open land at the delightful season of harvest, in the presence of the reaping husbandmen (for it was the hay month) who were gathering in the fruits given by God. The camel turned towards the Vogelsberg passing by the towns and villages lying to the left and right, and as if desiring some rest after its fatigues, it halted at the foot of the mountain. This spot offered comely and pleasant accommodation, partly because of the lovely green of the valley, partly because of the fresh and delicious water running down from the heights. Towards the east lay a long and large field, planted with vines that gave delight to the inhabitants; to the west lay the mighty chain of mountains on the summit of which was situated the church of St Odile as well as a monastery, extending far and wide; and not far thence lay the monastery of Niedermünster. Towards north and south stretched a lofty, dense forest, full of handsome and useful trees as well as other shrubs and plants, well fitted to give pleasure to both eye and heart.

Just in this spot, thus described, is situated a village, poor and lowly as to dwelling, but by reason of a church having been built in honour and in everlasting memory of St Nabor, the ancient martyr, it has derived great fame and, as it were, an immortal name through its association with this saint.

When the camel laden with its precious relics reached this spot it went down on its knees, just as if, in passing, it desired to pay homage to the Saint, and as if, furthermore, to refresh itself, it rested its whole body. This gave reason to surmise and to conclude that here, in truth, dwell people whom God had chosen and visited by raising in their midst the sign of salvation and blessing. In such thoughts and devout conjectures men took counsel how they might best meet God's grace and how best honour and glorify Him, and what necessary preparations to this end should now be made. Meanwhile, the stranger, feeling its strength restored, arose forthwith and began to pursue its way, climbing to the summit of the aforementioned mountain, over stones and rocks, with undoubted design of raising to greater heights and exalting the Holy Cross. Having reached the centre along uneven paths and arriving at a spot where two roads separated, one of them leading to the monastery in the middle of the mountain, the camel turned to the left to the aristocratic convent, situated somewhat lower, and continued its journey (both religious houses observed the rule of St Odile). Once more thoughts and conjectures arose, everybody believing that it had found and undoubtedly discerned the spot chosen by Divine Providence. Forthwith they began to wish good luck to the house and to deem it fortunate that so great a grace was to be bestowed on it.

The longer the hue and cry lasted the further it spread, till at last the convent for noblewomen was filled with it, and the nuns felt obliged to do their duty by the approaching bridegroom (i.e. the relic) and to go to meet and greet Him with all due honour. Much might be recorded of the joy pervading the convent, but this can be gauged by each one individually. Undoubtedly the sole care of these noble virgins inhabiting the aforementioned convent was the thought: 'How the Lord of Glory could be given the most magnificent introduction and reception.'

How the Holy Cross was Laid Down in the Convent of Niedermünster and How Joyously it was Received

(Chap. VII) This was the ever-spreading cry and it had gone so far that it seemed likely that the conjecture would become truth, more especially because the camel departed neither to the right nor to the left, impressing its footsteps into the hard rock as if it were mere wax,[61] which might easily have led the closely following devotees to surmise that here was the spot where the strange guest would halt. Whereupon they followed it all the more fervently until, guided and directed by the tracks left in the Niedermünster region, they clearly perceived the convent on the hill. The stranger, led until now by Divine Providence, stopped in view of the convent as it was nearing, just as if it wished to gaze at the building in wonderment—but presently it again pursued its way and when it came again to the gate of the lordly convent to which allusion has frequently been made, it stamped on the ground with its feet and knocked at the gateway by means of a ring which hung thereon, in order to enter in by the doors of justice and rest therein. In those days the convent had an Abbess, renowned for her noble birth, virtue and holy life, who, having heard of the ambassador guided by Divine Providence now standing before the door, ordered all doors and gateways to be opened straightway to the dear guest, and the gifts that it bore to be carried in and received with supreme reverence. Whereupon the stranger now entered, giving over the heritage entrusted to its care and demanding, as it were, a token or a testimony of its accomplished task. Meanwhile its escort that had followed it from afar in order to bear witness, as well as the crowds who had gathered together from all parts—all the witnesses of this miraculous proceeding—were now arriving and the whole courtyard was filled with strangers. Not to mention the noble maidens who had been disturbed in their devotional exercises by this great bustle and who hastened from their prayers to witness the miracle of which they were being told that they might learn the whole story more fully and truthfully. When all were assembled to listen to the message with greatest ardour and fervour, one of the five (knights) stepped forward into the centre and began his speech as follows: 'Very reverend and gracious Abbess! Duke

12. Niedermünster
    (a) *Ruins of Niedermünster Church in which the Blood-Relic, which Hugo of Tours received from Charles the Great, was preserved* (b) *The St Nicholas Chapel* (c) *The Hochburg on Odilienberg*

Hugo of Burgundy and Dame Aba, his spouse, our gracious Duke and Duchess, have made God Almighty, the King of Heaven and Earth, the Heir of all their wealth and have given over into His hands the power to take possession of this heritage when and through whom He may so choose. In order, however, that the actual delivery of the heritage—accepted by God, as we hope—may take place and pass on to the next inheritor substituted by Him, we are seeking the same everywhere with this our leader and guide, but it seems as if, notwithstanding all our proclaiming and heralding throughout the journey, no such claimant has yet been found. But whereas this messenger by Divine Providence now stands still in this habitation of God and clearly seems disinclined to leave this spot, we conclude therefrom that the heritage is your due, and belongs to you. May you, therefore, receive and accept the Divine Grace that will bring the whole convent happiness and blessing, and the gifts which my gracious masters have marvellously acquired at great expense to the eternal memory of all faithful Christians, and for their refreshment.' After the speech was ended the burden was lifted off the camel's back, the box was opened and the Cross glittering with gold, silver and precious stones was uncovered for adoration of all those present. After great joy and marvelling, the Holy Cross was then carried under pious escort to a worthy spot, in order that it might subsequently be placed among other sacred objects. Meanwhile the above mentioned Abbess took counsel with those in her charge as to what could best be prepared and done in honour of the newly arrived sacred treasure. After this the doors of the great church were flung open, the walls were covered with costly carpets, incense and candles were kindled, bells were rung and everything planned and arranged in the best order. With beautiful sweet music the holy Cross was carried into the church and set upon the altar and humblest thanks were offered to God Almighty for His Grace; health and happiness were wished to the two princely persons, the special benefactors, and blessing was given to the people assembled in devotion. Thereupon those who as witnesses had escorted the holy Cross took leave and bade farewell—the camel, unwilling to move, remained on the spot it had at last reached.

Roman and Grail Christianity at the Carolingian Court
(The circle of friends around Waldo and Hugo)

This legend as well as the first one we related brings us into the circle of Charles the Great and shows the Knight Hugo as the recipient of a relic of the blood of Jesus. He received in this relic 'the first outpouring of his rose-coloured blood.' This legend is a later production than the Waldo legend but it again draws attention to an important personality—Hugo—in a way that is different from ordinary history.

It is therefore a pertinent question whether any kind of connection can be found between Waldo of Reichenau and the Count Hugo of this legend. This connection is actually there, for the Count Hugo and his wife Aba—also called Bava—who are mentioned in the legend, meet us again in the biography of St Odilie where the later descendants of her race are mentioned.[62]

This genealogy is to be found on page 59 of *The History of Hohenburg or St Odilienberg* by P. Dionysio Albrecht, Schlerstatt 1751.[63]

So it was easy to identify more accurately Count Hugo of the legend. It is, as the writer of the legend already surmises, Hugo of Tours, a prominent official of Charlemagne well known to history. So there can be no doubt that a connection exists between Hugo and Waldo, who are contemporaries, both of whom are intimate counsellors of Charles the Great, and both of whom are described as recipients of a blood relic. But history does not mention this connection, and indeed, as we must believe, for a very definite reason.

We have already mentioned that Philipp Heber in his interesting book, *Waldo, Charlemagne's Spiritual Counsellor, and the ancient Waldensers* (Book VI. Vols. 4 and 5 in Marriot's *Der wahre Protestant*, Basel 1857), has expressed the conjecture that Waldo and his friend Hunfrid stand opposed to Einhard the biographer of Charles the Great, and that the tendencies which the two men *Waldo* and *Einhard* represent stand in express opposition to one another. Heber says on page 302: 'If therefore Einhard in his life of Charles never mentions Waldo it need not surprise us. This man is the chief opponent and rival at the Court, as the legend shows, and the method he uses of annihilating him by silence is the same method which those of the Romish current successfully used later to annihilate him (Einhard), as we shall see.' Heber so regards the matter that he says, 'At the Court of Charles the Great, Einhard represents the *Latin* or *Romish* tendency; Waldo on the contrary was zealously concerned in cultivating the *Germanic* nature'. There is also historical proof of this—for example that in the library of Reichenau for which Waldo had taken the greatest pains, there existed: *De Carminibus Theodiscae*, Vol. I, also Vol. XII *Carmina Theodiscar linguae formata*, also *Carmina diversa ad docendam Theodiscam linguam*. Heber points out, quite correctly, that from the time when Waldo became the prevailing influence at the Court of Charles the Great, he ceased to favour the Latin speech and earnestly pursued the study of the German language, that he wrote a German grammar, made a collection of ancient songs and sagas of heroes and gave the winds German names.

Without wishing to follow Heber in every detail, we must nevertheless say that he has drawn attention to an important point. But the contrast of which he speaks was not merely that of the Latin and German tongues but rather the contrast between *Romish* and *Grail Christianity*. Hugo of Tours, Waldo of Reichenau and others closely connected with them, for example Count Matfrid, undoubtedly belonged to a circle which cultivated a different spiritual life from that of which Einhard is a representative. It is not necessary here to give a fuller biography of Waldo for this has already been done excellently by P. Emmanuel Munding, O.S.B., a Benedictine of the Archabbey Beuron in his comprehensive work: *Abt-Bischof Waldo, Begründer des Goldenen Zeitalters der Reichenau*. We find there actually everything that has been recorded about Waldo, only precisely the connection with which we are here concerned is not taken into consideration. On the other hand Heber was aware of it, for after giving a short summary of the Reichenau legend, he writes: 'Within this legend of the sacred blood there indwells, though undeveloped, the same nucleus which is also in the Grail Saga.'

Here we will only specially note a few things which are important in our present connection and which may be read up in detail in Munding's work where all the sources are given. Waldo is descended from a noble family and is a relation of Charles the Great. Munding on p. 14 in summing up his studies says: 'Now we know that Waldo was related to Wetti of Reichenau' (this is the personality who had had the mighty vision which may be looked upon in a certain sense as the precursor of Dante's vision) 'and through Wetti with the brothers Grimald and Tietgaud.' (This is Tietgaud who plays a role in the history of Pope Nicholas I.) 'He (Tietgaud) as Archbishop of Trier was the successor of his uncle Hetti, while his Aunt Warentrudis was Abbess and his Aunt Hulindis was a nun of the renowned convent of Pfalzel near Trier. Pfalzel, again, was a foundation of the Merovingian Kings and its first Abbess was Adela, a descendant of the royal house or related to it, while her sister Irmina was superintendent at Oehren near Trier which was likewise a foundation of the royal Merovingians. In this region, however, there were Carolingian possessions. Pfalzel undoubtedly was one of these for it belonged to Pippin II . . . Prüm too, in the Eifel, was Carolingian property; it belonged to Bertha, or Bertrada, the wife of King Pippin. She, and probably also her grandmother of the same name, lived in the north in the neighbourhood of Trier, between the Sauer and the Kyll. Bertha and her royal husband Pippin had possessions from Trier to Prüm and even to Blankenheim and Rheinbach near Bonn, especially in the strip of land between the rivers Prüm and Kyll, as well as to the north-east of Trier near the Moselle. Therefore also these two, Bertha and Pippin, are related to one another, for both inherit from their parents part of the same possessions and even their remaining properties are intermingled. They devoted their wealth to the founding of the convent in that place. Closer by lay their family possessions on the north-west side of the Moselle in the Charasgau (in the present province of Prüm), in Mosellegau, Bidgau (a village near Luxembourg), Eifelgau (in the province of Daun, in the regional province of Trier), Ripuariergau (Rheinbach near Bonn), Prüm (in the regional district of Trier). These were all in Austrasian territory in the hereditary district of the Carolingian house. Pippin, with his wife, built the convent on their own estate. Bertrada the Younger, wife of Pippin and mother of Charles the

Great, is probably the granddaughter of the elder Bertrada, who founded Prüm from her own resources and whose son Heribert or Charibert, Count of Laon, was the father of the younger Bertrada.'

This Charibert, Count of Laon, the father of Charles the Great's mother, is, however, as Conrad Fleck relates in his poem 'Flore and Blancheflur', none other than the Knight in red robes who appears under the roses and seeks the beautiful Lily, Blanchefleur. Concerning the connection between this Flore and the Parzival Saga we shall presently have to speak in detail. So in following up the Carolingian relationships of Waldo we have come upon a track which, as we shall see, stands in closest relation to the Grail. For the connection which we are here pursuing it is important that Waldo was Abbot of St Denis in Paris, where in a specially intensive way the works of Dionysius the Areopagite were studied, and his teachings stand in closest connection with Grail Christianity. Waldo also played a special role in Italy. Munding says correctly on page 74 that he was the mediator between Charles the Great and his young son Pippin in the affairs of Lombardy. Waldo was actually a kind of teacher and guardian of the barely ten year old son of the King and acted as regent for him during his minority. Waldo was also Bishop of Pavia and also of Basel, of which more can be read in Munding. It is necessary, however, to place a somewhat different value on some of the facts which Munding mentions. He says, for example, on page 89 where he is speaking of Waldo and his position in Basel: 'Waldo was never canonically appointed Bishop of Basel *for the authoritative sources do not mention him*... Yet Waldo cannot be quite passed over in silence, for other sources which have a certain value do mention him. Moreover, between the names of Baldebert (751–778 at latest) and Heito (805–823) there is a *striking gap*. It is precisely the time during which it is a question of Waldo having been Bishop of Basel.' Must we not regard such a striking fact in the same way that Heber regards the other facts concerning the memory of Waldo in St Denis? Thus on page 328 of his work on Waldo, Heber shows how Waldo's name has been erased from history. He writes: 'The legend of Reichenau says ... that Waldo's body was buried in a side chapel of the Abbey-Church of St Denis, further, that up to our time lights had been kept burning around it by the younger monks and it was so revered and venerated that the author of the legend, in accord with the tribute of homage thus paid to Waldo, exclaims: [and now Heber quotes the saying which Munding also has placed as motto at the head of his work] 'Never shall thy memory grow old in this place, and so long as this fleeting world continues will thy name without ceasing be honoured, oh thou holiest man.' But Heber adds: 'The existing records of the monastery prove however on the contrary that from the 12th century his memory was wiped out and they knew how to hide the fame of his name under a bushel.' Heber relates[64] that during some repairs Waldo's memory was completely obliterated: 'For the bones of Waldo no longer was any place found, either by the ten altars of the upper Church, or the ten small altars in the side chapel, or the five in the Crypt.' From now on his light was extinguished in the Church. There is no mention of him either at the twenty-five altars or anywhere else. Indeed to bring about a complete forgetfulness of him his name is omitted from the list of Abbots without the succession of names appearing to be broken.' Is it possible that perhaps Heber was right and that the memory of Waldo and his friend was not expunged from the history without a purpose? Perhaps we may suppose that the following has happened and it will be the task of further investigation to prove this.

We shall see presently,[65] as the legend of Flore and Blancheflur shows, that Grail Christianity was present with the grandparents of Charles the Great on his mother's side. This flowed down through two generations as far as Charles the Great. He however (even if not out of free will) formed an alliance with the Roman Church which was expressed by the Pope's crowning him as Roman Emperor of the West. Did not Grail Christianity, whose representative was Charles the Great, here enter into an alliance with the Roman element? Did not a more esoteric current here mingle with one that was exoteric? Rudolf Steiner has indicated that this was so. He said that in Flors and Blancheflos there lived the wish to maintain esoteric Christianity in its purity, while in Charles the Great it was united with exoteric Christianity.

Let us call accurately to mind the solemn act of the coronation of Charles the Great as Emperor on 25 December A.D. 800. King Charles was present at high mass in St Peter's in Rome at the Christmas festival in 800. As he was kneeling before the altar of St Peter, Pope Leo III placed the imperial crown on his head. The people shouted, 'To the divinely crowned Emperor Carolus Augustus, long life and victory.' Charles's biographer Einhard says that Charles was unpleasantly taken by surprise.[66] That he was unpleasantly surprised we can understand. For Charles had for a long time so thought of the protectorate of Rome that he had intended having a decisive voice himself in the choice of the Pope and concerning the Pope's Government. Had not Frankish arms only recently brought back to Rome the Pope who had been driven away? No wonder then that Charles, who had thought out his position in relation to the Pope quite definitely, felt disturbed when the Pope anointed him. But he quickly regained self-possession and adapted himself to the situation. We may presume that he had the intention of not changing his relation towards the Pope, but he may well have adapted matters in such a way that from now on he should so express his will and deed as to give it the character of being the will and deed of the Pope, and that through his being the one to carry out the Pope's will, he himself would thereby gain a special authority. We may regard what then happened either as a passing over of the Empire from the Greeks to the Franks or else a renewal of the Roman Empire in the West. The latter was the Pope's view which he emphasised on coins, inscriptions and seals (c.f. p. 85, Vol II of Cardinal Hergenröther's handbook of general Church history). Charles found, however, that through accepting the crown he had offended the East

Roman Church and in the year 811 it was precisely Hugo of Tours whom he sent to Byzantium to conciliate the Byzantine Emperor and to bring him to acknowledge his coronation as Emperor of the West. What else could he do when everything had happened as it did? But this coronation meant the pouring of a spiritual stream into Rome which formerly had been kept far from it.

In the environment of Charles the Great, there were, however, as we know, personalities who did not consider this conjunction with the Latin stream to be right but had originally quite other purposes. And to these personalities belonged also Waldo. It has already been pointed out that it is symptomatic and significant that Waldo was made Abbot precisely at St Denis, i.e. he was placed at that spot, whether purposely or through the guidance of destiny, in which there was a connection with the writings of Dionysius the Areopagite. In 827 Michael the Stammerer of Byzantium sent the writings of Dionysius the Areopagite to St Louis the Pious. They were passed on to Abbot Hilduin, Waldo's successor at St Denis (c.f. 1 Durantel, *St Thomas et le Pseudo-Denis*). Nowadays everything possible is brought forward to prove the non-genuineness of these Dionysian writings. Rudolf Steiner, however, has showed that Spiritual Science in its method of investigation finds the content of these writings genuine. In the writings of the so-called Pseudo-Dionysius are reflected—of course written later—the content of the teaching of that Dionysius the Areopagite, who is mentioned in the Acts of the Apostles and who was an intimate pupil of St Paul. The pupils of this Dionysius took over from him each time the teaching and the name, and one of these pupils wrote down the work that has come down to us. Waldo, at least in his destiny, is closely connected with this stream of Dionysius the Areopagite.

This kind of Christianity which desires to cultivate Christianity in the native language we find also in Ulfilas, of whom extraordinarily little is known but of whom it is recorded that in his translation of the Bible he left out the Book of Kings because it seemed to him too warlike. This mood characterises the kind of mind Ulfilas had. There hovered before him a Christianity that strove not for outer power but rather to live itself intimately into the various *folk souls*. Therefore he did not give the Bible to his Goths in *Latin* but in the *Gothic* language. And we see in Waldo the same impulse to bring Christianity close to the heart of the people out of the forces of the language of the people. So we slowly gain an insight into the nature of the striving of that circle of friends who, at the Court of Charles the Great, sought to continue what we find revealed in the story of Flore and Blanchefleur in the form of a legend, and also to win Charles the Great for it. Therefore we will next study this legend which hands down to us in a different way that which has not come through the channel of history.

3
Flore and Blanscheflur

Conrad Fleck relates the Saga of Flore and Blanscheflur as we give it here in extract. This poem, translated from the Middle High German by Karl Pannier, is to be found in the *Universalbibliothek* No. 5781-5783 in the Philipp Reclam edition in Leipzig. Karl Pannier correctly says in the preface: 'Even if the original nucleus of the Saga must be sought in the Orient yet the standard form in which it spread to the West certainly arose in Northern France. The oldest form which has been preserved of this ancient French poem of Flore and Blanscheflur is edited by Edélstand Du Méril.' Only quite general motives have been taken over from the Orient. There is no doubt that the concrete saga which we have here, intermingled perhaps with sundry Oriental motives, proceeds from the European West. We will now relate the story as given by Conrad Fleck.

Conrad Fleck refers to an original French manuscript by Ruprecht von Orbent (verse 140) but it has not been possible to trace this author.

> 118 Of Love will I tell you so well as I may
> And through this legend you shall learn
> How once there were two children
> Whom Love brought to grief
> The two loved one another already
> So the adventure relates
> When they were not yet five years old.

Thus it is of heart's sorrow that came about through love of which the poet tells. And of a wonderful pair of children whose love blossomed in great purity long before they reached the age when they would be capable of feeling passion. This poem has the same aim as the Parzival poem of Wolfram von Eschenbach, for here too the prize is awarded to fidelity and steadfastness, to *Staete*:

> 274 Hear what to you I wish to say!
> Those who make plaint concerning love
> And, full of woe, strive after her
> Should, whatever else betide,
> *Steadfast* for evermore remain.

In just such constant faith were Flore and Blancheflur devoted to one another. And now the poet tells us that from these two Bertha was descended, and, as may be read in the ancient books, from her and Pippin was born later Charles the Great:

> 273 Then to this loving pair
> A child, a lovely maid
> Was given, named Bertha with the foot[1]
> From this Bertha, as we find in the old books
> And from Pippin, was born later
> Charles.

So *the Legend of Blancheflur*, grandmother of Charles the Great on the mother's side, likewise belongs to the circle of those documents with which we are here concerned. We shall see that *in the form of a charming story the greatest world-historic impulse of the eighth and ninth centuries comes to expression in this legend.*

> 290 Know ye Flore was a heathen
> But a Christian was Blancheflur
> Yet this difference if you only believe it
> Divided them not in their lives
> For Flore received baptism
> Through his love to Blancheflur
> Who never knew doubt.

The poet tells us where Flore had his Kingdom: he ruled in Hungary, in Vergalt (Norgalt) and in Greece. The legend makes him ruler of Greece because it is related of Bertha the Mother of Charles the Great that she was the daughter of the Emperor Heraclius. Thus the legend identifies the Greek Emperor Heraclius with our Flore (cf. the introduction of Du Méril). The poet says that he inherited Hungary from his Uncle. The father of Flore is Fenix the King of Spain. He also came into conflict with a host of pilgrims who belonged to a Carolingian Count who, with his daughter, was taking part in a pilgrimage to Santiago de Compostella. This Count was then killed in battle so that his daughter who was expecting a child and whose husband was dead, remained behind alone. This lady is the mother of Blancheflur. Taken prisoner by Fenix she came into his land. She disembarked at Naples and Fenix presented her as a gift to his wife, the Spanish Queen. She was lovingly received by the Queen and so it happened that the Queen of Spain bore her son at the same moment in which the Carolingian Countess bore a daughter, Blancheflur.

> 307 These two of whom I tell you
> Were both born on *one* day

> In *one* house, in *one* hour
> And what the legend says is well attested
> And *one* nurse brought up both.

It was on a Palm Sunday that both of them came into the world. But Palm Sunday means: Blossoming Easter—paske florie as Conrad Fleck says. Therefore they were called Blansche*flur* and *Flore*. And now it is related how dearly the two loved each other and how they went together to school. When, however, the King observed the love of the two children, who were growing up, he wished to separate them. Indeed, in his first anger the King desired to kill Blanscheflur. The Queen however pacified him. She advised him to restrain his wrath and to take her good advice. But she perceived that Flore could no longer remain there and continue to go to school with Blanscheflur. Rather must his interest be diverted far away. So it was decided to send Flore to school in Muntore in Andalusia. There lived the Queen's sister Sibylle and her husband Gurass. Flore set out on this journey but only on condition that Blanscheflur should be sent after him as soon as her mother, whom she remained behind to nurse, could spare her. As Blanscheflur did not arrive at the time promised, Flore returned home to fetch her. Meanwhile, however, the Queen had sold Blanscheflur to merchants. These merchants from Babylon halted at Lunquit. They gave as her price gold and treasures. Among these treasures there was a *goblet* which had been made by the God Vulcan himself. On it the meeting of Paris with Pallas Athene, Juno and Venus was portrayed. The Goddess of discord, who was not invited to the feast of the Gods had thrown an apple amongst the Gods which bore the inscription 'for the fairest'. Paris was to decide to which of the three Goddesses the apple belonged by right. Juno promised him *power*, Pallas Athene *wisdom*, Venus *beauty*. Paris decided in favour of beauty and so kept Helen.

Through this arose the Trojan war. All this was portrayed on this cup, the lid of which was crowned by a carbuncle and which had the quality of giving health for a year to him who drank from it. The carbuncle moreover shone by night. Blanscheflur was exchanged for this vessel and other treasures. The Amiral[2] bought her from the merchants and shut her up in a tower. Now when Flore returned home he was assured that Blanscheflur had died, and he was shown her grave. The memorial stone was made of marble and borne by four bronze lions. It was decorated all round with pictures of various animals which have their dwelling place in the elements:

> 1887 On the stone the eye astonished saw
> So many beasts formed by a master hand
> That lived on *earth*, in *water*, or in *air*.

This work had been created by the God of *fire*, by Orphanus and Vulcan.

Over the first stone lay a second, gaily coloured. In the radiance of the Sun four things shone forth:

1906   Gold, silver, precious stones
           And fair colours—these are four.

Above were to be seen two figures, one masculine and one feminine:

1912   A clever master had devised a picture,
           Two children laughing—
           Fair, playful, filled with happiness.
           Blanscheflur the gentle maid
           Resembled the one picture,
           Which was fashioned beautifully of rich gold.
           The other picture exactly resembled Flore.

The pictures appeared as though living.

1922   One saw how Flore daintily, tenderly
           Offered the friend a *rose*,
           Skilfully fashioned of red gold.
           Then graciously the friend held out to him
           A lily of burnished gold.

Both figures wore crowns. In Flore's crown was shown a carbuncle. At the four corners of this work of art were four pipes which gave forth four different kinds of wind. It was a miracle of workmanship, the like of which did not exist; for the lightest breath of wind lent the figures life and movement. Indeed, they could even speak and the marvel was that the figures remained united in love as long as the wind blew. They kissed one another and, as long as the wind persisted, found no rest. This monument stood before the door of the minster. Four Gods were planting four trees around the grave which were evergreen. An *olive* tree stood at the maiden's head, a tree of *balsam* at her feet. On Flore's side stood a tree of *cloves* and a tree from which streamed a *sweet perfume*. Of the tree of balsam it was said that it yielded an oil for anointing, with which youth could be sweetened. The clove tree was proof against fire. The aromatic tree bore red blossoms and from these came the scent.

    This marvellous tomb however was empty, for Blanscheflur was not dead but only snatched away. When Flore became acquainted with the report of Blanscheflur's death he determined to kill himself. So there was nothing for it but to tell him where she was. When this was done he set forth to seek her. Magnificently armed and accompanied by the wondrous vessel Flore rode forth. His *horse* was white on one side and on the other red. Quite sharp and clear was the distinction between the colours on the body of the horse. Quite equally too were the colours divided on the animal's body and there was a strip of black, of the width of three fingers, where the red and white surfaces met. This strip of black began at the forehead and went right along the back down to the tail in which it also appeared, for the tail displayed the two colours as well. On the sides of the horse stood the inscription 'Only he is worthy to ride me who is worthy of a crown.' This marvel was not a human invention but a *work of nature*. The charger's saddle too was wonderful and fashioned so that its *weight* was *equally* divided. Everywhere the right measure was preserved and everywhere was attained the correct medium between too high and too low. Anyone who reads the description of this horse recognises without difficulty what appears in all alchemistic writings, the different colours and the warning to observe the right balance, etc.[3]

But we must return to our story. The mother after she had equipped the son for the journey, gave him at the very last a ring which had the wonderful power of overcoming all enmity.

After many adventures, Flore who had still to wait for a favourable wind, crossed the sea towards Baldag. So after a fourteen day sea voyage he reached his goal in the land that was *ruled by seven kings*. In it was situated a tower with seventy chambers and in each of these chambers dwelt a fair lady. And here Blanscheflur was imprisoned. The interior of the tower was most wonderful—gold, lapis lazuli and gleaming crystals decorated it:

> 4074 The tower's summit had no roof
> For in lieu of a roof there glittered
> A shining knob of red gold,
> A wondrous arched dome
> Which rayed down light
> And when the hot sun was seen thereon
> The knob blazed and flamed with such resplendence
> It seemed, if one looked up,
> As if flames would burst through.

Leading up to this knob was a golden tube on which rested a carbuncle. This illuminated the whole castle. Deep below, however, there was a magic spring.

> 4100 And this Spring's source
> To a pillar is led
> Inwardly hollowed with cunning and art
> Upward the pillar strives high as the tower,
> In its hollow is a pipe,
> With *silver* all inlaid;
> Through this ascends the little Spring
> Within the pipe remaining bright and clear
> And wondrous cool *through all the year*.

>   Within a pipe of chaséd lead
>   It would have been impaired, the Spring's Perfection fair.

This Spring supplies all seventy chambers with water.

> 4127 Embracing all this pipe around
>   A man stood formed of bronze,
>   Whose mouth is open, whence there flows
>   A stream of water constantly,
>   A stream, received in its descent
>   Within the hollow pillar.
>   *First* was it led the upward way,
>   But *now* descends within the pipe.

This remarkable circulation too is always described in alchemistic descriptions.

So Blanscheflur lives in this tower and Flore has to rescue her from it. Four sentries guard the tower in which the seventy ladies dwell. They all serve the Amiral. Two, however, especially, Blanscheflur and her friend Claris.[4]

> 4193 When he[5] retires to rest at night
>   And rises early in the morn
>   Then instantly one ready stands
>   To hand him water
>   When on his stately couch he rests—
>   Such is the Master's habit—
>   And following her another waits
>   To hand at once a towel.

A sentinel guards the only door. And Flore must in some way win him. He wins his favour by presents and, after a game of chess, which he (Flore) wins, he not only excuses him his debt, but gives him an equivalent sum as a present. Thus he finally gets into the tower. Clothed in a garment of *red*, in a mantle of red blialt, concealed under *red roses*, the servants of the watcher carry him up the steps in a basket of flowers:

> 5277 He had delicate *rose* blooms
>   And grass and other blossoms fair,
>   As ladies love to see them,
>   Assembled in eight baskets wide;
>   For that was the joyous time
>   Of blossoms.
>   Beneath this he concealed

With bold and cunning art
In a large basket, Flore.

Now it is humorously described how the servants, swaying under the immense weight of the basket, set it down a floor too low. But fortunately Flore by this means was admitted to the presence of Claris who was so well disposed towards Blanscheflur. She, after recovering from the shock of seeing the red knight emerge from the basket, called her friend Blanscheflur to come. So the red knight found his white bride.[6]

5928 After so long a pain, in love
Forgot was all the woe experienced
Through long long hours.
As without fear the loving pair
So near each other once more were
And on the couch together sat,
No rapture nor desire forgot,
Forever sprang forth love anew
Which all who love enjoy so gladly—
Up to the point of that *one* game
Which th' only aim of savage man is . . .
What satisfies a right true man
A loving word, a sweetest kiss,
He (the savage man) finds no delight in.
Forsooth for *such* award of love
No thought came near this purest pair,
Nought here prevailed but quite pure love
And purest love was all its aim.

This joy however did not last long, for very quickly Flore's presence in the tower was discovered. It happened that one morning Blanscheflur did not wake at the right time to perform her service for the Amiral and was still asleep when Claris, already in her place, observed Blanscheflur's absence with fear and trembling. So at once a messenger was sent to her, and when he came back with his news the Amiral himself went to see what had been told him. When the messenger saw the two lying side by side he did not know whether it was a maiden or a knight who lay at Blanscheflur's side.

6160 Too soon came then the messenger
Where, arm round neck, the lovers lay
In bliss and rapture close embraced
And fast asleep.
Cheek pressed to cheek and mouth towards mouth
As true love teaches ever,
Love such as in their two hearts dwelt.

> And as the messenger saw this
> And gazed on Flore in amaze
> He quaked, nor in that moment's gaze
> Could tell what kind of being Flore was,
> If man or woman who could say?
> For like maiden's was his lovely body
> No hair was on the lip or chin
> Thus he stood there in fear and doubt
> Unwilling them to waken or alarm,
> And so he let them lie, and in his heart
> There conquered pity as he saw the pair,
> And quick reported he how all things were.

As soon as the Amiral heard the news he hurried, sword in hand, to the chamber where the two were asleep. He entered full of rage. But he himself was filled with astonishment and could not well decide who it could be that lay there with his lady love. When however he became convinced that it was a young knight, he gave him a rude awakening. Without further regard or consideration the two were placed in the large hall of the tower in order to face execution for what they had done. With drawn sword the Amiral asked Flore his name. Flore requested that the Caliph might do them the honour to hear the complaint which the Amiral might bring against Flore and also to hear what he might say for his justification. Thereto the Admiral agreed and proceeded to give notice far and wide that on the following day he would hold a Supreme Court of judgement.

> 6923 Straightway there rose in Babylon
> A noise and uproar everywhere.

Now as the dreaded morning dawned and the two were led to judgement, Flore suddenly remembered the little ring which his mother had given him. He took if off in order to send it to Blanscheflur for protection. But she sent it back. He pressed it upon her. She threw it away. A Duke who, as guard accompanied them in order to bring them to the tribunal, witnessed this extraordinary conflict, and gathered from the conversation of the two the qualities and powers of the stone. So he stooped and picked up the ring. Then in the course of events the two were being judged and this Duke appeared in defence of Flore and Blanscheflur. He said to the Amiral that never before had he found two so true, so of one mind, so bound to each other in deepest love, who, at the same time were so young and inexperienced. And then the Duke related how neither of them would keep for himself the ring that could save. This led to the Amiral examining the two but without relinquishing his rage. Flore now told his name and where he dwelt, but refused to say how he had obtained entrance into the tower. Finally he begged that he alone might be slain, for Blanscheflur was guiltless.

But Blanscheflur protested that Flore had come on her account and only *she* should be killed. The Amiral however remained unmoved and commanded that his sword should be handed to him:

> 6977 Hand me my sword! he then commands
> And quickly draws the naked steel,
> With rage consumed, above her head.

And now it happened that whenever one of the two laid their head on the block the other pressed forward and pushed it aside.

> 7016 She drew him forwards, he drew back
> His head to offer to the sword
> This strife and counterstrife went on
> Till for this woeful pair
> All hearts were seized with pity.
> Whoever watched this sorry sight
> For very grief the tears ran
> Adown the cheeks of man and woman.
> Had anyone a heart of stone
> He must have mourned the noble strife.
> Never in future nor in the past
> Had such a judgement taken place
> That even manly hearts embraced
> With such a woe and mourning.
> Indifferent was the Amiral
> And never thought of grace or goodness
> Until his heart all filled with wrath
> Waxed slowly, slowly weak and weaker,
> Until at last his stubbornness
> Gave way and vanished, and his wrath
> On which his mind had hardened,
> And to his right senses he returned.
> From every quarter came the call
> Use mercy Lord! for now 'tis time,
> See how before thee lies the maid
> For whom thyself hath often yearned,
> How can for thee the sword avail?'

And so at last the Amiral had pity on these poor children.

> Then a memory came into his mind
> Of all her service and his love,
> And how she once had pleased him well
> And so in thought's reaction
> *There fell the sword from out his hand.*

Thus here again there occurs what we have noticed in the story of the Knight Hugo.

Conrad Fleck relates at the close of the story the marriage and return of the pair. Flore's father having meanwhile died, they returned as rulers of Spain. Claris remained behind as wife of the Amiral. Happy and making others happy, Flore and Blanscheflur lived to their hundredth year, entering into divine blessedness in the *same* hour and on the *same* day. 'One grave enclosed the two bodies but their souls took flight into God's eternal realm of bliss. Never could false love enter where these two came. And all said "Amen!"'

Thus we see handed down in this legend a story which has an unmistakable similarity with that of the Knight Hugo. But it did not take place at the time of Charles the Great but two generations earlier. Yet this legend also leads us into the realm of Charles the Great, viz. to his mother and to his grandparents on the mother's side. Of these two whom the legend names Flore and Blanscheflur, history knows at least Flore. He is Charibert von Laon, the son of that Bertrada who founded the monastery of Prüm on 23 June 721.[7] The legend makes this Charibert to be the son of Fenix, King of Spain.[8]

That the race of Bertha, mother of Charles the Great, was Frankish is expressly stated by Pope Stephen II. (Codex Carolinus No. 45 in Dahn's *Urgeschichte*, Vol. 3, page 855—Oncken's *Allgemeine Geschichte*.)

Charibert von Laon must have still been alive at the time of the marriage of Pippin and Bertha for he bequeathed to them a part of Rumersheim (op. cit. Dahn, p. 834). The marriage took place about 741, for Charles the Great was born 742. At the time of the sending of the embassy by Pippin to Al-Mansur, Charibert appears to have already died, for it is his successor Froidmont who is mentioned in 763 (cf. Melleville, *Histoire de Laon*, Laon 1846, Vol. I p. 400). The legend speaks of his reaching the age of one hundred years. *Since the legend makes Charibert von Laon himself travel to the East, it seems likely that he was the inspirer of the journey which took place in 765.*

A reality is reflected by way of a legend in this journey of Flore to the East. The soul of Europe sought something in the East. It desired to fetch something from there which it felt as belonging to it—Blanscheflur.

Concerning this, Rudolf Steiner has said that in the story of Flore and Blanscheflur the quest of the world-soul for the human soul is portrayed. They are not an external couple. Lily (Blanscheflur) is the soul that finds its higher Egohood. So Flore who represents the European soul travels to the East to rescue what is man's highest treasure.

Anyone reading the poem of Conrad Fleck carefully and knowing the kind of language used by alchemists of the Middle Ages easily recognises that the poem is a description of the alchemistic way of knowledge. It is shown in the emphasis laid on the four elements—Earth, Water, Air and Fire—and in the descriptions of colours mentioned in the poem and more especially in the reference to the aromatic scent of the red substance.[9]

Further all that is said about the wind and the remarkable provision for water in the tower shows what knowledge is referred to. We find an exact correspondence in all alchemists. In the journey to the East it is a question of fetching over knowledge derived from the primeval wisdom which comes to light later especially in the literature of the *Rosicrucians*. The emphasis on the ROSE[10] points also to this kind of wisdom.

Thus our story of the legend of Flore and Blanscheflur has led us to the discovery of a quest towards the East two generations before Charles the Great. The spiritual stream running beneath the surface of profane history gradually becomes visible.

The following chapter will show from the point of view of world-history what has here been indicated in the form of a legend: *The rescue of the original wisdom of Charibert of Laon* before it was completely laid hold of by Arabism.

4
Orient and Occident

The Mystery of Golgotha came to pass at the moment when Christ's blood flowed down upon the Earth. Then the Spirit of the Sun passed over into the earth.[1] Then the heavenly Logos had not only become flesh but it had also passed from Jesus, the man, into the whole Earth organism. What occurred at that point had been in preparation for a long time, and the whole pre-Christian history is the history of the descent of the Divine down to Earth. In a marvellous way the descent of the Sun Spirit had been foretold prophetically by the founder of the Persian Civilisation, Zarathustra. He composed the wonderful words:

> The mighty promise-bearing [kingly] Sun–Aether–Aura, the God-Created, we worship in prayer
> Which will pass over to the most victorious of Saviours and the others, His Apostles.
> Which brings forward the world,
> Which causes it to conquer old age and death, corruption and decay,
> Which assists it to Eternal life, to Eternal prosperity, to free will [to Lordship in will]
> When the dead shall arise
> When the living Conqueror of Death comes
> And the world is brought forward through Will.
> (German trans: Dr Hermann Beckh, *Die Drei*, Year V, Vol 10, Stuttgart)

When the Persian looked up to heaven then he knew that behind the surface of the sky, hidden by the darkness of the heavens, shines the Spiritual Sun. At one spot it becomes visible, where the Sun's disc appears. Out of this wonderful radiant background of gold appear the coloured forms of the Gods seen in imagination. This experience is reflected in Persian art, as Dr Steiner has shown, for example in the Persian mosaics, where the most beautifully coloured pictures appear on a golden background. The sun is the door, but is also the Guardian before the door, for in looking up to this Guardian the earthly glance perishes. He who later spake the words, 'I am the door' and 'No man comes to the golden radiance of the world foundation (to the Father) but by Me.' He was still experienced in cosmic space, as the Sun Spirit in the most ancient Persian time. Stepwise, *gradalis*, He descended thence to the Earth, and His descent, the descent of the World Saviour, down into the darkness, is reflected in the history of the oriental religions. What then descended was experienced as the cosmic Word, sounding from all directions of space which in shining sounded, and in sounding shone. The light radiating into the depths must penetrate the forces of nature and these forces were felt in the image of the Bull. Mithras conquering the Bull is one of the imaginations for the primeval Word in its descent. This Bull was experienced as spreading through the whole space of heaven, for its head was where the constellation of the Bull is, and its tail where the constellation is of the Virgin bearing the ears of corn. This tail ended in three ears of corn. From below, from the constellation of the Scorpion, the sub-earthly force of the Scorpion lays hold of the Bull. So, to begin with, the heavenly Bull was spread out in the Zodiac. Mithras thrusts the golden dagger into the neck from the constellation of the Twins. Later we find as picture of heavenly events on Earth the gleaming Plough thrust into the Earth's neck.[2]

Thus was the descent of the primeval Word perceived in manifold imaginations, and the Mysteries cherished the memory of the original revelation of the Divine out of the heights as a wondrous primeval wisdom. A picture which later passed over into the cycle of Christian concepts, we see emerge in Wolfram von Eschenbach. We will seek to bring it in all its fulness before our souls. From lofty starry regions there shines towards the depths the figure bearing the fiery sword, which in Christian nomenclature is called *Michael*. He treads underfoot the falling Spirits. The light bringer, Lucifer, falls downwards. Through his descent into earthly regions he brings man the light, brings him knowledge, is able to say to him: 'Thine eyes shall be opened, and thou shalt discern light and darkness, good and evil.' But what falls downwards is not only Lucifer, it is a whole corona of Beings who accompany him. And the legend speaks of this corona as being the crown of Lucifer. And then Michael with his flaming sword strikes *one* Spirit out of the Corona of Spirits, out of Lucifer's crown, a Spirit different from all the others. *One* Spirit took the path from the heights to the depths, not as one falling, but accompanying the falling Spirits out of free will in order to bring salvation to the men who were to be delivered over to these Spirits. This being of *Angelic nature*[3] prepared the way for the Lord who followed him, for the world Logos Himself took the same path which the falling Spirits took whom Michael trod underfoot. Concerning this Being who prepared the way for the World Logos, the legend says that He had shone as a wondrous jewel in the crown of Lucifer. Michael struck this stone from Lucifer's crown, he then came down to men, formed himself into a vessel, became indeed the vessel destined to receive the Blood of Christ. This became the sacred Chalice which held within it the Sun-Host. Beings of Wisdom were they all who took their way from the heights into the depths. Wisdom that willed to become the vessel of love, such was the one Being. At first—so says the legend—it was preserved in a Mystery [centre] of Hercules, a Plutonic Sun Hero, i.e. in a Phoenician Mystery centre in Tyre,[4] in the City of Hiram. It then came to the Queen of Sheba, the Queen of the Star Wisdom; she brought it to Solomon. In this picture it is the path of wisdom that is described. Then this vessel came into the house in which Christ partook of the Last Supper with His disciples and the power which flowed over from Him to His disciples streamed forth from this holy vessel. A Jew brought it to Pilate, for Christ was led before Pilate. And when, after the Mystery of Golgotha, Joseph of Arimathea begged the body of Christ from Pilate, Pilate committed to him this precious vessel and he and his descendants became guardians of the Grail.

Thus the history of the Grail is the History of the wisdom descending from above downwards, the wisdom which was to become the vessel of love, and which became so the more, as it took its way from East to West. Preserved as it was in the various Oriental Mysteries this primeval wisdom found its last pictorial expression in the magnificent mythical pictures of the Platonic philosophy. In *the Symposium*, in the Banquet of Plato, there still live Grail mysteries, and in the discussion it appears how the love of Diotima must supplement the wisdom of Silenus. Plato is the last oriental, his pupil Aristotle the first westerner. We know from the spiritual investigations of Rudolf Steiner that an important conversation took place between Plato and Aristotle,[5] in which Plato demanded from Aristotle that he should henceforth transmit the whole of the primeval wisdom divested of pictures, in the form of concepts used in the West. And the history of Aristotelianism is the history of the further spreading of the primeval wisdom. While the Mystery of the Logos becoming flesh in the Christ was gradually being fulfilled, while it came to pass that the Kingdom of Heaven drew near and the mind of mankind was changed, there arose in the spirit of Aristotle the reflection on earth of the World Logos as recorded in the writing of the stars, viz. logic.[6] While the Logos Himself was descending there grew within humanity the faculty of knowledge to comprehend the Logos. It was with the thought-structure of Aristotle, that is with the metamorphosed primeval wisdom, that the Middle Ages sought to understand the Christ impulse.

At first the course of world evolution was such that no people on earth were so adapted to understand Jesus of Nazareth as the Persians who had prophesied of Him. Christ the Risen One however could be understood in a grand way by the Greeks. *By a union of the Persian and the Greek nature* an understanding for the Divine-human was rendered possible. The capacities of the different peoples are differently distributed. To the Jews was given the mission of providing a body for the Christ, of building the Temple of God; they could do this because the Phoenician stream added the faculty and power to carry things out. To the Romans the power was given to spread Christianity; the Greeks had the capacity for spiritual understanding, as Rudolf Steiner showed. The Persian, however, could recognise the nature of the Sun-Hero Who, like Ormuzd, is surrounded by twelve Amshaspands, his twelve apostles. But that which had been prepared by a wise world guidance did not come to pass. The Greek nature did not unite with the Persian impulse but with the Arabic. And Arabism came to the West via the Arabs. This reversal, this decision of fate, must be perceived if we wish to understand European spiritual history.

In the world of Asia Minor, there lived, in the third century AD, an extraordinarily important personality: Mani, or Manes, the founder of Manichaeism. He appeared when the sun was in the constellation of the Ram, when King Shapur began his reign in the year AD 242. He taught in a great way the descent of the primeval light, the Sun Spirit into the darkness. He described in thrilling words the penetration of matter by the Spirit. A grand moral conception of the overcoming of evil, not by conflict but by love, lived in his teaching. Mani *spoke* what Christ *did*, and he desired to teach humanity to live according to this deed of Christ. In his thinking, feeling and willing he was entirely filled with the Holy Spirit who spoke through him, and we shall perhaps best learn to know him if we can experience the conquering power of his word.

The following are rendered freely but in a way truly characteristic of him:

'Evil has not existed as evil from the beginning but only in its elements. For what is good and right is different for different times. Thus, what at first worked for good because it belonged to the time, later works injuriously. Taken merely in its elements evil is of the same origin as good, and it too therefore is without end. As evil it does end. But it determines its own end, being placed in a position to do so by the sacrificial act of the good which freely mingled with it. In order that good shall be able to redeem evil, it develops to the extent that, while separated from it, it has the power, through partly uniting with evil, to place it in the position of becoming good also, out of free will stimulated by the radiant light of the good. Now because evil has five members while good has seven, the good only remains by itself at the beginning and end. But during the middle period of its evolution it dips down into the five and redeems the harmony of the twelvefoldness. [Here reference is made to the seven light and the five dark constellations in the sun's course.] Therefore the Godhead, King of the Paradise of Light, adopts five members. His members are, Gentleness, Knowledge, Understanding, Silence and Penetration. Five other members are, however, concerned with the heart [das Gemüt]: Love, Faith, Fidelity, Bravery, Wisdom. As the evolution of the world brought about the severance of the world of the Light, of the heights, from the dark flood of the depths, there arose Satan from the depths. He was not himself without beginning but was nevertheless without beginning in his parts and elements; thus it was these parts which came together out of the elements and formed themselves into Satan. His head was that of a lion, his trunk that of a dragon, his wings were like those of a great bird, his tail was that of a water animal, his four feet however resembled those of a land animal. As this being had formed itself out of the darkness it was called the Dragon, the old Serpent. Then he began to destroy, to swallow and to injure other beings, stalking hither and thither to right and left and penetrating down below into the depths where he continually brought injury and destruction to all who sought to overpower him. Thereafter he darted upwards into the heights and catching sight of the radiance of the light felt a repugnance towards it. When he further saw that this radiance was only strengthened by coming into contact with its opposite, he was alarmed, crumpled up together limb by limb and withdrew into his basic elements.

But now once again he darted up into the heights, and now the Light-Earth observed the activity of Satan and his intention to attack and destroy. And as the Earth observed this, behold the world of Insight, the world of Knowledge, then the world of Silence, then the world of Understanding, then the world of Gentleness also observed it. Thereupon the King of the Paradise of Light observed it and considered by what means Satan might be met.

His hosts truly were powerful enough, but in the realm of light there was only good. Therefore He with His righteous Spirit, with His five worlds and with His twelve elements, created a race—the original race of men. This race he sent below that it might mix itself with darkness. And this race was to fight the Dragon.

Then primeval man armed himself with his five supporters, the five Gods—with the lightly fluttering breath, with the wind, with the light, with the water and with the fire. The first thing with which he clothed himself was the breath. Over the fluttering breath he wrapped the mantle of light that undulated downwards, and over the light he drew the veil of welling water and protected himself with the blowing wind. Then he took the fire as a shield and lance in his hand and hastened to descend from Paradise.

Then the Dragon armed himself with his five supporters—with the smoke, the flame, the darkness, the scorching wind, the suffocating fumes—he armed himself with them, took them for his shield and went forth against primeval man. They fought for a long time and the Dragon won the victory over man, devoured some of his light and surrounded him with his supporters and his Elements. Then arose the storm, the whirling dance and death, and hell consumed itself. Thus arose the human race. Man however recognised the Friend of Light, the King of the Paradise of Light and this radiance filled him with delight. For the light of primal man that the Dragon had swallowed caused the Dragon to feel pleasure in light. "May light be kindled by light" rejoiced man, and the abyss rose ever higher and higher, radiating, sparkling, shining and emitting light like a Sun. Thus were the Spirits of darkness, together with all their dependents and their substances redeemed, uplifted, illumined and warmed, so that gentleness proved stronger than hatred. In man gentleness redeemed the Dragon from hell.'[7]

This description is able to give us a fundamental feeling of Manichaeism. Through the horrible death of its founder and the intensive persecution of its adherents very little of this lofty outlook has come down to us. The enemies of this spiritual current have only handed down to us broken fragments of this teaching in their writings against it and yet Manichaeism still continues to live through the centuries and is also to be found in Goethe's *Faust*, although in a weaker form. It is precisely Goethe who in his Prologue links up with the fundamental conception of the Persians, and the problem is no longer expressed with such depth as in the Persian tradition itself for the question is not how Faust can protect himself against Mephistopheles but how Mephistopheles himself is to be redeemed. The fundamental thought of Manichaeism lives also in the Grail poem. For instance, in Wolfram's *Parzival* most clearly and plainly it is said that it is possible to transform the Evil:

If unfaith in the heart find dwelling
Then the soul it shall reap but woe;
And shaming alike and honour
Are his who such doubt shall show,
For it standeth in evil contrast
With a true man's dauntless might
As one seeth the magpie's plumage,
Which at one while is black and white.
And yet he may win to blessing,
Since I wot well that in his heart,
Hell's darkness and light of heaven
Alike have their lot and part.
(Opening stanza of Wolfram's *Parzival*.)

We further find the same idea in the Order of the Templars who do not admit merely the pure but who above all seek to lead evil-doers back to the Good. Hence also the remarkable regulation that one who is excommunicate, if joining the Order of Templars, shall be considered as freed from the curse. Again we find the same idea in Goethe's fragment, *Die Geheimnisse* [The Mysteries]:

We admitted none who young in years
Too early had the world renounced
Only when we had known life's joys and woe

And no more blew the wind within our sails
Was it allowed that we with honour here should land.

This is the meaning of the Grail: The pure fool does indeed find the Grail, but he is not worthy to possess it; only if he brings the black-white brother, the human brother, with him to the Grail, only then does he become King of the Grail. Parzival has to leave the Grail Castle. When he enters it a second time he brings with him the human brother Feirefis, who cannot see the Grail but can see very well its bearer and who through love of the Grail-bearer is brought to behold the Grail itself. In true Manichaeism there lives a wonderful moral impulse, a true Christianity, but with a special and peculiar concept of sin. That sin is something that can be made good again, this is the faith of Manichaeism. It is destined to penetrate Christianity ever more and more with the teaching of reincarnation and karma. Of the writings of this Manichaeism little more remains than the titles. We will name a few of them: The Mystery, the Epistle, the Gospel, the Thesaurus.[8] The writing concerning the Mystery treats of the Son of the Widow, the seven spirits, the four spirits, transitoriness, the three and a half days, the prophets, and the resurrection. The Epistles treat of light and darkness, of the Great Initiates, of the seal of the mouth, of comfort, of Paradise, of time, of fire, and of the Cross.

If this selection alone is read the wish arises that one might possess the whole document. Instead of this there is an extensive literature pouring out wrath and curses on Manichaeism amongst which these titles are scattered. The great aim of Manichaeism is to regard evil under the image of the *black coal*, but never to forget that black coal and the transparent *diamond* are the same substance. But the road to this is hard, and diamond is the hardest stone. In the Founder of Manichaeism we have to do with one of the highest initiates. In his lecture cycle No IX,[9] Dr Steiner says of him, 'Mani is still higher, still more powerful than Scythianos, mightier than Zarathustra or Buddha. Mani in his wisdom may be called an exalted messenger of the Christ.'

The will of Manichaeism is entirely directed towards the future; towards that future of which Mark speaks when he says (Chap. XIII, verse 24) 'But in those days, after that tribulation, the sun shall be darkened and the moon shall not give her light. And the stars shall fall from heaven and the powers that are in the heaven shall be shaken. And then shall they see the Son of Man coming in clouds with great power and glory. And then shall He send forth His Angels and shall gather together His elect from the four winds, from the uttermost part of the earth, to the uttermost part of heaven.' And Thomas Aquinas says in accordance with Isaiah XXX, verse 26, 'After the advent of Antichrist the structure of the world will be changed and the stars will fade in the exceeding light of Christ. Even sun and moon will for a time lose their light as at the death of Christ. After the day of judgement however the light of the moon will be as the light of the sun and the light of the sun will be sevenfold.' Thus does the herald of Christianity in very truth, in words full of power, point to that which lives in Manichaeism of which only a travesty has been handed down.[10]

When we have sufficiently felt this in its full weight, we may imagine what a turn world history would have taken if the ancient Mystery Wisdom concentrated in *Aristotelianism* had in its fullness streamed into the Persian culture renewed through Manichaeism. We can depict to ourselves what a complete synthesis would have come about between the heathen religions and Christianity. If we seek to follow this out in thought we may well feel blinded by the radiance displayed. This complete synthesis did not come to pass. But the wonderful dispensation by which, always at the last moment, the thin thread of continuity is saved shall here be described.

From 754–775 there ruled as Abbasidian Caliph, Abu Gafar al-Mansur, which signifies the Victorious. He had chosen as administrators men out of the Persian family of the Barmacides. The appellation used for such a minister was 'Vizier'. This word is of Persian origin. We may compare with this what Huart says in the first volume of his history of the Arabs, translated into German by Beck and Färber, p. 228. Huart[11] writes, 'So it came about that from the beginning the Abbasidian Caliphate took on a distinctly Iranian colouring. The Caliph was not only head of the Musselman community, but the successor of the ancient Kings of Persia.' We actually find also in the original documents which record the sending of an embassy from the Franks to the Caliph that the Caliph is called 'Rex Persarum'. The family of Barmacides which became so important under al-Mansur was descended from a family 'which for centuries had been employed in the service of the fire priests in the fire temple at Balch' (Huart, op cit.). The Government of al-Mansur is important because under him the connection with the wider world was sought. He conducted his government in a cosmopolitan way. He completed the Persian postal service which had already existed from ancient times. He looked after the caravan routes and improved the canals. In short, he did everything to make intercourse easier and to enable strangers to learn the Arabic tongue. Let us see what Huart says (p. 290): 'Under al-Mansur the teaching of the Arabic language became a science through the exertion of the two schools of Basara and Kufa. The first of these two towns boasts a Chalil and Sibawaihis, the latter being of Persian origin. Kufa is connected with the name of al-Kisai. The Arabic tongue, the official and commercial language of the kingdom, was learnt increasingly by foreigners who cherished the wish to learn its inner structure. From this arose the learned researches which under the stimulus of these great Masters quickly arrived at giving a fixed form to the rational structure which this masterly work displays.' Further Huart relates that now under al-Mansur the Persian Book of the Kings was translated into Arabic and under the successors of al-Mansur the Arabic poetry became more and more powerfully influenced by Iranian thought and was thereby entirely altered in its nature. He says further: al-Mansur founded Baghdad in 762 at a spot which lies exactly on the border between the Arabic and Persian regions and gave it a Persian name. Bagh-dad means 'Given by God'. He says concerning this founding: 'It signified a balance between the victorious Arabs and the conquered Persians who however were again raising their heads.' Under this rulership of al-Mansur, the first Frankish embassy, sent by Pippin and Bertha, the parents of Charlemagne, arrived in Baghdad. This embassy departed from the land of the Franks during Christmas 765 and returned in 768. In connection with Pippin's wife stands her father Charibert of Laon. He it is of whom Konrad Fleck speaks in his poem of Flore and Blanscheflur. We have already suggested that Charibert of Laon had inspired this embassy. We may say, after all, that the reason for sending this embassy was for the sake of forming a connection with the court of the Caliphs, because the Arabs who had arrived from Spain and who stood in opposition to this court of the Caliphs were regarded as a common enemy. This is undoubtedly correct and is also the reason why the saga of the Red Knight makes Flore the son of the Spanish king.

But the saga intends to tell us more on this subject. It desires to point out how the Red Knight, the Knight with the roses, the Knight who then later inspires the figure of Parzival, sought a connection with the Persian culture-element. And no one will understand the figure of Feirefis, whose birth is placed in Africa, the place where the European and Arabic nature come up against one another, who does not perceive this search of Orient and Occident. The excellent author *Heeren* expresses his conviction that the development within the land of the Franks and in Baghdad ran exactly parallel, only that with the Franks the officials overpowered their kings—the Carolingians overcame the Merovingians—whereas in the court of the Caliphs the rulers exterminated their ministers. This occurred under the rule of Haroun al-Raschid. It is one of the most remarkable occurrences that have ever happened. Of this Huart writes (page 292):

> Haroun al-Raschid found no pleasure in Baghdad. His favourite abode was a castle at Anbar on the Euphrates. There he settled in the beginning of the year 187 (803 AD) after returning from his pilgrimage to Mecca, and one day he summoned the head of the police so that he might give him certain secret orders. For many days he was sunk in thought and distracted and neither ate nor drank. On Friday, the last day but one of the month Muharram (27 January 803), he accompanied Gafar to the chase. No one could guess the terrible event that was being prepared. Whilst Gafar, having returned home, was giving himself up to music and song, he suddenly saw Masrur, head of the eunuchs, and Hartama Ibn Ajan, chief of the bodyguard enter. They tore him violently from his seat and dragged him outside. When half an hour later the Christian physician Gabriel, who until then had been in the company of Gafar, came before the Caliph, he observed that the severed head of the Barmacide lay on a dish before the chief of the

believers. This was the sign for the downfall of the family. All who belonged to it were taken captive that evening and thrown into prison. Messengers were sent in haste and by order to overthrow their authority in the provinces and all their possessions were taken from them. Only Muhammed, the son of Chalid, and his family were excepted.

Huart is quite right when he seeks for the real cause of this unexpected treatment in the fact that Haroun discovered one day that he was completely dependent on the family of the Barmacides. He says:

The real reason is to be sought in the feeling of dependence which Haroun experienced in relation to the powerful family who held the whole kingdom in their hands. And to make himself free of this, nothing remained but a *coup d'état* in which every precautionary measure that could possibly be used in such a case was used. The head of the police was secretly sent forth from the ruler's palace in order to carry out the orders which were to be communicated to none: likewise messengers with similar secret express letters were sent in all directions. The might of the Barmacides had become a danger to the ruling race, possibly to the Musselman community. For the Iranians, filled with the memory of their fatherland which had fallen into decay, could only dream of one thing, namely of the reinstatement of the Mazdain Kingdom and—who knows?—perhaps even of the renewal of the Zoroastrian faith.

The head of the Persian Prime Minister in the dish is the world-historic symbol, the concrete imagination of that which is the opposite of the Grail. I was once able to ask Dr Steiner the question: What does it signify that in some stories of the Grail there appears the picture of the bleeding head on the dish? Dr Steiner answered, 'It is the picture of black magic in its contrast to the pure Grail forces.' Through the beheading of the Persian Minister, through the extermination of the family of the Barmacides, a stream of culture was destroyed. It is the stream of the continued influence of the Zarathustra element which Manichaeism wished to renew, to Christianise, and which in its union with the Greek wisdom would have brought about a synthesis between Christianity and the ancient Mystery wisdom. Julian the Apostate was also seeking for this synthesis when he journeyed from Strasbourg to Gondishapur. Already then, the attempt was made to draw that world-historical line along which alone the Grail Mysteries could be unveiled. But on the way to Gondishapur the Initiate of the macrocosmic Eleusinian Mysteries, thrust through the liver by a spear, was prevented from uniting the sub-earthly Mithras Mysteries with the Eleusinian (see Note 45 to Chap. 5).

Once again was world history faced with the question whether that which

Mani had attempted, which Julian had striven for, which Charibert of Laon had longed for, must be destroyed. And once more fate offered an opportunity. For when, after the death of Haroun al-Raschid, the decision as to his successor became imperative, there were present two aspirants to the throne. His eldest son Abdallah would have succeeded him had he not been the son of a Persian slave. For this reason Muhammed, who was also named al-Amin, and was the son of the legal wife (Zubaida), was given the preference (Huart, p. 297). Once more the question had to be faced as to whether the Persian or the Arabian element should take the lead. Abdallah, the son of a Persian, called also al-Mamun, possessed lands in the East. In the fight which developed between him and his Arabic rival he came forth victorious. On 25 September 813, Amin was killed and the son of the Persian reigned. Now what Tabari relates is remarkable, viz. that this son of a Persian had a vision in which Aristotle appeared to him in a dream, and through this he was induced to renew the Greek element of culture, especially Aristotelianism. And if this had happened then the essence of the Greek Mysteries and Aristotelianism would have united and been able to take up Christianity. The cup of the half moon would have been able to be filled with the Christ substance. Hans Heinrich Frei has written about the historical impulse of Gondishapur (in *Die Drei*, Year IV, Nos 10–12). He there relates the dream of al-Mamun: 'There once appeared to the Caliph Mamun in a dream the figure of a man most beautifully formed. He asked him, "Who art thou?" "I am Aristotle." He asked him the cause of his beauty. He answered, "This lies in the beauty of reason's laws." It is to this dream that we owe the translation of the Greek classics into Arabic.'

Most significant is this appearing of Aristotle to the spirit of al-Mamun, and in order to grasp it in all its significance we must place it by the side of another historical event. When Lessing wrote his *Faust*, he was led into a curious train of thought. He said to himself, 'Faust knew that man does not solve the problem of evil by turning his back on it, but it is so that man must unite himself with evil without falling prey to it.' Now he saw that Faust was worried by scholastic doubt. And he said to himself, 'There is only one who can explain this doubt and that is Aristotle.' It occurred to him, however, that once the learned Venetian, Hermolaus, conjured the devil in order to ask him about the eternal nature of Aristotle. Peter Crinitus relates that Hermolaus boasted of this. Lessing's Faust wishes to repeat this. He utters the conjuration. But behold! Not the devil but Aristotle himself appears. This is a remarkable story, that Aristotle appeared to Lessing in a real vision when he conjured the devil (for he is describing himself in the Faust figure). We must connect this event with the vision of al-Mamun, and we must ask ourselves, what has Aristotle to do with evil? If we study his philosophy in this light we find in it the thought of *transubstantiation*. It is the idea of the transformation and spiritualisation of the substance of nature. The thoughts of Aristotle have the power of *spiritualising matter and evil* and changing them. That is why Christianity absorbed the thought world of Aristotle, for the central point of the Christian Mystery, the *transmutation of substance in the Mass*, can only be grasped with Aristotelian ideas. But that it is precisely the figure of Faust in whose discussion this appears has a profound reason. For Faust is that Manichaen bishop whom Augustine met. He is a last follower of that Manichaeism which went forth from Gondishapur. Augustine was bound to deny this Manichaeism for here he already encountered a representation of it that could no longer teach it in its original purity. And yet this Manichaeism in its true form was what he, as a true Christian, must have desired. For true Manichaeism, as has been already said, the Faust problem was not, 'How can man save himself from evil?' but rather, 'How is evil itself to be redeemed?'[12] Thus we see how intimately Aristotle is linked up with those thoughts which were fitted to unite closely heathendom and Christianity and just through this very union to redeem the evil, to spiritualise the hardened, to Christianise what was anti-Christian.

So too must we regard the dream of al-Mamun. It was precisely to the one who had Arabianised the whole of Aristotle that this Aristotle appeared and the great world-historic question was put as to how the stream of the primeval Mystery Wisdom should flow further. Al-Mamun during the course of his reign brought about political changes in a remarkable way, which might be described in a picture. This change of policy was expressed by the setting aside of the green colour of the apparel and banners of his court, and replacing them by the black garments and banner of the Abbasidians. In this change of colour may be seen the transition to Arabism. But this was only the prelude to the fast oncoming displacement of Arabism by the Turks. One only needs to study the history of the bodyguard of the Caliphs in order to see plainly the course which evolution took. We find in Huart's *History of the Arabians*, Vol. 1, p. 302, the following passage: 'The bodyguard of the Abbasidians at first consisted of Persians who had been brought from Chorassan but who became largely Arabic through the influence of the surroundings—they only continued to show traces of their Iranian descent as a race. Finally, the constant war and strife beyond the Oxus and the Jaxartes provided the market abundantly with Turkish slaves. From them the Caliphs very quickly supplemented their bodyguard.' So at that time decisions of world-historical importance occurred and we can comprehensively state what became necessary for European development thus: *The soul of Europe had to rescue from the court of the Caliphs what was really its own soul-bride*. This is what is expressed in the story of Flore and Blanscheflur. And we can become aware that in this chapter we have touched upon the same theme as in the previous chapter on Flore and Blanscheflur. What may not have worked in the soul of that personality in whom the thought arose at the time of al-Mansur of sending the first embassy from the Court of the Franks to the Court of the Caliphs? Did he not see that it was important to rescue a wonderful wisdom and to preserve it as a *Mystery*, since at that time it must not become the universal property of all mankind because humanity was not yet prepared to receive it in the right way? We can only admire the wisdom of the Spirits who inspired the idea of this embassy. They knew history and they led it, and we stand before the wisdom of this guidance with the very greatest wonder. This same wisdom-filled leadership of humanity gave humanity the story of Flore and Blanscheflur, not in the form of history, but as poetry.

Novalis also desired to lead humanity to experience and to form world history in the same way. Hence this poem:

> When no longer numbers and figures
> Are keys to all creatures,
> When those who sing or kiss
> Know more than all the learned scholars,
> When the world returns to itself
> In a life of freedom,
> When once again the light and shadow wed
> And these united give the real clarity,
> When man can know the true world story
> In myths and in the form of poems,
> Then will the whole deformed being
> Vanish before one single secret word.
>
> (*Heinrich von Ofterdingen*, Part II)

5
Wolfram von Eschenbach's *Parzival*

Wolfram von Eschenbach's poem also fits into the frame of the Grail narrative of which we have spoken, for Wolfram implies that he thinks of Parzival as living in the ninth century. He does not say this in so many words, yet he expresses it in a way that leaves one in no doubt. Wolfram says that eleven generations have elapsed between the time of Herzeleide and his own time. The verses referring to this are in the Third Adventure, line 281. They say of Herzeleide:

> ... This root of all goodness
> From which the shoot of humility has flowered.
> Woe! that there have not remained to us (ôwê daz wir nu niht enhân)
> Her children to the eleventh generation (ir sippe unz an den eilften spân!)
> So much is false around us (des wirt gevelschet manec lip)

Thus according to the statement of Wolfram von Eschenbach, Herzeleide, Parzival's mother, lived eleven generations earlier than Wolfram himself, i.e. about 870.

It is therefore quite natural and appropriate at this point to enter into a closer consideration of Wolfram's *Parzival*. This poem has not only a historical importance, but an educational importance as well, for it is Wolfram's version that is read in Waldorf schools and, as a matter of fact, in the eleventh class. That it is important for growing boys and girls to read and discuss this poem I have indicated in the Introduction. I shall add much that will provide material for teachers; the analysis is not given solely from a pedagogical point of view, but I shall at least endeavour to represent what has developed out of many years' work with the children, and which has been fruitful too for my own reflections and experiences.

To begin with I should like to make a few preliminary remarks about the structure of the whole poem. Wolfram von Eschenbach tells his narrative in sixteen Adventures. This is no mere chance, but is according to a law which is rigidly observed. For in all spiritual poems (for example Dante's *Divine Comedy*), and in this one also, the structure is strictly according to number, and this would be destroyed if even the smallest part were eliminated. Some of the chapters devoted to Gawain are today considered to be on the whole of less importance to the poem; for instance, we find that in one very fine edition, which is otherwise a model of excellence, these chapters have been published in a separate supplementary volume as *Gawain Episodes* (Kürschner's: *Deutsche Nationalliteratur*). Such a procedure completely destroys the meaning of the poem, as will be shown in due course. Wolfram von Eschenbach's poem is not intended to be merely a fanciful composition. On the contrary it creates in us a delicate subtle, spiritual organ of knowledge whose very lawfulness requires to be met by the lawfulness which is found in the architectural structure of the poem. Much in the poem is treated with a certain secrecy; and indeed it is a secret which has caused the poet to build up his tale in a definite architectural manner. He touches upon this secret in the first Adventure, in the description of the City of Patelamunt, for Patelamunt is nothing less than Wolfram's poem as a whole. He describes this city as having sixteen gates.

> ... so rode they around the wall
> To sixteen gates, and they told him not one of them might they close. (I: 470-71)

Round this city a conflict was taking place to avenge the death of Eisenhart, the owner of some wonderful armour, who lost his life as he rode out one day at the bidding of Belakane, whose suitor he was. The battle of the sixteen gates is carried on by two armies. A white and a black army each lay siege to eight of the gates:

> At eight of the gates they beset us true Eisenharts gallant knights,
> And evil shall they have wrought us. I: 475-476)

The army of Eisenhart consists of knights who are all in black:

> Dark as night were the people who in Zassamank dwelt. (I: 267)

And of the other army Wolfram says:

> Proud Friedebrand's Scottish army doth to eight of our gates stand nigh
> Baptized men from over the waters. A prince doth each portal hold
> And forth from the gate he sallies, with his banners and warriors bold. (I: 488-490)

This is the army of the white knights.

The city of sixteen gates; the battle round each of its gates; the different character of the conflict of each group of eight; the darkness of the one army, the clear brightness of the other; all these are pictures of spiritual realities. In his *Parzival* poem Wolfram von Eschenbach wished in his own way to show humanity a path leading to higher knowledge. He describes the organ of this kind of knowledge and the process of its development. He who develops it gains insight into the hidden rule of destiny. In his book, *Knowledge of Higher Worlds*,[1] Rudolf Steiner describes this organ in a manner suited to the present age. He explains how certain qualities of the soul are connected with its development. It is formed by sixteen different activities, eight of which belong to a very ancient period of human evolution, when man exercised them instinctively in a dulled and darkened state of consciousness; while today it is possible for him to complete the development of the other eight qualities in a state of consciousness that is clear and awake. Buddha describes them in his 'Eight-fold Path'. If these qualities are exercised, then the eight activities of the forces that were developed earlier, will bear fruit themselves. In the figure of *Friedebrand*, Wolfram describes the forces of the Eight-fold Path, and in *Eisenhart*, the earlier qualities formed when the state of consciousness was dim. Eisenhart is dead.

But in the events in and around Patelamunt, Wolfram describes, as though in a wonderful summary, all the sixteen adventures of his poem. He who draws strength from them by receiving with enthusiasm the conceptions pictorially presented therein, acquires the organ that can receive revelation concerning the secret laws of the ruling destiny:

> The heathen, Flegetanis, could read in the heavens high
> How the stars roll on their courses, how they circle the silent sky,
> And the time when their wandering endeth—and the life and the lot of men
> He read in the stars, and strange secrets he saw, and he spake again
> Low, with bated breath and fearful, of the thing that is called the Grail,
> In a cluster of stars was it written, the name, nor their lore shall fail.
> And he quoth thus, 'A host of angels this marvel to earth once bore,
> But too pure for earth's sin and sorrow the heaven they sought once more,
> And the sons of baptized men hold it, and guard it with humble heart,
> And the best of mankind shall those knights be who have in such service part.' (IX: 3369–378)

The Grail narrative can create the organ of the knowledge of fate, of karma-recognition. How it also evokes all other human forces will become more and more apparent as we go on.

After these introductory remarks, we will now consider what the poet's real intentions were. The following is a free rendering of the opening words, from which it will become apparent what the poet especially desires to place in the foreground.

When the human heart awakens from *dullness* into *doubt*, the soul draws itself together within. The brave and manly soul feels itself, at one and the same moment, both in dishonour and adorned with grace, like the enchanted bird the magpie which seems to be half dove, half raven: yet one thus bewitched may hope still to win *security of soul* once more (saelde), 'if only in his heart, Hell's darkness and the light of Heaven alike have their lot and part' [J.L. Weston. *Parzival*, Book I:6]. The lower of these companions has raven blackness in his soul and will also show black without. But he who has steadfast thoughts that are infused with moral force, cleaves to the whiteness of the dove. They who still live in dullness will scarcely unravel this fleeting parable, when in its ambiguity it rises up before them and like a frightened hare, springs now right, now left. Tin as the reflecting surface of a mirror, and the dream of a blind man also give pictures of outer appearance. Yet no true permanence will this gloomy wavering light possess, and it brings forth a joy that is but short-lived. What reasonable man would seize me by the hair where no hair grows, on the palm of the hand? He who would do that must indeed grip closely! His action would be as futile and aimless as that of a man who for horror can only cry out the little word, 'OH!' Were I to do the same it would be as wise as to seek for fidelity or truth where they have no abiding place, in the waverer and the doubter. Can I find fidelity where it must perforce disappear, as fire in the brook, or dew before the sun?

However wise a man may be, he will assuredly be glad to know what are the guiding thoughts in this narrative and what are the moral impulses it would impart. He who seeks to gain instruction from this tale, must not wonder at the contrary elements brought to light therein. Here he must learn now to flee away, now to chase, now to avoid, now to return, now to blame and now to praise. In him alone who is expert in all these possibilities, will wisdom be confirmed. If he sits not overlong, neither errs in his steps, but understands, then only will he reach his goal. He who enters into all kinds of falsehood in his disposition is led thereby into hell-fire; he destroys all his good fame as a hail storm destroys fruit. His fidelity has a tail as short as a cow's, for when she is bitten in the forest by a gadfly, she is hard put to it to ward off every third sting because of the shortness of her tail.

These are Wolfram von Eschenbach's words. They contain a very great deal. A little may be said now as to their meaning. Here we find already the three stages of development through which Parzival must pass. He must evolve upwards from *dullness*, through *doubt*, to the third stage, *Saelde*. This is the evolutionary path of each individual, as it is also the evolutionary path of humanity in history. Men live in dullness when they are given up to the bodily nature. Fichte mocks at such men who live in a kind of stupor, when he says that they were not taken into acount in the plan of the ennoblement of mankind, and that for their sake he hopes kindly Nature will watch over

13. The four stages of man's inner development
   (*Basilius Valentinus, 'The Twelve Keys'*)

the anchor, and on reaching the mainland of Europe he resumes his old blazon of the panther that he had inherited from his ancestors. He now marries Herzeleide (as told in the second Adventure) but soon forsakes her in the same way. While he is on his journey back to the Baruch again, Parzival is born to Herzeleide. Parzival is the true hero for whom the task is reserved of winning steadfastness and faithfulness, as inner qualities.

The historical conditions described in the first adventure are similar to those which prevailed in the second third of the ninth century. We must assign what is described here to the rule of the Aghlabites, the Emirs of the Caliph, in Africa. The conditions prevailing then in the East were actually those experienced by Gahmuret.[7]

Summing up the contents of the first chapter in their moral significance, we may say that Gahmuret endeavours to learn steadfastness and fidelity from life but does not fully succeed.

The second Adventure no longer depicts for us the man who would 'learn from life', but a human being who must learn by being thrown upon her own resources in her loneliness. We find this characteristic in Herzeleide.

As we read Wolfram's *Parzival*, we have the feeling that the opening chapters were written last, and this has been noticed by the commentators on Wolfram's *Parzival*. To obtain a complete survey of the poem, we must picture the sixteen adventures arranged diagrammatically in a circle, so that when the circle is complete the first Adventure seems to be the continuation of the last. This kind of architecture will be found in all medieval spiritual writings; beginning and ending seem to be connected in a peculiar way; for example, Basil Valentine says, 'O beginning of the first beginning, remember the end, and end of the last end, remember the beginning, and allow the middle portion to be commended to you in all good faith. Thus will God the Father, Son and Holy Spirit give unto you what you lack in Spirit, soul and body.' This unison of beginning and end is shown, for instance, in the fact that the mention of the pied magpie with which the poem begins, only receives its full explanation in the Feirefis Adventure. Let us now turn to the second Adventure.

Adventure II

Here Gahmuret appears equipped with the results of his achievements at Patelamunt. He brings with him a marvellous tent and some splendid armour. But he does not bring with him the possibility of keeping his recently acquired coat of arms. As we hear in the course of the tale, Gahmuret learns that his brother Galoes has been killed by a knight called Orilus. This knight plays an important role later. Through the death of his brother, Gahmuret becomes lord of his brother's Kingdom of Anschau:

He hath won him another heart-grief as his brother's death is told,

And he spake aloud in his sorrow, 'Now mine anchor hath found its hold
And its haven in bitter rueing,'⁷ᵃ and the badge he did lay aside. (II: 533-535)

A later passage particularly tells us that he took the panther badge again:

Then the panther the badge of his father on his shield they in sable laid; (II: 674)

Characteristically, he immediately feels himself impelled to leave Herzeleide, whom he had married in the meantime. In the second Adventure we become acquainted with a number of knights who appear and reappear in the course of the tale. We are told that Herzeleide is maiden and widow. Her first husband, Kastis, died immediately after the marriage. She has announced a tournament:

For the queen of the Waleis country⁸ had ordered at Kanvoleis⁹
That a tourney fair be holden, and they ordered it in such wise
That a coward had little liked it—for whoever would seek such strife
At his will doth it chance but seldom! She was maiden, not yet a wife,
And herself and two lands she offered to him who the prize should hold; (II: 25-29)

The lands are Waleis and Norgals. Gahmuret wins them both and their queen besides. He now possesses three lands, Waleis, Norgals, Anschau. These are the lands which Parzival later inherits from him. This inheritance is disputed by Duke Orilus, the knight who killed Gahmuret's brother. We shall hear later how Parzival is led to meet him. In this second Adventure, Arthur and Klingsor are mentioned but only in parenthesis. In the list of knights we read:

Here Uther Pendragon fighteth, and with him his Breton host;
One grief as a thorn doth vex him, his wife hath the hero lost,
The queen who was Arthur's mother; a clerk who all magic knew
With him hath she fled, and Arthur doth after the twain pursue;
'Tis now the third year since he lost them, his son alike and wife
(II: 117-121)

The clerk[10] mentioned here is Klingsor. How Arthur regains his mother is told much later. It is brought about by Gawain, Parzival's friend, who conquers Klingsor's castle, Castle Merveil.

As the tale continues we learn something of events in the Orient, the Baruch has been beset by two brothers in front of Babylon:

And the one he was called Ipomidon, and Pompey his brother's name

(For so hath the venture told me), a proud man of warlike fame.
('Twas not he whom Julius Caesar had driven from Rome of yore).
His uncle was Nebuchadnezzar, who in books found the lying lore[11]
That he himself should a god be, (o'er this would our folk make sport)
And of noble race these brothers nor of strength nor of gold spared aught.
From Ninus they came who was ruler ere ever Baghdad might be,
Nineveh did he found[11a]—Now an insult and a shame vexed them bitterly,
The Baruch as vassals claimed them—so the combat was won and lost,
And bravely the heroes battled, and on each side they paid the cost,
Thus Gahmuret sailed the water, and aid to the Baruch brought,
And gladly he bade him welcome; tho' I weep that that land he sought!
(II: 685-696)

Thus Gahmuret forsakes Herzeleide (whose son Parzival is born in the meantime) and fights at Baghdad for the Baruch, and there meets his death. He is accompanied by his young friend Schionatulander, to whom Wolfram dedicates a separate poem. Something will be said later of this remarkable personality and his fate. Gahmuret's death is briefly related here in the second Adventure. Ipomidon kills Gahmuret; his spear cleaving helmet and brow:

For the spear cut sheer thro' the helmet, and it pierced through my master's brain
(In his head did they find the splinters), yet the hero still held the rein,
And dying he rode from the combat, o'er a wide plain his way he'd take,
And his chaplain knelt above him, and in few words his shrift he spake.
And he sent here the shift and the spear-blade that hath robbed us of our friend. (II: 757-761)

The head squire, Tampanais, brings these tidings back to Herzeleide, and tells of Gahmuret's burial at Baghdad according to Christian custom, and how the grateful Baruch adorned his tomb with gold and jewels, and ornamented it above with a costly ruby, and reared the Christian cross upon it, wrought from an emerald. The Baruch paid the cost, although the heathens could give no instructions as to how all this should be done, for they do not know the Cross.

And there in his diamond helmet an epitaph did they grave,
And last to the cross they fixed it o'er the tomb of that hero brave,
And thus do they run the letters: 'Through this helmet a joust hath slain

>This hero who bare all manhood, and Gahmuret was his name,
>As king did he rule o'er three kingdoms, in each land the Crown he wore
>Whom mighty princes followed—Anjou's land this hero bore,
>And he lost his life for the Baruch at the city of Baghdad fair.
>And so high did it soar, his honour, that no knight may with him compare,
>Howe'er ye may test their dealings. Nor is he of woman born,
>(I mean of the knightly order) to whose hand he his strength had sworn.
>But help and true manly counsel to his friends did he steadfast give;
>And thro' women much grief he suffered, for he would in their favour live.
>Baptized was he as a Christian tho' Saracens mourn him yet,
>(This is truth and no lie)—All his lifetime since his years were on wisdom set
>His strength strove for fame and honour, till he fell in his knightly pride,
>Wish him bliss who here lieth buried! 'Twas by treason's hand he died!'

This is Gahmuret's epitaph, showing that he gave love and devotion in equal measure to Christians and to pagans. But he had not achieved steadfastness. Parzival is the first to develop steadfast fidelity.

It is related how the painful tidings came to Herzeleide. One noontide the queen lay in a restless slumber. Suddenly she started up in terror. It was as if she were carried up into the air by lightning, and as if flash after flash passed through her. Crackling fire singed her hair; she heard the rolling thunder, and tears poured down her cheeks. As she came to herself on awakening, the dream passed over into a vision in which a griffin seized her right hand:

>And lo! it was changed, the vision, and wondrous things befell;
>For then did she nurse a dragon, that forth from her body sprung,
>And its dragon life to nourish awhile at her breast it hung,
>Then it fled from her sight so swiftly she might look on it never more;
>And her heart it brake for the anguish, and the terror and grief she bore. (II: 722–726)

She awoke with a cry. Four maidens spring to her aid, and wakened her completely. Then Tampaneis came in and recounted Gahmuret's death. We learn that Gahmuret had taken off his helmet on account of the heat. The knight accomplished his aim through sorcery. With the blood of a he-goat he made the adamant or diamond that protected Gahmuret soft and spongy. The softened diamond is really the cause of Gahmuret's death: he died an alchemist's death. Herzeleide's grief on hearing the tidings is described. Fourteen days later Parzival is born:

> And when fourteen days were ended a babe lay the queen beside,
> 'Twas a son, and so great and goodly that the mother had well-nigh died.
> Now 'tis cast the die of the venture, and here doth my tale begin,
> For now is he born who henceforward this song for his own shall win.
> (II: 841-844)

In grief and tears Herzeleide bears the son who is the real hero of the tale, and who shall accomplish what his father Gahmuret was unable to achieve.

Adventure III

Queen Herzeleide—as Wolfram relates in his third Adventure—wished to bring up her son in a sequestered spot far removed from knightly adventure and the temptations of the world, in the wilderness of Soltane. Parzival was really heir to three kingdoms; from Herzeleide's first husband he inherited Waleis and Norgals, and from his father Gahmuret, Anschau, but at first he is not allowed to know of it.

> But Queen Herzeleide only, she left her fair estate . . .   (III: 55)

She charges her people not to speak of knightly deeds when the boy is near. She will not have him suffer his father's fate:

> For the knightly deeds ye vaunt of, and the glory and pride of war,
> Have wrought me but heart's affliction, and trouble and anguish sore,
> So, lest I yet more should suffer, I pray you, my servants dear,
> That ye speak no word of knighthood, lest my son perchance should hear!
> (III: 71-74)

So the boy grows up far away from all the culture of his time.
Parzival is the son of Gahmuret, whose father was Gandein, named after the town of Gandein:

> And the town lieth near the river, where Graien and Drave they meet,
> And the waters, I ween, are golden . . .   (IX: 1117-1118)

On his paternal grandfather's side Parzival is descended from knights who live where the Greian flows into the Drave near Pettau.[12] (M. Haupt; Zeitschrift für Deutsches Alterthum, Vol. II, 1859, p. 42 et seq.).
It is approximately the same country as that ruled over by Duke Arnulf of

Carinthia. Gandein's coat of arms is the black panther. A white panther on a green field is the coat of arms of Styria (p. 376 Vol. 10 of Simrock's *Collected Works* published by Hesse.) Parzival was the heir to certain lands, for the possession of which Duke Orilus and his brother Lähelein fought against those knights who sought to defend them for Parzival. Parzival's lands are in part identical with the lands of Charles III (or Charles the Fat), who was supplanted by Arnulf of Carinthia. Parzival's connection with these circumstances explains the relationship so prominent in Wolfram's poem between the Frankish royal house and the region Carinthia and Styria.

Far removed from all knowledge of his royal rights, the boy grows up in the wilderness. He shoots at the birds and does not understand why those he hits stop singing. When he bursts into tears his mother decides to have the birds trapped for causing the child pain. But the boy protests.

> Then the boy spake, 'Now sweet my mother, why trouble the birds so sore?
> Forsooth they can ne'er have harmed thee, ah, leave them in peace once more!' (III: 105–106)

The mother reflects and exclaims:

> ... 'Perchance I have wrought a wrong.[13]
> Of a truth, the dear God who made them, He gave unto them their song. (III: 107–108)

The boy asks, 'God, Mother? Who may God be?' The mother's answer gives a profound glimpse into her religious views. The Christianity with which Herzeleide is imbued is represented as a kind of Zoroastrianism. For her, God is a Being of Light.

> 'My son, He is light beyond all light, brighter than summer's day... (III: 111)

She warns her son against the spirit of darkness and to beware of doubt. The meeting of Parzival and the knights is now described. Three knights ride by, closely followed by a fourth. They pursue Meljakanz, the son of Poidikonjonz (III: 220), who has carried off Imäne of Bellefontaine. Karnachkarnanz, the fourth knight hopes to rescue the captured damsel and asks Parzival if he has seen the robbers. From the description given by Chrétien de Troyes of this scene, it is clear that Parzival's whole attention is devoted to the world spread out before his senses.[14] He admires the knight's armour, but is quite unable to make their interests his own. Instead of answering he asks questions himself and so he learns from them what knighthood is, and that it is bestowed by King Arthur. From this moment his great desire is to become a knight. With a heavy heart his mother gives him his equipment

14. Portrait of Empress Richardis, wife of Charles the Fat

Portrait of Charles the Fat
(From: Palatius, J., 'Aquila inter Lilia . . .' 1671)

and bestows on him for the journey a sorry steed, fool's clothing, and good advice. He hears for the first time of his royal rights, and that Lähelein, the brother of Duke Orilus, has killed Prince Turkentals, who was defending Parzival's lands. Parzival promises to avenge his death.

Then he rides away and Herzeleide's heart breaks as her son leaves her. The widowed mother dies of heart's sorrow (Herze-leide). Here the poet remarks that if Herzeleide's family continued to descend through eleven generations, his own contemporaries—or her descendants—would have been better men. Herzeleide must therefore have lived eleven generations before Wolfram. Parzival rides impetuously away and meets with Jeschute, the wife of Duke Orilus of Lalande. The description that follows is a historical occurrence transformed into poetry. The guileless Parzival in all innocence brings Jeschute under the suspicion of having been untrue to her husband. Wolfram's version is that the foolish youth finds the sleeping Jeschute in a splendid tent and (all too literally following the counsel of his mother, to honour all beautiful ladies with a kiss) awakens her with a kiss. Jeschute in deadly terror has to give the simple youth her ring and clasp, which he demanded from her in accordance with his mother's advice. Then he falls hungrily upon the food in the tent, taking no more notice of Jeschute. Orilus returning holds Jeschute to be dishonoured, and repudiates her, forcing her to ride behind him as a penitent, clad in rags and mounted on a miserable horse, until Parzival later establishes her innocence by an oath. Prior to this, however, Parzival meets the Red Knight, Ither of Gahevies, the husband of his father's sister, and kills him. Henceforward Parzival donning the Red Knight's armour is himself called the Red Knight. This 'Red Knight' is the subject of a legend, the text of which is inserted here. This legend is to be found in Strasburg in the district archives of Lower Alsace under the number ME R IV. This is the source used by Bécourt (Andlau), Schöpflin, Königshoven and others. Bécourt believes that the document was printed in 1660.

St Richardis, or Richarda, was born in Scotland of noble Christian parentage, in the year of the Lord, 860.[14a] Her father was Gregory,[14b] the legitimate son of Don Galli, King of Ireland, the fifth of that name, crowned King of Scotland in 872. The nobility of Richardis' birth was even surpassed by the nobility of her faith and chastity. From her youth she was bred in all modesty and virtue by her parents. Having attained to womanhood she was asked in marriage by the Frankish King, Charles the Fat. With the assent of her noble parents she was wedded to him in the year 874. When she reflected on the close relationship into which this marriage had brought her with the mighty Emperor Charlemagne, now dead—(of whom Jacobus Gaulterius writes in his 'Chronographia' that in the year 788 he concluded with Achaius[15] a bond of eternal friendship which united the Franks and Scots, and that it was Charlemagne's greatest joy to build houses of God and to

15. Entrance to Andlau Church at the foot of Mount Odilie in which the Lazarus Relic, brought there by St Odilia from Constantinople, was preserved.

16. Detail of carvings round the door of Andlau Church (Alsace)

increase the number of His servants) she rejoiced, and with his son's son, Charles the Fat, endeavoured to follow in the footsteps of his grandfather, Charles the Great. In 876 they built the monastery of Stiffach for the maintenance of the thirteen Canons Regular in honour of St Peter, Prince of the Holy Apostles.

Love, says St Gregory,[16] is never idle and doeth great things wherever it be—and so, soon after this, St Richardis was resolved, with the consent of her spouse which was willingly given to establish a convent for virgins on her own estate at Andlau. They were both desirous to begin all things in God and to do nought without His pleasure. Charles, although eager to devote himself to religion and to the service of God, was still much taken up with the affairs of his realm, whereas Richardis, who had more opportunity for the service of God, gave herself up to prayer and betook herself to the nuns of Hochburg, that is, of the mount of St Odile. For Richardis, as well as her friends amongst the nuns, had a great veneration for St Odile, by reason of her holiness as well as the manifold miracles wrought by her. There she prayed to the Almighty Lord, for the sake of the merits of St Odile, to reveal unto her the spot where He desired her to accomplish the work she had planned. And behold, she had a vision and revelation that she was to found the convent at the foot of the hill on her estate where she would find a bear with its cubs scratching at the ground. As soon as she awakened she started joyfully on her way, and with her nobles and attendants descended from the mountain to her lands near Andlau and came to the spot where the bear with its cubs was scratching at the ground just as if it wished to show her the site where she was to build the convent. There in the year 878[17] she laid the foundation of the convent, first building a crypt in honour of the Blessed Virgin, then the Cathedral and finally the cloisters together with the convent which she and her spouse Charles piously dedicated to St Peter, Prince of the Apostles. As soon as the convent was completed she installed Adelheid as its first abbess and filled it with pious and devout virgins, servants of God. Meanwhile they were not forgetful of the first convent, at Stiffach, for Charles admonished and counselled his Richardis to endow it with good lands, which she did joyfully, confirming her gift in the year 879 by a deed that is still in existence.

Moreover, all those who strove to further God's honour and service were honoured likewise by the Lord, as it is written: 'Whoso honoureth me, him will I honour'; this proved itself true in the lives of Charles and his Richardis. Victorious in battle, Charles journeyed with his Richardis to Rome where he was given 'God's welcome' by the Senate as well as by the people. Charles was received with great pomp and rejoicing and was anointed by Pope John VIII on Christmas Day 881, after which he was crowned Emperor and Richardis was crowned Empress. For this honour received at the hands of the Vicar of Christ, the august Senate and the people of Rome, Charles and Richardis were not lacking in gratitude and, having returned to their own land, they sought fresh opportunity to serve God. There was a church[18] in Lüttich (Liege) in Braband sacred to the Heavenly Queen and Blessed Virgin Mary and to Saint Lambert[19] where Franco was Bishop: this church, being in extreme poverty, was endowed by Charles[20] with his farmstead of Magdera[21] in the village of Scarpone, which endowment was confirmed by brief and imperial seals in accordance with the exhortations of his beloved spouse Richardis as well as his faithful Lord High Chancellor Luithard, Bishop of the holy church of Vercell. For, as Pliny says, it is the nature of generosity once begun never to cease its bounties. But Satan the envious spares no pains to place obstacles in its path even at the time, and within those hearts of great price he sought every opportunity to do so. In order to distract Charles's thoughts he (Satan) aroused such unrest in Italy and France that Charles knew not whither to turn. He received many letters from John VIII who desired to avert those troublous events and he knew not what reply to make. In the end Pope John resolved on other means and sought help of the Empress, hoping through her to find access to him. To her he poured out his laments and requested her to implore Charles her spouse in this bitter distress to come to the aid of the churches of Italy and France. She was to fall at the feet of Charles—which as an obedient and reverent daughter she would not fail to do—and she then humbly replied to the Apostolic letter. This was one thing instigated by Satan to thwart the good. The other thing was that he did all within his power to bring into disfavour and ill-repute the Lord High Chancellor and the Empress Richardis in the eyes of her lord. (This Chancellor is called Luiduuardum by Regino, Hermannus Contractus and Arnoldus Wion; Cuspinianus calls him Luituuardum; Aventius calls him Luithardum and Caesar Baronius calls him Lintuuardum.) Lintuuardus had been Charles's most faithful and beloved Chancellor, and had given him the best of advice and counsel and he had therefore been considered by Charles as his best and most confidential counsellor whom he entrusted with the ruling and administration of his kingdom. So much favour did he find in the eyes of the Emperor that he was granted everything he ventured to ask. Amongst the powerful nobles of his Kingdom the Swabians[22] were worst, and among these nobles was one who was called the Red Knight[23] who, inspired by the Evil One, cherished hatred against Lintuuardum, for he was angered that the Emperor accepted and followed the Bishop's counsel in all things. By reason of this he kept a diligent eye on the actions of Lintuuardus and the holy Empress Richardis. This resulted in the banishment of both Lintuuardus and the saintly Empress.

There was a Bishop on the Isle of Cyprus who, knowing Richardis's great love for Jesus the Crucified, gave her a crucifix made from the wood of the true Cross and adorned with precious jewels. This crucifix was held in her high esteem and great honour and she gave it to Lintuuardo, her own and her dear husband's most faithful Chancellor and most devout Bishop, so that he might hang it round his neck during the Mass according to the customs of Bishops. Whenever he celebrated Holy Mass she was wont to adore the holy Cross hanging round his neck[24] and with a lay sister approached him from behind that she might touch it most reverently with her virgin hands. When this was seen by the Red Knight he perversely misrepresented it. Her reverence was misconstrued into an inordinate affection for the Bishop and, as she had to consult him frequently about the building of God's houses and the spread of the divine office, he took occasion by false insinuations to arouse in the Emperor the suspicion of adultery. The Evil Spirit lost no time in playing his malignant trick on the saintly Empress and Bishop Lintuuardo, the faithful servant of God, by inducing the Emperor to lend his ear to the evil Red Knight and to pour his wrath on the Bishop, his Lord High Chancellor, and his own wife. He dismissed his Chancellor and banished him,[25] heaping insults upon him and well-nigh making an end to his life, so that he was obliged to seek for help in Italy. The Evil Spirit was well pleased with this and goaded the Emperor on to summon Richardis in great wrath and to threaten her with vengeance. He held a diet with the mighty ones of his Kingdom before whom Richardis had to appear and in her presence he testified that he had not touched nor known her throughout the twelve years of their married life. Now it had to be proved that she was innocent of any other man's touch. Richardis was willing to submit to any test which he desired. In fulfilment of his wish she was put on a wax shirt, which was set on fire at the four corners, but it would not burn, whereupon glowing coals were laid down and she stood on them with bare feet. This was done on condition that, having stood all these tests, she would be acknowledged free of the marriage bond and able to serve henceforth none but her beloved Jesus.

After she had stood on the fiery coals which not only did not burn her but, on the contrary, were thereby extinguished, the saintly virgin took her holy crucifix into her hand (that had been returned to her by the Lord High Chancellor at his approaching death) and said, 'Well, My Lord, thou hast confessed that thou didst not know me throughout all the twelve years of our married life, and this thou hast well and rightly said. Now I too have gone through the test proving that I have not been known by any other man either. God speed thee, Charles; henceforth I am wedded to Him whom the angels serve, whose beauty is admired by the sun and the moon. I was faithful to thee and to that Only One, who will recognise my fidelity better than thou hast done. I shall be true, for I have given myself entirely to Him and have commended myself to Him in all reverence. The kingdom of this world and all that adorns it I now despise for the sake of His love, for this have I seen, Him have I loved, Him have I believed, to him have I given all tokens of love, God bless thee, Charles! I shall now go to the convent in my land which we built for St Peter and gave to Him, and I shall go into the house of my spiritual sisters, dedicated to God, the house I have dedicated and given to them. I shall now betake myself to the convent of Andlau which I built from its foundations and there will I serve God remaining a virgin-queen always. May the Holy Cross protect thee, and may God forgive thee. Have pity on the Red Knight, my Charles.

Thus St Richardis went forth and forgave all men. But God, avenging His elect, sent a great punishment to Charles so that he was despised and rejected by all men and he had no maintenance, neither that which came to him from the Bishop of Mayence nor that which Arnulph the King of Rome, who was reigning in his stead, had paid him as a tax. He went to the convent of Neidingen (situated in Baar near Fürstenberg). There he fell ill and was strangled by his own men. Thus he scarcely lived on for more than a year. His body was transferred to the monastery of Reichenau where it was buried in the year 888 as the inscription on his grave testifies.

Thus St Richardis was liberated from her matrimonial bonds. She went, as already mentioned, in great joy to her virgins in the convent; and she, who was shortly before this a virgin-wife, now became a virgin-widow. She went to Rome to visit St Peter and St Paul, the Princes of the Apostles, as well as to other holy places; from there she journeyed to the Holy Sepulchre and to men of saintly life, in order to collect a goodly store of relics and sacred things for her convent. From Rome she sent—according to the ancient legend of Andlau—an iron grill which she ordered the Evil Spirit to carry home. (Just as Theodulus, bishop of Vaudois, had made the Evil One carry the bells given him in Rome to his bishopric.) When he arrived laden with this iron grill as the last Mass was being celebrated, he rested on a stone so that the traces of the grill are seen and shown to this day, which stone is now called the grill-stone. From there he took the grill to the convent, and a beautiful miracle-working object it is. This iron grill is the tall grill that is to be seen behind the upper Altar of the Holy Cross. Then she journeyed to Constantinople to which place had been brought only three years previously, in the year 886, on 17 October the holy body of St Lazarus, Bishop of Cyprus (whom the Lord raised from the dead), for whom Leo the Greek Emperor had built a beautiful church in Constantinople. This sacred body was given to St Richardis and she held it in greater honour than all the rest of her possessions. She also brought with her many other sacred objects and found great joy in them at her convent in Andlau when her pilgrimage was completed. In memory of the translation of the sacred relics of St Lazarus the date of 29 October was specially celebrated and the bells were rung for a whole hour in the evening. Recognising, in accordance with the Apostles' teaching, that she should rejoice with them that do rejoice and weep with them that weep, she rejoiced in these sacred objects; but with the dead of whose peace she was not certain, she wept. On her return to the convent she learned that God had called hence one of her friends from this vale of woe. She gave order that the body should be carried down and interred in her Cathedral, in order that she might weep over her according to her desire. She followed the hearse and was present herself at the burial.[25a] Likewise she ordered that her father and mother who had already been buried at the Hohenburg should be disinterred. Their bodies were placed in a coffin and were buried in her convent according to the Catholic rite, with a procession of priests carrying a cross, followed by St Richardis with her own Cross, as well as by many other worthies of the world. As she was fain to stay with her parents, desiring to die and be buried with them as a virgin-queen, it can be easily surmised how much comfort she received from the great treasure of the holy relic and the presence of her dear parents' remains. Here she served God with vigils, fasting and prayer, striving to gain the crown of immortality in unceasing holy converse and saintly life unto her death.

Having adorned her convent with all that could make it beautiful and precious, and having endowed it with various estates, she became aware that the hour of her death had come. She lay down on her death-bed, placed the crucifix on her breast and devoutly repeated the 51st Psalm: the 'Miserere', reading it out of a book that was held in front of her. Then, according to the custom of all the righteous, although she had led such a holy life, she confessed her guilt where there was no guilt, and received the Blessed Sacrament, while the Bishop and all the sisters of the convent were present at her pious end. She passed away into the glory of the Lord on 18 September 903.'

The foregoing legend from the county archives of Strassburg will be found on page 107 et seq. of E. Bécourt's excellent work, *Andlau, Son Abbaye, Son Hôpital, Ses Bienfaiteurs*, Strassburg (Fischbäch) 1014/21. Together with a detailed bibliography and commentary there appears the figure of the Red Knight, taken from some old paintings. A document of 1660 of the Strassburg Library entitled *The Life of the Virgin Empress, St Richardis . . .* which was mentioned by J. Rietsch in 1904 in the Strassburg Diocesan Journal, Vol. XXIII: No 9 contains an exact description of these paintings. The legend describes the Red Knight as bringing ill-fortune to Richardis and at the same time causing Luitward, the Lord High Chancellor of Charles the Fat, to pass through very severe trials. If these events are traced further, it becomes clear that a wise Providence ruled both over the repudiation of St Richardis and the expulsion of Luitward, for the difficulties experienced by Richardis are fundamentally related to the special character of her inner life, and Luitward's banishment, driving him as it did to Arnulf of Carinthia,[26] was probably important for the whole subsequent development of history, (cf. p. 721 in Böhmer: *Regesta Imperii*, 2nd Edition, 751-918, Carlovingians). We may naturally assume that when Arnulf became head of the Empire by supplanting Charles III, Richardis's husband, he found an excellent advisor in Luitward, who for years managed all the affairs of the Empire.

We need not take exception to the fact that the Red Knight appears in this legend as the instrument of Evil. The writer of the legend could hardly describe him otherwise if he knew only one of the many deeds of the Red Knight, namely that he was the cause of the defamation and disfavour into which the Empress Richardis was brought. We, however, who know the other deeds of the Red Knight realise at once that we have come upon the same motif as is found in the Parzival legend. We know that when the youthful Parzival rides impetuously out into the world, he meets the wife of Duke Orilus. He finds her in her tent, embraces her and kisses her, yet still remains the pure fool. In the Parzival legend this woman is called Jeschute. Parzival plunges her in misfortune, for her husband Orilus, returning home, perforce believes that his wife is faithless. Later on Parzival finds Jeschute again and is able—according to the legend—to establish her innocence on oath at the altar of Trevrezent. The question must be asked: Is it mere chance that the Red Knight suddenly appears in the history of the Empress Richardis, or is there a real connection between *Richardis* and the *Jeschute* of the Parzival poem? Let us compare what both legend and history have bequeathed to us.

There is an important difference between the legend and what is contained in history in the fact that Parzival is Jeschute's supposed partner in guilt and at the same time brings disgrace upon her. While *Luitward*, who in history *plays the part of Parzival*, is not, in the Andlau legend, identified with the Red Knight but is distinguished from him. Again Parzival is not called 'the Red Knight' until after he has vanquished Ither of Gahevis, although he meets Jeschute before this adventure. In spite of all these differences there still seems to be a suggestion of the Parzival legend in the Andlau story, and in any case we have sufficient reason to consider legend and history side by side.

In this way we approach a chapter that is of the very greatest importance for the investigation of the history of the Grail; for in the Empress Richardis we find a personality who came very closely into touch with the stream of esoteric Christianity. The excellent researches made by the late pastor of Andlau, J. Rietsch, reveal the great importance of St Richardis. In his *History of the Family of Bethany after the time of the Gospels, and of the Lazarus relics at Andlau* (pp 297 et seq., Vol.21, No 8 [Aug. 1902], Strassburg Diocesan Journal), Rietsch says that Richardis was given the Lazarus relics by the Emperor Leo VI while on a journey in Palestine.[27] She presented them to the Convent of Andlau, where they are still preserved. A photograph of this

17. The 'Head of Lazarus', brought by St Odilie to Andlau at the foot of Mount Odilie

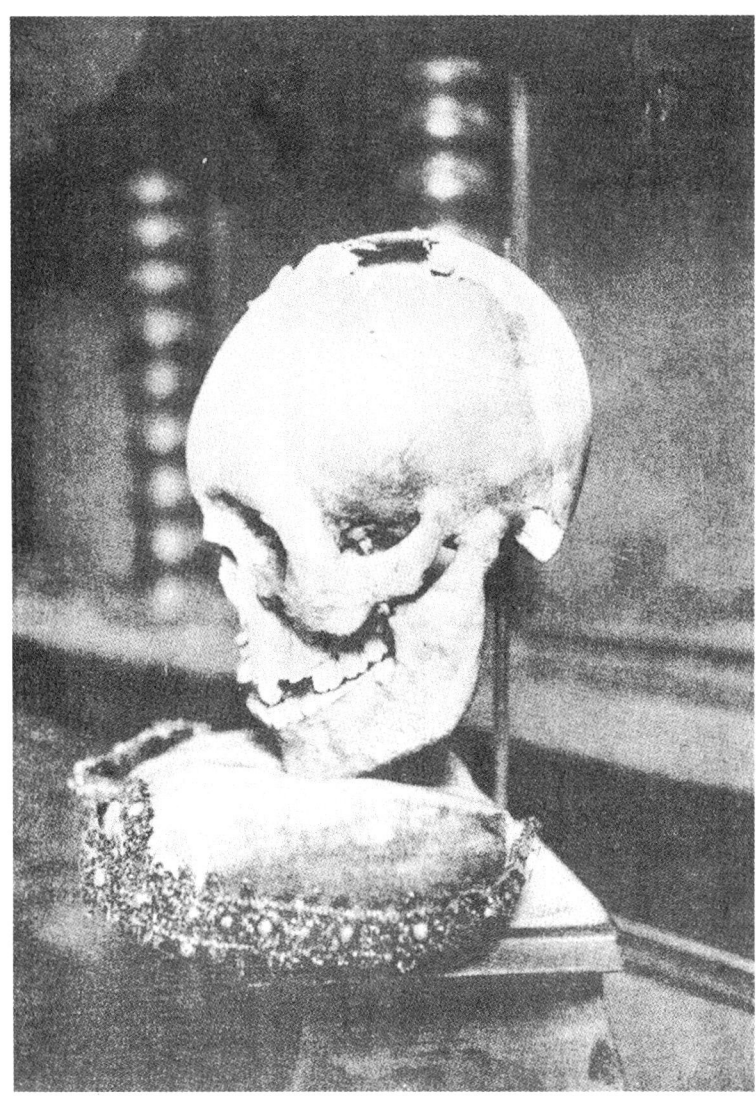

18. The 'Head of Lazarus', brought by St Odilie to Andlau at the foot of Mount Odilie

head is reproduced along with the other illustrations. Rietsch[28] has rendered signal service in showing the historical foundations for the belief that the head now at Andlau is the one that Leo VI possessed and which was on the island of Cyprus before it came to Constantinople. Zacharius Werner mentions this head in his drama, *Die Söhne des Tales*,[28a] and Molay in the drama holds it in his hands as a holy relic. We cannot of course consider the question of whether or not the head is really that of Lazarus. Here we can only consider, with the means at the disposal of the historian whether the presence of this head in Andlau is a proof that the Empress Richardis wished, spiritually and psychically, to unite herself with the Lazarus stream, which is the same that passed over into the traditions of the Order of the Templars. The researches of J. Rietsch show most distinctly that the Lazarus cult was alive in Andlau up to recent times. This is the historical fact that is of importance for us, and the genuineness of the relic may remain an open question so far as our present enquiry is concerned. Thus according to the legend, it is the future guardian of this relic to whom the Red Knight is guided, and he was the cause of her downfall. It is perhaps not irrelevant to note in this connection that the cross upon Luitward's breast, that Richardis touched (the action that caused her repudiation), had come from Cyprus, as had also the head of Lazarus.[29]

Richardis meets us in history as the virgin wife of Charles III. The latter, tormented by unremitting headaches, sought release from pain by undergoing a peculiar operation on his head. He had it cut open. But he died soon afterwards and was buried at Reichenau. Charles the Third's empire had suffered considerable downfall. The Normans were flooding the whole country, travelling up every river from its mouth. Arnulf of Carinthia saved his country by opposing the invasion. He had supplanted Charles III in the rulership, an act to which the Empire owed its existence. Luitward fled to this same Arnulf. Everything that tradition has preserved concerning Luitward will be found collected in Dümmler's *History of the Empire of the Eastern Franks*. He relates that Luitward was the highest of all the Emperor's Swabian favourites, that he assisted the King as his Chancellor in the first years of his reign and very soon received the office of Lord High Chancellor. In an unusually large number of documents, Luitward appears as the beloved Chancellor and trusted adviser of the Emperor and as intercessor or pleader who looks after the presentation of evidence. Dümmler says, 'We may therefore believe a contemporary, who writes that like Haman under Ahasverus, he was feared and honoured by all more than the Emperor himself.' 'He was united in a close and confidential relationship with the Empress. Thus the records often show them appearing as intercessors together, and John VIII often seeks to assure himself of their combined intercessions.' Luitward was owner of the Chapel Birminga in Allemannia, but exchanged it for a cell in Reichenau (cf. Dümmler, op. cit. p. 283; and Pupikofer, *History of Thurgau*, Vol. I, Appendix 3, B 970). This shows that Luitward is also very closely connected with the traditions of Reichenau. He must have known all that has been related about Waldo. Besides, Luitward's brother belonged to the village of Langdorf, where Swanahild had rested with the Reichenau relic of the Sacred Blood. This is a proof that all these traditions are also locally connected with one another. Throughout an entire epoch the history of his time was really guided by **Luitward**, and his spiritual influence was extraordinarily great. He died on St John's Day, 24 June 900 in a battle against the Hungarians in Italy.

Is the connection between Luitward and Arnulf of Carinthia to be ascribed to mere chance, in view of the fact that **Parzival** carries the arms of Styria—the panther—that he inherited from his father? We will leave this question open and content ourselves with placing the historical and legendary material side by side. Was not Luitward the real ruler, and Charles III merely the apparent head of the government? Do we not find here the same relationship that existed between **Parzival** and **Orilus?** However this may be, a more exact examination, from this standpoint, of the biography of Luitward affords the student of history a task of the greatest interest.[29a] Let us now return to the Parzival narrative and try to throw yet more light upon it. This we can do when we see that Orilus, Jeschute's husband, is connected with that part of the narrative which we have now to discuss. We will accompany Parzival further upon his journey.

Wolfram von Eschenbach tells us that soon after Parzival leaves Jeschute, he meets Sigune. Let us first hear the poet's account of it:

Thus rode he, our lad so foolish, adown a mountain side,
When a woman's voice before him from amid the rocks loud cried;
'Twas a cry of heartfelt sorrow, for her joy was in ruins laid—
Then swift rode the lad towards her—Now hear what she did, this maid:
She tore, the maid Sigune, her plaits of long brown hair
From out her head for sorrow; and the lad he beheld her there,
And he saw Schionatulander, the prince on her knee, he dead,
And the maiden she wailed above him, and her joy had for ever fled. (III: 433-440)

This meeting of Parzival with the maiden bride who is holding her dead bridegroom in her lap does not occur haphazardly immediately after the Jeschute adventure, for the youthful hero Schionatulander has been killed by Jeschute's husband, Duke Orilus. This can be seen from the following lines in which Orilus boasts of his death:

As today in the early morning . . .
I have fought, and a prince hath suffered, for joust he towards me sped,
But my spear-point so sorely smote him that he lay there before me dead! (III: 390-392)

Orilus therefore has killed Schionatulander. Strangely enough, Orilus had not intended to kill him; he really wanted to kill Parzival. He says as much in speaking of his sister Kunneware:

> Her lips may not move to laughter till the day that her eyes shall light
> On him who of all shall be reckoned the fairest and bravest knight.
> Would he come unto me, that hero! Ah! then should a strife be seen
> As today in the early morning already my lot hath been.
> I have fought and a prince hath suffered, for joust he towards me sped
> But my spear-point so sorely smote him that he lay there before me dead!

We know that Parzival is the hero who was acclaimed as the fairest and bravest knight, since Kunneware smiled upon him when he appeared at King Arthur's court. Orilus really means to kill *Parzival* and kills *Schionatulander* instead. It is important to be clear about this, because we then understand that the sight of the dead Schionatulander must have had quite a special significance for Parzival, for Schionatulander died *for him*. Schionatulander was the comrade-in-arms of Parzival's father, Gahmuret, and after Gahmuret's death he defended the young Parzival's lands from Orilus, who tried to seize them. In this sense also Schionatulander gave his life for Parzival.

Here we must interpolate a detailed account of Schionatulander's career. It is possible to do this because Wolfram von Eschenbach has written a separate poem about Schionatulander, and on the other hand Albrecht von Scharfenberg has also a good deal to say about him in his *Titurel*.

Schionatulander is the grandson of Gurnemanz of Graharz, who later on becomes Parzival's instructor. Gorgegris, the son of Gurnemanz, married Mahaute, the sister of Count Ehkunat. Schionatulander was the child of this marriage.

Schionatulander: li joenet u l'alant, der Jüngling mit dem Hunde = the young man with the dog.

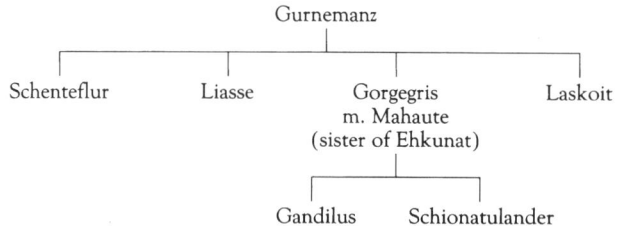

The young Schionatulander served Queen Anflise, of France, as Squire. Queen Anflise gave her squire to her lover Gahmuret, the father of Parzival. Schionatulander, as Gahmuret's squire, acted as his messenger in carrying letters to and from Anflise. When Gahmuret married Herzeleide, Schionatulander made the acquaintance of Sigune who was under Herzeleide's care. Sigune was the daughter of Kiot of Catalonia, and Schoisiane. Her mother died at her birth. The feudal territory held by Kiot was now transferred to Sigune. Kiot gave up the service of the sword and withdrew with his brother Manfilot to lead the life of a hermit. Kiot held his lands in fee to King Tampentaire, who now adopted Sigune and educated her with his own daughter Kondwiramur. Kondwiramur later married Parzival.

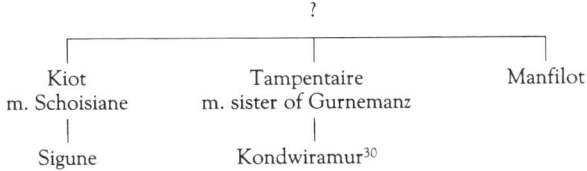

These events took place at the time of the death of Herzeleide's first husband Kastis, who died immediately after the marriage ceremony. When Tampentaire also died, five years after Sigune had entered his household, Herzeleide took Sigune to her home and here Schionatulander found her.

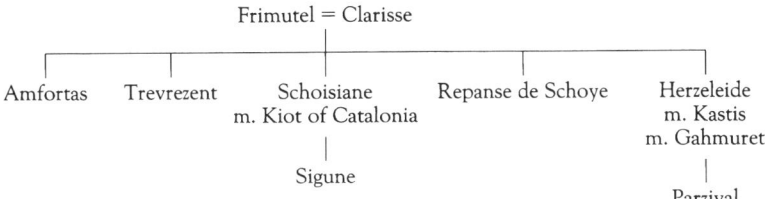

When Gahmuret left Herzeleide to serve the Baruch Ahkarin,[30a] Schionatulander accompanied him, while Sigune stayed behind with Herzeleide. Albrecht von Scharfenberg gives a beautiful description of the love of Schionatulander for Sigune. He it is who teaches her and he can do it well, having learnt 'Minne' in love-service, as the messenger between Gahmuret and Anflise. Sigune says:[31]

> Minne, is it a 'he'?
> Can you teach me about him?
> Is it a 'she'? If she comes to me
> How shall I best show her friendship?
> May I keep her myself, with my dolls?
> Or perhaps she will easily fly,
> Out of my hand to the wilderness?
> (She means like a falcon).
> I shall know how to charm Minne   (Titurel: Chap. 7, Verse 64)

119

Thus, in all innocence, she converses with Schionatulander. Their relationship is wonderfully described. The poet tells how Schionatulander speaks to Gahmuret in distant lands of his love for Sigune, and at the same moment Sigune, at home with Herzeleide, confesses that she loved Schionatulander.

When Gahmuret is killed in the east, it is Schionatulander who witnesses it all and brings home the news. Before starting on his journey to the East Schionatulander took leave of Sigune with these words: 'My departure is inevitable, but may God send the angel who shielded Elizabeth, kinswoman of the Christ, to protect thee from suffering and to take thy life and thy chastity under his protection.'

So Schionatulander sallies forth bearing on his escutcheon an anchor, the arms of the Baruch. The poet tells us that the Baruch was descended from Ahasver and, as we have already mentioned, he was called Ahkerin and figures in Wolfram von Eschenbach's poem, '*William of Orange*'. The poet strangely enough recounts that Schionatulander has to fight two knights who tell him that they are Philip and Alexander of Macedonia, and that they live, not upon earth, but in Paradise. Philip of Macedonia, the father of Alexander the Great, wants to win the hand of Sekundille who afterwards marries Feirefis. Ehkunat, whose sister Mahaute is Schionatulander's mother, stands by and listens in astonishment to the tale of Alexander the Great. Thus it is that Schionatulander is he of whom the poet relates that he met Alexander and his father.

The love of Schionatulander and Sigune was not destined to bring them earthly happiness. Wolfram von Eschenbach relates their tragic fate in his poem 'The Hound Gardevias', the hound whose name signifies, 'Guard the way' [included in the story of *Titurel*, Chap. 10].

One day Sigune and Schionatulander were in a tent in the forest when suddenly 'Guard the Way' sprang upon them. He had escaped from the Palgrave Ehkunat who was, as already mentioned, Schionatulander's uncle. The hound belonged to Ehkunat who had sent him to his beloved, Klauditte von Kanedig, as the wild bearer of script. Upon his leash (twelve fathoms in length, and made of twisted strands of four colours, yellow, green, red and brown, the colours changing at the end of every span) mystical writing appeared if the strands, held together by pearl rings, were drawn aside. The writing began on the dog's collar, continuing along the leash, and was formed of emerald, ruby, diamonds, chrysolite and garnet. The inscription was:[32]

> She to whose name of Kannedig is added the name of Klauditte, sends Ehkunat this letter which contains her loving greeting. The wild bearer of this letter is called Gardevias, Guard well the way. Let him remind thee above all to guard the way that leads to the love of God. This commandment is above all others. Guard the way, therefore, that you may gain a heavenly crown. Beware lest desires of the flesh lead you into shameful ways, but choose, rather, the way that may end in happiness. Speak courteously to priests and holy men, honour and revere them,

hold fast the faith as it is taught thee by the Church. Guard well the way, that thou mayest attain to blessedness through penance and confession. Be merciful in thy judgement of widows and orphans and wield thy power with pity and humility. Guard well the way, that the angelic host may not shut thee out from among them, and be just that the judgement of God may not turn thee from Him. Guard well the Order of Knighthood that it may bring thee salvation, and if thou seekest worldly praise in knightly deeds, then take good heed lest thy modesty should suffer. Honour women with pure love. If a man does not revere women and priests, then the anchor of his honour sinks into a slough of infamy whence it can never be raised. Women bring us into the world, priests bring us to God; so guard thou well the way that, both here and in heaven, thou mayest have happiness and joy. Let thine eyes be like those of the ostrich whose piercing glance has power to hatch her eggs; be wary that thou mayest escape harm; carry watchfulness in thy heart, even as the lynx, lest any should seek to befool thee. Let thy neck be flexible as that of the crane on the watch against betrayal or fraud, but hold thy head modestly like the dove. Two-fold is the nature of the eagle; let thy left hand practise its mildness and thy right hand its justice. Let thy heart be like the lion, strong and sublime. Plant thyself firmly upon thy feet, even as the bear, that thou mayest stand fast in adversity as in prosperity. Twine for thyself a garland of twelve flowers in the day of festival. The first flower is purity of behaviour, the second chastity, the third mildness, the fourth fidelity, the fifth temperance in all things. By two kinds of intemperence, lust and greed, man's virtue becomes endangered, for both spell death to body and soul. The sixth flower is care and foresight, the seventh bashfulness, the eighth modesty, the ninth perseverance and the tenth humility. This—humility—Lucifer forgot; now guard well the way so that thou be not cast into hell with him. Patience is the eleventh flower, and the twelfth is love. Now guard well thy way for the last flower—love—will guide thee to the singing of the angels.

We may see from the writing on the leash that he who receives it should learn to keep strictly to the path, that is to say, the path to the spiritual world, the way whereby he may learn to read the writing of the stars which has its reflection in the virtues of man. The hound, moreover, is of strange appearance: on one side it is vermilion, on the other like ermine, black and white.[33]

Sigune caught the hound and began to read, but he broke away from her. This is what happens to many who begin to read the starry script; they cannot read it to the end. And here we come to the tragedy. Sigune says to Schionatulander: 'Catch the hound for me, for I cannot belong to thee until I have read the writing to the end.' The poet gives us a beautiful picture in this striving of Sigune who strives with greater intensity for knowledge of the spiritual world than for her earthly love. But the hound escapes and the leash becomes entangled in a thorn bush. King Teanglis of Texag and Tamilone perceives the hound and, capturing it, sets it onto a deer in the neighbourhood of Duke Orilus. The latter now catches the hound and makes good his capture by overcoming Teanglis. Meanwhile, Schionatulander meets Teanglis and conquers him also, and the story of this victory is told at Arthur's court. Thence, heroes set out to avenge the defeat of Teanglis, but Schionatulander is victorious over them too. Last of all comes Kay. He it is who struck Kunneware when, hearing Parzival praised, she laughed. Now Kay, too, wants to fight Schionatulander. When a hound leaps past them Schionatulander, taking it for Gardevias, rides after it and Kay thinks he is fleeing for fear. But Schionatulander was in pursuit of the hound which, alas, was the wrong one. It is remarkable that the knights take Schionatulander for the disguised Red Knight, Ither of Gahevies—saying he had a green coat. He thus appears to them like the counterpart of the Red Knight, in the complementary colour. Orilus now sends the hound to his spouse Jeschute, but in the meantime he has met Schionatulander who is responsible for the Kingdom of Gahmuret. They fight for the possession of the dog's leash but Jeschute, wanting to end the conflict says she will send it as a present to Sigune. Schionatulander, however, opposes this and says he will fight for it. Then he rides away meaning to return to fight later. Jeschute now sends the leash to Sigune, hearing which Orilus vows death to Schionatulander. Meanwhile a huntsman brings Jeschute a ring and a clasp which Parzival had previously taken from her. A pilgrim as he was dying handed them to the huntsman with the words, 'For the prince of Waleis', which could only refer to Parzival. But the huntsman not understanding this brings the treasure to the unlawful possessor of Waleis, Orilus.

Meanwhile Schionatulander rides away in search of adventure and wounds Lähelein, brother of Orilus. These two brothers have taken possession of Parzival's lands and made themselves lords of his realm. By this time Sigune and Schionatulander have come to the woods of Picimont de Kluse where Orilus meets them and, in accordance with his vow, kills Schionatulander. As Schionatulander dies Orilus says to him, 'Both lands I give back to thee.' Parzival now appears, to find Schionatulander dying and Sigune weeping over him.

Only now are we able fully to understand what it means to Parzival to see the dead Schionatulander in the virgin Sigune's lap. He sees this woman who, rejecting earthly aims, ever strives towards the spiritual, and on her knees her bridegroom who has suffered death on his account. It is this same woman who first called him by his true name, and first told him who he was.

Wolfram von Eschenbach relates the story in his poem, 'The Hound of Gardevias' in the following words:

The Duchess Sigune
Read the beginning of the tale:

> The name of the hound is the phrase
> Dedicated to what is worthy
> Man and wife who honourably guard the way
> Will find profit in this world
> And also reward in heaven.
> She read still further on the collar
> Though not as yet on the leash:
> 'He who ever guards the way
> Will never sell his honour.
> For he is so strengthened in purity of heart
> That no one's glance will ever detect him
> Wandering and unstable
> About the market-place.' (Titurel: Book X, verse 144)

So speaks the poet of this Guardian of the way, signifying that he leads us on the path to constancy, to unchanging loyalty.

This Guardian of the way, this wakeful watcher, is no ordinary hound. He is a symbol for the starry script. Socrates used to swear by him when he said, 'Yes, by the Dog.' He is the constellation of the Dog, called by the Egyptians the wakeful watcher. Whoever wishes to understand how to read the starry script must first know the love story of Sirius which was known even in old Egyptian times. There is a suggestion of the Isis tragedy[34] in the story of Schionatulander and Sigune.

In this narrative the mysteries of the third Post-Atlantean period of culture are presented to us in medieval, Christian form. Parzival, approaching Sigune, reads in the earthly realm the writing of the stars. Sigune, the silent, the dumb, is the widowed human soul. Every man must meet her, and from her lips the seeker of the spiritual must receive his true name. Sigune asks Parzival his name but he does not know it. Like the majority of mankind he is ignorant of his eternal reality. So he answers:

> At home all who know me call me 'Bon fils, Cher fils, Beau fils!'
> (III: 462)

He refers here to his mother. By his tone of voice rather than his words Sigune recognises the voice of Herzeleide. She feels as if Herzeleide were hovering around the beautiful youth:

> Ere ever the word was spoken, the maiden she knew his name—
> Now hearken aright his title, that hereafter ye own his fame
> Who is hero of this my venture, who now standeth the maid beside—
> And her red lips they spake unfaltering, 'Thou art Parzival,' she cried,
> And thy name it shall mean 'to pierce through', for thy mother's
>   faithful heart

With furrows of grief was riven when she from her lord must
 part. (III: 463–468)

Thus Parzival learns his true name. It is the name of the spiritual force of light that penetrates darkness. Mysteriously does this name stand in starry script in the Easter sky, when within the sickle of the moon appears the dark yet luminous Host. Then appears the light that has power to penetrate, the light that shines in shadow, spiritual light, and this light writes the word 'Perceval' in the writing of the stars.

And now Sigune tells him that his mother is her kinswoman, that he was born at Kanvoleis, that Schionatulander has suffered death for him, and how much suffering has been brought about by the leash of the hound. Parzival wants forthwith to rush away to avenge Schionatulander, but Sigune shows him a false path fearing for his life. This path leads Parzival to a fisherman who gives him shelter in return for Jeschute's clasp, that same clasp which the huntsman brought back to Jeschute, as we have already heard. He received it apparently from the fisherman. The next day Parzival meets the Red Knight, Ither von Gahevies. As he appears in red that means that he is wearing the armour of love (XII: 42). By these steps had Parzival to be led. First he saw death, and fidelity that goes beyond death, then only did he encounter the Red Knight.

The Red Knight is Ither von Gahevies. His wife is Lamire, sister of Gahmuret. He is thus closely related to Parzival.

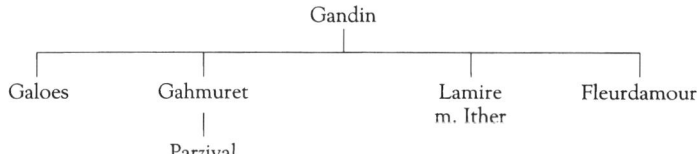

The poet describes Ither in the following words:

All dazzling red was his armour, the eye from its glow gleamed red:
Red was his horse swift-footed, and the plumes that should deck his
 head,
Of samite red its covering; redder than flame his shield;
Fair-fashioned and red his surcoat; and the spear that his hand would
 wield
Was red, yea, the shaft and the iron; and red at the knight's desire
Was his sword, yet the blade's fair keenness was not dimmed by the
 raging fire.
And the King of Cumberland,* stately, in his mailed hand did hold

* See note 95a

> A goblet, with skill engraven, and wrought of the good red gold—
> From the Table Round he had reft it—All red was his shining hair
> Yet white was his skin ... (III: 550-558)

Thus does this Knight stand before Parzival, with his white skin and his red hair. The Red Knight had stolen the cup from Arthur's Round Table, and inadvertently, in his haste, had spilt the wine in Guinevere's lap. He hoped by the theft of this cup to lay claim to land withheld from him. Now he asks Parzival to make this known to Arthur and to demand of the Knights that they should retrieve the golden cup. Parzival promises to fulfil this errand and rides to the town of Nantes where Arthur is staying with his knights. He meets first the Page Iwanet.

Parzival who still, in a childish way, follows his mother's instructions, begins by asking for Arthur and says:

> 'But here see I full many an Arthur! Who of all these shall make me
>   knight?' (III: 590)

This childish manner excites the merriment of the Knights. Then Parzival delivers the Red Knight's message, saying:

> That he spilt o'er the queen the wine-cup that sorely doth grieve the
>   knight—
> Ah! if I his gear so goodly from the king's hand as gift might take,
> (III: 601-602)

The Knights ask Arthur to let the youth meet the Red Knight in combat which Arthur at length allows. Here we are told how all the knights and ladies want to witness the fight, and how Kunneware, who had taken a solemn oath not to laugh until the coming of the one who was to win the highest honour, now laughs at Parzival. Kay, in his wrath, seizes and strikes her, upon which Antanor, who had sworn not to utter a word till Kunneware laughed, begins to speak saying to Kay, 'because you maltreated Kunneware de Laland on this boy's account, therefore will joy be changed for you into sorrow.' For these words he also received a blow from Kay. Parzival now rides off to the Red Knight and kills him with his javelin, thrusting this little spear-like weapon in between helm and visor. With the Page Iwanet's help he takes possession of the Red Knight's armour, but when Iwanet is helping him to put it on, he cannot make up his mind to discard the many-coloured coat given him by his mother. Iwanet does not put the javelin into his hand for, as yet, Parzival has not been knighted. Except for this he is now fully armed and goes back again to Arthur to return to him the reclaimed golden cup. We are told further how Ither is buried amid the great sorrow of Arthur's court. The name Ither can be traced in history. About 781 lived an **Ither** who was Abbot of Tours, and belonged to Charlemagne's Court (Dahn, *Urgeschichte*, Vol. III, p. 991). Thus the name was familiar in the entourage of Charlemagne.

Meanwhile Parzival rides off with great speed until at close of day he arrives at the castle of Gurnemanz de Graharz, who now becomes his teacher in all that pertains to the custom and conduct of knighthood. Gurnemanz teaches him not to be always quoting his mother, for that is not becoming in a knight. He also persuades Parzival to lay aside his fool's motley garment. In this way Gurnemanz separates him from his mother. Parzival undergoes, in a kind of adventure, the experience that every man goes through in the course of his inner development, and we recognise in Gurnemanz the power that leads the youth to independence and places him into external, conventional life. Detailed description is given of how the hero bathes in water into which *roses* have been thrown and, further, how he is then clothed in a white garment. After this Parzival relates his adventures to Gurnemanz who recognises that the slain Red Knight is none other than Ither von Gahevies. Gurnemanz now passes on the name 'Red Knight' to Parzival:

> And the name of his guest he asked not but 'The Red Knight' he called him still. (III: 957)

And he gives him much good advice:

> An thou follow henceforth my counsel far wiser the ways I'll teach! (III: 961)

The advice culminates in these words:

> Thou shalt learn a fitting measure ... (III: 976)

We may, perhaps, at this point be allowed to draw attention to the remarkable architecture of Wolfram's poem. The succession of events is shown in such a way as to suggest that in Parzival we have to do with a Sun Hero. As the Sun passes through the signs of the Zodiac, so does the narrative pass through particular adventures which show the sway of the forces of the various signs. The words, 'the true *Measure* shall be your rule', lead us into the constellation of *Libra*. Previously to that, Parzival experienced the meeting with *Virgo* in the Sigune-Jeschute adventure. Before that was *Leo*, for out of the constellation of Leo comes the power to grasp the world of the senses. The adventure which relates to this is clearly set forth by Chrétien de Troyes. It has to do with Parzival's encounter with the Knights in the forest when he is completely fascinated by the appearance of their shining armour and more interested in such details than in the questions of the Knights. This adventure was preceded by another, the mood of which corresponds to the constellation of *Cancer*. This is the mood we find in the wilderness of Soltane where Parzival grows up completely shut away from the world. All the events preceding the birth of Parzival are steeped in the atmosphere of *Gemini*. We have the double marriage of Gahmuret with Belakane and Herzeleide, and the black-and-white Feirefis, Parzival's half-brother. And in the beginning of the poem where mention is made of the black-and-white magpie, the forces of heaven and hell, we have the same suggestion.

Adventure IV

As the Adventure in Gurnemanz's house proceeds, the hero is offered by Gurnemanz the hand of his daughter, the beautiful Liasse. Parzival declines and rides away. But the opening lines of the next (the fourth) Adventure show us that in spite of this the course of the narrative has led into the realm of the constellation of *Scorpio*. For it begins:

> Thus Parzival parted from them, and courteous he now might bear
> His knightly garb, and he knew them, the customs of knighthood fair.
> But alas! he full sore was troubled with many a bitter pain,
> And the world was too close, and too narrow the width of the spreading plain,
> And the greensward he thought was faded and his harness had paled to white;
> So the heart the eye constraineth and dimmeth awhile the sight.
> For since he had waxed less simple somewhat of his father's lore,
> The desire of the man for the maiden, in his wakening heart he bore;
> And he thought but of fair Liasse . . .   (IV: 1–9)

Parzival has lost his simplicity and is captured by Minne. Yet he is the hero who must stand in a new relationship to love. He is predestined to win the force that his ancestors were not ready to achieve. It is he who can first realise and preserve *Fidelity*: This comes to expression in his wonderfully pure relationship with Kondwiramur, which translated, means Bringer of Love (San Marte: conduire amour). Parzival rides into the Kingdom of Brobarz and enters the town Pelrapäre. Here lives Kondwiramur the daughter of King Tampentaire. She was Sigune's playfellow before Sigune came to Herzeleide. Kondwiramur is besieged in her town by a most unwelcome suitor. The proud King of Brandigan, Klamide by name, seeks her in marriage. She does not want to be his wife, so he besieges the town.

Wolfram describes the pitiful condition of the townsfolk in the following words:

> 'Twas a sorry host, for as ashes some were grey, some were pale as clay,
> (My lord the Count of Wertheim[35] sure had starved on such scanty pay!)

> Thro' want full sore they hungered, nor cheese, nor bread, nor meat
> Had they, and their teeth were idle since naught might they find to eat.
> And their palate knew naught of the flavour of the wine-cup, or red or white,
> And their doublet hung loosely on them, and wasted each limb of might,
> And their skin like wrinkled leather on each limb hung gaunt and grim,
> For hunger their flesh had wasted and driven from every limb.
> (IV: 77–84.)

As Wolfram von Eschenbach describes it, his own poverty strikes him and he cannot help telling us of it. He says:

> At home in mine house, with trouble e'en the mice shall their portion steal,
> Nor oft for their food be joyful! Nor need they the bread conceal,
> Unhidden, I scarce may find it—Yea, oft doth it happen so,
> And I, Wolfram von Eschenbach, ofttimes such comfort as this must know,
> But enough of my lamentation, once more ye the tale shall hear
> (IV: 93–97)

Whither has the poet led us? Are we in the land of Scorpio? Yes and No. We are in the land of renunciation. Parzival is destined to spiritualise and ennoble love. In the land of renunciation he meets his bride Kondwiramur. At first he sits silently opposite her, following all too literally the counsels of Gurnemanz, who said to him:

> Nor be thou so swift to question—Yet I would not that thou withhold
> An answer good and fitting to the speech one with thee would hold.
> Thou canst hear and see, I wot well full five shall thy senses be,[36]
> An thou use them aright, then wisdom it draweth anear to thee.
> (III: 982–985)

Rudolf Steiner once told me that Mephistopheles lurks behind Gurnemanz. This is patent here. None other than Mephistopheles would speak of the sense of smell in this use of the word (*draehen* = 'to smell' in Middle High German). And the advice not to ask so many questions is also Mephistophelian. Later, when Parzival comes to the Grail, he has to suffer for having had Gurnemanz-Mephistopheles as his teacher.

The effect of it is not so bad with Kondwiramur. At first Parzival sits down before her and contemplates her beauty:

> And the thoughts of the knight will I tell ye, 'Liasse *there*, Liasse *here*,
> God will free me from care since I see here Liasse that maiden dear, the

> child of a gallant father!'—Yet her fairness was nought I wot,
> 'Gainst her beauty who sat beside him, in whom God no wish forgot.
> The maiden was queen of the country. Yea e'en as by morning dew
> Refreshed, the rose from its calyx forth buddeth in beauty new,
> And is white and red together[37]—and grief to her guest if wrought
> To whose courtesy nought was lacking since Gurnemanz's side he sought,
> And his words had from folly freed him, and had bidden him questions spare
> Save only when they were needful—so he sat by that lady fair,
> And never a word his lips spake, tho' he sat close the maid beside.
>
> (IV: 139-149)

Kondwiramur realises that he is silent from good manners and begins the conversation herself. In the evening after a frugal meal which is the bounty of Sigune's father, Kiot of Catalonia, Parzival goes to bed.

The scene now described by the poet will never be understood rightly unless Parzival is pictured lying there upon his couch, without shoes, fully robed. The bed is surrounded by candles and the sleeping Parzival offers more the aspect of a dead man on his bier, than of a sleeping man. During the night Kondwiramur enters the bedchamber. She approaches to beg for Parzival's help against Klamide. The poet is emphatic that:

> Pure was she aye, the maiden of whom this venture spake   (IV: 210)

Softly she comes in:

> To his bed she turned her footsteps, and she knelt low his couch before,
> But no thought of love unlawful the heart of either bore.
>
> (IV: 223-224)

Parzival lying upon a bier in the light of the candles experiences the meeting with his soul bride. The same figure here appears to the Red Knight whom Chrétien de Troyes calls Blanscheflur. The poet now describes how she weeps at the bedside, then kneels and her tears flow down upon Parzival. At last he awakes:

> And waking, he looked upon her, and sorrow and joy he felt,
> And he rose up, the youthful hero, as the maiden before him knelt,
> And he spake to the queen, 'Say, Lady, wilt thou make a mock of me?
> To God only, and never to mortal methinks should'st thou bow the knee.
>
> (IV: 229-232)

Then he invites her to sit beside him, or to lie upon his couch:

'Lay thyself down where I was lying, I will seek me some other place!'
But she spoke, 'Thyself wilt thou honour, and shew honour alike to me,
And by never a touch wilt shame me, I will e'en lay me down by thee.'
Then the knight he spake by his knighthood he would e'en do as she should say
So down on the bed beside him in peace the maiden lay.

(IV: 234-238)

And now Kondwiramur confesses to him that she would rather kill herself than become Klamide's wife, for Klamide slew her lover Schentefleur, a son of Gurnemanz and brother of Liasse. Parzival trembles as he hears the name of Liasse. Then he vows to Kondwiramur that he will save her.

And so the day breaks. Parzival arms himself and goes into battle. He vanquishes Klamide's seneschal, Kingron, and charges him to seek out Kunneware and consider himself her prisoner. Meanwhile fate is kind to the besieged city, for two ships laden with provisions sail into the harbour. It is now night again, and according to the customs of the time, as a matter of course, the queen becomes the wife of her deliverer:

To the marriage couch they bade them, 'twas the will both of king and queen,
Yet throughout the night so courteous he bore him, in truth I ween,
He little had pleased those ladies who now, in these latter days,
In passions heat forget all that should win for a woman praise.

(IV: 365-368)

The poet describes more fully the customs he must deplore. But the good breeding he esteems he describes as follows:

But the steadfast knight and faithful guards himself at every hour,
And well knoweth to spare a woman and she chanceth within his power.
For he thinketh, and thinketh truly: 'Tho for many a lonely year
For her favours I'd serve this lady: now, behold the day is here
When her will is to reward me, and here we twain do lie—
Had I touched with bare hand her vesture I were blessed to eternity.
And I vantage take of her slumbers to myself untrue I seem.
Methinks we were both dishonoured did I waken her from her dream,
For a woman's sleep is holy, and all men shall own its sway.'
Thus the Waleis, who ne'er had feared him lay still till the dawn of day.
Thus he whom men call the Red Knight, a maiden he left the queen,
Yet surely she deemed in the morning his wife she o'er night had been
And for love of her lord her tresses she bound with the morning light

> As matrons are wont to bind them. And he won him, the gallant knight,
> Castles and lands around them from the hand of his maiden bride,
> But her heart was ere this his guerdon, and in peace did the twain abide.
> Thus glad in their love they held them two days till the third night fell.
> (IV: 371-387)

We later learn that the boys Kardeiss and Lohengrin are the children of this marriage. The poet here goes on to relate that after the third night Klamide receives the news that his seneschal has been conquered, so he rides out to take vengeance—as he thinks—upon Ither, the Red Knight. Parzival vanquishes him also, but does not kill him, for mindful of the counsels of Gurnemanz he exercises mercy. He charges him to ride to Gurnemanz. The King of Brandigan implores him not to enforce this, since he killed Gurnemanz's son. Then Parzival sends the king also to Kunneware. The poet describes how Klamide comes to Arthur's court and meets his senschal Kingron who, when he saw his master, began to wring his hands so violently that—as Wolfram says—'As dried twigs they cracked amain' (line 646). Klamide remains at Arthur's court. Parzival has now sent two knights to Kunneware, and as a result the Round Table pronounces Parzival as worthy of the highest honour and Kay to be in the wrong for having struck Kunneware. The poet then returns to Parzival. He is now king of the land of renunciation. Yet he does not stay with Kondwiramur. The poet says of her:

> The worth of her lord and husband her heart might scarce fail to know.
> And each found their life in the other, and each was the other's love.
> (IV: 708-709)

And yet they must part.

> Thus courteous he spake one morning (and the knights stood their lord beside),
> 'Lady, an it so please thee, give me leave that I hence may ride
> And see how my mother fareth . . .   (IV: 713-715)

And so he is permitted to ride from Kondwiramur. He seeks his mother, and he finds the Grail. There is a deep mystery here, for no one can find the Grail who is not led to the place where Parzival's mother was. Parzival's mother was dead, although he did not know it. Not on earth but among the stars must he seek her, and as he sought for his mother, he found the Grail, for the Grail can only be found where the stars work in earthly matter or in man himself. An important point is indicated by the poet when in the fifth

Adventure Parzival is brought to the Castle of the Grail while still seeking for his mother.

Adventure V

With extraordinary swiftness Parzival follows his path.

> ... so far did he ride that day
> E'en a bird had been outwearied, and its flight were fain to stay.
> An the tale hath not betrayed me, no further the knight did fare
> When Ither he slew, or from Graharz rode swiftly unto Pelrapär.
> (V: 13-16)

In the evening he came to a lake, where some fishermen had anchored a boat. He saw the boat in the middle of the water, and in it he could see a richly dressed personage with a hat of peacock's feathers. He took him for the *Fisherman* and asked for shelter. We can see from this account, that the poet's allusions to the Zodiac are continued. We have seen how Wolfram von Eschenbach's poem leads us from constellation to constellation, from Gemini through Cancer to Leo, Virgo, Libra, and Scorpio. We know that Parzival withstood the trials which each stage of this course laid upon him. The poet now speaks of the tremendous speed with which the hero rides. He rides through the constellations Sagittarius, Aquarius, Pisces (the *Fishes*). In a day he rides further than is usually ridden in one day, and so we find him with the *Fisherman*, when the poet once more takes up his tale in detail. When he asks the Fisherman for shelter the latter replies:

> ... 'Nay, Sir Knight, I know not for full thirty miles around,
> By land alike or water, where dwelling may yet be found
> Save one house, I would bid thee seek it, for it lieth in sooth anear,
> Thro' the livelong day wert thou riding, none other thou findest here.
> Ride there to the high cliff's ending, then turn thee to thy right hand
> Until to the moat thou comest and thy charger perforce must stand.
> (V: 27-32)

Parzival is guided to the chasm that must be bridged by the traveller who undertakes the ascent from the deep valley, where he meets the Fisher, to the lofty castle of the Grail. He is led into the castle by the forces of the Ram (Aries). As Parzival comes to the Grail castle this mystery is not fully clear to him. He does not know what forces he needs. It is easy enough for the Grail seeker to miss the right path between the Fisher-King and the Grail-Castle, for the seeker after the Grail-Castle must ascend out of *the depths of humility* and yet must not lose the inner activity of his soul. The Fisherman points out to Parzival that the forces found in the valley of humility, where *water* washes over the *feet*, are those which in the heights above guard the Grail. He says:

> ... I myself will thine host be, an thou fail not to find the way,
> Be thy thanks then as is our tendance—as thou ridest around the hill
> Have a care lest the wood mislead thee, such mischance would but
>   please me ill. (V: 36–38)

Parzival comes from the region of earthly love. He has passed through renunciation and humility. The Fisherman warns him against a false path, and Parzival rides on. He finds the chasm which yawns between the depths and the heights, between the depths of humility and the heights of knowledge, between love and wisdom. He finds the drawbridge raised by which access is gained to the castle. If all peoples of the earth joined together to storm the castle, they could not do it in thirty years.

> ... its folk they had held the hall
> And mocked at the foe, if all armies thirty years long beset the
>   wall. (V: 45–46)

A squire espies Parzival and asks him what he seeks. Parzival answers:

> ... 'Tis the Fisher who hath bidden me ride to thee.
> With all courtesy[38] have I thanked him for the shelter he proffered free
> 'Tis his will that the bridge be lowered and I ride here the Burg
>   within. (V: 49–51)

The squire recognises the humility in Parzival and answers:

> 'Sir Knight thou shalt here be welcome, and the way to the Burg shalt
>   win
> Since the Fisher so spoke—and honour would we show unto thee his
>   guest!'
> Then the squire he left fall the drawbridge for so was his lord's
>   behest. (V: 52–54)

None may enter here, into the Castle of the Lamb, into the Mystery Temple of Christianity, who has not come filled with love from the vale of humility. Few walk this path, and the grass in the courtyard is not trodden down; the fire of the heart does not carry many into the bright thought world of the head.

> So the hero came to the fortress, to a courtyard so broad and wide,
> By knightly sports untrodden—Nor oft would they journeys ride,

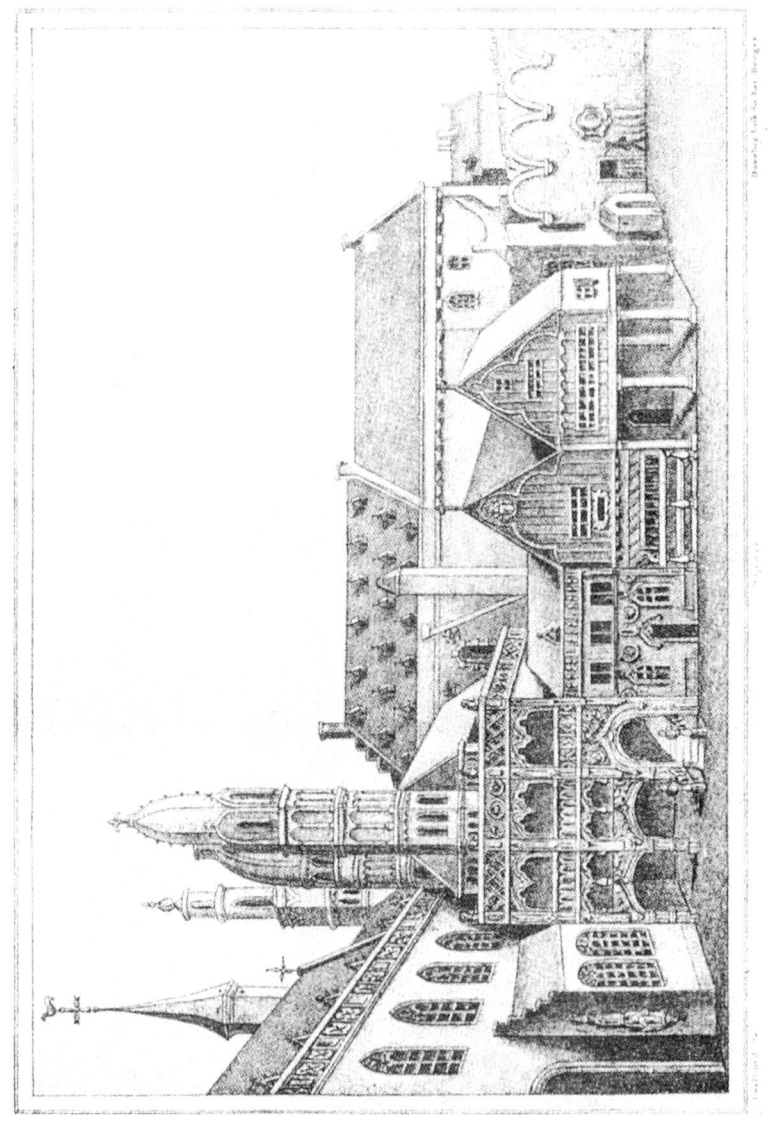

19. Chapel of the Sacred Blood in Bruges, in which the Relic brought by Dietrich of Alsace from Jerusalem was preserved (an early picture)

20. The Relic from the Chapel of the Sacred Blood in Bruges, to which the tradition underlying Chrestien's poem is attached

(By short green turf was it covered) and but seldom with banners
   bright
As on Abenberg's field did they ride there, as fitting for gallant
   knight. (V: 55–58)

Wolfram von Eschenbach calls our attention to the difference between the place we now enter and that in which the affairs of everyday life take place. And he now describes to us what was revealed to Parzival's gaze—Mysteries at the same time of man and of the Cosmos.

We possess two versions of the Grail story—that of Chrétien de Troyes and that of Wolfram von Eschenbach. Their versions are different because their standpoints are different. Chrétien de Troyes draws his knowledge from Count Philip of Alsace, whose father Dietrich is a recipient of a relic of Christ's blood. Dietrich of Alsace takes part in the Second Crusade, which was inaugurated through the preaching of Bernard of Clairvaux, who had given Statutes to the Order of Templars. Through Bernard's sermon in Speyer on Christmas Day, 1146, Konrad III resolved to begin this Crusade from Regensburg. Dietrich followed with the Flemish, joining the French who were streaming into Metz. From here in the middle of June 1147, Louis VII led the Crusades.

Meanwhile a sermon of Bernard's at Cologne had stirred a company of knights to join the Crusade. On 27th April 1147 a fleet set out from Cologne and on 20 May reached an English harbour where it found the Count of Arscoth[38a] with about 200 English and Flemish ships. These troops, Westphalians, Frisians, Netherlanders and English, landed eight miles from St Jago de Compostella on the day before Whitsunday, on which day the burial of St James is celebrated. On the eve of the feast of St Peter and St Paul they landed at Lisbon. The king of Portugal, Alfonso I, son of Henry of Burgundy, persuaded them to help him to free Lisbon from the Moors. On the feast of the Eleven Thousand Virgins they succeeded.[39] Then they travelled further to the Holy Land, where Dietrich of Alsace, who had travelled through Germany, waited with his men. Dietrich remained in the Holy Land until the spring of 1148. He returned home in 1149. Dietrich's wife was Sybilla, the sister of Baldwin III.

When he returned home, Baldwin III, with the consent of the Patriarch of Jerusalem, gave him a part of what was said to be the Blood collected by Joseph of Arimathea. This relic he gave to the town of Bruges (cf. Franz Bender, *Illustrierte Geschichte der Stadt Köln*; also, H. Schäfer, *Geschichte Portugals*, Vol. I, and A. Jox, *Die Reliquie des Kostbaren Blutes zu Brügge in Flandern*, Luxemburg, Peter Brück, 1880). Sybilla, who remained in Jerusalem, died in 1165 in the convent of St Lazarus. The son and successor of Dietrich of Alsace, Philip, was the heir to this relic and the owner of the book which Chrétien de Troyes mentions as the source of the Grail story. Chrétien dedicates his work to Philip and very likely wrote it at his court. This happened at the time when Barbarossa ruled in Germany. Philip's niece was Elizabeth of Hennegau who in 1181 married the young French King, Philip II, Augustus (1180–1223). Philip of Alsace was his trustee and guardian. Through him, therefore, whether in Bruges or in Paris, *at any rate in connection with a tradition bound up with the possession of the relic*, arose the poem of Chrétien de Troyes (cf. page 148, *Die Sage vom Heiligen Gral* by Eduard Wechssler, Halle 1898).

The blood of Christ it is which inspires the version of Chrétien de Troyes.[40] He represents the microcosmic aspect. For this reason, says Rudolf Steiner, the approach to the Grail Castle, the penetration into the mysteries of the human body which are revealed to the soul which experiences the microcosm, are nowhere so wonderfully described as in the poem of Chrétien de Troyes.

Wolfram von Eschenbach's version is quite different. His informant is not the owner of a blood relic but Kiot, through Flegetanis, the possessor of the wisdom of the stars. Not in earthly script but in the script of the stars is written the original of the book from which Wolfram von Eschenbach draws the tradition which he uses. Perhaps it is significant that he expressly says that he cannot read. Wolfram von Eschenbach had a good reason for quite clearly emphasising the fact that he could not read:

> ... no maker of books am I!
> But a singer of strange adventures, and of knightly prowess high:
> Stripped bare will I be of all honour, naked and reft of fame,
> Ere I trust my renown unto letters, and give to a book my name!

(Wolfram's 'apology' occurs between Books II & III)

Whether the medium is a written or an oral tradition, Wolfram's ultimate source is the star writing.

Now the poet describes what the inhabitants of the Grail Castle suffer. And he describes this suffering from the *macrocosmic* aspect. He describes it expressly in relation to the constellations of the stars. It is true this mystery is not revealed until Parzival comes to the Castle of the Grail for the second time. The first time it remains hidden. It is just this that is lacking in Parzival—he cannot read star-writing, he does not find the words which are inscribed on the Grail sword, he only looks at what is revealed to him in *Imagination*, he does not rise to the reading of this picture-writing, to Inspiration. What the human being sees when he enters the Grail Castle is himself. It is precisely the question for him when his own being confronts him and asks: 'Brother, what is wrong with thee?' No one else can answer this question—only he himself can do it. For the answer to this Parzival-question is: 'I myself have caused all this suffering that I see here...'

Parzival must learn that Amfortas suffers because he, Parzivial, has not recognised himself to be the cause of his suffering. Who sees the imagination of the Grail and thinks that he sees anything other than the slaying of what is noblest through his own imperfection, cannot redeem the suffering Grail

King. The *question* is what brings redemption. But there we anticipate the second visit of Parzival to the Grail Castle, for between the first and second visits lies a long path of inner development. The human soul must find the way to imaginative vision, and must nevertheless lose it again, for not until it reveals itself to him for the *second* time does he see it aright. One can study this in the mystics, for example, Jacob Boehme. he too had to lose all his visions, as Rudolf Steiner told us, before he was able, after straying for a long while, to experience them anew, penetrated now with inspiration. Rudolf Steiner has again and again called attention to the necessity of going through this stage of knowledge. Inspiration, the reading of the picture script, the recognition of the significance of the imagination, depends upon a kind of conscious voluntary forgetting.[41] Only in the soul which has been emptied of imaginations, does the language of the stars resound;[42] and then are seen anew imaginations which form the spiritual starry heavens, the macrocosmic aspect of the Grail Castle.[43]

Wolfram thus describes the suffering of the inhabitants of the castle:

'Twas long since they might disport them in such pastimes of warlike skill
For sorrow lay heavy on them, and mirth it beseemeth them ill.
(V: 59–60)

This sorrow of heart lies in the fact that all the Knights of the Grail share the suffering of the Guardian of the Grail. Parzival now draws near. He who will approach the Grail cannot do so with the forces of earthly understanding. He who thinks he can ride to the Grail in proud self-consciousness on the horse of intellectualism, makes a mistake. So we are told how Parzival alights from his horse. No one can approach hither without purifying himself from all that clings to him through his outer sheaths, through that within which he is born. That is why we are told that Parzival washed off the rust of his armour. Parzival is really not fully in the condition to go through the Grail adventure. The poet expressly tells us that he cannot yet wear any of his own garments, as he who wishes to approach the Grail must do. So Repanse de Schoye sends him a purple cloak of reverence [cf. *The Twelve Keys* of Basil Valentine, The Third Key. Paul M. Allen, *A Christian Rosenkreutz Anthology*, Rudolf Steiner Publications, New York, 1968]. It is her own cloak. The chamberlain who brought it to him says to Parzival:

She hath lent it while fit robes they for thee prepare. (V: 76)

Now we are told that Parzival's own armour is taken away from him. He who draws near to the Grail must separate himself from the armour in which he is clad by earthly forces. That is difficult for the soul, and although Parzival had ridden through the valley of humility, he flies into a passion:

> For he laid his hand on the swordhilt—when he found it not by his side
> Then he clenched his fist so tightly that the clasp wrung the blood drops red
> From beneath his nails, and crimson to the sleeve of his robe they spread.
> (V: 90–92)

He is, however, pacified when they ask him to be friendly, and tell him he need not be afraid, that all the events which he sees are only indications of the fact that the forces and powers that he had encountered in the valley have now reached the heights of the Grail Castle.

> That the Fisher hath come to the Castle, nought else shalt thou here have heard
> Now do thou to our lord betake thee, here art thou an honoured guest,
> And the load of thy heavy anger be banished from off thy breast.
> (V: 96–98)

And now the poet describes to us what is active from above downwards, the forces of illumination:

> To the palace hall they gat them, where a hundred crowns hung low
> With many a taper laden ...
> (V: 99–100)

We are told that even the walls are furnished with candles, and that there are a hundred couches along the sides of the walls. Each couch bore four knights. In the middle of the hall Parzival sees three altars erected. On each of them burns a fire, the burning wood of which spreads a clearly recognisable and pleasant odour.

The rest of the description is in a picture-language which resembles that which once prevailed in medieval alchemy. In every book in which the alchemistic process is described in detail, the three fires are mentioned (as for instance: *Geheime Figuren der Rosenkreuzer*, Berlin 1919—Barsdorf, p. 6). They are what stimulates the forces in the threefold human nature. In thinking, feeling and willing we learn to recognise that to which these three fires supply the stimulus. The sick guardian of the Grail took his place before the middle fireplace. He invites Parzival to seat himself by his side. His illness consists in his being unable to bring to fulfilment the process of inner development that he has begun. The alchemists are accustomed to indicate the stages of this process by the colours which are revealed to imaginative knowledge. One can refer to any alchemistic book and find that the series of colours here referred to begins with black and grey, and then passes on to red and white. Here one finds something similar:

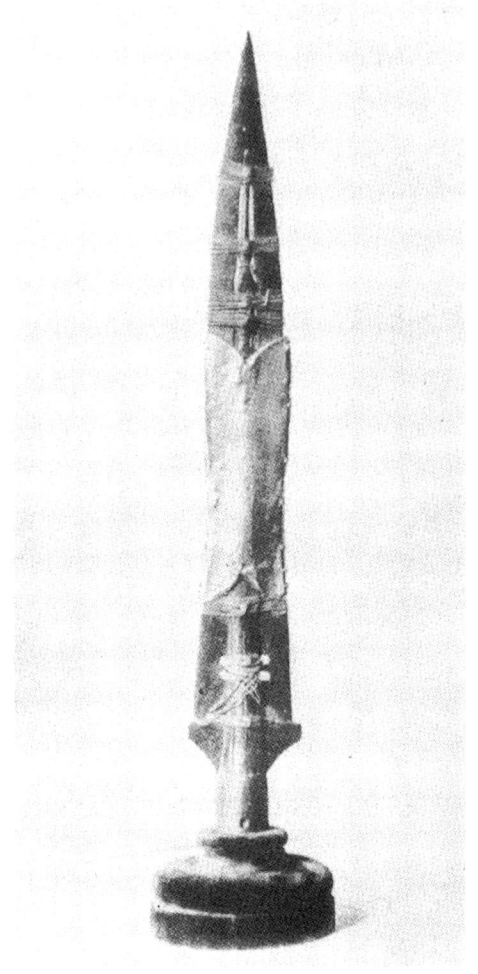

21. The Imperial Lance, Imperial Treasure House in Vienna

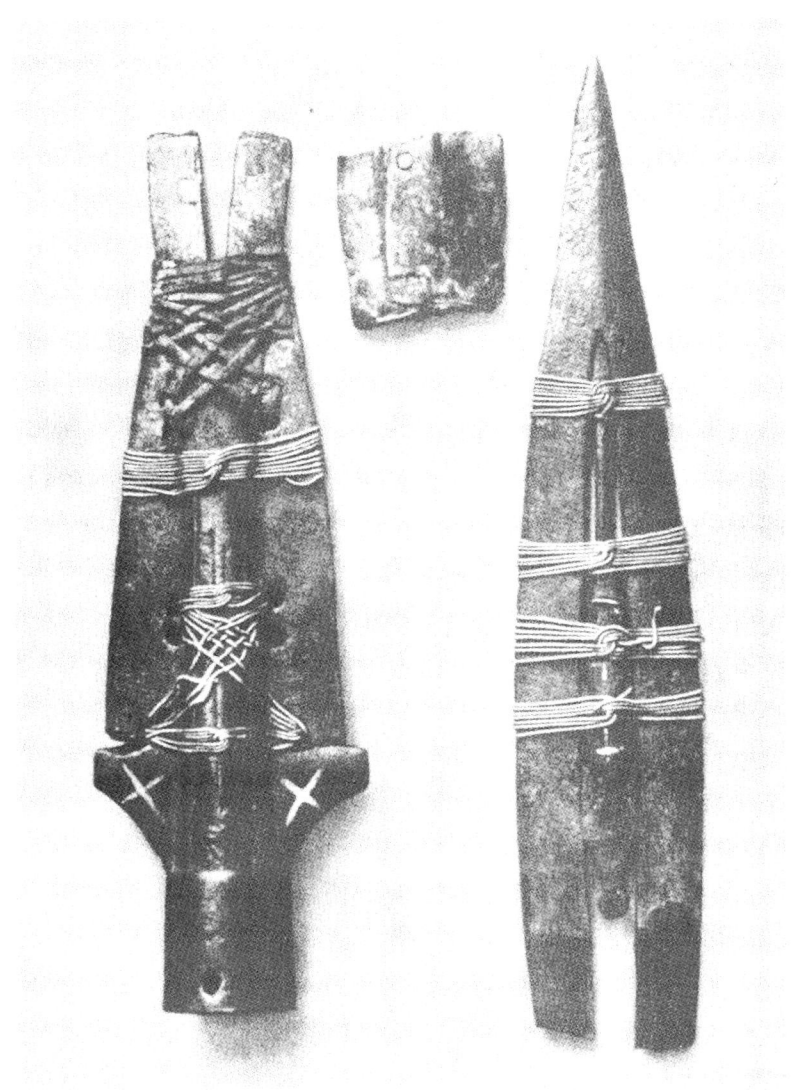

22. The Imperial Lance, Imperial Treasure House in Vienna (taken apart)

> And the host he craved through his sickness great fires, and warm
> robes would wear. (V: 119)

This is the manner in which the alchemist expresses himself. We read, for example, in the alchemistic instructions of Basilius Valentinus: 'Make a big fire'; or 'Do not make too great a fire or everything will escape up the chimney'. These are figures of speech which relate to inner soul processes which at the same time have their physiological counterparts. The play of colours here referred to is indicated in the following words:

> And the poorest skin was costly, and black was its hue and grey,
> And a cap of the selfsame fashion he wore on his head that day,
> 'Twas within and without of sable, with bands of Arabian gold
> Wrought around, and a flashing ruby[44] in the centre might all
> behold. (V: 121-124)

With this last is indicated the stage that Amfortas has not attained, and because he did not attain it, we are told, there is great lamenting among the knights and squires. A bleeding lance is brought in, from the point of which blood drips.

> ... from the point did the blood run fast
> Adown to the hand of the holder, till 'twas lost in the sleeve at last.
> And then thro' the lofty palace was weeping and wailing sore
> The folk of thirty kingdoms could scarce have bemoaned them
> more. (V: 127-130)

It is the sight of the spear which causes the Grail Knights such grief. When Parzival enters the Grail Castle for the second time and delivers Amfortas, the spear is no longer there. It is the spear, carried round the four sides of the hall, which is the indication that the true goal has not yet been reached. In the spear we learn to recognise the forces which kill the higher man. The poet lightly touches upon what later he plainly says: that the spear is a picture of Saturn forces. We shall later see clearly that whenever Wolfram mentions the spear, he is referring to Saturn constellations. When the spear disappears, the people's lamenting is stilled:

> And thus to each of the four walls with the lance in his hand he drew
> Till he reached once again the doorway, and passed him the portal
> thro',
> And stilled was the lamentation, and the grief that this folk must know
> When the squire bore the lance before them, and thus bade them think
> on woe. (V: 131-4)

The people recognised the spear with which the body of Christ was pierced,⁴⁵ so that water and blood flowed from the wound by which the death of the Saviour was recognised. And now is put before us a detailed picture of the Grail procession.⁴⁶ The number and order of the persons taking part in it, each in their appropriate colour, is described with great precision. First appear two children, maidens with wreaths on their flowing hair. Each bears a golden candlestick, and in each candlestick burns a light. They are the Countess of Tenabrock and her companion, their garments are of brownish red, and they wear girdles. Now follow two more women, a duchess and her companion. They carry stools of white ivory, and their lips glow red. All four bow, set down the stools before the host, who is seated before the middle altar, and retire. All four are clad alike.

Now there appear a further twice four women, that is eight, so that with the previous four there are now twelve. Four of the eight newcomers carry tall candles: the other four carry a precious stone which is transparent. It is a granatjacant,⁴⁷ and so translucent that one could almost hope to see the sun through it.

It had been formed into a table top, from which the host was in the habit of eating. The eight maidens approach the host, inclining their heads slowly as if in greeting, and the four who bear the table to place it upon the snow-white ivory stools. They then bow and pass to where the first four women are standing.

The first four women are clothed in brownish red, the eight women now mentioned are clad in green. Their robes are of green samite. They too wear girdles and wreaths of flowers on their heads.

After all this has taken place, two more women come, the daughters of Counts Iwan of Nonel and Jernis of Reile. These two bear two knives with silver blades, gleaming brightly.⁴⁸ They are so sharp that they could cut steel. In front of these, four women bear lights, so that the women who bear knives and those with the lights together make six. The two maidens now lay the silver knives on the table and retreat into a circle of twelve, four of whom as we have already said are clad in brownish red, and eight in green. Thus the two handmaidens who had carried the silver knives joined the twelve. When they had all taken their places, there were eighteen women standing together.

Immediately after came six more women. Their garments were made half of blialt⁴⁹ and half of bright silk from Nineveh. These last six, and the previous six were clad in two colours. After these however came the queen. She was clad in tissue from Arabia, and she carried on a cushion of green silk a thing which is called the Grail.

. . . a thing which men call 'The Grail',
The crown of all earthly wishes, fair fulness that ne'er shall fail!
(V: 189–190)

When she had brought it in there followed the six maidens bearing lights, in which balsam burned. The queen now set down the Grail before the host.

Parzival watched all this, and was himself enveloped in the cloak which she had lent him. The Queen and the six maidens who carried the lights, making seven, now joined the other eighteen, and these twenty-five women were so arranged that the queen stood in the middle with twelve women to the right and twelve to her left. The poet lays so great a stress on the exact description of all these complicated proceedings that we can scarcely suppose it to be merely the play of poetic fancy. The Grail appears in a circle of twenty-four lights. They are the twenty-four elders with the lily wreaths of whom Dante too speaks in his *Divine Comedy* (Purgatorio 29, v. 83), described in medieval symbolism in the twenty-four books of the Old Testament. They represent high spiritual beings, leaders of human evolution, as Rudolf Steiner once explained; leaders of twenty-four stages of world evolution, usually called Thrones in the Middle Ages. They encircle the force of Christ, of the Lamb, and bask in the sight of Him, but their light is outshone by the Grail. Simrock expresses this when he says: 'The Grail is the fullest ray of earthly blessing.'

There is no philosophy, no religion, that is not superseded by the Grail, for the Grail embraces them all. Goethe expressed this in his poem, *Die Geheimnisse*. And Rudolf Steiner rightly says that had Goethe completed *Die Geheimnisse*, which however, remained a fragment, the whole of the mystery of the Grail would have been expressed in it. Goethe wished in his poem to show that wisdom, sacrificed by the teachers of the world on the altar of humanity rises again as love in the heart of the One who can unite the many rays of many-coloured light. The transmutation of wisdom into love is what he wishes to show. And it is healing love which Parzival out of true knowledge has to develop.

Now we are told how the knights sat at the tables. Four sat at each little table, and there were a hundred tables. So there were four hundred knights, and each knight was allotted a squire to serve him, so that there were four hundred squires as well.

> And wherever there stood a table there four squires were ready right
> To serve the four who sat there and their service they knew aright,
> For twain would carve, low kneeling, and twain to the knights would bear
> Of food and drink as needful, and thus for their wants would care.
> (V: 215–218)

Four wheeled carts brought vessels for drinking. Four knights set the tables, and a steward followed behind whose duty it was to gather up again everything that had been distributed, when it had done its service, and to put it upon the trolley. A hundred squires received bread from the Grail in white cloths and divided it up. One could obtain anything from the Grail, for that is its peculiar characteristic, that it gives to each individual precisely what he needs. It is so universal that it contains potentially in itself everything, and gives to each just what is necessary for him.

> What of food or drink desiring, each one might stretch forth his hand.
> Food warm or cold, or dishes that known or unknown shall be,
> Food wild or tame— (V: 228–231)

Thus the Grail worked a great miracle. It gave the food which we venture to call the bread of heaven. Christ gave of this food to His disciples, and they became thereby a community, for the Grail bestows what is individually received and through which one becomes a member of a single being. The poet describes clearly how the knights also received with the food three kinds of condiments corresponding to their threefold human nature—Salt, Agrass [gooseberry juice] and Pepper. But also three kinds of drinks—Morass [mead], Wine and Sinopel [red wine].

When Parzival saw all this, he might have said, 'There I see the Holiest surrounded by twenty-four lights; there too I see the bleeding lance, there I see what brings death, what destroys the mystery of the Saturn force, and on the other hand the rebuilding force which overcomes it.' And then came the moment in which he had to show whether he was ripe. A squire advanced and brought to him a sword in a costly sheath. The shaft was of ruby and the blade truly wonderful. The host handed it to him and said, 'This sword often helped me in the greatest need, before I through God received so severe a wound. I give it to you—may it secure for you what you cannot acquire merely by gazing at what you here enjoy.'

> ... now with this shalt thou be repaid
> If ought hath in care been lacking—Henceforth shalt thou bear this blade
> Whatever chance befall thee, and when thou its power hast tried
> Thou wilt know thou art fully armèd, whatever strife betide.'
> (V: 251–254)

Had Parzival recognised the peculiar nature of the sword (we have already spoken of this in the introduction to this book), then he would have known it was the Word-Sword that was given to him, in the presence of the twenty-four flames and the highest force. He would, in the *radiance* of the lights, have recognised the harmony of *wisdom*, and would have received *strength*. This was what could not yet be given to him. He did not read the sentence on the sword. The gift of the sword was the challenge to ask.

> Ah! Woe to the guest that asked not, I am sorrowful for his sake,
> When his hand clasped the sword 'twas a token that his silence he well might break. (V: 255–256)

The appropriate question was, 'Why do you suffer? Why does the sword which has so often helped you in need serve you no more? Why have you lost the sword? Why have you lost the Word?'

All Parzival's further experiences serve to lead him to this question and to the answer that he alone can give: 'I myself am guilty of humanity's suffering; only if I reach my highest goal, not for myself, but in the service of the Word, can I bring forth the force of healing.' But Parzival does not understand this, and so he sees what there is to see, but then is obliged to leave the Grail Castle. Everything now happens again in reverse order—more or less backwards. Here Parzival experiences things backwards.

> ... each maid to her task was fain
> From last to first ...
> (V: 261-262)

They turn to the Grail with the Queen, the Queen bows, and the maiden bears the Grail forth again. Parzival gazes after them, and when he sees them disappear he can see in the antechamber which they enter a wondrously beautiful old man. He knows not who is this wondrous aged man.

> Who he was shalt thou know hereafter, when a fitting time shall be,
> The host, his Burg and his kingdom, yea, all will I name to thee.
> (V: 269-270)

Wolfram means that the time is not yet ripe to impart this. This is the law of the Grail, to reveal nothing, except in circumstances in which it can be fully grasped. We are prepared by much which goes before, to understand the meaning of it all. But the same thing does not hold good for the commentator as for the reader who takes his Parzival in hand for the first time and has read up to this point. We venture therefore to reveal here what the poet says at a later place. But we should like at the same time to point out the great value the poet lays on coming to everything in the Grail narrative in its proper time and place, and on giving nothing to the unprepared. The poet compares one who tells of the venture of the Grail to a man who draws a bow. He must not too soon release the arrow from the bow.

> But he who this story aimeth at the ear of a fool shall find
> His shaft go astray, for no dwelling it findeth within his mind.
> Too wide is the road I think me, and that which he chance to hear,
> Ere yet he may know the meaning, flies out at the other ear.
> For rather at home I'd bide me than in such ears my story tell,
> A beast or a stock, I think me, as a hearer would serve as well.
> (V: 281-286)

To be sure, the poet is not in favour of wandering too long in devious ways.

> For it goeth straight to its ending, while he who aside shall stray,
> Though his goal at last he reacheth, findeth all too long his way.
>
> (V: 277–278)

We may certainly reveal here, without altogether ignoring the poet's warning, that the old man whom Parzival saw is *Titurel*, he who brought the Grail down from heaven to earth. Before him angels bore it in the heights. He built a covering for the Grail, within thirty years he built the Castle, he built the Temple, he did it in his own being. Then the Grail sank into the Temple. Thus came down to men what the angels had guarded. Parzival only perceives the bearer of this Mystery in the background. Thus he sees the wonderful pictures gradually vanish. The host says to the guest—'Now your bed is ready, so I advise you to retire to rest. The poet deplores the fact that Parzival acquiesces. Oh, if only he had asked! But he takes his leave and gets him to bed. The bed was richly decked. It gleamed so wondrously, that Parzival thought it glowed with fire. Parzival only saw one bed, so he bade the knights who accompanied him to go to rest. As formerly in the Castle of Kondwiramur the bed and the bedchamber resemble more the bier of a dead man than an ordinary bed. Once more candles surround the couch. But still brighter than the candles shone his countenance. With the help of the maidens he laid aside his garments. Four more maidens entered to see if he is well cared for and if his couch is soft. Before each of these four maidens a squire carried a candle. As they entered, Parzival drew the coverlet over him. They, however, said to him, 'Will you, to please us, remain awake a little longer?' As they said this, he lay under the coverlet and his face shone like the sun. The maidens could not but be aware of his beauty. Three bore spiced drinks, mead and wine [according to San Marte]. The fourth maiden bore apples from Paradise. She knelt low before him as once Kondwiramur had done. He bade the maiden be seated as once he had bidden Kondwiramur. But she said, 'Allow me, seated I cannot serve you, but we have come to serve you.' Then he spoke sweetly to her, as once to Kondwiramur. He drank and ate from the food that she offered him, then she departed. Parzival lay there and the candles illumined his bedchamber, and he slept. But he lay not alone.

> Yet Parzival lay not lonely, for until the dawn of day
> Heart-sorrow would lie beside him, nor passed with the dawn away.
> And every coming anguish its herald before would speed,
> E'en so did the fair youth's vision outweigh e'en his mother's need
> When she dreamed ere the death of her husband. As a carpet unrolled his dream
> The centre of fair jousts woven, while the edge was with swords agleam.
> And in slumber his foemen pressed him, and would swiftly upon him ride;

So fearful his dream that, wakened, thirty times had he rather died.
Thus fear and unrest awoke him, and the sweat streamed from every
    limb.
(V: 333-341)

Parzival goes through a kind of death experience. The skeleton-man stands before his eyes. Although he thus develops a body-free consciousness, he is yet not capable of rightly entering the spiritual world because he has not asked the question. He therefore experiences the entry into the spiritual world not as a loving union of himself with the world of the elementary spirits, but in fear. And so he is obliged to return into his ordinary sense-consciousness, to leave in the morning the Grail Castle.

The daylight shone fair through the windows, yet not voice had called
    on him;
Then he spake, 'Where are now the pages, who stood before me of
    late?
Who shall hand unto me my garments?' Then awhile would he patient
    wait
Till slumber o'ercame him: none spake, none aloud would cry,
Vanished the folk . . .   (V: 342-346)

Therein lies the tragedy that Parzival must experience. His sleep remains the ordinary sleep. The pictures of the Grail Castle reveal themselves to him no more. We are told how he springs out of bed, and how he finds on the carpet before him two swords, the Grail sword and the sword of the Red Knight, of Ither of Gahevies. He still possesses, too, the Queen's cloak. As he finds no one to help him, he arms himself and girds both swords to his side. In front of the house he finds his horse, his shield and his spear. All his shouting is in vain. As he rode into the courtyard, the grass and earth were trodden down. Many knights must have ridden forth. The doors were open, the tracks of the horses and those on foot marked the exit of the knights. The bridge was down.

    Parzival rode across the drawbridge. Then suddenly the bridge was drawn up. Parzival could not see the squire who did it, but it was done so suddenly that his horse stumbled and almost fell. So it is if a human being seeks the transition from the spiritual to the physical world, and is unable to control by his will all that is involved. Then the person experiences how the picture world by which he felt himself unborne, begins to fall away. He who experiences things thus, sins against the inner sun, against the force which illuminates human beings in sleep. The force of the dove is lost to him. So the squire calls after Parzival, 'Henceforth shalt thou hate the sun—thou art a goose. Ah, if only thou hadst exercised activity and asked the question.' The squire means that love and sympathy ought to have been stronger in

Parzival than the conventionality that Gurnemanz-Mephistopheles had taught him!

When Parzival turned round and asked for an explanation, no one heard him and the door slammed. Then he sought to follow the tracks of the hoofs. But so it happens to man, when on awakening he tries to hold fast the pictures which have fled. The more he tries, the more they hide themselves. Parzival following the track of the hoofs is forced to realise that the path vanishes. At last he loses it altogether. What else has he now to encounter but self-knowledge! Self-knowledge confronts him in the form of Sigune. That is different self-knowledge from that which Amfortas offered him. Amfortas showed him the suffering guardian of the Grail—Sigune holds the dead knight on her knees. Embalmed, he lies in her arms.

We have already pointed out that from the moment when Parzival neglects to ask the question, all his experiences go backwards. Parzival has now to experience everything again, but in a different form. The poet only describes the outstanding events of this retrospective life. He who wishes to be cleansed must pass through his life backwards. He will attain to true self-knowledge in no other way. No wonder that Parzival encounters again the maiden with the dead knight. Parzival has nothing left of all his experiences in the Grail Castle except the cloak and the sword. The cloak protects him from many things. The sword reminds him, through the sentence on its blade, of what he has neglected. That he has not found the right relation to the Word, must be brought to his consciousness. Sigune asks him where he was last night. Parzival answers, 'A mile from here lies a noble castle, I have just left it.' Then says Sigune, 'That cannot be true, there is no house for thirty miles around. But thirty miles from here there is certainly a castle. Who seeks it, cannot find it, it only reveals itself when unsought. Unconsciously it must happen, if anyone is to see this castle. Yet this castle cannot be known to you. Monsalvasch it is called, the kingdom where its lord ruled is called the land of Salvasch. Titurel is the name of the king who bequeathed it to his son Frimutel.' And now she tells of the race of the Grail. Frimutel left four children (the fifth is not mentioned because he died during the lifetime of Frimutel). Three are now rich, the fourth chose voluntary poverty. Trevrizent is his name. The poet Albrecht von Scharfenberg in his *Titurel* has told us the other name of Trevrezent. He calls him the 'Tatenschnellen' (Quick-Doer). A man of action is he, who brings his activity to bear wherever it is a question of securing proper balance. Because others do not maintain the balance, he often appears to shoot beyond the mark. If he is considered only in himself, he would not be rightly judged or understood. What he does only has sense and significance in that he holds the balance for the deeds of another. When he learned that his brother Amfortas, contrary to the law of the Grail, erred in the service of love, he wished to maintain the balance by contrary action. He renounced all honours, renounced proud knighthood and the joy of life, and became a hermit. It by no means lies in his nature to be an ascetic. He perseveres in this onesidedness, feeds on roots and herbs, sleeps on a bed of moss under a rocky wall, which but poorly protects him from rain, in a poverty stricken hut, because he creates the balance for the deeds of Amfortas. And so much of what he does is related to what takes place in the Grail Castle. He has the external service.

This is interpolated as a help to the understanding of the character of Trevrezent. But the poet goes on to say:

> ... Amfortas, his brother, hath grief enow,
> He can neither stand, nor be seated, nor walk, but must aye recline.
> (V: 434-435)

Then Sigune continues, 'Alas! If only you had been in the Grail Castle. You would have been able to free the host.' Then said the Waleis, 'I was indeed there, I saw the wonders, I saw the women.' Then she recognised the speaker by his voice. Then she pronounced his name. 'Thou art Parzival. Sawest thou the host? Tell me!'

> Ah! tell me the joyful tidings, may his woe at last be stilled?
> Well is thee that the blessed journey thou hast ta'en, now shall earth be filled
> As far as the winds of heaven may blow, with thy fair renown.
> Nought on earth but shall do thee service, fulfilment each wish shall crown.
> (V: 443-446)

Then says Parzival, 'How did you recognise me?' And the maiden answered, 'Look, I am the person who made my plaint to thee, and who told thee thy name. Thy mother is related to me, she is my aunt.' Then Parzival recognises her too. Then he realises who is before him. For he had not recognised Sigune, so deathly pale was she. And he begged her to allow him to help her bury the dead.

He does not perceive that destiny brings him face to face with the affianced maiden who bears the dead knight in her arms so that by means of an outer experience he should gain an inner one. He does not perceive that his own soul too is widowed, that he has allowed the writing of the stars which he bore in his soul to die. Sigune however knows what he needs and calls his attention to it. She points to the Grail sword and asks, 'Knowest thou its gifts?' And she told him who had forged it. Trebüschet was the name of the smith, in the country of King Lac (Lac is the father of Jeschute). There is to be found a fountain, near Karnant:

> The sword will withstand the first blow, at the next it will break in twain,
> An thou to these waters bring it, from their flow 'twill be whole again.
> Yet where at its source the streamlet flows forth from its rocky bed,
> Shalt thou seek those healing waters ere the sun stand high o'erhead.

> Lac is the name of that fountain. If unsplintered shall be the blade
> Then press thou its halves together, from the waters shall it be made
> Not whole alone, but stronger the blade and the edge shall grow,
> Nor their brightness and fair adorning be dimmed by the water's flow.
> Yet a spell thou first must master, ere thou draw that sword of might,
> Thou hast left it behind, I fear me! ... (V: 477-486)

We have already at the commencement of this book explained this passage. Sigune draws Parzival's attention to the force of inspiration, he must become conscious that he bears two swords. That he is knight of the sword but also a knight of the *Word*. And the *Word*-sword is broken for him if he does not learn how to perpetually *renew* it. He who cannot renew the spiritual Word where runs the spiritual stream, where the bright sun of daylight does not shine, he who only receives it in *fragments* through *tradition*, he *cannot be a Knight of the Grail*. He can certainly come to the Grail, but he always has to leave it again. And this is what Parzival has to learn. He must learn to read the imaginations that spread themselves over the starry heavens. He must read the star writing.

Now in reply to Sigune's questions Parzival tells her of his omission; then she scolds him. Then he quoth, 'Nay, I asked no question!'

> Then the maiden laments. Then she calls him dishonoured and accursed.
> Now thou livest, and yet I tell thee to bliss art thou henceforth
>   dead! (V: 504)

And then comes to pass what a human being experiences if he is obliged to acquire self-knowledge in this way. The pictures speak no more and disappear.

> And never a further answer or word shalt thou win from me (V: 509)

His experiences however go backwards—inevitably. From experience to experience he must march. What he has to make good is placed before his eyes. But they are not merely inner experiences that the poet describes, they are outer events. That is characteristic of the destiny of a Grail seeker, that he has ever before him in outer and inner experience the same picture. He is celebrating his own destiny. From stage to stage he rises and falls, and he must recognise it, until after long wandering and false paths he reaches the Grail.

Parzival encounters Jeschute. In all innocence he sinned in respect of her. Now he meets her again. He must make good again also the mistake that he unwittingly and involuntarily committed. The poet gives a horrifying description of the appearance of Jeschute. Cast off by her husband she rides on a miserable horse. One can see the horse's bones through its skin, and its ribs stand out. It is as colourless as ermine. The halter is of hemp, the mane matted and untrimmed. Its eyes are sunken within deep sockets. Tormented and worried, the horse limps along. It had to suffer hunger. It was a wonder that it was still able to get along. Its trappings are narrow and poor, its bells and saddle shattered, instead of proper girths there is only a hempen cord, and this was torn by thorns and briars, as was also Jeschute's robe. Only rags covered her skin. When she saw Parzival, she recognised him at once. She blushed, for he was the most handsome man in the countryside, and she remembered her first encounter with him. He said, however, that he had not the least intention or wish to shame her, and that he was distressed at her sufferings; then she wept. But he rode after her and said:

> ... Now lady, of true service from mocking free,
> In God's name take thou here my surcoat, a covering it will be for
>   thee. (V: 561–562)

It is easy to overlook this passage. But it is important. For what he offers her is the mantle of the Grail-bearer. It is indeed no trifling gift. In expiation of guilt, the human being must give all, were it the highest. Destiny is inexorable. She however rejects it for fear of her husband, for she dare not wear the cloak of a strange knight. And it is well for Parzival that it was so. Then she asks him to ride away, otherwise they would both come in danger of their lives. Parzival asks her to whom she refers. And she tells him about her husband, Orilus who has cast her off. Orilus rode in front of her, and after the two had been talking together for a long while he turned round and saw them. Full of anger he sprang forward with couched spear. The spear which was now aimed at the breast of Parzival had belonged to Gahevies. This is apparently an unessential detail that the poet tells us. In reality it is a deep principle. Parzival killed Ither von Gahevies, and Gahevies's spear is now turned towards him. The poet teaches us of the mercilessness of destiny. Parzival had not asked the question as he should have done, and as the sword reminded him. Trebuschet had forged it. The helmet that Orilus wore came from Trebuschet. What is it that is directed against Parzival? What is it with which he must now fight? It is his own guilt, reflected by the stranger's soul. Much that tends in the same direction is worked by the poet into the following lines. We cannot explain all the allusions. But the poet becomes still clearer. Orilus has his own peculiar armour. On his shield he bears a serpent. Over his helmet hovers a dragon. On his armour are many figures of dragons wrought in gold and set with precious stones, with eyes of rubies. With countless dragons must Parzival fight when he fights with Orilus. The poet expressly says that:

> And Parzival won him honour, for here hath he rightly shown
> How before a hundred dragons, one man might well hold his own.
> (V: 675–676)

Yes, he even describes precisely how Parzival wounds the dragon which hovers over the helmet of Orilus. Orilus would not believe otherwise than that he was fighting against the man who had dishonoured his wife. He had not the slightest idea that she was innocent. Then the fight reached its crisis. Parzival was the victor. Now Parzival demands that Orilus should forgive his wife:

> Then Parzival quoth, 'Right gladly, Sir Knight, will I let thee live,
> If favour and love to thy lady thou swearest again to give!'
> (V: 675–676)

Orilus refuses. He offers a great deal, he offers two countries, one which his brother Lähelein rules. Again destiny speaks: they are countries of which Orilus has robbed Parzival. Parzival declines all this, and demands that Orilus should go to Britain where he would find a maiden who had been struck on his (Parzival's) account; to this maiden he must bear greetings otherwise he must die. Arthur too he is to greet. Parzival has no suspicion that Kunneware is the sister of Orilus. How gladly does the latter ride to her! Destiny is kindly, reconciliation is at hand. Parzival is able to make good what he has done. He says:

> But first will I see that thou givest to this lady thy homage meet.
> (V: 702)

And he says that he is ready to swear that his wife is innocent. At that Orilus rejoices. Then the three ride together to a cell hollowed out of the rock. They ride thither because Parzival has seen a reliquary there.[50] On this sacred object will Parzival swear to the innocence of Jeschute. It is Trevrezent's cell. Once again Parzival will return here on his way to the Grail Castle, when he has paid the price of his guilt. Meanwhile, however, he has yet much to suffer. There at the altar he is seized by the force of destiny which is to be his guide through a long period. It arises from the depths of his soul. The poet describes it in pictures: a coloured spear leans against the altar. This coloured spear has deep significance. In it the poet is referring to Saturn in its many coloured rays.[51] It is the forces of Saturn with which Parzival unites himself. This Saturn-force gives to men the unconscious guidance of destiny. So Parzival swears to the wife's innocence:

> ... A fool and no man was I
> Nor yet had I waxed to wisdom—and sore did she weep thereby,
> And anguish and grief she suffered; yea guiltless was she that day—
> And forfeit my bliss and my honour, if the words be not truth I say!
> (V: 735–738)

And with these words Parzival restores to her the ring he had stolen.

According to Scharfenberg's version Orilus had already received the ring and clasp. Then Parzival takes his leave. Orilus rides with his pardoned Duchess to Arthur and to his sister Kunneware. He finds the latter guarding a fountain; on this fountain is to be seen a dragon which has its claws half round an apple. It hovers above it as if in flight, but it is held by four ropes. The Prince recognised in the figure one similar to that which he bore on his shield. Thus he recognised his sister. His wife Jeschute is here called, 'Jeschute of Karnant'. For her father is King Lac of Karnant. The fountain in which the broken Grail sword is again to become whole is in fact situated in his kingdom. And the guardian of the fountain is Kunneware. Parzival sends every conquered hero to this fountain, to Kunneware. So the misfortunes of Jeschute end happily. And Parzival himself, without knowing it, as if overtaken by absentmindedness, takes with him the coloured spear. It is the spear of Troy, which Dodine's brother, the wild Taurian, had forgotten and left there. We can call it the speak of forgetfulness, and we shall have much to say about it. With this spear Parzival goes forth, to encounter fresh and harder experiences.

Adventure VI

In the *sixth* adventure we learn to know a great danger which Parzival, through a wonderful guidance of destiny, happily escapes. Parzival is not predestined to be an Arthurian Knight, a Knight of the Sword. It is much more part of his destiny to become a Knight of the Word, a Knight of the Grail. When therefore the poet tells us that Arthur sought to attract Parzival to his Round Table, that indicates a grave danger for Parzival. Parzival has to endure an experience of great pain in this chapter of his life. But it is just this painful experience, his banishment from Arthur's Round Table through the curse of the Grail messenger, which brings him healing. But before we narrate the details of this story, let us preface a few general remarks on the architectural structure of the poem.

We have now accompanied Parzival through many and manifold adventures. They reveal themselves in such an order that we can recognise Parzival for a true Sun Hero. The poem passes through the signs of the Zodiac, beginning with the Twins. We were led through the signs of the Zodiac one by one as far as the Ram. When Parzival entered into the Grail Castle, the narrative reached the mood which corresponds to the Ram. We then learnt how Parzival, after he had left the Grail Castle, begins to experience things backwards, and how the hard law of destiny takes hold of him. This corresponds to the mood of the *Bull*. In the ensuing chapter we enter once more into the sign of the *Twins*. Parzival becomes a doubter, he denies God. As if in spiral ascent, the poem runs through the Zodiac for the second time at higher level. But when it begins to rise to this repetition at a higher level, the poet unites with the forces of the *Zodiac*, those of the *Planets*.

And all that follows is filled with the activity of the planets. Later, when Parzival becomes King of the Grail, this will be clearly expressed; here at this stage, it is only hinted at. He who is able to follow sufficiently well the whole course of the poem will note that the mention by Wolfram of untimely summer snow is combined with a reference to Saturn. The alchemistic writings of the Middle Ages say that Saturn is connected with cold.[52] Saturn however is not to be looked upon simply as the bringer of cold. Wolfram's remark (Book XV, 786–790), that the planets fought against and checked the course of the heavens, certainly in the first place refers to relations of movement, but is perhaps also intended to show that Saturn is mentioned in connection with unaccustomed cold because it counteracts this. We have already drawn attention to the connection of the coloured spear with Saturn, which in all alchemistic writings, e.g. in Basil Valentine, is called the 'many coloured'. We must also realise that in the following lines the poet refers to a constellation which Saturn calls into activity.

> ... Now hear ye how Parzival,
> The Waleis, rode near unto them: thro' the night did the snowflakes fall,
> Light they fell, yet lay thickly on him, yet if well I the tale may know,
> And the singer aright hath sung it, it was never the time of snow;
> For whate'er men have sung or spoken of King Arthur at Whitsuntide,
> Or when May blossoms deck the meadow, these marvels did aye betide.
> For sweetly the springtide bloometh, and many a garb, I ween,
> Shall it bear, this song of my singing, tho' snow-clad it now be seen.   (VI: 25–32)

Arthur's falconers had been hunting. By the river of Plimizöl the falconers of Karidöl had lost their best falcon. It had overeaten itself. (Line 13, Stanza 191, in the German shows the significance of the word überkröpfen.)

> Ueberkröpfung verbrocket[53]
> Dass kein köder mehr ihn lockte.
> Er blieb die Nacht bei Parzival.

Transl.: His crop so full that no dainty tempted him further
       He passed the night with Parzival.

Parzival and the falcon are in the dark wood. They do not know their way and they are suffering from the frost. At sunrise the paths were covered with snow. Then in the early morning a flock of geese took wing so that their cry was heard. The falcon pursued one of these geese. It just managed to escape him, though he wounded it. Then fell three drops of blood in the snow. That is the peculiar thing about Parzival's destiny: what takes place in his own soul, is at the same time placed before him as a physical experience. The squire at the drawbridge of the Grail Castle had called after him: 'You goose.' Now he saw the flock of geese. Was he not as much wounded as the goose? Was not his soul to be linked to that of a wandering falcon? He gazes at the picture—and as he gazes, something takes place in the depths of his soul. Let us try to express it in words. The poet is silent about it. Nor had Parzival these thoughts in his soul, they remained below in his unconscious; in his consciousness rise up only pictures and feelings. Nevertheless, let us try to express these thoughts. He might have said something like this: 'There was I in the Grail Castle—if I had stood the test, I might have become a Knight of the Swan. I did not stand it, so the Squire was able to call after me in scorn, "Knight of the Goose." But here is my soul being. In the picture of the falcon I experience it. It has swooped down upon that force in me which has not become what it ought to be, which is goose instead of swan. Something in my innermost being is wounded, my life-organisation is wounded through my soul-organisation. My soul-being has erred, and has wounded the life in me. Now I must reflect, I must discover the reason why this has happened. I must call to mind the things which are still forces of desire in my soul. The forces of selfish desire, which want to possess my beloved as my own, these are they which have prevented me from passing the test in the Grail Castle.' All this he does not think clearly, he only feels it, he dreams of it, and when he dreams, pictures rise up before him. And at the same time the dream stands before him as reality. He sees the three drops of blood on the white snow. Then his longing comes to consciousness, and he breaks forth into the words, 'Kondwiramour, here lies thy image.' And that robs him of consciousness. Out of the depths of his unconscious soul-life something rises up against this coldness of soul. It robs him of consciousness. What takes place in Parzival's soul, takes place also in nature. When in springtime the plants sprout, they are conjured forth by the forces which unfold themselves fully in summertime. But these forces cannot yet act fully. The snow and ice of barren winter hinder them. Then Saturn intervenes and quenches the cold. This Parzival must inwardly imitate. Now to the force of spring, not the cold of winter, may he surrender his soul. He must call up the clear, cold world of thought against the feverish desires, but then temper this cold to thought life, warmed by the soul. What Saturn does when untimely snow falls, he must inwardly do. He cannot yet do it. One day however he will approach the Grail Castle with the force of Saturn. Now however his longing robs him of consciousness.

> '. . . in this snow that so spotless lies,
> 'Gainst the blood drops, that ruddy gleaming, glow crimson beneath mine eyes,
> Red as blood drops and white as snowdrift it rejoiceth me evermore!'
> Then her sweet face rose before him, in that night she first sought his side,

> When on each cheek a teardrop glistened, and a third to her chin did glide. (VI: 57–62)

In the three blood-drops he sees again these tears as bloody tears.

> And so true was his love and steadfast, little recked he of ought around. (VI: 63)

We have tried to imagine his thoughts.

> But wrapped round in love and longing, saw nought but the bloodstained ground.
> Frau Minne with force constrained him, as here on his wife he thought,
> And by magic of colours mystic, a spell on his senses wrought.[54] (VI: 64–66)

The force which robbed him of consciousness overtook him at the altar of Trevrezent. There, where he joined in love the reconciled Orilus and Jeschute, it came over him that he too had a wife, but it did not once come to him as a dream, but in the deepest depths of the unconscious. Then thoughtlessly he took the coloured spear of the Knight Taurian. Perhaps in this word 'Taurian' is concealed the word 'Bull' (Taurus). Parzival now has to become a bull-conqueror. Now he has to overcome the forces of desire. These forces, which exist wholly in the service of the body, rise up in him, rise up into his blood, and produce for him bright pictures of desire. This he must learn to overcome. His sun path must lead him to the force of Mithras victorious over the Bull. Not outwardly, but inwardly he must conquer these forces. Over the desire-world of summer's warmth, he must lay the snow which falls from the cold star spaces of thought. But he must penetrate the cold of thought with warmth. He cannot yet do it. He is not yet capable of uniting the above and the below, of warming thought with love from above. So he stands there in the wood, his summer-like nature covered by snow, hot blood upon cold snow. Heat and cold he feels at the same time, and his consciousness vanishes. So he stands there asleep, losing consciousness, the coloured spear held aloft.

Then comes Kunneware's squire. He has no idea that the Knight whom he sees in the wood is his lady's most faithful servant. He only sees the spear held high aloft, he can but think—'There stands a knight who is seeking battle.' So he hurries away. He whistles on two fingers, and the poet imitates his whistling. Fi fi, fi! Fi o, fi! Thus he summons the Round Table. He calls out that they will be dishonoured if they do not resist the knight who seeks battle. Thus is happens to men in such a soul condition as Parzival's. The forces which strive outwards into the whole world and seek for adventure will become rampant if the forces of desire are not subdued. Parzival experiences this inwardly, and at the same time it is enacted outwardly before him. Then they all come, one after another, these knights of Arthur's Table. And the first is Segramor. But he dare not forthwith enter upon the adventure, for the Grail Castle is near, and Arthur has forbidden them to be drawn into battle. He fears that one of his knights might come to blows with a guardian of the Grail. So he has forbidden his knights to fight, and Segramor must first secure special permission. To his request Arthur gave Segramor the answer:

> If thou to a joust now ridest, hereafter shall many a knight
> Crave leave of mine hand to ride forth, and seek for fame in fight.
> And 'twere ill thus our force to weaken, for know thou that near at hand,
> Amfortas of Monsälvasch with a mighty host doth stand.
> This wood of his he guardeth, and since we but little know
> Where he and his force shall hold them, such chance well might work as woe. (VI: 107-112)

Arthur and his Round Table serve a ritual in which the forces of the stars are represented on earth. The force of the sun in Arthur, the force of the moon in Guinevere, the host of the stars in the knights—so we are told by Rudolf Steiner, and it is confirmed by all the descriptive epithets which are given to the persons in the poem. Guinevere is beautiful as the moon. Arthur is connected with the Sun force of springtime. Guinevere wishes Segramor to have permission to fight. Arthur is against it, but yields. The moon forces are victorious. So Segramor rides out.

> Parzival remained rooted to the spot, lost to all around.
> Such was the power of the three blood drops and of that relentless love.
> [Trans. by Mustard & Passage, Vintage Books, p. 155.
> In preference to Jessie Weston's translation.]

Now Segramor rides towards Parzival. He threatens him but Parzival does not notice it.

> ... for Frau Minne so fair and young
> In a sorer conflict held him ... (VI: 141-142)

Segramor turns his horse round, and gallops so forcibly against Parzival that the latter is driven by the impact in another direction.

> And ever he gazed on the blood drops; as his charger turned him round
> Awhile from his eyes they vanished, and fame in their stead he found!
> For swift as the blood drops crimson thus passed from his dazzled sight,
> He hearkened the voice of the foeman, and braced him anew for fight.
> Then as Segramor rode against him, Parzival sought afresh the spear

> That he found by the woodland chapel with blazon of colours clear;
> For tough was the clasp and he gripped it, and he held the point full low,
> As his foemen dashed fair against him, his shield rang with the ringing blow.
> (VI: 145-152)

Segramor falls and lies on the snow. Parzival, whose spear remains intact, rides to the place where the blood drops lie. When he saw them again he lost consciousness once more. But Segramor's horse trotted back home. The conquered Segramor returned on foot. When the knights see that, they hasten to meet him. He however receives them with rebuke and praises Parzival's strength. He says that it may easily happen that a man be conquered once. Now Kay asks to be allowed to fight Parzival. He too rides out. Wolfram von Eschenbach here interpolates a song to Frau Minne. In it he calls Frau Minne almighty.

> Since all wisdom shall be thy portion, since against thee nor spear nor shield
> Nor charger nor guarded fortress their vaunted power can wield.
> I know not what shall withstand thee, nor on earth, nor on the sea!
> He who feareth to face thy conflict, say whither shall he flee?
> 'Twas thy mystic power, Frau Minne, that dealt thus with Parzival
> And reft him awhile of knowledge, and wrought with him as a fool.
> (VI: 239-244)

Kay has now approached. He sneers at Parzival. He advises him to attach himself to a dogleash, so that he can be led at the end of it into the presence of the King. But Parzival remains silent. The force of Frau Minne constrains him. Then says Kay, 'Wait, I will waken thee—upon the snow shalt thou be laid.' Then the poet asks, turning again to Frau Minne:

> Frau Minne, now bethink thee, for sore this shameth thee,
> For an one should wrong a peasant in this wise his speech will be,
> 'My lord will sure repay thee.' Vengeance from thee he'd seek
> Methinks, this gallant Waleis, an thou wouldst let him speak.
> (VI: 2271-274)

Now Kay throws his lance. Parzival's horse turns round and round. He loses sight of the blood drops and comes to himself. The two ride to an encounter. Kay pierces a great hole in Parzival's shield. Parzival retaliates, and Kay falls, his horse lies dead. In his fall the lord Kay breaks his right arm and his left leg, crushed between the saddle and a stone. Now Parzival has avenged Kunneware's ill treatment. But he is not conscious of this. Again his gaze falls on the blood drops and once more he loses consciousness.

> Thus he who knew nought of falsehood was guided by truth to know
> Her message in blood drops threefold on the white of the drifted snow.
> 'Twas teardrops not blood, that he saw there, and well might his senses fail,
> And the thoughts of his heart wax heavy, as he mused on the wondrous Grail.
> And surely the resemblance grieved him, that spake of his wife and queen.
> Yet though o'er the twain he sorrowed, the greater woe, I ween,
> Was the woe that Frau Minne wrought him, for there liveth not heart so strong,
> But longing and love united break its power, ere the time be long.
> Count we here these twain as ventures? Nay, 'twere better methinks to hold
> That they were nought but pain and sorrow, that vanquished the hero bold.   (VI: 293-302)

Now the poet says, 'Kay was not so bad as he was often represented, rather he was a faithful, valiant knight, who indeed loved his lord, and wished to render him the greatest glory. Now he lay there in a lamentable plight until someone raised him up.' And now came Gawain too. He is the knight with whom we shall now be concerned for a long time, who will soon be more important than Parzival himself, and whose story is now told at length, while Parzival steps into the background. Recent interpretations of Wolfram's poem speak of a Gawain episode, which is inserted in the poem. We shall show clearly that this is unjustifiable. So Gawain comes. Gawain is experienced. When he sees Parzival, he at once diagnoses the case aright.

> Thought Gawain, 'It may be Frau Minne dealeth so with this goodly man,
> As she dealt with me of old time, so claspeth him in the ban
> Of her magic spells fair-woven, that his spirit within the snare
> She holdeth fast entangled . . .'   (VI: 391-394)

But Gawain knows what must be done in such a case. Not to fight, but something quite different. He alights from his horse, takes a silken 'kerchief, spreads it over the three blood drops, and behold! Parzival awakens. The poet here places before our eyes in imaginative pictures a mighty teaching, he gives us a key which opens many a lock. For he gives us the answer to no less a question than this: how does the Grail-seeker become the ruler of his passions? A secret of human nature is now revealed. Instincts are at first stronger than the human being. Only in one way can he conquer them—on every other path he must lose. It is not fighting against passion that leads to victory, but control of the *world of ideas*. He who puts out of his consciousness the idea that stirs his longing (and that the human being can always do, for he is *ruler* of his world of ideas) knows how to make use of Gawain's silken 'kerchief. Parzival however cannot yet use it himself. What must take place within him, through *himself*, comes to pass *externally* through another. Through this he comes to depend on this other, and *it is for this reason that the Gawain episode is interpolated*. Gawain drives him out of the poem, and not until Parzival conquers Gawain, after lengthy experiences, does he again become lord of the adventure. From now until that time, Parzival goes through what has to be experienced by the human being who wishes to become ruler over his passions and desires. That Parzival will do. But in quite a veiled fashion the poet tells us this. For the mysteries of knowledge are open, but the mysteries of magic are hidden.

Parzival's path goes from the Castle of the Grail, where, *in the starry spaces*, he finds the forces of knowledge, through the *world of the planets*, where he dreams in feeling, into the *subearthly*, where he has to obtain mastery over his own will. These last are the adventures of Castle Merveil. Parzival laments:

> Alas! Who of thee hath robbed me, who erewhile was my queen and wife? (VI: 401)

And much more he bemoaned. But he finds the right word when he says, 'A vaporous film before mine eyes has taken thee from me in full sunlight—I know not how.' Then he quoth,

> 'Now, where shall my spear be, since I wot well I brought it here?' (VI: 407)

All the bright and beautiful pictures which stirred his longing, these he has lost. Gawain, his teacher, replies drily:

> ... 'A joust thou hast ridden, and splintered shall be thy spear.' (VI: 408)

Then asks Parzival, 'With whom?' Parzival has absolutely no consciousness of his opponent and still believes himself to be alone. And so he is; Parzival really is alone. It is the coming to an understanding with the forces of his own being which he is experiencing. Only because of his dullness it is placed before him as outer destiny instead of inner experience. Now Gawain tells him what has happened. That he has wounded Kay, that he has in fact fought a battle, he tells him. Parzival is greatly astonished to hear this. But then the knight tells him his own name, Gawain, and says:

> And fain would I do thee service, alike with my hand and name. (VI: 433)

This line must not be overlooked. The poet expressly says that Gawain places his name at Parzival's disposal. Thus one should not lose sight of the fact that behind the Gawain adventures of the Gawain episode, *Parzival himself is concealed*. Only Parzival, because he still lives in darkness, does not yet know that he must realise in inner experience what encounters him from without in Gawain. So now he asks with astonishment, 'What, art thou Gawain?' And so they ride back to Arthur's court. Parzival is received there with rejoicing. Kunneware, the guardian of the spring in which the Grail sword is renewed, receives him joyously. And now Parzival goes through a great temptation which consists in his wishing to become a knight of King Arthur. Arthur is willing to forgive him even the slaying of Ither. He is prepared to receive him at his Round Table. But if that happens, Parzival is lost. He will never return to the Grail Castle, he will never find Kondwiramur, nor his sons, Kardeiss and Lohengrin. But divine guidance does not forget him. His saviour draws near.

How strange a being is man, that he complains of a painful blow of destiny which he encounters, even when it is sent to him for his highest good. So it happens with Parzival. He ought to have recognised that his good angel approaches—and what does he see?

> For hither came one I must tell of, and faithful was she in truth,
> Tho' discourteous her ways, and for sorrow, I ween had she little ruth!
> And the folk for her message sorrowed—Now hear how the maid must ride,
> Her mule it was tall as a war horse, and branded on either side;
> And its nostrils were slit as is custom in the far lands of Hungary,
> Yet her harness and bridle were costly, with rich work broidered cunningly.
> Soft and slow paced her mule, yet the maiden was not as a maid, I trow.
> What sought she? She came as 'twas fated, and sorrow must Arthur know.
> And of wisdom forsooth this maiden might boast her a wondrous store,
> No tongue but she spake, French, Latin, and Paynim: in all such lore
> As men read in the highest heavens, Dialectics, Geometry,
> In all was she courteous trained, and her name it was called Kondrie.   (VI: 583–594)

Now she is described in further detail. She wore a blue cloak and a hat of peacock's feathers. Over her hat she slung her plait, black and thick, about as soft as the hair on a hog's back. Her nose resembled that of a dog. Two tusks projected a hand's length out of her mouth. The eyebrows terminated in thick tresses. Her ears were shaped like the ears of bears. The harshness of her face did not exactly invite tender yearnings. She carried a scourge with knotted cords. Its handle was made of a ruby. Her skin was the colour of a monkey's skin, and instead of nails she had a lion's claws. One can scarcely consider the maiden beautiful, and yet she is only the counterpart of what the human being bears in himself when he is still full of desire. And yet this being is the messenger of the Grail. Only he will be astonished at this who is not yet clear how beautiful the ugly becomes when it is transmuted. The most detestable lust needs only to be transformed into its counterpart to show itself as a glorious force. This Parzival does not yet know. He is obliged still to experience what this being says as a curse. He does not understand at all that she who appears here in the regions of Arthur in her opposite (counterpart) represents the good angel who protects him from becoming a knight of King Arthur. And so he hears her say:

> Thou son of high Pendragon, thyself and thy Breton host,
> By thy deed hast thou shamed—From all lands the noblest that they might boast
> Once sat here a gallant circle, but poisoned is now their fame.
> And thy Table Round dishonoured by traitor, and brought to shame. (VI: 629–632)

She means Parzival. A deceiver is here, for the Grail is his destiny, not the drinking vessel of Arthur's adventure-loving knights. He has to transmute the forces of the Knighthood of King Arthur. Out of the depths he has to raise himself to the heights. It is not without significance that the Grail Castle stands on the mountain where the eagles nest, while Arthur's tent is on the plain, in the valley, near the rivers. And so he hears himself cursed:

> ... Oh thou false and faithless guest. (VI: 651)

So she calls, in reproaching him for his lack of compassion in the Grail Castle.

> To hell shalt thou be predestined, by the Ruler of heaven high,
> And this be on earth thy portion, that true men thy face shall fly.
> And ban hast thou won for blessing, and for bliss shalt thou find but bane.
> For too late dost thou strive for honour, and thy striving shall nought avail
> And so feeble shall wax thy manhood, and thy fame it shall be so weak,
> That never shall soul's physician the promise of healing speak.
> And one to the oath should drive me, on thine head were I fain to swear,
> That never a darker treason was wrought by a man so fair.
> Thou hook in fair feathers hidden, bright serpent with poisoned fang

> Who ne'er of the sword was worthy which thine host at thy side did hang!
> The goal of thy sins, this thy silence, of hell's horde art thou now the sport,
> And dishonour upon thy body, Sir Parzival, hast thou brought.
> Saw'st thou not how they bare before thee the Grail and the bleeding spear,[55]
> And silver knives? Thy joy's destruction,[56] and thy shelter from grief were here! (VI: 655-668)

And now she warns him that he really ought to have asked, not only to redeem Amfortas, but also Feirefis. If he had asked, she says, he would have learnt of a town in a far heathen land, called Tabronit, which fulfils every desire. Then he would have heard of Feirefis of the race of Anschau (those who had won the hand of the Queen of that land) and who is at the same time both black and white.

Kondrie, the Grail Messenger, wishes to call into Parzival's consciousness the fact that he has a brother. Every human being has his brother, his brother man. That is the strict rule of the Grail. 'If thou wilt approach the Grail, thou mayest not come alone, thou must bring with thee thy brother man. Thou mayest not seek only thine own development, thou must seek it for the sake of other men. And thou must bring with thee not only those who themselves have the capacity to see the Grail, who already wear the white robe, but thou must also lead to the Grail those who appear still black and white, in whom heaven and hell have part. They cannot see the Grail, but they can see the Grail bearer, they cannot see the spiritual world, but they can perceive how he who does see it behaves in practical life.' So Parzival is warned that the important thing is to acknowledge the Grail in the conduct of one's life. And now two scenes take place, rapidly one after another. One between the Grail messenger Kondrie and Parzival, and the other between the messenger of another Kingdom, which is the polar opposite of the Grail Kingdom, and Gawain. Both are cursed, Parzival as well as Gawain, and the destinies of the two are closely bound up together. Of Kondrie's curse we have already heard. Now let us hear the other part of the story.

> Now sorrow had Kondrie brought them; and e'en as her way she went
> Another must ride towards them, on a warlike errand bent:
> (VI: 719-720)

The poet expressly calls attention to the close connection between Kondrie and this knight. As she rides away, the knight approaches. This knight is Kingrimursel. His lord Kingrisin, he says, has been treacherously slain by Gawain.[57] He had slain him in the act of greeting him. Therefore he now challenges him to a duel. He is to present himself in forty days before the King of Askalon in the capital city of Schampfanzon, and says that the

Round Table is dishonoured, for a faithless knight has a place in it.

Parzival's soul-task is to recognise that the loathsomeness of the Grail messenger has been brought about by his own imperfection. He must learn to transfer within what is without. Gawain's trial is the reverse of this. He has not to see his own self externally in another, but the deed of another is laid upon him as a burden, and he has to learn to bear this. At a much later point (VIII; 256-257) we learn that not Gawain but the Count-Palatine Eckunat is the guilty one. We know Eckunat or Ehkunat already. He is the individual who sent the hound Gardevias as a 'gamely-letter'[58] to his beloved. Eckunat is the brother of Mahaute, the mother of Schionatulander. He is related therefore to those persons whom we have found to be in the closest connection with the mysteries of the starry script. We shall be able to see more and more clearly that the destinies of Parzival and Gawain bear a wonderful resemblance, and yet at the same time are quite different. We shall likewise have to recount how Parzival, who follows the path of knowledge, is led through terrible doubt. Gawain does not take the path of knowledge, he takes the way of the heart, and does not become a doubter, but an object of doubt; he is slandered. And what we now learn, the false accusation against Gawain that he has killed Kingrisin, is only the first of a long series of accusations to which Gawain is exposed. In truth the poet describes in Parzival and Gawain only two diametrically opposite sides of human nature as a whole. And he who travels the path of the Grail will make the discovery that he has a close connection alike with Parzival and Gawain. It is not possible one-sidedly to walk the path of pure knowledge, and it is not possible to try to penetrate only into *the Grail Castle*, one must also take the way of the heart that Gawain takes. One has to go through the adventure of *Castle Merveil* as well. We shall therefore later see how Parzival and Gawain, when they fall into strife with each other, have to say that they felt as if they had been fighting with themselves. They represent different sides of human nature. Indeed, as the exposition of the Grail story advances we shall yet see that something quite similar applies to Feirefis. But let us follow the course of the story. Before Parzival leaves Arthur's court, he has once again to fulfil a piece of his destiny. By marrying Kondwiramur he has made King Klamide, who had wooed Kondwiramur, unhappy. Now he has to compensate for this deed. He is able to do it. He brings it about that Kunneware marries Klamide.

> Kunneware they gave to Klamide, who yearned for her love so sore.
> And he gave her, as her rewarding, himself, his body fair,
> And a queenly crown and golden henceforth on her head she
>   bore! (VI: 862-864)

When this had taken place, when Parzival had expiated another piece of guilt, then only does he experience something which carries him forward on his Grail journey. Eckuba of Janfuse says that Feirefis, of whom Kondrie had spoken, is Parzival's half-brother, the son of his father. She who tells him this is the daughter of the sister of Gahmuret's first wife.[59] This news proves later to be of the greatest importance, when Parzival meets Feirefis. Parzival thanks her for this enlightenment and for the attempt to comfort him. Then however he says, 'Peace is gone from me, I must find the Grail again. How can I find the way to make good again the fact that I did not ask the question? How can I help Amfortas?' Then he says, 'What need to remain longer here? I must get hence.' So Parzival decides to ride on. He takes leave of Kunneware. In the future he will send her no more knights, for she now belongs to another hero. Then he takes leave of Gawain. Gawain kisses him and says:

> ... Now ridest thou in warlike guise,
> And thy feet shall be swift to battle—God guide thee on thy way,
> And give me such strength to serve thee as my heart shall be fain
>   alway.   (VI: 934–936)

But Parzival cried:

> ... 'Woe is me! Who is He, this mighty God?
> Had He power, then methinks our portion had ne'er been this shame
>   abhorred!
> Small power shall be His! I served Him from the day I first knew His
>   grace.
> Henceforth I renounce His service; doth He hate me, His hate I'll
>   face!   VI: 937–940)

In this moment Parzival denies God. Doubt seizes him, as he says, 'Woe is me! Who is He, this mighty God?

Parzival goes through three stages—dullness, doubt and blessedness. Now he encounters the experience of the Second Stage. The poem began in the sign of the Twins, we have passed through the whole of the Zodiac; in dullness Parzival traversed it. As doubt takes hold of his soul, the poem stands once more in the sign of the Twins. For the second time must Parzival enter upon the path of the Sun hero, this time at a higher level, with doubt in his heart. Two heroes now stand before us, no longer one. Two heroes, who proclaim two sides of human nature: Parzival and Gawain. The poem will be complete when yet a third, Feirefis, is added to them. Kunneware says her last farewell to him. Up to this point, Parzival was the Red Knight. Now he becomes white. But not yet forever.

> For battle decked was his charger, and his sorrow must wake to life.
> And fair was the Knight to look on; and the harness he bare for strife
> Knew never a flaw, but was costly, and as sunshine 'twas white and
>   fair.   (VI: 953–955)

So he mounts his horse, radiant is he. One day he will wear armour made of the translucent diamond, when he becomes King of the Grail. Now he must pass through trials.

> And radiant with gold and jewels the corselet and coat he ware,
> But the helmet alone was lacking—ere he bound it upon his head,
> In the selfsame hour he kissed her, Kunneware the gracious maid.
> And this of the twain was told me, that the parting was sore to see
> Twixt those two who loved each other in all honour and loyalty.
> (VI: 956–960)

Parzival rides, renunciation in his heart, grief in his heart, doubt in his heart. The three accompany him. The poet however says something significant when he says:

> So hence let him ride, our hero, and what ventures a man may tell
> He shall measure them not with ventures that to Gahmuret's son befell,
> Yet hear ye awhile of his doings, where he journeyed and whence would ride.
> He who loveth not deeds of knighthood, if counsel he takes of pride
> For a while will forget his doings ... (VI: 961–965)

The poet says he who reads the poem superficially may think what is now related has nothing essentially to do with Parzival. He however who reads with deeper understanding, let him consider whether it does not seem to him that the so-called Gawain episode has to do with Parzival also. The direction the path now takes is briefly indicated by the poet when he says that many folk were striving towards this laborious goal, the Castle Merveil. Here the Greek Klias was overthrown by a Turkovite. We hear of the four queens in the castle, and we learn too that four hundred maidens are held in bondage there by a magician. Who will rescue them? The Saga of Castle Merveil now begins to sound in the narrative. It is the counterpart of the story of the Grail. The approach to the Grail Castle is difficult. It is difficult to get *inside* it. It is difficult to get *out* of Castle Merveil. That is the difference.

Now the poet tells us how the heroes disperse: Arthur to Karidöl, Kunneware and Klamide home towards Brandigan, Jeschute and Orilus to the same place, for the sake of Klamide. With that the Sixth Adventure closes.

Adventure VII

We must become aware that in the Seventh Adventure we begin in a certain way to go through the whole course of the narrative again. But not now from the aspect of Parzival, but of Gawain. Therefore the poet says:

> A while shall this venture follow the knight who to fly was fain
> From shame, nor with guile had dealings, that hero bold, Gawain.
> For many a one hath held him for as brave, yea, for braver knight
> Than Parzival . . . (VII: 1-4)

Thus Gawain rides forth for adventure. He has forty days. Then he must be ready for combat with Kingrimursel. The poet tells us something apparently of minor importance. He expressly points out what kind of horse Gawain was riding. As the narrative proceeds, however, we shall see that it is quite necessary to pay attention to which kind of horse Gawain and Parzival are riding in various parts of the poem. Gawain, for instance, is riding a Grail-horse. Lähelein had obtained it at the Lake of Brumbane. It belonged to a Grail-knight whom he had killed. Orilus, Lähelein's brother, had given it to Gawain. This horse had red ears and is called Gringuljet. Gawain possessed other horses besides. There is one other of which we know the name; Ingliart with the short ears. It is this one, not the Grail-horse, which later runs away from Gawain and becomes Parzival's horse (VII: 828). But Gringuljet too had its peculiar destiny, and we shall hear later how Gawain lost it and how, at the right moment, in a wonderful way it came again into his possession. All this is pointed out now so that when it appears in the narrative it may be observed.

As Gawain now rides further he encounters an army. The young King Meljanz of Li is leading this army against Lippaut, his vassal, who had also been his educator. They are going to besiege the Castle of Beauroche. Lippaut's daughter, the beautiful Obie, loves Meljanz, but has refused him the reward of love. Riding with the host of King Meljanz of Li is King Poidikonjonz[60] of Gross, the father of Meljakanz. This Meljakanz is already known to us. We met him in fact at the very beginning of the poem. (We have seen that we are going through a kind of recapitulation of the whole poem.) We heard at the beginning how Parzival grew up in the loneliness of the wood, far away from all knights. One day however he met three knights who were pursuing another knight who had carried off a lady. And the knights in pursuit ask Parzival whether he has seen the robber. He takes the radiant knights for God. These knights were at the same time in pursuit of this Meljakanz. We see Parzival at the beginning of his adventures meeting with the pursuers of Meljakanz. Gawain at the beginning of his adventures meets a host to which Meljakanz himself belongs. Of this Meljakanz the poet says:

> He beareth the brand unknightly, Meljakanz that prince is hight,
> He wooeth nor wife nor maiden, but their love will he take with might,
> And, methinks, men for that should slay him—Poidikonjonz' son is
> he. (VII: 95-97)

As he continues the poet speaks still more clearly:

> And here will he fight with his army, and he fighteth right valiantly,
> And dauntless his heart; but such manhood it profiteth naught, I trow—
> An ye threaten, perchance, her sucklings, she fighteth, the mother sow!
> And never a voice shall praise him whose strength lacketh knighthood fair.
> (VII: 98-101)

Gawain entered into conversation with a squire, who told him that the reason why this host is marching on Beaurosche was that King Schaut, the father of Meljanz, had called his princes around him on his deathbed, and bade Prince Lippaut to be his son's teacher, to act as regent for him and to take him into his house. There the boy, who was to be the future ruler, got to know Lippaut's daugher Obie. He loved her, but she refused him although she loved him. Enraged at this he was besieging the fortress and fighting against his teacher and guardian. We see that we have been led into a remarkable region. We find people here who do violence to women, others again who revolt against the one who has been their educator. In short, it is a strange mood that prevails here. In becoming aware of this we recognise at once the relative nearness of Castle Merveil. Gawain is led into this region in order to prove whether he can pass through it purely and nobly. This is the test which is set him. Gawain could only came to one decision, viz. to 'ride straight through the midst'[61] (VII: 208) of all this host, and to offer himself as helper to the besieged. The moral and rights of the case were obviously on their side. So Gawain turns towards the town.

> Then he thought, 'Must I e'en as a smuggler, in hiding-place bestow
> My goods, then the town is safer, methinks, than the plain below,
> Nor on gain shall my thoughts be turnèd, for this be my care alone,
> An fate will so far befriend me, to guard that which is mine own!'
> (XII: 217-220)

We see that Gawain thinks, like a merchant, of profit and loss. Yet again, he differs from a merchant, since he says expressly that he is not out for gain. Above on the battlements of the castle, stand the two daughters of Prince Lippaut; Obie, the elder, and Obilot, who is still a child. Then says Obie to her mother: 'See, Mother, here comes a merchant.' This is not true, it is slander. For Gawain is no merchant, he is a knight. Nevertheless there is something of truth in it for Gawain did think of profit and loss. Yet even in this he was no merchant, for he did not desire gain. But so it is with all slander; while untrue, yet something in the soul of the one slandered is connected with it. That is precisely the experience that Gawain must pass through.

The younger daughter, Obilot, now says the following:

'Surely he is no merchant! My knight shall he be straightway

> If his service here craveth guerdon, such debt I were fain to pay!'
> (VII: 237-238)

The elder daughter still continues to invent new slanders. After a while, as the younger sister praises him, she says:

> ... 'I see naught in that man below!
> He would that they well were guarded, the chests that his steeds do lade,
> And like to a brooding dragon, O foolish sister mine,
> O'er his treasure-chest he watcheth, this gallant Knight of thine!'

Gawain hears all this. The poet now describes how it fares within the town, where preparations are being made to withstand the siege. Then, however, his narrative returns to Obie, and he tells us that she sent a messenger to the Burggrave Scherules to inform him that a fraudulent merchant has entered the town.

> 'From knavery must we guard us,' quoth Scherules, 'I forth will fare.'
> (VII: 382)

When he comes to Gawain, however, he is so completely charmed by his appearance, and his shining countenance, that he says, 'Sir, thou art here our guest. We were out of our senses not to have received you with honour long ago.' But Obie is not pleased, and gets her father to say that there is a false coiner in the town. Expressly does the poet emphasise:

> Now guiltless in sooth was Gawain, 'twas but thro' his steeds and gold
> That suspicion on him had lighted ... (VII: 413-424)

Thus the object of the slander is to capture Gawain's possessions. We may say this is not comprehensible. The prince's daughter must have horses enough. But, if we speak so, we forget that Gawain was riding a Grail-horse. The slanders were directed to this. Scherules denies all this, and laughing, says:

> ... Nay, sire, they misled thee, they lied who thus told the tale
> Were it wife, or man, or maiden—Nor knighthood my guest shall fail,
> (VII. 415-416)

So we hear of the manifold trials which Gawain goes through. Gawain now fights as a knight of the younger daughter on the side of the besieged. This younger daughter Obilot offers him her love. He answers:

> 'Yet, e'en an I did thee service for thy love, still long years must fly,[62]

> Ere yet thou shalt be a woman, and my service might well approve.'
> Then he thought how Parzival trusted less in God than in woman's love,
> And the words he spake bare the message of the maid unto Gawain's heart;
> And he vowed to the little lady to bear arms on her father's part.
> (VII: 520-524)

At the time when Parzival renounced God, he had said to Gawain:

> And, friend, in thine hour of peril, as thy shield may a *wife's* love stand,
> Dost thou know her for pure and holy, then the thought of her guide thy hand,
> And her love from all evil guard thee... (VI: 941-943)

Here we have to understand that Gawain experiences Parzival's words like an inspiration which rises up in him and which he hears. So he becomes Obilot's knight. The question now was what could the little Obilot give to Gawain as token—she only possessed dolls. And now comes a remarkable verse:

> Then Lippaut the Prince o'ertook them half-way on the hillside green,
> And he saw Obilot and Clauditte, as up toward the Burg they sped,
> And he bade them stand still and await him ... (VII: 556-558)

Thus Clauditte, the Burggrave's daughter, accompanied Obilot. Is it only *by chance* that she is named Clauditte, like the beloved of Ekhunat, for whose deed (the murder of Kingrisin) Gawain is called to account? Obilot now tells her father that Gawain will fight for her. She sends him a sleeve of her robe as token and badge for his shield. And now something wonderful happens, for it turns out that in the other army—the outer one, there has suddenly appeared an invincibly brave hero. Wherever he comes victory is his.

> And he who the Burghers challenged his harness glowed red as flame,
> 'The Nameless Knight' they called him, for none knew whence he came. (VII: 733-734)

And further the poet says:

> For Maid Obilot's sake with the townsfolk a knight valiant deeds had dared;
> Without, a Red Knight fought bravely, and the fame 'twixt those two was shared. (VII: 801-802)

But this Red Knight is Parzival. How easily it might have happened that Gawain and Parzival might have fought together without recognising one another. A kind fate preserved them from this. It is remarkable that the Red Knight fights in the outer army on the side of the evil-doers and Gawain with the inner. He had become united with the inner army through his service for Obilot, and this had come about through the fulfilment of a prophetic charge of Parzival's. Is not Parzival here fighting against that which he himself as opponent placed there? Parzival accomplishes great deeds. He makes many prisoners. King Schirniel of Lirivoyn, his brother the King of Avendroyn, and Duke Marangliss of Brevigariess. He sends them back to the town in order to receive in return from Gawain his prisoner Meljanz. Parzival tells the prisoners that they may ride back to the citizens of the town and free Meljanz.

> ... or if they failed here, to help him the Grail to win
> But never a word could they tell him of where It was hid, the Grail,
> Save 'twas guarded by King Amfortas, but further, their lore must fail.
> When thus they spake, quoth the Red Knight, 'Then if it shall still betide
> That my wish find not here fulfilment, ye to Pelrapär shall ride,
> And assurance bring to the Queen.' (VII: 812–816) [Last line altered]

He now no longer sends his conquered knights to Kunneware, but to Kondwiramur, and tells them to say that he sorrows sore for the Grail, and yearns at the same time for her love. So the prisoners ride away. While this occurs, Parzival turns to a squire and says, 'I desire no booty, there is only one thing I ask, that you send me a horse, for mine is wounded.' Then he is given the horse that ran away from Gawain; Ingliart, with the short ears. So it comes to pass, strangely enough, that Parzival rides Gawain's horse. Through the next adventure, however, Gawain, as we shall see, is led to seek the Grail for Parzival. It is as though the heroes must exchange certain forces. Gawain now loosens the sleeve from his shield and gives it to Clauditte. She is to give it back to Obilot.

The poet further tells us how the knights come into the town by order of the Red Knight, in order to free Meljanz. Through the story told by the prisoners, Gawain learns what arms the Red Knight bore. Besides this, he hears that the Red Knight has demanded from them that they should help him in the quest of the Grail. Then Gawain recognised that the Red Knight was Parzival.

> And his thanks uprose to high Heaven that no evil did there befall,
> But that God apart had held them, and they met not in strife that day.
> And courteous I ween were those heroes that they tore not the veil away,

> But both of them there were nameless, and none knew whence they came,
> Yet I wot well the world around them rang fair with their warlike fame. (VII: 880–884)

Gawain had sent his prisoner King Meljanz to Obilot, and she sent him again to her sister Obie. So the conflict could end in peace, since Obie and Meljanz were reconciled.

> Frau Minne with power and wisdom again o'er their hearts held sway,
> And knit afresh the meshes, and fettered the twain anew.
> (VII: 936–937)

Thus there is a general reconciliation. To the great grief of Obilot, Gawain declares that he must ride hence. Obilot begs him to take her with him.

> ... and sore wept the little maid
> And spake, 'Now take me with thee,' but Gawain her wish gainsaid,
> And scarce might her mother tear her from the knight, as he farewell spake. (VII: 949–951) [Last words altered]

Gawain, however, went forth with sorrow in his heart. If we consider this whole adventure, we must acknowledge that it is most instructive. Many riddles stand before us here. How are we to explain that there are two armies, the inner which fights for morals and justice, which Gawain joins, and the outer, where injustice and wrong are present, but for which Parzival fights? How are we to understand that Parzival fights on this side? The right interpretation of this fact is of tremendous significance.

After repeated inward efforts to come to an understanding of these facts, the following has resulted. Parzival in his soul's wanderings enters the region of desire. He must pass through this realm. But he must choose a different path from Gawain.

Gawain stands opposed to evil and fights it. Parzival's way is different. He must connect himself with the Evil and stand on the side of the Evil, but turn all to good. Parzival's is the harder way. I should like to characterise the way that Parzival takes by a picture. The dragon may be fought in two ways. Externally, by actual fight, or from within, by allowing oneself to be swallowed by the dragon, and then be free within its organism to unfold the forces which transform it. The latter is a *Manichean idea*. If we wish to *fight* the Evil, then we shall become evil, for it requires evil means. If, however, we allow the world of light to be swallowed by the world of darkness, then by this means the Dragon of darkness will be illumined from within. This latter appears to me to be the way of Parzival. There seems to me to be no other explanation for the fact that Parzival fights on the opposite side. We are more especially led to this explanation through the fact that while

Gawain is being faced with the decision as to whether or no he shall join the inner army, he suddenly remembers Parzival's words, which prophetically gave him the decisive counsel. The test before which Gawain stands consists in trusting more to the inspirational voice of Parzival than to the outer appearance of things which places Parzival on the opposite side. Yet the test is made easier for him through the fact that only afterwards does he learn that Parzival is on the opposing side. We shall see in due course that Parzival takes part in all Gawain's adventures, but in a hidden way. We shall note this point by point. Thus there can be no question of regarding the Gawain adventures as an interpolation, and as not belonging to the whole.

Adventure VIII

In the seventh adventure we saw revealed a remarkable connection between Gawain and Parzival. Gawain's horse, Ingliart by name, had run away from him. The poet tells us at the beginning of the *eighth* adventure that it had all the good qualities which the horses of Tabronit usually possess. Tabronit is the city wherein every earthly wish is fulfilled. This horse has been taken captive and Parzival has selected it as booty. He rides Gawain's horse. Indeed, the two faced one another in battle, but a happy fate preserves them from fighting with one another. Yet in a certain sense Parzival has won Gawain's horse from him. We know that since Gawain freed Parzival from his spell by covering the three blood drops with a silken cloth, Parzival has become dependent on Gawain. Wherever Gawain goes, Parzival goes too. He follows him unconsciously from afar. He wins back his freedom bit by bit. First he wins Gawain's horse.

Gawain is thereby brought into a dilemma, for the time appointed for the fight with Kingrimursel draws near, and indeed the poet mentions this at the beginning of the eighth adventure, and emphasises the fact that in his fight Gawain will miss his horse. Gawain now takes his way to the land of Ascalon and the town Schampfanzon. He has to ride to this across high mountains, and through marshland. He finally reaches his destination and meets King Vergulacht riding on a Spanish war horse. This King Vergulacht is the son of the dead Kingrisin and of Fleurdamur, Gahmuret's sister.[63] Thus we have to do with near relatives of Parzival. Vergulacht is Parzival's cousin. The poet expressly emphasises here the descent of Vergulacht from Mazadan out of the mountain of Fay Morgan, for he says, Mazadan was descended from the Fays. We are thus in the realm of the Race of the Grail. It is important to notice this, for what we here meet with as morality would not of itself have led us to suppose that we are concerned with the Race of the Grail. But the poet feels it important to bring it to our consciousness. The situation in which Gawain chances upon King Vergulacht appears like an imaginative picture of his moral condition. He has just fallen into the bog as he rode after the falcon which he had sent forth. So deep in the bog has he sunk that he has even lost his horse and all his clothes are so badly soiled that he has to give them to the falconers. Is he not in a remarkable situation? Has not the same thing befallen Gawain? He has lost his horse, and Parzival, whose soul is represented in the image of the falcon, has received it. We are reminded here of what Parzival experienced before the three blood drops. Gawain arrives at the moment when he is giving his clothes to the falconers. Gawain has inwardly passed through what he now sees happening outwardly before him. Now the poet prepares us to hear of evil things, for he says:

> An ye will I cease my story ere the tale to its end be run,
> And for pity's sake keep silence ... (VIII: 70–71)

He resolves however to continue. The King asks Gawain whether he may ride on further or whether he must return to the house to receive Gawain. Gawain says that whatever the King chooses to do will please him. So the King says, 'Then will you go by yourself to Schampfanzon where you will find my sister. Her beauty will indeed suffice you. She will care for you in my absence.

> '... and she shall well entreat thee in my stead till I come again.
> And whenever I come, I think me, 'twill be sooner then thou art fain
> To look on my face, for gladly wilt thou spare me when thou shalt see
> My sweet sister, nor bemoan thee, tho' my coming o'er late shall
>   be.' (VIII: 85–88)

We can tell already by these words that Gawain is to be led through some test. And we can already surmise that in its essentials he will be able to endure it and yet through the few little failings which still insinuate themselves into his soul he will be subjected to the most terrible slander. The poet will show us as he goes along how in one who is seeking the Spirit, the smallest failings, even if only in thought, assume huge dimensions and tend to be poured out as horrible slander.

We are told that Gawain is received by the Queen Antikonie in a friendly manner. The Queen is extraordinarily beautiful.

And Gawain begins to court her.

> Unchecked he sat him by her and sweet words passed between,
> Soft spake they to each other; and oft renewed, I ween,
> His prayers and her denials. Yea, sorely, grieved was he,
> And fain to win her favour—Then spake she as I tell to ye:
> 'Bethink thee, Sir Knight, thou art wise else, with this I enough have
>   done,
> For I ween at my brother's bidding mine uncle Gahmuret won
> Less welcome from Queen Anflise than the welcome I gave to thee,
> An our tending were weighed together methinks hers would lighter be.

Nor know I, Sir Knight, whence thou comest, nor e'en what shall be
  thy name,
That after such short approving, thou shouldst to my love lay
  claim!' (VIII: 135-144)

Gawain answers that he will tell her of his descent, he is his Father's sister's brother's son. Herewith of course, nothing more is said than that Gawain's father has a sister. Thus he conceals his descent and adds:

'Wilt thou give me sweet love's rewarding, for my birth thou shalt not
  delay,
Hand in hand, and to equal measure it paceth with thine alway!
 (VIII: 147-148)

Although this is only a jest, yet we may observe that Antikonie belongs to the Race of the Grail, while Gawain belongs to the Race of Arthur. The two are placed here as of equal birth. The poet now describes how they remain alone and suffer much torture through their mutual love. Yet nothing occurs between them except that Gawain puts his arm around Antikonie. At this moment a Knight enters the doorway and he alarms the whole castle by calling out that Gawain will force the daughter of his lord. The slander here consists in the fact that Gawain's—perhaps even inwardly resisted—intention is stated as deed. Again and again the poet wishes to teach us: he who strives after the Spiritual must be extraordinarily on his guard; even the desires he represses, the fulfilment of which he denies himself, have their effects, in order to make him aware of these effects, the wise leading of destiny brings it about that the hero is slandered. The two now withdraw from the threatening knight, fighting their way to a tower from which they defend themselves, Gawain seizing an enormous chessboard and Antikonie the giant chessmen which she flings at the knights. The whole adventure ends when King Vergulacht arrives home and wants to proceed against Gawain. The poet mourns that shame will thus accrue to Gandein, the ancestor of Vergulacht (Gandein is King of Anjou and Parzival's grandfather) because Vergulacht has violated the laws of hospitality. And now something strange happens: the Landgrave Kingrimursel who had challenged Gawain to single combat at Schampfanzon, appears suddenly as Gawain's defender, for he had pledged his honour that Gawain should have safe conduct till the combat. His honour cannot allow that Gawain, being unarmed, should be attacked. He springs into the tower and supports Gawain. So the King stands opposed to his own Landgrave and the King's men refuse to fight against their own Landgrave.

Now Sire upon our Landgrave no vengeance we think to take,
Nor shall harm at *our* hand befall him—May God so turn thy mind

> That, instead of shaming, thou honour shalt from this venture
>   find.   (VIII: 240–242)

And now they enumerate the reasons why the fight shall not continue. First it is the case of a guest for whom the laws of hospitality must hold good. Further, Kingrimursel is a near relative of Vergulacht. So they propose a truce. They further point out to the King that Antikonie is guiltless, that she is his sister and that he himself sent Gawain to her.

> . . . Then the King bade those warriors brave
> To call a truce—He'ld bethink him how vengeance he best might take
> For his father's death—Yet all guiltless Gawain, for another's sake,
> Must he bear the shame; with a lance-thrust by Ehkunat was he
>   slain   (VIII: 254–257)

Now the innocence of Antikonie comes triumphantly to light. Vergulacht has to allow his Landgrave to bring the moral responsibility of his act home to him. It is not fitting that Gawain, the nephew of Arthur, should thus be treated, after being promised safe conduct and their pledged word having been given that he should not fight here with more than *one*. He, the Landgrave Kingrimursel, felt himself responsible for the whole affair. And now comes a most remarkable passage. Wolfram begins quite suddenly to speak of his secret source Kiot. We might have expected that he would have referred to this secret source with great solemnity, but we should not have expected that he would mention it in this connection.

> As he made an end of speaking stood a vassal the king before,
> And as Kiot himself hath told us, Liddamus was the name he bore.
> And I speak here of Kiot the singer, and so sweet was I ween his song
> That none wax of hearing weary, tho' the days of their life be long.
> And I rede ye to wit that Kiot of old was a Provençal,
> Who found writ in a book of the heathen this story of Parzival.
> And in French again he sang it, and I, if no wit shall fail,
> Would fain in his footsteps follow, and in German would tell the
>   tale.   (VIII: 315–322)

Who then is this remarkable Liddamus? Why does his name lead over to Kiot? If we read the following description of the poet this Liddamus appears at first as a boaster who uses big words but does little. Liddamus now speaks angrily of the necessity of taking vengeance on Gawain, the murderer of Kingrisin. Kingrimursel will have none of this.

> . . . yet Sir Liddamus, I know well
> This man were safe from thine onslaught e'en tho' shame at his hand
>   befell,

> For ne'er wouldst thou dare to avenge it, who yet dost so loudly
>   boast—
> And swifter were we to hearken if ever in battle host
> We had seen thee ride the foremost! But strife ever wrought thee
>   pain ... (VIII: 331-335)

Thus through Wolfram our attention is drawn to the fact that it is of just such people as these who talk much and do little that Kiot speaks. Does the poet wish to say Liddamus is one who talks much, and he does not wish to be a Liddamus—a chatterer? I know not, but one thing at least is certain, that he has told us little enough about Kiot. We shall have to return to the Kiot question. If however Kiot wrote about Liddamus, then since Liddamus lived at Vergulacht's court, he may well have busied himself with that circle to whom Vergulacht, Antikonie, Kingrisin, Fleurdamur and Gahmuret belong, for they are all closely related. We are told expressly in other places that he concerned himself about the Race of the Grail. The combat between Kingrimursel and Gawain was now postponed for a year. That this is not Gawain's fault the reader only comes to know through an incidental remark of the poet; for the persons concerned in the matter, his innocence is not yet clear. So the combat is to take place in a year at Barbigöl before King Meljanz. Through the mention here of King Meljanz the eighth adventure is linked up with the seventh, for we met with King Meljanz, the husband of Obie, already in the seventh adventure. Liddamus in a further speech shows that he has a quite exact knowledge of the King's kindred. He mentions among others Gandein, Gahmuret and Galoes. Then he emphasises that it is not his task to fight:

> ... yet for never a maiden's sake
> Will I evil entreat this body, or bid it such ill-road take.
> Nay, why should I be a Wolfhart? Since barred is the battle way,
> And no lust of strife hath beguiled me ... (VIII: 385-388)

He does not wish to be a Wolfhart thirsting for battle such as is portrayed in the Nibelungenlied. Rather than that he would prefer to be like Rumold the Burgundian cook who dissuaded King Gunther from journeying to meet Attila. Thus we see that Liddamus *is not really a coward, but obviously does not fight on principle.* Therefore Kiot must have written about the knight who will not fight. Perhaps on this account many suppose this knight to be the most fearful among men[64] without his actually having been so. Strangely enough, however, it is this same Liddamus who counsels that Gawain's deed shall be avenged by the sword. Now Vergulacht tells a remarkable story. In the wood Lächtamreis he had met a knight who conquered him, but granted him his life on condition he would promise to undertake the Quest of the Grail for him. This he had sworn to do within the course of a year. If he failed to do this within a year, then he was to go to Pelrapäre, to Kondwiramur and present himself to her as having been vanquished. Upon this Liddamus breaks in again and proposes that Gawain should take over Vergulacht's task; that Gawain should seek the Grail for Vergulacht. This closes the circle. Parzival rides on Gawain's horse and Gawain must take over Parzival's task. Something mysterious is at work between these two. And Liddamus, in keeping with his whole nature, has transformed the *armed combat* with swords into the quest for the Grail. Of just such a knight must Kiot have written, a knight who desired *peace* and not the *sword*.

> In such wise the strife was ended, Sir Gawain far hence must ride,
> And with sword and spear do battle, and woe for the Grail
>   abide. (VIII: 525–526)

That the Grail cannot be striven for the heroes do not as yet in the moment perceive. Now it is related that Gawain partakes of a meal in company with Antikonie and the others. Here Wolfram again refers to Kiot and tells us that Gawain became sad and felt pain in taking leave of Antikonie and for her too it was no better. Gawain is now dismissed by a kiss from the noble Queen. Gawain rides forth alone on the Grail horse Gringulet in quest of the Grail. This closes the eighth adventure.

Adventure IX

Wolfram begins the *ninth* Adventure with wonderful lines. Dame Adventure, experienced as a spiritual being, wishes to penetrate into the heart of the poet.

> 'Ope the portal!' 'To whom? Who art thou?' 'In thine heart would I
>   find a place!'
> 'Nay! if such be thy prayer, methinketh, too narrow shall be the space!'
> 'What of that? If it do but hold me, none too close shall my presence
>   be,
> Nor shalt thou bewail my coming, such marvels I'll tell to thee!'
> Is it thou, then, O Dame Adventure? (IX: 1–5)

We are now getting to the heart of the story. After a long time it comes back to Parzival. We are told that he has passed through many adventures on horseback, by ship and at sea. They are not, however, recounted to us. I once asked Dr Steiner, 'What kind of adventures are they, which are here referred to, and which the poet does not describe?'

Dr Steiner answered, 'They are those which represent pure imaginations, without anything corresponding to them in the physical world. Those which have a counterpart in the physical world are expressly told by Wolfram von Eschenbach, the others he keeps back and merely refers to.'

That is an important hint. For to these adventures belongs the one in which Parzival breaks the Grail-sword. Wolfram von Eschenbach says of this:

> The sword that Amfortas gave him, as ye once in this tale did hear,
> Sprang asunder one while, yet 'twas welded afresh in the mystic spring
> At Karnant, and much fame and honour the blade to its lord did
>   bring!   (IX: 34-36)

The poet Albrecht von Scharfenberg tells us something about this adventure. Parzival had been in Roumania, Cappadocia and Asia. At last he had come to Flordibale where Flordiprintze and the Lady Albaflore ruled. The daughter was Floramie. Frimutel, the father of Amfortas, had loved her and had fallen in battle on her account. In the effort to avenge him, Parzival's Grail-sword was broken. He had gone on fighting with Ither's sword. Then he hastened to Karnant: there at the fountain he repeated the words that Sigune had taught him. Then his sword was made whole again. Parzival however did not keep it, but gave it to Count Ehkunat. He is the person of whom we already know that he killed Kingrisin and that he owned the hound Gardevias. He, then, becomes another owner of the Grail-sword. He is an important and significant personality. We are told that he used the Grail-sword against Orilus to avenge the wrong done to Sigune. Soon after this Sigune died in the wood. Out of her mouth and Schionatulander's grew two vines which intertwined. Then Ehkunat killed Orilus and the latter was buried in the monastery of Prurin.[65] But Jeschute had taken the veil. This is told in the Titurel of Albrecht von Scharfenberg.

After Wolfram von Eschenbach had recounted the story of the broken sword put together again, he adds the lines:

> Who believeth me not, he sinneth . . .   (IX: 37)

At this point we must on no account neglect to call attention with all emphasis to the extreme importance of *Count Ehkunat*. The history of his time must have taken its imprint from him. He possessed the starry script, he possessed the Grail-sword, he had the closest link with Parzival. The innocent Gawain had to suffer on his account. He must have been a leading personality. One has to identify him historically through the statement that he killed Orilus. He must have come into contact with the descendants of Gandein of Steiermark and Kaïnten.

According to the description of Wolfram von Eschenbach, Parzival meets Sigune, who shortly afterwards dies. Schionatulander had already been buried. Sigune was mourning at his tomb. Parzival rode between high rocks. His horse came quite close to the hermitage. Upon untrodden sward he guided it. When he saw that there was a woman in the hermitage he was abashed to have ridden so close. He alighted and tied up his horse. The sword too he put aside. Sigune was wearing a little ring with a garnet[66] in this, which gleamed in the darkness, as if flashing sparks of fire. Round her head she wore a black band. Parzival sat down on a bench in front of the window. He asked her if she too would sit down within, then, without recognising her, he questions her and expresses surprise to find her alone in the wilderness. Then she tells him how every Saturday night, at the end of every Saturn's day, the Grail messenger, Kundry, the sorceress, appears, and brings her food for the whole week. Then he asks her about the ring, for he says, hermits surely renounce love. Then she replied that she was pure, that she mourned for a husband who had never received the reward of her love, for Orilus had slain him in battle; but that her fidelity endures beyond death, in God's eyes she feels herself united with him in a true marriage; she had not been otherwise betrothed.

Then he recognised Schionatulander and Sigune. And she recognised him when she looked into his face and saw his features beneath the rust of his armour. Then she asked him about the Grail, if he has now become aware of his strength, if he has found the way. Then Parzival pours forth his grief. He is mourning the loss of the Grail, and of his most beautiful wife as well. To the Grail he had never returned, he had never found the way. He asks her counsel. Then she advises him to follow the track of Kundry, the Grail messenger. It was not long since she had been there—the tracks of her mule must still be fresh on the ground. At the fountain between the cleft rocks she was wont to draw in her rein. Parzival follows her advice, but the track disappears, once again the Grail seems lost to him.

The encounter with Sigune always signifies for Parzival a piece of self-knowledge. He has learnt much. Kundry the sorceress already seems to him worth searching for.

He finds her track. He seeks out what has wrought him ill. He has learned to love deep sorrow, he does not yet find the way to the end. Something is still lacking in him. As he thus rides, he meets a knight. The latter stops him and tells him that he is in the land of Monsalväsch, and that no one must ride here armed. Then they both spur their horses to battle. Parzival throws the knight from his horse. A slope precipitates the knight backwards. Parzival's horse too falls, and he is hurled into the depths. He seizes hold of a bough and saves himself. Thus dies Ingliart, Gawain's horse. It must mean something that this happens. Parzival now mounts the horse of the Grail Knight. Now he too, like his friend Gawain who rides Gringuljet, rides a Grail horse. This must not be considered irrelevant. It is this horse that, precisely because it is a Grail horse and knows the way, leads hereafter to Trevrezent.

Mounted on this horse then, Parzival continues on his way. A few weeks pass, how many the poet cannot say, then one morning snow fell. Once again it was an unusual snowfall. On Saturn's day Parzival came to Sigune, and Saturn now works further: smitten to the point of death, shaken with cold, Parzival rides in the snow. Then he meets an old knight called Kahenis. His wife and two young daughters accompany him. This knight is surprised that Parzival rides armed at so holy a season. Then Parzival answers:

> ... 'Nay, I know not what the time of the year may be,
> Or how men the tale may reckon of the weeks as they swiftly flee.
> How the days shall be named I know not, long have I forgot such lore!
> Of old time I served a master, and *God* was the name He bore.
> But He bare unto me no favour, and for guerdon He mocking gave,
> Tho' ne'er had my heart turned from Him—Men said, "If from God ye crave
> For succour, He sure will give it;" but I deem well they spake a lie,
> For He who they said would help me, did help unto me deny!'
> (IX: 255-262)

No one can come to the Grail without the knowledge of the secret of time; Chronos, Saturn, teaches these secrets. The old knight warns Parzival that today is Good Friday. An iron garment such as he wears is unsuitable for such a day. He speaks of penance. But his daughters say, 'Do not scold him, but help him to warm himself in this cold, how cold he must be in his iron garment.' Parzival is moved by their loving plea, but he does not venture to join them. He aloft on his horse, and they on foot, that would not do. So he takes leave of them, and rides, rides in the track of the path by which Kahenis came. And now something remarkable happens. Immense sorrow sways the soul of Parzival. The reins fall from his hand, he wrings his hands in despair above his head and calls out of the loneliness of his soul to the highest Helper.

> Yet ever his soul waxed sadder, and there sprang up thoughts anew
> Of the might of the Maker of all things, Who hath made this earth of naught,
> 'How He dealeth with all creation, and still on His power he thought
> How might it yet be if God sent me that which brought to an end my woe?'
> (IX: 318-321)

Thus Parzival prays and at last he breaks into the words:

> 'If today be His Day of Redemption![67] Let Him help me, if help He can.'
> (IX: 326)

Thus he speaks out of the loneliness of his soul. Now for the first time he, the son of Herzeleide, feels sorrow in its full force, and then, as he wrings his hands, the wonder happens, the horse begins to trot. No rein restrains his course, he goes his accustomed way. He knows well the way, he has often traversed it. He is indeed a Grail horse. He penetrates to the source of healing, to the place where Parzival swore to Jeschute's innocence.

> ... bridle and bit he laid
> Free on the neck of his charger and spurred it adown the glade.
> Towards Fontaine-Sauvage the road led, and the chapel where once he sware
> The oath that should clear Jeschute—A holy man dwelt there,
> And Trevrezent men called him ... (IX: 335–339)

To the hermit in the hermitage comes Parzival. To the rocks his horse guides him, guides him to the place where dwells the man from whom he can learn the hidden secrets of the Grail. And here at this point we too learn the secret.

> And he, who of this hath asked me, and since silence my lips must seal
> Was wroth with me as his foeman, his anger might naught avail,
> Since I did but as Kiot bade me, for he would I should hide the tale,
> And tell unto none the secret, till the venture so far were sped
> That the hidden should be made open,[68] and the marvel of men be read. (IX: 346–350)

The now the poet speaks of his source, of Kiot. He speaks of it at that point of the narrative at which Parzival is led to Trevrezent. He first mentioned Kiot when Gawain had been led to the descendants of Gandein of Anjou. Now he speaks of him for the second time, in referring to Trevrezent. Why? Because Trevrezent had been there too. He says, then:

> In Rohas I sought for ventures, and Slavs were my foemen then,
> With lances they came against me and I trow they were gallant men!
> From Sevilla I took my journey, and I sailed o'er the tideless sea
> Unto Sicily, since through Friuli and Aquileia should my journey be.
> Alas! alas! woe is me, for I met with thy father there,
> I found him and looked upon him, ere I from Sevilla must fare.[69] (IX: 1075–1080)

We must look for Kiot somewhere along a line which goes from Steiermark through the land of the Franks towards Sevilla.

> For Kiot of old, the master whom men spake of in days of yore,
> Far off in Toledo's City, found in Arabic writ the lore
> By men cast aside and forgotten, the tale of the wondrous Grail;
> But first must he learn the letters, nor black art might there avail,
> By the grace of baptismal water by the light of our Holy faith,
> He read the tale, else 'twere hidden; for never, the story saith,
> Might heathen skill have shown us the virtue that hidden lies
> In this mighty Grail, or its marvels have opened to Christian eyes. (IX: 3551–358)

The master Kiot found in Spain, in Toledo, a book in Arabic script which contained the story of the Grail. In what form, we shall yet see. It must not straightway be supposed that it was in the form of a poem or of a romance. He was a Christian, whereas that which lay before him was not Christian.

'Twas a heathen, Flegetanis, who had won for his wisdom fame,
And saw many a wondrous vision (from Israel's race he came,
And the blood of the kings of old-time, of Solomon, did he share),
He wrote in the days long vanished, ere we as a shield might bear
The cross of our Holy Baptism 'gainst the craft and the wiles of Hell,
And he was the first of earth's children the lore of the Grail to tell..
On his father's side a heathen, a calf he for God did hold.
(IX: 359–365)

Here the question arises, 'Who is Flegetanis?' Flegetanis is not a name, but a Persian word that means 'a person familiar with the stars'. Flegetanis then was an astronomer. He was nevertheless not an astronomer who observes the heavens with external means, but one who had Imaginations of the heavens. 'He descended from Solomon' cannot refer directly to his physical origin. The word stands directly after the word 'vision'. It is possible that by this it is intended to indicate the character of his clairvoyance. There were different kinds of clairvoyance. One might be a follower of the prophet Jonah, or a follower of Solomon, by which different types of clairvoyance were indicated. Matthew speaks of this, Chapter XII, verse 39, and Chapter XVI, verse 4. Here he refers to the sign of the prophet Jonah, to the Fishes. One finds the same thing in Luke (Chapter XI, verse 29). But in Luke it is contrasted with the wisdom of Solomon. Rudolf Steiner has drawn attention to this contrast. He interpreted it as follows. There were two ways of reaching the supersensible; either through the sign of the Prophet Jonah, through *inner training*, or through the wisdom of Solomon, that is to say out of the *forces of heredity*. The passage in Wolfram only refers to the latter, hence the next line says, 'from Israel's race he came'. To sum up all this, a heathen able to obtain astronomical knowledge through visions, had acquired this power not through training but through his special heredity. He was the first who put into writing what was revealed in these visions, the Message of the Grail. The book in question is, therefore, an astronomical book (Rudolf Steiner specifically said this). Now we are told that this Flegetanis prayed to a calf, as if it were God. And to this is added that on his father's side he was a heathen, on his mother's a Jew. Further information about this personality is given in the poem called 'The Battle of the Wartburg',[70] which I unhesitatingly use as a source, in spite of its being relatively late, because its contents show that the person who wrote it possessed a profound occult wisdom. He refers to a book, there called the book of Zabulon, and says:

> And when the book was being written[71]
> By a Master who still a calf adored,
> He was a Jew on his mother's side,
> On his father's side a heathen,[72]
> And the first who hazarded the starry lore
> (Because I know the truth, your wrath I endure)
> One night in the stars he found
> How after the lapse of twelve hundred years,
> Into this world would be born a child
> In honour surpassing all the Jews.

Here is said in other, rather clearer, words the same thing as in Wolfram's *Parzival*. If we compare the passages word for word, we see that the visions were starry wisdom, and that the first message of the Grail was the message of a child that would be born in 1200 years. This child can be no other than Jesus. *Jesus, then, is the Grail.* He is the vessel in which the blood of Christ is to be found.

But who is Flegetanis? The information that on his mother's side he comes of the Israelitish race, and on his father's side from a heathen, points to Hiram of Tyre. The other information, that Flegetanis had prophesied the birth of Christ twelve hundred years before His coming, points to Balaam, whose story is given in the Book of Numbers, Chaps XXII-XXIV. He, though summoned by the enemies of the Israelites to curse them, blessed the people of Israel, when the Divine Being, who wishes to save Israel, speaks through his mouth. But who at that moment was Balaam's inspirer? Who is it that saves Israel just when it is destined to decline? In order to be able to answer the question, let us look at the position of Israel in the year 1200 before Christ. Moses, whom Osarsiph names Manetho,[73] leads the Children of Israel out of the land of Sinai towards Canaan. He preaches to the people the Moon God, Jehovah, but does not know the Christ, who goes before him as a cloud by day, and by night as a pillar of fire. As long as Manna suffices, the leadership of Moses endures. Before him moves his staff-bearer.[74] With the staff Moses strikes water from the rock. He does not recognise the Christ, the Sun God, who gives the people to drink. So Moses is superseded by Joshua, Je-hoschua. Originally he was called Hoschua, Hosea (Numbers XIII, 16). Moses, then, adds to his name the divine name. But Joshua is the same word as Jesus. When Joshua takes over the leadership, the transition from Jehovah to Jesus is achieved.

The Old Testament passes into the New. When Moses sent out spies into the promised land, ten came back again and announced that the country was not worth consideration. But Joshua and Caleb praised it and brought back a great bunch of grapes to prove its worth. Christ, who later speaks of Himself as the Vine, is here foreshadowed. Moses is the Moon-leader of the Jewish nation. Joshua commands both the Sun and the Moon (Josh. X, 12).

In this time of the transition from the Moon- to the Sun-leadership of the

Jewish people occurs the Christ-prophecy of Balaam. He says, 'I shall see him, but not now, I shall behold him but not nigh; there shall come a Star out of Jacob, and a Sceptre shall arise out of Israel, and shall smite the corners of Moab, and destroy all the children of Sheth . . . nevertheless, the Kenite shall be wasted'[75] (Numbers XXIV, 17 and 22). Balaam, who is meant to curse Israel, blesses them and prophecies the Christ. How is that? Michael stands in his way. The ass, destined one day to be the bearer of the Christ, recognises Michael and sinks to its knees. At last Balaam recognises him too. It is at this point that the Sun leadership begins. But Balaam is a devourer of nations. He prophesies for gold. The gift of seership is used by him in his own service. Therefore Phinehas slays him with a lance—Phinehas who, according to Jewish secret doctrine was born again as Elijah.[76] But who speaks through Balaam? Who blesses Israel? It is Hosea-Joshua, the bearer of the name Jesus, who here appears between Moses and Phinehas-Elijah, as in a foreshadowing of the Transfiguration. As later Hiram carries the Sun-Impulse to the Jewish people and sends the Grail to Solomon by the Queen of Sheba, so now Hosea-Joshua sends to the Jewish people his benediction. From these elements has the Saga welded the figure of Flegetanis. It is Hiram-Hosea, he who through the mouth of Balaam was the first to announce the Grail, i.e. the pouring-in of the Divine into the earthly vessel, into the body of Jesus, into the Temple of God.

Thus the figure of Flegetanis points to the Old Testament and particularly to Jewish sources. In them still lived something of the old star-wisdom. Kiot, the authority used by Wolfram von Eschenbach, had learnt to know this star-wisdom from old oriental sources. This star-wisdom flowed into the Hebrew writings in the form of genealogical books, in which Israel as a nation organised itself according to the laws of the stars. What is reflected in an earthly form in the twelve tribes, has its origin in the starry script. Blavatsky has already referred to the fact that the genealogical descent from Adam to Noah can be related to the Zodiac. She has shown how the ten generations from Adam to Noah correspond to the twelve signs of the Zodiac, for the Balance was introduced later and Virgin–Scorpion together formed a single sign. It is true that the sign of the Scales, symbolising the balance of day and night at the equinox, did not take the place of the Scorpion's claw until the first century BC. The great length of life that the Bible ascribes to the first patriarchs obviously cannot refer to individual men. There is here genealogical succession, but not a genealogy in the usual sense.

Rudolf Steiner has pointed out that the figures given for the age of the patriarchs are connected with the following remarkable fact. In ancient times the memory was not the psychological property of the individual in the same sense as is today the case. Memory reflected not merely personal experience, but in remembering, the person was plunged into the organic forces which act in the formation of his own body. But in these forces is reflected what is inherited from one's ancestors, and this is what one saw when looking into one's inner self.

Dr Steiner stated that the numbers which in the Bible expressed the ages of the patriarchs, gave the duration of time during which what was thus inwardly perceived continued to be passed on. The numbers, then, show how the forces of heredity live on further in the descendants.

But therein are again reflected higher cosmic laws of rhythm, which can very well be thought of as related to the cosmological development itself. Blavatsky deals with the subject in the second volume of her *Isis Unveiled*. She points out that every evolution goes through twelve transformations. The first six bring about a condensation, a becoming-earthly, the last six an etherealisation. In the middle, at the turning point *is placed the sign of the Balance, an expression of the point of balance* between descending and ascending evolution. This she says is shown in the Bible as the special place of the patriarch Enoch. In Christian terminology he corresponds to Michael. Thus the evolution from Adam to Enoch (who is the seventh in the succession of patriarchs) is in descending evolution; from Enoch to Noah it is in ascending evolution. Noah appears, then, as the person who, at the end of this mighty cycle, leads mankind over to a new phase of evolution.

The events described in the Bible are not however merely cosmological facts, but the Genesis-pictures show at the same time the evolution of *knowledge* in the cosmos. The words, 'Let there be Light' describe not only a cosmological process, but the *experience of illumination* of the seeker after knowledge. This 'Let there be Light' refers to the formation of imaginative vision. Rudolf Steiner describes the organ of Imaginative Knowledge in his book, 'Knowledge of the Higher Worlds—How is it achieved?' He discusses it under the name of the two-petalled lotus flower, which develops between the eyes. But he describes the development of the supersensible organ of knowledge in such a way as to make clear that when the development proceeds in the right way, it takes hold of the whole human organism from above downwards. This can be read in Rudolf Steiner's book.

Eliphas Levi in his *History of Magic*, p. 62 (Rider and Co, London, 1957 Ed. translated by A.E. Waite) basing his work on the Sohar, describes the cosmology thus: 'That synthesis of the word, formulated by the human figure, ascended slowly and emerged from the water, like the sun in its rising. When the eyes appeared, light was made; when the mouth was manifested, there was the creation of spirits and the word passed into expression. The entire head was revealed, and this completed the first day of creation. The shoulders, the arms, the breast arose, and thereupon work began. With one hand the Divine Image put back the sea, while with the other it raised up continents and mountains. The Image grew and grew; the generative organs appeared, and all beings began to increase and multiply. The form stood at length erect, having one foot upon the earth and one upon the waters. Beholding itself at full length in the ocean of creation, it breathed on its own reflection and called its likeness into life'.

That is a very externalised account compared with the description given in all concreteness by Rudolf Steiner; that can be summarised by saying that in a right occult training the way goes from thinking, through feeling to will, that is to say, leads from the head into the lower organisation. That corresponds to the stage from Adam to Enoch. When the human being has passed through his whole organisation, he enters the region that the Bible describes as Paradise, as the region of the four rivers of Paradise. Here grows the tree of Life, and the Tempter meets the human being. He who stands the test will be able to undertake the ascent. 'Enoch does not die, but is taken over living into the new cycle of evolution!' Thus is reflected in the work of six days the descent in six successive stages through one's own organism. On the seventh day man must rest. He must in his own development copy the work of divine creation, then he is ripe for the ascent. Thus it is in macrocosmic becoming; thus it is in the microcosmic copy of cosmological processes in the development of the human being. The Bible describes both in its genealogical trees. He who can read the secret of these genealogies finds that they describe the phases of world evolution and at the same time the stages of supersensible knowledge. Both these were classed together in ancient times in the expression, 'the starry script'. In the development of the organs of supersensible knowledge is reflected the rhythm of the great world-becoming, and as the latter advances from the Logos to the Logos made flesh, in order then to carry the earthly upwards again towards the spirit, so likewise proceeds the development of the individual man. First he creates, through developing his thinking, a preliminary centre in the head, then he carries into the depths of his organisation what must develop through feeling and will in order that at last with his whole being he may be able to undertake the ascent to the heights.

That what has just been said corresponds to the description given by Rudolf Steiner is seen by a comparison with his *Gospel of St Matthew*. Here he shows that in one of the two genealogical trees of Jesus, the stages of supersensible development are indicated. We cite these references to make clear what a genealogy is, in the sense of the Grail-Saga. In the Grail-Saga is hidden the successive stages of development. It expresses the way in which the human being advances from stage to stage (gradalis). For this reason, for instance, one of the versions of the Grail relates the following: *The Vulgate Version of the Arthurian Romances*, edited by Oscar Sommer, Washington 1909 (Vol. I, *Lestore del Saint Graal*) tells of a hermit who, seven hundred and seventeen years after the agony of Christ, experienced while asleep on a Good Friday a vision in which Christ appeared to him. Christ instructed the hermit about the Trinity and gave him a book that he himself had written. The book contained the race of his ancestors and information about the Grail.

This story shows us how genealogy and Grail are connected. We have tried to explain this connection. The mystery of the development of the world and of the individual stage by stage is contained therein.

But still another aspect of the matter is involved here. If the fact of repeated earth-lives is recognised and what has been given about repeated earth-lives out of anthroposophical knowledge has been assimilated, then it is found that while mankind evolves upon earth from generation to generation, the man who has passed through the Gate of Death prepares himself in the supersensible world for his next birth. This takes place in such a way that between death and a new birth the human being is membered into the rhythm of the stars just as during his earthly life he is membered into the earthly rhythm, that is to say, into the rhythm of the breathing or of the blood. Now what is experienced in the passage through the cosmic existence is quite individual. It is true that the rhythm of the stars can be calculated, and the rhythm of the cosmos follows external laws. Nevertheless the human being makes the transition from one part of the cosmos to another, from one planetary sphere into another in varying degrees of rapidity, according to his individual predisposition. Therefore his experience after death is quite individual. The human being passing through the starry spheres works at the preparation of his future earthly body, and therefore works down into the earthly, where within the succession of generations this earthly body is being prepared according to the laws of physical inheritance. *Thus the succession of generations reflects the starry script which the human being inscribes in the Cosmos between death and a new birth.*[77] This is what Flegetanis saw. He was able to prophesy the birth of a child twelve hundred years in advance, because he could see how the spirit-being of this child would pass through the cosmos. The child whose birth was so prophesied is the man Jesus, who at the age of 30 years became the Bearer of the Christ. By all the above considerations Joseph of Arimathea is shown to us in the Saga as the guardian of the mystery of the starry script. It is said of him that Vespasian encountered him when he was in prison. The main features of this story can be read in the summary by Paul Piper in the first part of the fifth volume of *Kürschners Deutscher Nationalliteratur*, pp. 86–87. Vespasian found the guardian of the mystery in prison. Something very similar, but without mentioning the name of Joseph of Arimathea, is recounted in the introduction to the Book of Jaschar in the edition of Bragadinus. There it is related how one of Titus' officers named Cidrus at the conquest of Jerusalem had released an old man from a walled-up chamber. But this old man—so the story relates—was the guardian of the ancient traditional wisdom and keeper of the genealogy of Adam, i.e. of humanity, and this mystery was recorded in the Book of Jaschar. On account of its importance we print in the appendix, translated from the original, the preface and introduction to this document. But we find there explained that the edition before us is not the original, but merely a feeble reflection of the book of the original mysteries. Wolfram von Eschenbach then, drew from this secret doctrine. He possessed the secret of the starry script and his authority Kiot perceived the connection between genealogy and starry script. He wished to do in the time after Christ what corresponds to the deed of Flegetanis in pre-Christian times. He wished, by the study of the chronicles of his country, to discover whether he could find a genealogical connection in which was reflected the starry script which he knew.

> And the heathen Flegetanis could read in the Heavens high
> How the stars roll on their courses, how they circle the silent sky
> And the time when the wandering endeth—and the life and the lot of men
> He read in the stars, and strange secrets he saw . . . (IX: 369–372)

This knowledge of the accord between the path of the soul and the succession of the generations was imparted to him when he observed the moon and what rested in the sickle of the moon as Sun-host

> . . . and he spake again.
> Low, with bated breath and fearful, of the thing that is called the Grail,
> In a cluster of stars was it written, the name, nor their lore shall fail. (IX: 372–374)

Written in the stars is found the name Perceval. The physical light is reflected by the moon, the spiritual light penetrates through it, the light itself writes the name Perceval in occult script in the stars. Rudolf Steiner discovered this.

> . . . 'A host of angels this marvel to earth once bore,
> But too pure for earth's sin and sorrow the heaven they sought once more,
> And the sons of baptised men hold It, and guard It with humble heart,
> And the best of mankind shall those knights be who have in such service part.'
> Then Kiot my master read this, the tale Flegetanis told. (IX: 375–379)

We learn that *Flegetanis* only spoke of the stars, and referred to *the birth of the Being in whom the Sun Spirit would dwell*. *Kiot* had a different task. He encountered in Toledo through the study of the Jewish secret doctrine the history of the *transition of the Jewish people from the moon-leadership to the sun-leadership*, and he knew that the wisdom which spoke through Balaam had to be renewed. It was not Balaam's wisdom which had to be revived for that was still self-seeking and connected with heredity, but the wisdom which used Balaam as its instrument. The medieval legend of Barlaam and Josaphat has reference to this wisdom, *the wisdom which works good through the mouth of evil*. It is clear from this legend of Barlaam and Josephat—and Rudolf Steiner has called attention to it—how clear a consciousness there was in the Middle Ages that the pre-Christian heathen stream had to become spiritually permeated with Christianity in the post-Christian era. Attention is even called in it to the permeation by the Christ of the Bodhisattva, who had become Buddha. But reference is also made there to Balaam. The Barlaam[78] of the medieval legend appears as the good inspirer of Balaam. Kiot was saturated with these things. How *in his own time* the Christ Impulse creates for itself a bearer, this is what he wanted to find.

> Then Kiot my master read this, the tale Flegetanis told,
> And he sought for the name of the people, in Latin books of old.
> Who of God were accounted worthy for this wondrous Grail to care,
> Who were true and pure in their dealings and a lowly heart might
>   bear.   (IX: 379-382)

He does not now seek for a single man in whom the cosmopolitan impulse of the Sun-Spirit could find a body. That only happened once in Jesus of Nazareth. Now he seeks for a people, for a whole racial community which would be willing to sacrifice its blood relationship to become the bearer of a cosmopolitan impulse.

> And in Britain, and France, and Ireland thro' the chronicles he sought
> Till at length, in the land of Anjou,[79] the story to light was
>   brought.   (IX: 383-384)

Anjou, in the form 'Anchan' first emerges as a name in Babylon. There it signifies a district. It is a Babylonian word. Anschan also is the name of a race of people living in France and also one in the region of Kärnten and Steiermark.[80] We shall have to deal more fully with the question of the Grail-race.

> There, in true and faithful record, was it written of Mazadan,
> And its heroes, the sons of his body ...   (IX: 385-386)

Mazadan is Macadam, Son of Adam. The Son of Adam is Cain; he reads, therefore, of the children of Cain. But he not only followed them up in the Old Testament, he followed them up to the time when that occurred, which had been prophesied by Balaam: a star was to go forth from Jacob, which would smite the princes of Moab and destroy all the children of Seth. All these he traced then, how it came to pass in fulfilment of prophesy, and then he was able to see how in David was foretold what later through Christ found its full realisation. Thus he was able to read of Mazadan and of his race, and he found the members of this race all described by name.

> ... and further the story ran,
> How Titurel, the grandsire, left his kingdom to Frimurtel,
> And at length to his son, Amfortas, the Grail and its heirdom fell:
> That his sister was Herzeleide, and with Gahmuret she wed

> And bare him for son the hero whose wand'rings ye now have read. (IX: 386-390)

That means, he traced the destiny of him who, in external history, a long time after, long after the Temple had been destroyed, rebuilt the Temple as announced by the angel.

Into the thirty-year-old Jesus the Spirit descended, and the body into which it descended he himself spoke of as being the Temple of God. This temple was destroyed. In *three* days he built it up again in resurrection. What took *thirty* years to build, and wherein he had dwelt for *three* years, he built up again in *three* days. Titurel too built the temple in thirty years. But this temple no longer stood visibly upon the earth, it was now built in such a way that it enclosed seventy-two choirs, corresponding to the seventy-two nations of the earth.[81] Just as Christianity came to the individual man at the time of the transformation of the earth by Christ, so henceforth it was coming to nations, to communities of men. In them the Christ was to gain a new kind of body. To the morality of the individual man, the morality of communities was to be added. When the Christ Jesus was born, then was peace announced to individuals of good will. Now this message was renewed. But not for the individual man but for communities of men and for nations. Around the altar of the Holy Ghost were the seventy-two choirs of the nations of the earth to congregate. And as the Lord had at Easter-tide awakened the dying body of Lazarus, so was the body of humanity which had fallen into corruption to be awakened through a new penetration of the Christ into the relations between nations. Titurel was the first to whom this was revealed. *The Temple of the Grail is not a medieval Saga.* It is still continuously in course of construction, and the Grail-Saga, far from being finished, is a *continuous living development.* It will take the form which fits the present time when the social ideas of Rudolf Steiner begin to be realised; for not by chance, but in full consciousness he named the spiritual science inaugurated by him the science of the Grail.[82] *We are at the point of time in which the Christ Impulse is being renewed, in which the Christ comes to the folk-souls* as he came to the *individual* human being in the events of Golgotha. The preoccupation in the Grail-Saga with the problems of Kiot, who interprets the starry script and the signs of the times—now however for the nations—is literally a burning present day problem. What the present can gain by a spiritual interpretation of history, this is what we wish to show: for no other reason would we engaged in research into the history of the Grail.

While we have formulated all these problems as they present themselves to the present time and for a renewed Quest of the Grail, so Parzival learnt them from the hermit, in the way which was suited to him. Now let us return to the adventures of Parzival.

He had to recognise again the place of his expiation. He felt himself laden with sin throughout his whole being, he alighted from his horse and begged counsel of the hermit. He learned that the old man whom he had met was

Kahenis, the Prince of Punturteis, and that he visited the hermit's cell every year at Easter-tide. The hermit hereupon describes to Parzival his simple, pure and spiritually-dedicated life. Parzival takes off his armour and remains as a guest of the hermit. He looks at the latter's books. He discovers the reliquary on which he had taken the oath. And he revealed to Trevrezent the reason why he had taken with him the coloured spear.

> And a spear, with fair colours blazoned, that did here by the altar stand
> I bare hence, and in sooth, I think me, right well did it serve my hand!
> Men say it much honour brought me, yet I wot not if it be so,
> For in thoughts of my wife had I lost me,[83] and naught of the thing I know.
> Yet, unwitting, two jousts had I ridden, and two foemen I overthrew, (IX: 471–475)

Parzival now becomes conscious of what had robbed him of consciousness at that time. Then he asks the hermit: 'How long is it since I took the spear?'

> 'It was Taurian,' quoth the hermit, 'who his spear in my care did leave,
> And much did he mourn its losing, and I with the knight must grieve,
> And four years and a half and three days shall have passed since we lost the spear'. (IX: 479–481)

Thus long has Parzival wandered about the world. How is it that he can now be aware of what earlier robbed him of consciousness? That is the work of time. Parzival has passed through the hard schooling of Kronos (Saturn). What was earthly in his love has been consumed.

Parzival tells Trevrezent of his despair and of his mistakes during the four and a half years. No church, no minister had he sought. In battle and in strife was he absorbed. And he bore hatred and anger in his heart against God, for he could not reconcile himself with his destiny. With sighs the hermit answered, that was a mistake. Parzival then had to recount how he fell into this conflict of soul. The hermit says that he is no priest, only a layman, but yet he is experienced. He admonishes Parzival to be faithful, God himself is faithfulness. God is also truth, and one ought never to begin to waver in thought. One gets nothing from God by anger. Now he instructs Parzival about the powers which lead men into temptation. He tells him of Lucifer. He was once an angel of Light, and then rebelled. In his inner being man is bound up with the rebellion of Lucifer and his expulsion from the heavenly heights. For as Lucifer sank into Hell, at that moment the human being came into existence. Out of clay the Godhead fashioned Adam, out of the form of Adam came forth Eve, who hearkened not to God and brought trouble upon the world. From them sprang Cain and Abel. The sin of Cain consists in the fact that he deprived his ancestress, the earth, of her virginity, by sprinkling her with blood. It is instruction about evil that Trevrezent gives to Parzival, but he presents the thoughts in such a way that the whole attention is directed to the earth. In *The Golden Legend* of Jacobus de Voragine similar thoughts are expressed in the story of St Silvester.

> For the *Earth* was Adam's mother, of the *Earth* was Adam fed,
> And I ween, tho' a man she bare here, yet still was the Earth a maid.
> And here will I read the riddle, he who robbed her of maidenhood
> Was Cain the son of Adam, who in wrath shed his brother's blood;
> For as on the Earth, so stainless, the blood of the guiltless fell,
> Her maidenhood fled for ever! And true is the tale I tell.
> For wrath of man and envy, thro' Cain did they wake to life,
> And ever from that day forward thro' his sin there ariseth strife.'
> (IX: 549–556)

Against the earth Cain sinned, with the earth he remained united, and the earth he must redeem.[84]

> Think how pure are maidens, God himself was a maiden's child!
> The Virgin Earth bore two men, and to show himself to man,
> God took on human likeness: consider it who can![85]

Thus he says, from Adam's race evil and blessedness alike have fallen to the lot of man. Through Adam we are related to the divine and then thrust down again in the depth of sin. The Lord himself however descended into these depths and of his goodness became man, for our salvation. Parzival should think of this, then his anger would disappear. Trevrezent exhorts Parzival to remember Plato and the Sibyls.

To this Plato passage Johann Heinrich Jung (called Stilling) has referred in the 11th volume of his *Collected Works* (Stuttgart, Scheibles Press, 1842, p 251 et seq.). In the Second Book of his *Republic*, when he foretells what an absolutely just man has to expect from humanity, he says: 'They will tell you that in the case described the just man will be scourged, racked, bound—will have his eyes burnt out and, at last, suffering every kind of evil he will be impaled.'[86] Jung-Stilling[87] comments, 'Is not this a pretty accurate description of the life and passion of Christ? Instead of burning out his eyes, a crown of thorns was pressed upon his head. The wise heathen had a pretty clear idea how the perfectly virtuous man would have to live and suffer.'

One finds similar prophesies in the Sibylline books, which have appeared in a German translation.[88]

The Saviour foretold in this fashion possessed the true Love, the divine Love. Of the difference between earthly and heavenly love Plato speaks in his *Symposium*. It was Christ who realised heavenly Love.

> For Plato alike and the Sibyls in their day spake words so true,
> And long years ere the time had ripened His coming they did foretell

> Who made for our sin's Atonement, and drew us from depths of Hell.
> God's Hand from those torments took us, and God's Love lifted us on high.
> But they who his Love disdained, they yet in Hell's clutches lie!
> From the lips of the whole world's Lover came a message of love and peace,
> (For He is a Light all-lightening, and never His faith doth cease).
> (IX: 572–578)

That is what the message announces, that one can win for oneself either God's hate or His love. The sinner flees from the divine goodness. But he who wishes to make good his transgressions, gains the favour of the Most High. He it is who penetrates the thoughts of men. The rays of the sun cannot illuminate thoughts, they are hidden and the ordinary human consciousness is not penetrated by the sun. But to the Divine Light human thoughts are manifest. The Light shines into the night of the heart. Before thoughts have escaped the human heart in which they were born, God has already penetrated and fathomed them. If He finds them to be pure, He guards them. If then God can discern thoughts, how must the evil-doer fear him. He who loses God's protection through an evil action, he who denounces God, must lose the game itself. Therefore, bear no hatred towards God, but change your disposition.

Then says Parzival, 'I thank you warmly for having made clear to me how the sway of destiny is penetrated by divine force. I have lived in ceaseless sorrow because I have not thoroughly understood that.' Then the hermit asks him what he thinks was the cause of his sorrow. Then Parzival answers that two things gave him grief. His greatest sorrow is because of the Grail; then next to this he mourns the fact that he has for so long been parted from his wedded wife. He yearns for both. Then the hermit answers, reversing the order of these sorrows, 'Yes, you are right to grieve at being separated from what you love. That is a real sorrow, to be separated from what one loves.' With that the hermit says something which is a saying of Buddha's. You are right, says he, to feel longing in such circumstance, but to bear desire towards the Grail, that is not right.

> ... for thou shalt know
> That none win the Grail save those only whose names are in Heaven known.
> They who to the Grail do service, they are chosen of God alone:
> (IX: 616–618)

The hermit wishes to say to Parzival that there is no sense in seeking for the Grail. The only sense is in fulfilling with enthusiasm the demands of the Grail—to work upon oneself and to serve the world. Whether one comes to the Grail or not, that one must leave in the hands of God, that is a grace. He gives to what he says a still greater force, by mentioning that he has himself seen the Grail. Parzival asks him—were you there? The hermit says that he was. Then Parzival was silent. He could not find the courage to claim that he too had been there. And so he only asked about the Grail. He says: 'At Monsalväsch there is a castle where the Grail is cared for by the Knights-Templars. These knights have gone through many adventures. The purpose of all their journeys is to fulfil the demands of destiny. All these valiant knights live by the power of a stone. It must be a noble kind of stone. What is it called?'

'Lapis exillis is its name.' (IX: 630)

The word is obviously derived from lapis exilii. Du Cange, 'Glossarium mediae et infimae latinitatis' defines the word *exililum* as 1) dissipatio, destructio, 2) Peregrinatio. *Lapis exilii* must therefore be translated 'stone of destruction', or 'stone of death'. Basil Valentine speaks of the stone, produced from fire, in the fourth of his 'Twelve Keys'.

> 'When ashes and sand are thoroughly baked for just the right amount of time, the master makes a glass out of them which henceforth will always resist the fire and resembles in colour a transparent stone and can no longer be recognised as ash. To the ignorant that is a great mysterious art, but not to the wise, for by knowledge and repeated experience it becomes a handicraft . . . At the Last Judgement the world will be judged by fire—fire that has been created by the Master out of nothing—the world must again become ashes through fire; out of these ashes will the Phoenix at last bring forth her young. For in such ashes is verily concealed the true Tartarus, which must be dissolved, and from a solution of which the solid castle of the kingly dwelling can be revealed.'

That means, man then comes to body-free, pure soul-spiritual experience.

The next lines that the poet gives us have to do with the experience of death. When the human being becomes free of his body and passes out of his body, a remarkable experience confronts his inner gaze. Human capacity for feeling is such that it penetrates the flesh but not the bones. When through becoming free of the body the capacity for feeling is released from its dependence upon the body, i.e. to express this in anthroposophical terms, when the astral body leaves the physical body, and the human being in imaginative experience is confronted by his astral body, then the space that the bones had occupied appears as a hollow space, as unoccupied space. That means that the human being has in imagination the skeleton in front of him. The picture is brought about just as a negative on a photographic plate. Rudolf Steiner explained this experience to me in the following way.

If the capacity for feeling the astral body presses against the bones, the inner part of the bones, which otherwise would have remained unconscious, become conscious. The fine cancellous tissue within the bones is perceived and in the moment when this is experienced, no other word can be found for the experience than *ashes*. Because the experience appears with especial strength in the region of the teeth, one speaks of the ashes that the dead have in their mouths. The next stage of this experience is that not only the bony structure is experienced but the blood in process of formation in the marrow of the bones is experienced too. As soon as this occurs, the bones begin to shine. The poet now describes this:

> . . . by its magic the wondrous bird,
> The Phoenix, becometh ashes, and yet doth such virtue flow
> From the stone, that afresh it riseth renewed from the ashes glow
> And the plumes that erewhile it moulted spring forth yet more fair and
>   bright.   (IX: 630–633)

So the poet describes the stepping out of the body, the becoming free of the body, the passing of the living body through the Gate of Death, the entrance into the spiritual world. But it is not actual death, it is the experience of death which is vouchsafed to successful inner schooling on the way into the spiritual world. Hence the poet emphasises that this illness is not unto death, but to the glorifying of the divine in man.

> Yet he dies not that same day that his eyes behold the Grail
> —Nor yet in the week to come—and his features stay unchanged.[89]

As they certainly would not do were he really to die.

> His colour fadeth not,[90] if he daily sees the Grail,
> But remaineth pure and bright as in youth or maidenhood.

He who has this experience notices that he has lived through it before in childhood as if in prevision. But then he could not understand it. The explanation of this experience too I owe to Rudolf Steiner. The poet refers to this fact:

> His hair would not turn grey, tho' he gazed two hundred years,
> Such strength it gives to man, that both his flesh and bones
> Are quickened to new life: *this stone is called the GRAIL*.

When the human being experiences the approach of body-free consciousness, when he experiences the stepping-out of his supersensible organisation, the weakness of death overtakes him, but he does not die, he is led to the point of looking at the birth of the light-forces out of the skeleton man, the Light of the World illuminates death. If he has this experience, his bodily

23. The Imagination which arises when one becomes free of the body
    (*Basil Valentinus, The Twelve Keys*) (*Fourth Key*)

organisation becomes penetrated with new force. What then is the Grail? It consists of the vessel and of the substance within it. The vessel is the skeleton and the substance is the blood-penetrated marrow within it.

THIS STONE IS CALLED THE GRAIL.

That is the microcosmic aspect of the Grail, experienced for the whole man. The experience can also be made in the head, as Rudolf Steiner has often described. There are in fact many ways of encountering the Grail. The experience here described is the one Trevrezent had. He says to Parzival that he had indeed stood before the Grail. We shall see in the course of the narrative how the poet tries to describe the experience from ever new aspects, when he tells us how different types of men are led to the Grail in different ways. Parzival himself takes a different path from Trevrezent, but through his encounter with Trevrezent an experience awakens in him which leads him further. Basil Valentine at the end of his fourth key, in which he describes the experience we have just given, writes:

And however many masters their attention turned to me,
Yet few have got so far as to fathom my true force.

And in his *Treatise on the Preparation of the Great Stone* [Philosopher's Stone] Basil Valentine says: 'Now follows the extraction of the golden salt according to the teaching of the Fourth Key.'

Then he describes how the extraction of the soul-spiritual out of the physical-bodily takes place in three days and three nights. He describes this experience as the 'third work'.

In order that the various aspects of the Grail should be better understood, the following interpolation is perhaps appropriate, There is a certain correspondence between what is microcosmic and what is macrocosmic which, though often only faintly indicated, plays a part in the manifestations of the most divergent epochs. Thus one experiences the moon in the cosmos, for example, as something which corresponds to the skeleton in man. As the skeleton represents death, which already during life we bear within us, so the burned out slag in the moon represents the same thing for the cosmos. This feeling exists at the same time as another, that represents the rhythm of the moon as precisely the life-giving element in the cosmos. This rhythm certainly acts in all embryonic life, in short, in all becoming. On the other hand what is formed into blood within the marrow of the bones corresponds to those forces of the sun which are active in shadow, whilst the blood that has emerged from the marrow corresponds to the forces of the sun which work directly. Now in the Grail one has to do with a protective sheath, and a blood substance to be found within it. In the passage of which we speak, the Grail is called a stone. The protective sheath, i.e. in the aspect here discussed, the inwardly-experienced skeleton, is viewed from outside the body. It is for this reason that the Grail in this passage is called *lapis exilii*.

Parzival is prepared through still more stages for this experience. Such a preparation he undergoes in the Grail Castle. Then comes the line:

His veins and bones poured sweat.[91]

Such a line is to be taken absolutely literally. It is a quite definite and precise inner event that he experiences.

In his conversation with Trevrezent he had to become aware how the forces of renewal of life (life renews itself in man in the blood-building within the marrow) are woven into the course of time. It is this which Parzival is unable to see, so long as he remains in a state of doubt. Not until he conquers doubt, or at any rate begins to overcome it, does he notice the real position of the human being and of nature within the course of time.

It is a fact of cultural history that the people which was most beset by the experience of doubt, the Persian people with its cult of light and darkness, was the people which had to discover the calendar. The understanding for what is connected with the calendar comes directly out of the experience of doubt, by the conquest of it. Parzival has to learn to understand how sun, moon and stars are related to the vegetative earth processes. That is why he is so urgently reminded that Good Friday is a special day. On no other festival could he experience what is here called to his notice, for Easter is the only moveable feast, the only one fixed according to the sun and moon constellations—the Sunday after the spring full moon. The significance of the Easter festival is indeed an extraordinarily real one. He who observes nature notices that there are years when the growth, the formation of flowers and fruits, in short the whole vegetative process, begins earlier, and again other years when all this begins later. To my question as to the precise connection of all this, Dr Steiner once answered that this too depended upon the constellation by which the Easter was fixed.

One can say that Parzival was faced with the task of studying the life of the earth, he was told that the blood which Cain had shed had deprived the earth of her virginity, that the blood which Christ had shed had restored again the pure virginity of the earth. Every Good Friday is enacted afresh between earth and cosmos, the event through which the earth is requickened. This event is the spring. It is not without significance (Dr Steiner too called attention to it) that Richard Wagner got the first idea for his Parzival whilst gazing at the scenery and wonderful sprouting blossoms of spring.

Parzival is in search of his mother. He thinks that he has to look for his earthly mother, but she is dead. She lives now in the starry spaces. That is precisely the mystery that the Grail seeker has to penetrate, how the heavenly mother and the earthly mother at certain times meet one another. All this is implied in the description that Trevrezent gives of what takes place on Good Friday. He says of the Grail:

'And Its holiest power, and the highest shall I ween be renewed today,

For ever upon Good Friday a messenger takes her way.
From the height of the highest Heaven a Dove on her flight doth wing,
And a Host, so white and holy, she unto the stone doth bring.
And she layeth it down upon It; and white as the Host the Dove
That, her errand done, swift wingeth her way to heaven above.
Thus ever upon Good Friday doth it chance as I tell to thee;
And the stone from the Host receiveth all good that on earth may be
Of food or of drink, the earth beareth as the fulness of Paradise.'
(IX: 641–649)

In every foodstuff there operates what the earth receives into itself at Eastertime as cosmic impulse. We have already explained that Wolfram describes things from the macrocosmic point of view. He speaks therefore of the starry script, he speaks of the earth, and he speaks of the *whole* man. Chrétien de Troyes, as Dr Steiner has said, describes things more from the *microcosmic* aspect, he describes what is connected with the human *head*, and the renewal of its life every night.

Thus in Chrétien de Troyes, the Grail Saga is given more from the point of view of waking and sleeping, while on the other hand Wolfram von Eschenbach shows it in relation to the course of the year and to birth and death.

Moreover, Wolfram's authority Kiot looks less at the events which take place within the individual man, he is more concerned with the human *relationships* which serve the Grail impulse, it is the *Grail Race* which interests him.

It is now necessary to make a few explanatory remarks about this Grail Race.

In the Grail are always united sun forces of a spiritual kind and moon forces of a physical kind. Every blood-relationship through which a particular heriditary tendency is passed on further is under the influence of the moon; that is why Gabriel, who is connected with the moon influence, always appears as the announcer of birth. The sun-impulse is to be seen wherever there is intermingling of blood, where the cosmopolitan Being dissolves the moon- or blood-relationship, the tribal relationship, where everything is directed to the production of a unified humanity over the earth. Michael, the Sun Spirit, both in medieval descriptions and also in all historical descriptions of Rudolf Steiner, is shown as the leader of the great Cosmopolitan movement. *The Grail Race is then the race which uses its family and blood ties and the forces of heredity to serve universal ends.* Kiot had set himself the task of scrutinising the history of the world to see if he could find a line related by blood descent which furthered not family impulses, but the needs of humanity. He had found one, through a purely historical examination of the history of the world, and for this research we propose to make his method our own. It is not so important to find the book of Kiot, for the book does not so much consist of leaves of paper covered with letters, but one has to call the Book of Kiot a book in the sense in which the word book is used in the Bible. There 'book' signifies racial succession, the sum of life-forces. *Those blood-relationships which further world-purposes form the book of Kiot.* Whether he also wrote down in an actual book what he read in this book is a matter of indifference to us. In anthroposophical terminology, the Book of Kiot is an etheric body in which the starry script has been imprinted; that is to say that there was a people on the earth whose history, whose genealogical connections correspond to macrocosmic events. The inspirer of Balaam had in his time looked upon these macrocosmic starry happenings. He (as we have already shown) is the personality named Flegetanis. He directs attention to a genealogical tree which points on the one hand to David and on the other to Christ.

Kiot had set himself the task of making researches into the history of the Christian era—therefore by a Christian method—a thing which the inspirer of Balaam in his own way had also done. Through these researches he is led to the Grail Race.

> 'Now hearken, the Grail's elect ones, say who does their service claim?[92]
> On the Grail, in a mystic writing, appeareth each chosen name,
> If a man it shall be or a maiden, whom God calls to this journey blest. (IX: 653-655)

This writing is clearly a starry writing: to the Grail Race belong children who are not born just on any day, but on a fixed day in harmony with cosmic rhythms.

> And the message no man effaceth ... (IX: 656)

This effacing happened often enough in the records of external history as regards the names of those persons about whom there were Grail legends. The example of Waldo of Reichenau, whose name has been deleted from the list of Abbots makes this clear. In the cosmos however the name of a Grail-bearer remains inscribed.

> But when all shall the name have read there, as it came, doth the writing go:
> As children the Grail doth call them,[93] 'neath its shadow they wax and grow.
> And blessèd shall be the mother whose child doth the summons hear, (IX: 657-659)

The call to the Grail came through birth. Forces of heredity were first active. But they are placed in the service of something which will bring forth a *new* relationship between men. Christ referred to this new relationship when his relations came to him, to speak with him. On that occasion, ignoring their petition, and pointing to the people, he said, 'these are my brothers and my sisters'.

In these words one can recognise the transition from the moon-impulse to the sun-impulse, from Gabriel to Michael. The nation which is placed specially under the leadership of Gabriel which bears on its shield the lily, has to express the Grail-Saga most powerfully of all in its microcosmic aspect. It was not by chance but by cosmic law, that Chrétien de Troyes wrote his work in Old French.

Nothing in the history of the Grail is accidental. All is permeated by a higher law. But the watchword of the Grail Knights was 'seek to come from Gabriel to Michael'. Through this watchword they became the leaders from the fourth into the fifth post-Atlantean culture-epoch, from the epoch of the Lamb into the epoch of the Fishes. When the Lamb was born who bore the sins of the world, Gabriel heralded His birth and with it the nature of the whole culture-epoch. Roman Christianity arose. It is based upon a Gabriel principle, it rests upon tradition. What passes from generation to generation on the earth through apostolical succession is protected by Gabriel. The fifth culture-epoch has created for itself a Christianity without tradition, and this Christianity bears within itself the force to become universally independent of blood-ties, hereditary relationships, nations and religious denominations.

It becomes ever clearer to us what the symbol of the sun-host resting in the moon-chalice signifies, that it is the sign for the transition from the fourth into the fifth culture-epoch, in the language of Anthroposophy, from Roman to the Anglo–Saxon–Germanic.

Thus, then, Parzival is instructed by Trevrezent about the Grail Race. But Trevrezent has to add something else. He has to add that the Luciferic powers have interfered in what has brought humanity down into earthly birth. Hence he comes to speak of the sublime and mighty battle between the Trinity and Lucifer.

Let us remember that Trevrezent gives this teaching at a time which is eleven generations before the time of Wolfram, that is to say, if one takes into account what Wolfram says about these eleven generations, about the year 869 or 870.[94] It is the time when humanity, just like Parzival, who represents human experience, had begun to doubt the Trinity. At this time the eighth Oecumenical Council occurred. Rudolf Steiner's recognition of the importance of this Council was his central discovery. At this Council the Trinity within the human being was extinguished. No longer was one to speak of body, soul and spirit, but only of body and soul, and to the soul were to be ascribed some spiritual qualities. Wherever the true Christianity is propagated in esoteric tradition, trichotomy has been retained. Read for example the works of the enlightened Basil Valentine, and besides the breath of a wondrous Christlike love, you will find trichotomy. We stand then at the point of time at which humanity began to doubt concerning the Trinity.

In Chapter 6 of this work we shall show the whole connection of the Grail history with the year 869. Here perhaps the reference may be allowed to suffice.

A most remarkable passage follows containing teachings of Trevrezent, remarkable because Trevrezent himself later says that his teaching about the Trinity was false. The lines in which he says this run as follows:

> ... Yet aforetime in sooth I lied,
> For I thought from the Grail to bring thee, and the truth I from thee would hide.
> Do thou for my sin give me pardon, henceforth I thy hand obey,
> O my King, and son of my sister!—Methinks that I once did say
> That the spirits cast forth from Heaven thereafter the Grail did tend
> By God's will, and besought His favour, till their penance at last did end.
> But God to Himself is faithful, and ne'er doth He changing know,
> Nor to them whom I named as forgiven did He ever forgiveness show.
> For they who refuse His service, He Himself will, I ween, refuse
> And I wot they are lost forever, and that fate they themselves did choose.   (XVI: 185-194)

Later, then, we shall be told that the following doctrine is false. Trevrezent wished to dissuade Parzival from following the Grail. Thus prepared, let us now listen to the words:

> When the battle was fought between Trinity and Lucifer[95]
> The whole heavenly host with its shining wings
> Had to descend to the stone, there to serve that same stone.

These words refer to Chapter IV, verse 11 of the Gospel of St Matthew. There it says, after the story of the Temptation, that the divine spiritual hierarchies ministered to Jesus. We have already called attention to the fact that Jesus is the chalice which contains the blood of Christ. If then it says here that the angels ministered to the stone, this refers to Jesus. At the same time however we recognise that the angels who served Jesus after the story of the Temptation are the very powers who tried to tempt him, and whom, through resisting temptation, he made into his servants. It is Lucifer and his hosts who minister to Jesus. Now we can understand the lines differently:

> When the battle was fought between Trinity and Lucifer
> The whole heavenly host with its shining wings [the Luciferic angels]
> Had to descend to the stone, there to serve that same stone
> It must be very precious and sublime.

And now came the words which Trevrezent later withdrew:

Whether God remitted their guilt, or whether he later wholly rejected them,
He must do as seems Him well. To them whom God since called to serve the stone, He sent to them *His* angel.

Thus Christ sent his angel to those Luciferic angels who were chosen to find their way back to the Christ angel, the precious stone in Lucifer's angel-crown. They and the true angels minister to the Grail. But if they become servants of the Grail, they must renounce strife. Trevrezent however leaves Parzival under the delusion that the Grail can be striven for. At that time, in the time of Trevrezent, humanity had fallen into uncertainty over the question of the redeemed and rejected angels, that is to say, over the cosmic intelligences. The solution to this question however is fundamental, and we shall have to discuss at length what happened to the Luciferic hosts after the Sun-Spirit had descended upon the earth; what became of Lucifer the Light-bringer when the Light of the World walked the earth as man and rejected the temptation of Lucifer? Those Luciferic spirits who were willing to abandon the conflict were then redeemed, those who persisted in battling and strife were banished for aeons. What was good in the fall of Lucifer became through Christ Jesus united with the development of humanity. And until 869, the spirits had a respite in which to become converted. That means that the Luciferic spirits had to make the decision whether they would in the future serve the Grail, or whether they preferred to remain what they were, rebellious spirits.

In the time of doubting, in the time of Parzival, men were aware of this separation of the spirits. But Parzival by bringing humanity to blessedness (Saelde) had the task of overcoming this doubt, which was not merely a subjective experience of the human soul but an objective fact of the world, i.e. division in the realm of the spirits. All this will become perfectly clear to us when we come to describe the year 869 with all the historical events connected with it, in their historical aspect: the year of momentous decisions for the life of humanity, when humanity had to choose between acceptance and rejection of the Trinity.

After Trevrezent had explained all this, he says to Parzival... 'and so standeth it with the Grail—' (IX: 672). Then Parzival says that in future he will, in right knightly fashion, seek to pursue noble strife, and that, when he had learnt to wage such warfare worthily, God would call him to the Grail. Then Trevrezent answers that he must guard against pride; pride must ever come to downfall. At these words, Trevrezent was so moved that he began to weep, and he told Parzival about Amfortas. He too met his downfall owing to pride, for he had pursued unbridled love. He who wishes to approach the Grail may not do this. No one comes to the Grail without being called. Only one person came there without being called, but he underwent frightful experiences there. Trevrezent refers to Parzival. And now he says that yet another knight got as far as the Lake Brumbane—Lähelein, the brother of Orilus. There he killed the Grail Knight Libbeals, the son of Prienlaskoss. In this way Lähelein had looted a Grail horse. We know that Parzival had done something similar, by exchanging the dead Ingliart for a Grail horse. The only difference was that Lähelein had killed the Grail knight, whereas Parzival had not. Then Trevrezent asks Parzival 'Are you not Lähelein, since I see on your saddle the turtle-dove which is a Grail token? You ride a Grail horse, who are you, what is your race, whence come you?'

Then Parzival answers that his father was Gahmuret, but that he is not Lähelein. Murder he had not committed, at least not to secure a horse. But he had acquired his armour thus, for he had slain Ither of Kukumerland[95a] for it. Then Trevrezent calls Parzival his nephew, and laments that Parzival has killed a near relation. Ither von Gahevies' wife was indeed Lammire, the sister of Parzival's father, but possibly the relationship was closer than that through marriage, for Trevrezent says that Ither and Parzival are of the same blood. From what we know of this relationship it lies three generations behind Ither and four generations behind Gahmuret, thus five behind Parzival.

Both races spring from Mazadan and the Fairy Terdalaschoye in Feimurgan. We have seen that Mazadan is MacAdam, the son of Adam, who is Cain[96] [Verse 464]. But the fairy Feimurgan is the Persian Peri Mergiana as Blavatsky has already pointed out in the second volume of her *Secret Doctrine* (p. 398 in facsimile edition). Thus the relationship lay in the fact that they were both children of Cain. With Blavatsky's observation in this passage that this genealogy relates to epochs of humanity and not to individuals we are quite in agreement, more especially as we notice that the two descendants of Mazadan have names which point to what is universally human. For the one descendant Lassalies from whom Parzival's family derives is called something like 'Uniter of the Blessed', whereas the other descendant, from whom Ither, Arthur and Gawain spring, is called Brikus, which means something like the 'Unfortunate'. Two children of Cain—one from the family of the Blessed, Parzival, the other from the family of the Unfortunate, Ither, the Red Knight, thus come to battle with one another, and Parzival has slain his human brother. Trevrezent instructs Parzival that through his act he has forfeited his life. World-justice now demands his life of him. What Trevrezent prophesies here becomes fulfilled later in Parzival's fight with his step-brother Feirefis, who is of course not a red knight but a black and white one. In this battle Ither's sword is broken. And Parzival's deed is only expiated when Feirefis and he recognise each other as brothers, and Feirefis, who would never have been able to come to the Grail out of his own forces is led to the Grail by Parzival.

In Feirefis someone attains to Blessedness who by himself could never attain to it. But Feirefis at least on his father's side springs from the Family of the blessed. As to the descent of Belakane his mother, we know nothing.

Now Trevrezent calls to Parzival's consciousness the guilt with which he has burdened himself. And so he tells him too that by his hasty departure from her, he caused the death of his mother, Trevrezent's sister. Parzival now learns this, a thing which he did not know before.

Moreover, Trevrezent gives Parzival further information about his relations. We can best reproduce what he told him in the form of a genealogical tree.

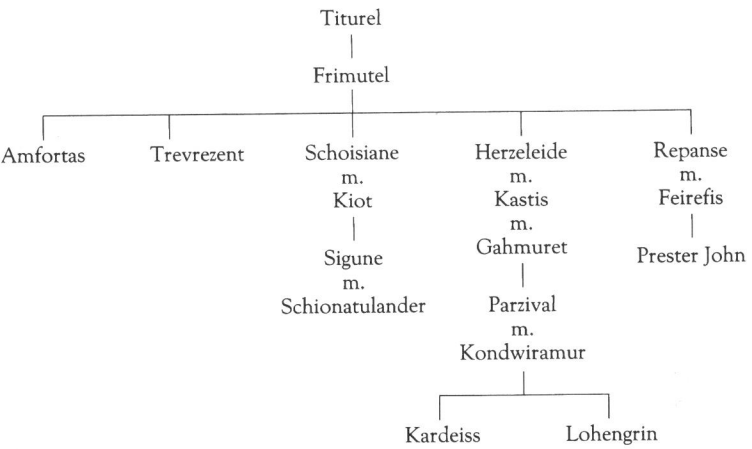

What he says about Kiot, Schoisiane and Sigune, we know already from the chapter about Schionatulander. He tells him too, what we also know, how Repanse de Schoye tends the Grail, and about the lot of Amfortas. Amfortas, although he served the Grail, indeed was even King of the Grail, committed the sin of daring to choose a mistress who did not feed him on the Grail. We know that Trevrezent refers to Orgeluse. Thus his battle-cry was 'Amor', which is not exactly an inducement to humility. One day when Amfortas had ridden out to seek adventures, something happened which was the cause of his severe wound. The poisoned spear of a heathen borne by Ethnise from Paradise, pierced him to the pubic bone. The name of the heathen was engraved on the spear. So deeply had the iron of the spear penetrated into the wound that it could not be easily withdrawn. The doctor's examination showed that the spear-point was hollow, and that poison ran out of it. The doctor had to draw out the splinter very skilfully. Thus Amfortas, through his carnal desires, fell sick with an incurable wound. In order to restore the balance in the universe, Trevrezent had been willing to renounce all those things which Amfortas in his uncontrolled passion had done to excess. He renounced the service of the sword and became a hermit.

Later on Trevrezent tells the means that were tried to cure the wound. All was in vain. The wound was ever wet with the poison. What was found in the medical books was of no avail. Neither did the various snake poisons help. Even an expedition to the four streams of Paradise, to see if perchance the healing herb was borne along by one of them, was fruitless. Nor again was the bough of any avail that the Sibyl gave to Aeneas on the way into the underworld, as a protection against the dangers of Hell. And it was no better when one had recourse to the blood of the pelican or to the carbuncle which is found beneath the horn of the unicorn. Neither was the herb that is called Trachonte and that springs up in the blood of slain dragons and has a mysterious relation to the course of the stars, any use as a remedy. In short, neither in the knowledge of the great demons (Ecidemon, as the 'Battle of the Wartburg' tells us, is the angel or the daimon of the human being, and is referred to here as snake poison, that is, as the gift of a snake, of one who knows) nor in the four-fold forces of the bodily organisation (the four streams of Paradise) nor in the region of the forces of the physical body (the descent of Aeneas into the underworld) nor in the ego (the blood of the Pelican) was any remedy found. Not even those substances which man obtains through alchemistic processes (the carbuncle of the unicorn) nor the earthly substances which were specially penetrated with heavenly substances (the herb Trachonte) helped. But through the last, they came very near to the peculiar mystery of the wound, for the pain of the wound increased when certain stars came round to certain points in their course, and the phases of the moon in the same way made themselves felt. The wound of Amfortas is then a kind of organ of knowledge for the course of the stars. But Amfortas has not succeeded in forming this organ as it ought to be, but experiences in suffering the mystery of the connection between the microcosm and the macrocosm. Only one thing can bring healing—the knight who asks the question. We already know that this knight, when to mere picture-vision he adds the question, produces that which heals, namely, inspiration.

At this point Trevrezent breaks off the conversation. He has brought it up to the point where Parzival stands. The rest he can leave to the self-knowledge of Parzival. In the lines which follow we are told about the simple meal, the simple dwelling of the hermit. After they had eaten, Parzival confesses that he is the unhappy one who beheld the Grail and the plight of the King, and yet had not asked. And then he learns from Trevrezent what he has to know, if he is to unravel the knot of destiny. Trevrezent says:

> Through my mouth would God teach thee wisdom; now say didst thou see the spear,
> In that wondrous Burg of Monsalväsch? As ever the time draws near!
> When Saturn his journey endeth[97]—(that time by the wound we know,
> And yet by another token, by the fall of the summer snow)*
> Then sorely the frost doth pain him, thy king and uncle dear,
> And deep in the wound empoisoned once more do they plunge the spear.
> One woe shall help the other, the spear cure the frost's sharp pain,

* See note 97a

And crimson it grows with his life-blood ere men draw it forth again!
When the stars return in their orbit, then the wailing it waxeth sore,
When they stand in opposition, or each to the other draw.
And the moon, in its waxing and waning, it causeth him bitter
    pain.   (IX: 963–973)

It is a mysterious wound which is produced in the human being, because he misuses egoistically the highest forces that nature gives him, the creative forces. In the human being there is a part of his organisation in which what takes place follows not earthly but starry laws. How destruction and upbuilding there take place in secret starry rhythms remains unknown to the ordinary consciousness.

Let us examine from this standpoint the laws of Saturn. Saturn completes her circuit in about the same number of years as the moon in days. She advances from quarter to quarter in approximately seven years. In four times seven years she traverses the whole circuit of her course. That is expressed in the human being in the process of advancing age. Every seven years the metabolic system in the human being changes. In the first seven years the teeth grow. Then a certain process is finished for the head organisation. In the second seven years occurs puberty, and then the process is closed for the middle man and begins in the lower man. In the third seven years is fulfilled a process which for our time is less easily observed, for it is not experienced bodily, but in the soul—the process in which the twenty-one year old human being (it varies in different nations) reaches his coming-of-age. In the twenty-eighth year the circuit is completed. All these processes which take place in the rhythm of Saturn are hardening processes, which find their whole expression in bone-formation, in sclerosis. We know that lead, used in medicine, produces the same symptoms as sclerosis. It is this which the Middle Ages called the action of Saturn. The cutting of the second teeth, a bone-process, the slight ossification of the larynx in the male at puberty, which causes the change of voice, both these are Saturn processes. Saturn gives men inner solidity, the inner skeleton, the upright position.[98]

Another force, entirely opposite to this one, is that of the moon. The rhythm of the moon acts everywhere where the phenomenon of ebb and flow in fluid appears. In the human organisation this force comes to light in the rhythm of the female organism. Whilst in the man Saturn is more active, and in the woman more the moon, nevertheless the two forces are active in every human being whether man or woman. They are the forces of birth and the forces of death. How in the human being forces encounter one another which build up and destroy in accordance with the rhythm of the stars, and how this meeting in harmony with starry laws is disturbed if the human being egoistically seeks pleasurable experience for himself out of the processes in the depths of his organisation, this it is which forms the sickness of Amfortas. What heals this sickness? Only the knowledge that love must be unselfish, that the human being is only the steward of divine heavenly forces within his own organisation. Anything else that is told about the illness of Amfortas, is only the pictorial amplification of what has just been said. The silver knives of the smith Trebüschet (looking at the matter from the macrocosmic point of view) are connected with the moon, as the spear is with Saturn. The upbuilding moon forces, i.e. the silver knives, must continually renew in the human being what Saturn's spear destroys. Saturn is connected with heat and cold, just as the moon is with fluidity and ice.

> His flesh thro' the frost it groweth colder than e'en the snow,
> But men know that the spear sharp-pointed doth with fiery venom glow,
> And upon the wound they lay it, and the frost from his flesh so cold
> It draweth, and lo! as crystals of glass to the spear doth hold,
> And as ice to the iron it clingeth, and none looseth it from the blade.
> Then Trebüschet the smith bethought him, in his wisdom two knives he made,
> Of silver fair he wrought them, and sharp was the edge and keen—
> (A spell on the king's sword written had taught him such skill I ween,) (IX: 975–982)

We know already about this 'spell' that it contains the power to put together again what has been broken in pieces. Plato in his own way expressed the same thing in his Symposium. He shows there how in the male and female sex the unity of Primeval man is split up, and how love (to begin with the lower kind of love) is an attempt to bring about again this original unity. While this attempt however, as Plato shows, can never succeed, yet the aim of the higher purified love is to reach that essentially human quality in human beings which, high above all differentiation, reveals a unified primeval being in man. This of course lies beyond the force of birth and death, in the eternal. That is what Parzival must strive for. A true science of man will understand rightly the contrast between male and female, in that it knows that the male organism is constituted more out of the destructive forces, while on the other hand the female organism is formed more out of the upbuilding forces. Where both these seem to be overcome and neither of them stands out in its one-sidedness, in the regions beyond birth and death there is the world where what was once separate finds perfect union. In this world a lower love can no longer exist.

Perhaps from such a standpoint, derived from anthroposophical knowledge of man, it will be possible to understand in a worthy manner the problem of the sickness of Amfortas.

The poet then goes on to tell of asbestos, which burns. Really it is supposed to be unburnable. It is clear that this has some connection with the fire of desire. The comparison is borrowed by Goethe in his *Faust*, where in the second part, he says:

Earth's residue to bear
Hath sorely pressed us;
It were not pure and fair,
Though 'twere asbestos.
When every element
The mind's high forces
Have seized, subdued, and blent,
No Angel divorces
Twin natures single grown,
They inly mate them;
Eternal love alone,
Can separate them.
[Bayard Taylor's translation of Goethe's Faust, Part II, act V, last scene]
       'Chorus of the More Perfect Angels'.

Goethe means (and he lets the more perfect angels say it) that no angel could separate the united two-fold nature of higher spiritual force, which had joined itself to the human body. Only eternal love is capable of severing the immortal from the mortal. Thus Karl Julius Schröer explains these lines.

Thus too we can interpret the following lines of Wolfram von
   Eschenbach:

Tho' no flame on earth can kindle Asbestos, as men do tell
And never a fire may harm it, if these crystals upon it fell
Then the flame would leap and kindle and burn with a fiery glow
Till th' Asbestos lay in ashes, such power doth this poison know!'
                                                                (IX: 983–986)

All this only happens so long as man has not purified his lower nature. When he has purified it, then he overcomes all separation. Then he reaches the region in which all contrasts disappear, and the unified human being finds himself in his eternal nature. *Amfortas has not achieved this ascent to the heights.* When his pains overtake him, he seeks out *the depths*. He has himself carried to the Lake Brumbane in order to fish there, so people believe, but, burdened with all his torments and sufferings, he has never been able to catch enough to suffice him for a single meal. To try to get heavenly food by a descent into the lower nature is a hopeless enterprise.

Then Parzival says that he knows that; that he too had met the King at the Lake Brumbane, he had just come from the land of renunciation, from Pelrapäre. Although the Grail Castle was so well-guarded, he had nevertheless got through to it, he had entered into the castle, and the spear too he had seen. Then answers Trevrezent that the King had never experienced such grief as at that time.

> Then answered the host, 'Far sorer than before was the monarch's pain,
> In this wise did he learn the tidings that Saturn drew near again,
> And the star with a sharp frost cometh, and it helpeth no whit to lay
> The spear on the sore as aforetime, *in* the wound must it plunge alway!
> When that star standeth high in heaven the wound shall its coming know'
> (IX: 1013-1017)

At that time, then, Saturn was at its zenith. At that moment Saturn and the Sun-hero Parzival found themselves together. It was indeed the force of Saturn with which the Sun-hero came. But it was not yet time, he could not yet ask the question. When will the day come, when the star-constellation, and that which is produced out of the inner being of man will meet in full freedom? On that day Parzival will know that the suffering of the King is caused because he is unable to create this harmony.

After Parzival has been able to acquire so much self-knowledge, he then learns through Trevrezent of the life of the Templars. Chosen as children by God, they are called to the service of the Grail. If anywhere in the country after the death of a king another king is wanted, and the people desire an emissary of the Grail, then the Grail sends to such a people a king. But he has to keep silence about his origin. If on the other hand there is a country that desires a maiden from the Grail, then the Grail grants the maiden, without her origin being in any way kept secret.

> 'God sendeth the *men* in secret, but the *maidens* in light of day
> Are given unto their husbands; thus none spake to his wooing, Nay,
> When King Kastis wooed Herzeleide, but joyful our sister gave.
> (IX: 1043-1045)

A remarkable custom: the men are silent about their origin, as we know too from the story of Lohengrin, but not the women. Therein too is concealed a mystery of the nature of male and female. Rudolf Steiner has told us that the forces of heredity work in such a way that they are in fact inherited through the male, whilst the woman rather works against heredity, and through what she gives, transmits to the children forces which are more universally human characteristics, which are derived from the whole cosmos.

One must not enquire of a male messenger of the Grail who was his father or his mother; for it is just what runs through the generations that is unessential, so soon as he becomes a Grail knight. In the case of the woman, what she brings with her out of the hereditary connection is the essential thing. The Grail has the tendency to dissolve the blood relationship and to replace it by relationship of soul. Hence the man must free himself from what works in him as heredity, the woman on the contrary must surrender herself to the forces of heredity, because in her case and in virtue of her womanly nature these are already forces working against heredity. That is why in all the Grail genealogies more stress is laid upon descent from the mother than upon the descent from the father. Let me give one example to illustrate this. Those writers for example who wish to emphasise that Charlemagne was the bearer of a spiritual mission lay stress on the fact that his grandparents on his mother's side were Flore and Blanscheflur. Compare the poem of Konrad Fleck. It is a question of his maternal descent. That is the meaning of the line:

God sendeth men in secret, but the maidens by light of day. The mysteries of the Grail genealogies are unveiled for Parzival in his encounter with Trevrezent, his relative. The poem then goes on:

> Thus the Grail Its maidens giveth, in the day, and the sight of men,
> But It sendeth Its knights in the silence and their children it claims again,—
> To the host of the Grail are they counted, Grail servants they all shall be,
> So the will of God standeth written on the Grail for all men to see.
> He who would to the Grail do service, he shall women's love forswear;
> A wife shall none have save the Grail King, and his wife a pure heart must bear,
> And those others whom God's hand sendeth, as king, to a kingless land.   (IX: 1053-1059)

Trevrezent tells Parzival how he too had known love, how he had been in its service in Europe, Asia and Africa, how he had ever been led to Gaurivon, and to the mountain Feimorgan and to that of Agremontin. He had been obliged to fight with fiery men, he had struggled with the force of passion. But one day when he had come to Rohas in Steiermark, i.e. to the Rohitsche Mountain in Styria, he met a party of Wends. Then he came from Seville towards Sicily, through Friaul as far as Aquileia. But in Seville he met Parzival's father. We see at this point that Trevrezent considers it important, amongst various mythical places, to mention Steiermark. And this fact, together with the other, that Gahmuret, bears a shield which resembles that of Steiermark, is not unimportant. We have already referred to the connection between the Carolingian territory and Steiermark. Trevrezent speaks more clearly of this in the following lines. He says:

> ... unto Rohas I took my way.
> From Rohas I took my journey and unto Gandein I came,
> ('Twas that town from which first thy grandsire, his name of Gandein did take,)   (IX: 1112-1115)

He says then that this town lies where the Greia empties itself into the Drave. M. Haupt ('Zu Wolframs Parzival' in *Zeitschrift für Deutsches Altertum*, Vol.

II, Berlin 1859, p. 42 et seq.) identified Rohas as the Rohitsch Mountain in Saangau in Styria and the Greia, which is mentioned later, as the Grajena Brook which flows into the Drave near Pettau. The town Gandein lies in the basin of the Drave near Pettau. The coat of arms of Gandein, the black Panther, resembles that of Steiermark which has a white Panther on a green field. Parzival's family comes from this neighbourhood. At the time which we have identified as that in which the Grail Saga took place, living connections existed between the Carinthian–Styrian region and the country of Charlemagne. In our references to Liutward, to Richardis and to Arnulf of Carinthia, we have drawn attention to this connection.[98a] In this passage we learn too that Ither was the husband of the daughter of Gandein, Trevrezent's squire. Ither was given to Trevrezent by Parzival's father. Gahmuret gave Trevrezent at the same time a green stone, out of which the reliquary was carved on which Parzival swore to Jeschute's innocence.

Trevrezent reproaches Parzival for having killed Ither and for having caused the death of his mother. Also for having taken a Grail horse. Then Parzival tells him that he had received a Grail cloak and a Grail sword.

Parzival remained fourteen days longer with Trevrezent. In conversation he learned that the old man whom he had seen in the chamber within the Grail Castle was Titurel. We learnt that at an earlier point in the narrative. Then Parzival and Trevrezent took leave of one another.

> Now this day was the day of parting—Trevrezent to our hero spake,
> 'Leave thou here thy sins behind thee, God shall me for thy surety take,
> And do thou as I have shown thee, be steadfast and true of heart!'
> Think ye with what grief and sorrow the twain did asunder part.

Adventure X

The next chapter leads us again to Gawain. In the *tenth* Adventure Gawain passes through experiences which run parallel to the experiences of Parzival. For example, Parzival finds the dead Knight in Sigune's lap. Gawain finds a wounded Knight in the arms of a woman and heals him. We point this out at once in order to draw attention to the fact that it is a question of learning to recognise in the following chapters how different are the paths of Gawain and Parzival. Gawain's goal is the Castle Merveil (Magic Castle). Parzival's goal is the Grail Castle. There is a polarity between the two. We shall study this more closely.

If we observe the content of the tenth adventure the opening verse at once makes it clear to us that we have entered the realm of Klingsor. Here there rules the opposite of '*Staete*' (steadfastness). Towards the end of this chapter we read:

> ...'So is here the custom, in the forest as on the plain,
> As far as Klingsor ruleth, be he coward or valiant knight,
> "Sad today, tomorrow joyful,"[99] so it goeth for peace or fight.'
> (X: 728–730)

So it is ever in the land of Klingsor. This is noted in the opening verse:

> Now tell we of strange adventures thro' which joy shall be waxen low,
> And yet pride shall grow the greater, of the twain doth this story
> show. (X: 1–2)

Thus we can have no kind of doubt that we are not dwelling in the heights where the Eagle of thought builds its Eyrie, rather have we descended into the depths where the Dragon of desire rages. We are reminded that Gawain enters this region well armed through the poet's mention of the fact that Gawain and Vergulacht have become reconciled. Gawain moreover is guiltless and has done none of those things of which he is accused. Both, however, Vergulacht as well as Gawain, are, quite apart from one another, seeking the Grail. So while Parzival rides Gawain's horse, Gawain has taken over Parzival's task. We find Gawain, who is in quest of the Grail, in the region of Castle Merveil. We find—as we shall see—that Parzival in a mysterious way takes part in Gawain's adventure.

Now of Gawain it is related as follows:
One morning Gawain rides forth and finds on a grassy plain a horse bearing a woman's saddle. Thereon hung a shield. Ah! thinks he to himself, 'What kind of a warlike woman can it be to whom these arms belong? The shield was even hacked.' As he thought thus to himself he saw a lady sitting by the mighty trunk of a linden tree. And now an experience is described which throughout corresponds to Parzival's encounter with Sigune, only now in the way it happens in the realm of Klingsor. A knight who has been wounded lies in the woman's lap and his blood is flowly freely. Gawain who is versed in the art of healing, dismounts, tears off a piece of the bark from a bough of the linden tree, twists it to form a tube which he thrusts into the knight's wound and bids the woman suck until the blood flows towards her. Thus he knew from what the knight suffered. Almost immediately the knight revived, thus proving Gawain's diagnosis to be correct. It says:

> 'The wound is not all too dangerous, but the blood on his heart doth
> press'. (X: 52)

By this we understand that the illness of the knight consisted in having been in too close accord with what is earthly. Schionatulander had died in the service of the quest for the writing of the stars. The knight here suffers from being full-blooded to excess. It is what springs from the blood that troubles him. The knight whom he thus heals warns Gawain. He is called Urian, as we shall see later. He is hardly a model of virtue. Gawain recognises him, as we find it expressed later on, as one with a passionate and chaotic nature. Gawain became acquainted with him just as he had forced a maiden to his will against her own will and the knight had been called to answer for it before Arthur's Round Table. He was sentenced to death and only because Gawain had interceded for him was the lesser penalty prescribed of eating from one trough with the hounds and house-dogs for four weeks. This knight, whom at first Gawain does not recognise, warns him that all kinds of unpleasant adventures may be experienced in this neighbourhood. It was Lischois Giwellius who had treated the wounded knight so badly. We shall see later who is hidden behind the name of Lischois Giwellius. It is a knight who treats people of Urian's nature badly. At all events a personality that has nothing in common with such deeds as Urian's. Let us bear this well in mind for we shall see later that we shall need this knowledge. Gawain now bound up the wound and spoke a blessing over it. Then he rode on. Before his gaze there appeared the citadel. The castle hill towered up in a spiral and seemed to turn in a circle. It is clear that in the picture of this landscape the human soul is indicated which here has the quality that is displayed when as in a whirling dance of intoxication it is given up to passion. Here there was a spring which flowed from a rock on which a lady was seated of whom the poet says that only Kondwiramur could be compared with her for beauty. She was called Orgeluse of Logrois. Gawain saw her and at once proferred his love, she however rejected his courtship with no uncertain words. Among other things she said:

'Thy desire is but empty folly, thou shouldst other service seek!'

(X: 114)

But Gawain declares that he regards himself as her captive. And since Gawain will not allow himself to be repulsed, Orgeluse sets him a task. He is to go down to the garden where he had seen the horse and bring this horse to Orgeluse. Gawain springs from his charger, but does not at first know how he can leave his steed. Orgeluse then offers to hold it. As he is about to place the reins in her hand Orgeluse declares she will not touch the place where his hand has rested. She will only hold the horse if in handing her the reins, he can show her a part that his hand has never touched. The whole conduct of Orgeluse is that of rejection. The people in the garden warn him. He however strides courageously to the olive tree to which the horse is bound. Here Gawain perceives a knight who is leaning on a crutch and who has a grey beard. He weeps as Gawain approaches the horse. He too warns him not to undertake the adventure and he curses the lady. But Gawain does not allow himself to be dissuaded. We may here observe that Gawain has dismounted from his horse just as Parzival did at the Grail Castle, and as Parzival met a young squire, so Gawain encounters an aged knight, and as Parzival, after his failure at the Grail Castle, hears the words, 'You Goose', called after him, so Orgeluse welcomes Gawain as he approaches her with the horse thus:

> 'Now welcome, thou goose! for of all men most foolish art thou, I ween,
> All too bent shalt thou be on my service, wert thou wise thou wouldst let it be—'
> Then he quoth, 'Yet shalt thou be gracious who now art so wroth with me,
> For so harshly thou dost chastise me thou in honour must make it good,
> And my hand shall be fain to serve thee till thou winnest a milder mood.' (X: 198–202)

As Gawain offers to lift her onto her horse she repulses him and with one spring is on its back. She further orders him not to ride behind her but in front of her. At this point the poet warns the reader not to blame Orgeluse; the reader does not as yet know what her character is and he should at least be on his guard and determine whether he has truly recognised what is in her heart. The poet takes pains to make clear to us that we are concerned with a test of Gawain and that Orgeluse plays some kind of predestined role. Very rapidly do the experiences take place, the action hastens on much faster then before when the experience of Parzival was being described. For we have already arrived at the place where Kundrie encounters Parzival at Arthur's Round Table in order to curse him. Only here of course it is not Kundrie but her brother whom Gawain encounters, a monster named Malkreatur. We are told that Kundrie was his beautiful little sister.

> And e'en such a face as the sister, I ween, did the brother bear.
> From his mouth, as the tusks of a wild-boar, stood the teeth out to left and right,
> Unlike was his face to a man's face, and fearful in all men's sight
> And the locks of his hair were shorter than those which from Kundrie hung
> Adown on her mule; stiff as bristles, and sharp, from his head they sprung.
> And beside the river Ganges, in the land of Tribalibot,
> Dwell such folk . . . (X: 236–242)

The poet tells us how such hideous malformations come about. Adam, who had given names to all beasts and plants, was well versed in the knowledge of the forces of roots. He warned his children against the lack of temperance and moderation as they approached the age of puberty. Specially did he warn them of certain herbs which upset and pervert the fruit of human kind. But, says the poet, the women were just women and could not control their desire and therefore, to the woe of Adam, are human beings thus fashioned. The charming figure of Malkreatur is thus also presented to us by the poet for the purpose of self-knowledge. We learn that the Queen Sekundille had presented Kondrie and Malkreatur to Amfortas and that Amfortas again sent Malkreatur to his beloved Orgeluse. The poet calls Malkreatur the Son of Stars and of roots. The poor creature rode a wretched mare that was lame on all fours. Even Dame Jeschute rode a better steed. Malkreatur now insultingly warns Gawain against further adventures. He will be thrashed as a common servant. Gawain, becoming furious, seized the hideous dwarf and thereby was deeply cut by his sharp hogs-bristles. He threw him from his horse, so that the horse ran away and then, somewhat disconcerted, he observed his bleeding hand. Orgeluse laughed heartily and expressed her gratification at this quarrel. Then they came to the place where the wounded knight was. Gawain had picked a root for healing the knight and it may be supposed that Malkreatur, who is named a Son of the stars and roots, is in some way connected with this plucking of the root. Also the story of Adam who knew the force of roots and warned his female posterity of certain herbs must in some way be connected. However this may be, Gawain bound the roots on the knight's wounds. The wounded knight warns him once again of Orgeluse. Gawain however says that he will gladly help the wounded knight to reach a hospital of which he had spoken. The knight thereupon requests him to lift him and his lady on to a horse which is standing ready. And now, while Gawain lifts the lady onto the horse, the wounded knight, who was only feigning, sprang with one bound onto Gawain's horse and rode off. Orgeluse laughed and continued to inflict on Gawain what he had already suffered at the hands of Obie. She had called him a merchant, a trader. Now Orgeluse says:

> 'First wert thou a *knight*, then, in short space, I thee for a *leech* must take,
> Now art thou become my *footman*! yet thou shouldst in no wise despair,
> Such skill sure should bring thee comfort! Wouldst thou still in my favours share?' (X: 326–328)

Gawain however avoids a mistake and answers, 'Yes.' Then the wounded knight turns round and makes himself known to Gawain at Urian. Now Gawain remembers how in Arthur's Court he saved Urian's life and obtained for him the milder punishment of eating from the same trough as the dogs. Urian answers with a moral proverb of Castle Merveil!

> 'Who saveth the life of another, that other shall have for foe'
> And I do as a wise man doeth—'Tis better a child should weep
> Then a full-grown man, and bearded,—this charger mine hand shall keep!' (X: 356–358)

And now he rides away on Gawain's Grail horse, Gringuljet. For Gawain, there only remains the limping horse of Malkreatur. The squire, however, had slunk behind and Gawain could hear that Orgeluse addressed him in Arabic. The horse actually belonged to a poor knight from whom Malkreatur had taken it. Gawain now had to be content with it and to accept the scorn of Orgeluse. Gawain was much too heavy for the horse to carry so he laid his shield and spear on the horse and had to lead it by the bridle. Orgeluse renews again the scoffing of Obie.

> Then his shield on the mare he fastened, and she spake, 'In such guise wouldst go,
> And carry thy wares thro' my kingdom? A strange lot is mine, I ween,
> Since *footman*, and *leech*, and *merchant* in turn hath my comrade been!
> Of the toll hadst thou best beware thee, or else, as thou goest thy way,
> It may chance they who take the toll here on thy merchandise hands may lay!' (X: 454–458)

Gawain however bore all scorn quietly. It is all brought about by Cupid and Amor and Venus. The poet here interpolates a little song concerning the tyranny of love. He says he would gladly free Gawain but can do nothing. Gawain must just endure this penance. The lady rode, he walked on foot. Finally they came to a wood and to a boulder. Gawain mounting this, carefully set himself on the limping horse, for he dared not venture to spring on its back. Then they came to the castle from whose windows four hundred ladies looked down. And here Gawain encountered a Knight, Lischois Giwellius. Upon this Orgeluse says: I have warned you from the beginning that you will only experience dishonour here: I have sworn it and shall remain true to it. Guard yourself while you can. A ferryman now came and took the Duchess into his boat. Gawain however he would not take as the Duchess refused to have him. On this Gawain was very sad, but Orgeluse said: If you conquer Lischoise Giwellius you will see me again. But it is useless to trust to that! Then the conflict began and Gawain was victor. For a moment he considered whether he should slay the knight who lay on the ground, but he relinquished the idea and decided to grant him his life, although the vanquished warrior would give him no security. Then it occurred to Gawain to compensate himself for the conflict by seizing the knight's horse and so he sprang on it. But oh! wonder—no sooner was he seated thereon than he recognised it to be his own horse, Gringuljet, of which Urian had robbed him. And herewith the poet sets us a riddle, for obviously Lischois Giwellius must by some means have come into possession of this horse. How this has happened remains at first an open question. Now they both fight again. Once more Gawain is victor and once more the temptation presents itself to kill the one vanquished. He spares him however on the following consideration. He says to himself: If I now kill this hero who fights at the command of Orgeluse I shall certainly lose her love.

To please her I will spare him. So they make peace. They sit far apart. Then the ferryman came bearing a yearling falcon and said: It is the custom here that the horse of the vanquished warrior shall belong to me. But Gawain was angry and said: Am I a merchant that I should pay you toll? But the ferryman said he must receive his rights.[100] In true knightly joust has Gawain won for him, the boatman, this charger. We see that Gawain is in a sorry plight, for it is his own horse that he must give up although he is the victor. For the knight whom he had conquered was seated on Gawain's horse. Then the ferryman spoke these strange words:

> Your hand has o'erthrown him to whom until this day with truth
> The world ascribed the highest prize . . .
> [This is a more exact translation than J. Weston's at X: 679–680]

These are words that can apply only to Parzival. For since Parzival caused Kunneware to laugh he is the Knight to whom the highest prize is accorded. Has Gawain overcome Parzival? That Lischois Giwellius is a different person from Parzival is clear from Book XIV: 833, where Lischois Giwellius marries Gawain's sister and Parzival is present. Yet it appears nevertheless in the present passage as if Parzival is hidden behind the mask of Lischois Giwellius. If this is so then we can understand the joy of the ferryman when Gawain proposes that instead of the charger he shall retain the Knight.

> Then joyful I ween was the boatman, and with smiling lips he spake,
> 'Now methinks that a gift so costly it hath ne'er been my lot to take,
> And I deem myself all unworthy—Yet, Sir Knight, be he mine indeed,
> Then the guerdon is more than I asked for and o'er my deserts my
>   meed.   (X: 699–702)

The ferryman still further gives expression to his great delight but demands that Gawain shall convey the Knight across and bring him into his house. And this happens. Gawain answers:

> . . . 'Yea this will I do, and more,
> To thy boat first, and then from out it will I lead him within thy door,
> And there will I lead him captive' . . .   (X: 707–709)

The ferryman then says, 'Tonight you shall be my guest.' Just as Parzival meets the fisher so Gawain meets the ferryman. As Parzival spent the night with the fisher up in the castle, so Gawain, in the realm of the Castle Merveil spends it with the ferryman. Here we shall interpolate a few explanatory remarks. From much that Rudolf Steiner has said we know well the extraordinary significance of Goethe's fairy tale of the Green Snake and the Beautiful Lily. There too appears a ferryman to whom all toll must be paid and there too a river has to be crossed. What Goethe then describes is part of an adventure of Castle Merveil. We find the same scenery in Dante's *Paradiso*. Dante too comes to a stream and sees on the further side the procession of the Hierarchies. Dante calls this region the Earthly Paradise. Goethe knew quite exactly the experiences of this region, and in many respects had to take Gawain's Path. It is not so much Parzival as Gawain who has the same kind of experiences as Goethe. From this standpoint much in Goethe's life can be understood. Thus perhaps this parenthesis is justified.

So Gawain stays with the ferryman but suffers sorely the pangs of love. It is Orgeluse he means when he cries out:

Alas! I had found a treasure, yet but loss hath it brought to me.
(X: 720)

Thus he cries out in the region of the ferryman.[101] The Boatman hears it and comforts him by saying that he is in Klingsor's land where one is 'sad today, tomorrow joyful'.

But now the sun is setting and it is time they went back home.
Then Lischois he was led by Gawain, and never a word he spake,
And the boatman he followed after and the steed by its rein did
    take. (X: 735–736)

Gawain spends the night with the ferryman. The ferryman's son looks after the horse. He also brings the beds. The ferryman's daughter Bene takes the greatest possible care for Gawain's comfort. She brings him three larks as food. Not very satisfying! Especially when the maiden requests him to leave one for her mother. Purslane and lettuce in vinegar presented by the hand of one of the ferryman's sons completes the sparse meal. After having eaten, the ferryman leaves Gawain but sends his daughter back to him.

Men say that alone with Sir Gawain the maiden her watch did keep,
And I think if he more had prayed her she never had said him Nay—
Then he slept, for he well might slumber, God keep him till dawn of
    day! (X: 804–806)

Adventure XI

In the *Eleventh* Adventure it is related that in the morning Gawain arose from his bed and passing through an open door found himself in a beautiful orchard where birds were singing. From here he could observe the Castle wherein dwelt the four hundred ladies. They were already up. But he thought it was too early and he would go back again to rest—perhaps, he thought, the ladies would then also retire again. So once more he returned to bed and the maiden's mantle served him as coverlet.

He quickly slipped beneath it and did not notice that the daughter of his host entered the room and was waiting there patiently till he should awaken. As he opened his eyes and thanked her for being there on his account, she assured him that they were all most heartily grateful to him. And then in conversation he asked her who the ladies in the Castle were. At this she shrank back in terror and said that although she knew she dared not tell him. And she begged him to not renew the question. We see that here the conditions of the Grail Castle are reversed. There it is expected that Parzival shall ask, here in Castle Merveil Gawain's questions are taken ill.

> But Gawain he would ever ask her, and ever an answer pray,
> What ladies were they who sat there, and looked from that stately hall?
> And the maiden she wept full sorely, and aloud in her grief did
>   call. (XI: 40-42)

Attracted by the noise her father entered. He found his daughter sitting on the knight's bed, but was not angry, neither did he further enquire what had passed between them. The poet adds that whatever might have occurred the father would not have taken amiss. So it was at Castle Merveil.

> ... Then her father he mildly spake,
> 'Now weep not so sore, my daughter, for if one a jest doth make
> Whereof thou at first art wrathful, yet I ween ere the time be long,
> Shall thy sorrow be changed to gladness, and thy wailing to joyful
>   song!' (XI: 47-50)

But Gawain says that nothing has occurred of which he cannot speak quite openly. He had only pressed the maiden with questions which seemed to terrify her. But Gawain was still desirous of the answer. He enquires concerning the fate of the ladies. Then the ferryman says, 'By God don't question me as to their fate, for the most terrible distress prevails there and if you feel sympathy for these ladies and do not cease from questioning, you will begin to desire to fight for them and this will bring you into deadly danger and will bring us extraordinary suffering.' Gawain however insists on the answer. So the ferryman says, 'Since you will not cease to question I will lend you a fair shield with which you must be armed for you are here in "Terre Merveil" and here stands the "Lit Merveil". No one yet has been able to endure the adventure concerning which you ask.' Gawain says he does not fear this adventure, only he asks the ferryman what it involves. The ferryman says, 'If you are able to endure the fight then you will be lord of this land and you will deliver the ladies who are imprisoned here by magic and also many noble Knights.' Then he says, 'Your prize is great, for you have conquered Lischois Giwellius. He is so brave that no one can be compared with him except Ither of Gahevies.' And now the ferryman says something most remarkable which is of extraordinary importance:

He who at Nantes slew Prince Ither my ship bare but yesterday,
Five steeds hath he given unto me (God keep him in peace alway)
(XI: 107–108)

Thus the ferryman says that only yesterday he carried Parzival across the water and received from him five steeds. Parzival then must have conquered five knights and must likewise be in Castle Merveil. We hear more precisely of this further on (XII: 548). Parzival had conquered five knights and given their horses to the ferryman, and Orgeluse, who saw this, had ridden after Parzival and offered him her love.

Parzival however had refused it. Thus we see that Parzival and Gawain go through a similar adventure. In Gawain's case, however, tortured with the pains of love, there is no coming to meet him on the part of Orgeluse. To Parzival on the contrary Orgeluse offers herself but he will not have her. The poet tells us expressly that Parzival has been led here in his quest for the Grail. When Gawain has heard the story he asks if Parzival was informed how matters stood with these ladies. The ferryman answers that he was not. Now it is clear that Orgeluse must have had the encounter with Parzival before the ferryman took her across the water—up to that time however Gawain was constantly by her side—thus in the story there is no room for this encounter with Parzival. There remains nothing therefore but to look upon this encounter as woven in a concealed way into the story. And this is what we have attempted in suggesting that Parzival is hidden behind the figure Lischois Giwellius. It is remarkable too how suddenly the poet passes from Lischois Giwellius to Ither and to Parzival in XI: 100–106. The five horses still remain a problem. But we know that something must have happened, for suddenly, and for us quite inexplicably, Lischois Giwellius is riding Gawain's horse of which Urian had robbed him. Therefore a fight must have taken place between Lischois Giwellius (Parzival) and five knights, of whom one was Urian. Who the other four are we are not told. If this explanation is the right one we might ask: why does the poet hide such a simple event so mysteriously? The reason is quite obvious. The adventures of Parzival in the region of Castle Merveil are regarded as hidden. Only those of Gawain are openly described. I will try to explain why this must be so.

Man lives in his head principally as the man of knowledge. But the activity of thought is mysteriously interpenetrated with will activity. In his limbs or lower organisation man lives principally in his will yet in the limb- and metabolic-system there works in a hidden way—though of course unconsciously—knowledge. In the Biblical expression, 'Adam knew his wife', the genius of language, as Dr Steiner once said, brings something of this mystery to expression. For the poet, Parzival is one who seeks the spiritual world along the path to knowledge. Gawain, on the contrary, seeks the way into the spiritual world out of the forces of the heart which are closely related to the will. Here the knowledge-forces only vibrate *in sympathy* and are more difficult to observe. Therefore in the region of Castle Merveil, Parzival must step into the background. Even if one is not prepared to accept that the poet conceals Parzival in Lischois Giwellius, yet what is essential in this suggestion remains as a fact, viz. that Parzival in a mysterious way takes part in the adventures of Gawain.

Now as Gawain arms himself the ferryman offers him counsel and advises that he should leave his steed with the merchant at the door. We have already seen how again and again Gawain is described as a trader or merchant. It was a slander and yet there was a certain grain of truth in it, for through the conquest of Castle Merveil it is just the wares of the merchant that become Gawain's possession as we shall see later. Amongst these were some very costly treasures which we shall hear of later in detail. Then Gawain is instructed by his host that the Lit Merveil is a bed that runs on four rollers. On this bed he will experience the most terrible adventures. But he gives him the good advice never to let shield or sword go out of his hands.

As the ferryman had said, so it came to pass. He dismounts from his horse. He finds the merchant and examines his wares. He allows him to show him clasps and girdles, and he sees what otherwise no man had seen, for only ladies had been here for a very long time. Usually only women looked at what he is now looking at. The merchant tells him: All this will belong to you if you conquer. Trust God! Did Plippalinot the ferryman direct you here? Just as Parzival was asked whether the Fisher had directed him to the Castle, so here the merchant asks about the ferryman. Gawain now enters the interior of the Castle on foot. The roof was gaily coloured like peacocks' feathers and glimmered in all hues. The interior of the Castle was richly decked. The mullioned windows supported high arches. Within there stood a great number of couches, while carpets covered the walls. But Gawain saw nothing of the ladies. Finally he came to a large room the floor of which was as slippery as glass, and in this stood the Lit Merveil. It ran on four wheels that were made of rubies, and the ground in accordance with the advice of Klingsor was inlaid with sardis, jasper and chrysolite. The peculiarity of the bed was that as soon as a person was seated upon it, it started into motion. Tempestuously it rushed along striking violently against each of the four walls. This was the test which Gawain had to endure here.

Everyone who enters the region of Castle Merveil learns to know this Lit Merveil. It is an imaginative picture for a mystery of human nature. Whoever enters the world which is indicated here must first leave his ordinary power of forming ideas, his world of memory, behind him at the door. He must leave this at the merchant's shop which he will only have rightly made his own after having endured the adventures. The mental images of the ordinary consciousness present themselves separately as static pictures. They are not in movement. They present themselves to the consciousness as mental pictures and one beholds them in peace. But if a man inwardly enters upon the realm of Castle Merveil he has penetrated into the moving world of life-processes which is otherwise withdrawn from intellectual consciousness, so that he now no longer has pictures *before* him, but *is himself picture* in a world of pictures, as in dreaming. But these pictures are in motion and it is not the man himself who calls forth this motion, rather it is the case that the pictures have their own motion. In ordinary consciousness this world pours in everywhere but we are protected from knowing it in its full content. A simple experiment can show us this world. If we look at the sun and then shut our eyes, we have within the closed eye a complementary picture of the sun before us. But we cannot hold this picture fast, it starts at once into motion, it changes its colour and also its place. That which changes this picture and drives it to a different place in the field of perceptive consciousness, that is the region where the soul-processes cross the life processes. The sun formed the eye. In experiencing the complementary colour we observe half dreamingly the growth processes of the organism.[102] This experience which everyone has can be extended. The totality of the whole upbuilding process of growth can enter man's consciousness in moving pictures. He can in this way perceive the peristaltic movement of his intestines, he can behold the blood formation, or how the lymph is prepared, or the process of reproduction. Then he is within Castle Merveil. If he learns to know this he understands why it is always said that it needs much courage to lie on the moving bed of Lit Merveil. Man is of course protected from realising anything of this organic process. If it does press into his consciousness then there arises in him the urge to regulate it from his consciousness. But no sooner does he attempt to do so than he discovers that he is by no means wise enough to interfere in this process. The difficulties relating to this are shown immediately after in the picture-form of a fight with a lion. If a man mounts the Lit Merveil, he learns to know something of human nature. He does not of course experience the moving picture-world localised in the lower organism, far more does he experience it raised above his head; he finds that the life processes of the lower man are reflected above the head. If this inner experience is studied more closely, the discovery is gradually made that what is experienced above the head as a reflection of the lower metabolic activity is the thought world of man. Herein of course there exists a mystery of human nature. It is not the peaceful, but the life-filled thought-world, the world of imagination that has been entered, and we discover that it requires a long inner path of schooling if the mastery over the leadership of thought in this living world is not to be lost. Goethe passed through this experience. In his fairy tale of the Green Snake and Beautiful Lily he describes the passage over the water. He also knows the experience of the lifting of the lower man above the head. The wife of the old man with the lamp carries a basket on her head. What is dead within it she does not find heavy, but what is living is heavy almost beyond bearing. If the experience is familiar one knows this to be a correct description. And because Goethe knew it he was able to grasp the idea of the

24. 'Riding on the Lion'
    Stone sculpture from Andlau Church, Alsace

25. The Eleventh Key from the Twelve Keys of Basil Valentinus
    This represents the augmentation or multiplication of the Philosopher's Stone; through the attainment by the soul of ever higher stages of unselfishness it produces essential matter out of itself as the sun does to the planets which belong to it, or the lion to its cubs. Every piece of substance thus produced becomes an organ of perception for a sphere of the macrocosm. The soul-substance of man becomes the higher self which has subdued the lower forces by means of development. (See Rudolf Steiner, Cycle XXVII, lecture 10.)

archetypal plant. It is a mobile idea and he who wishes to think it out must endure the mobility of the Lit Merveil. On the path to this mobile thinking, however, a man passes through many trials. They will be exactly described and we will enter into them point by point.[103] The poet describes what a deafening noise and uproar is caused as the bed, in rushing round, bangs against the walls. Like thunder or a great number of trumpets played together in a hall. Gawain commends himself to God and covers himself with the ferryman's shield. Now the bed stands still and the uproar ceases. For the understanding of this it is important to nôte that Gawain only has a weapon of *defence* which he uses in this situation, viz. the shield, and through what he accomplishes—i.e. through following this process out to the end—that which was previously in motion comes to a standstill. The trials are however by no means over; they only suffer metamorphosis. Immensely heavy stones are hurled at him, likewise numberless arrows. Over his whole body he feels bruised and cut. To crown all there now enters through the door a mighty peasant who was clothed all over with fish skin, his cap also was of the same and his cloak. This is a figure which we know well from Babylonian representations. This giant carries an immense club. He assures Gawain that what he has to fear will not come from his side but from another quarter. Upon this Gawain quickly lays hold of his sword and with it breaks the shafts of the arrows which have stuck fast in his shield, and now he hears the mighty roar of a gigantic lion which comes bounding in and with savage fierceness springs upon him. Its talons pierce Gawain's shield. Gawain hacks off one of its legs so that it springs about on three. It comes close enough for him to feel its breath. He finally succeeds in killing the lion but he himself is left in a swoon. We shall understand this description if we regard it as a continuation of what was previously explained. In entering the spiritual world what is first of all experienced is a peculiar kind of reflection. It is as if one were seated at the central point of a reflecting globe. What proceeds from a man as feelings and thoughts he does not experience as going forth from himself but as crashing down upon him. It is again nothing else that is here described than an act of self-knowledge. Gawain must recognise how clumsy his thoughts and how harmful his feelings still are. The thoughts appear to him as heavy millstones, his feelings as sharp arrows. The experience of this process of reflection may, however, be accompanied by a secondary physiological process. (This properly should not occur but it does usually occur at the beginning.) If the process is accomplished normally then all remains purely as imagination, but if it is accompanied by the slightest feeling of fear then the imaginative process becomes half physiological and the bodily rhythms fall into disorder. The rhythm of breathing and of the heart are disturbed. And this is described quite in accordance with facts by those who represented it in the Middle ages as the 'Meeting with the Lion'. The Bible also knows this experience and describes it in the picture of Samson. In all alchemistic representations this experience emerges in some kind of picture-form. This test is effectually endured if the lion is not in any way fought but if with one swing its back can be mounted.[104] Basil Valentine describes this proper way of experiencing the test in his *Twelve Keys*. There we find the rider of the lion who holds a heart in his hand. Similar representations are to be found on many Rosicrucian figures. Dr Steiner also indicated that this is the true way of absolving this experience. Through his explanation the representations of the Middle Ages first become comprehensible. To swing oneself onto the lion's back means: to confess that one has far too little wisdom to dare to interfere with the wonderful course of the breathing and blood activity, and to commend oneself to God for all that may happen. If this can be successfully accomplished then the trial of courage has been endured and the lion tamed. Gawain does not fully stand the test. He kills the lion, i.e. the heart stands still, the whole bodily activity is lowered, the Lit Merveil stands still. Gawain falls in a swoon and is more dead than alive. Had the inhabitants of Castle Merveil, the imprisoned Queens, not come to his aid he would have died. The wise Arnive, the wife of Uther Pendragon and mother of Arthur, hastens to Gawain's help. She first sends two maidens to see if Gawain still lives. One of them unfastens his helmet and lifts it from his head.

> And she saw a light foam gathered upon his lips so red,
> And she waited a space and hearkened, if perchance she might hear his breath,
> For but now had she thought him living, yet she deemed it might well be death.
> And his overdress was of sable and the mystic beasts[105] it bore . . .
> (XI: 366–369)

His sable the maiden quickly tears off and holds before his nose to see if he still breathes. She finds that he does. Water is fetched and the maiden, placing her ring between his teeth, succeeds in getting him to swallow a little. So he gradually comes to himself. And then he finds that the trials are over; he has endured them sufficiently. What is still lacking he will have to supplement by the adventures that have yet to be described. The fact that Gawain lacks the courage to stand the test completely is due to his not yet having silenced his passionate nature. Parzival had done this, therefore a similar experience in Parzival's case is not described. Because he did not desire Orgeluse, but on the contrary she offered herself to him and he refused her, Parzival experiences no difficulty from the lion. Strong of heart and lion-like in courage as he is, he only takes part in the adventures of Gawain which follow, not, however, in the battle with the lion. Parzival does not suffer from the illusion that what proceeds from the self and in the mirrored reflection is seen approaching, is something *foreign*. Through the wonderful way in which he is led he has acquired the faculty of recognising his own being in its reflection. His path always allows him at once to make good the evil he has done. Gawain, as we have said, does not fully endure the

MONS PHILOSOPHORUM.

The soul of men everywhere was lost through a fall, and the health of the body suffered through a fall. Salvation came to the human soul through IEHOVA, Jesus Christ. The bodily health is brought back through a thing not good to look at. It is hidden in this painting, the highest treasure in this world, in which is the highest medicine and the greatest parts of the riches of nature, given to us by the Lord IEHOVA. It is called *Pator Metallorum*, well known to the philosopher sitting in front of the mountain-cave, easy to obtain for anybody. But the sophists in their sophistic garb, tapping on the walls, recognise him not. At the right is to be seen *Lepus*, representing the art of chemistry, marvellously white, the secrets of which with fire's heat are being explored. To the left one can see freely what the right *Claris artis* is; one cannot be too subtle with it, like a hen hatching a chicken. In the midst of the mountain, before the door stands a courageous Lion in all its pride, whose noble blood the monster-dragon is going to shed; throwing him into a deep grave, out of it comes forth a black raven, then called *Ianua artis*, out of that comes *Aquila alba*. Even the crystal refined in the furnace will quickly show you on inspection *Serrum fugitirum*, a wonder-child to many artists. The one effecting this all is *Principium laboris*. On the right hand in the barrel are *Sol* and *Luna*, the intelligence of the firmament. The Senior plants in it *Rad. Rubeam and albam*. Now you proceed with constancy and *Arbor artis* appears to you, with its blossoms it announces now *Lapidem Philosophorum*. Over all, the crown of the glory, ruling over all treasures.

Be diligent, peaceful, constant and pious, pray that God may help thee. And if thou attain, never forget the poor. Then thou wilt praise God with the legion of the angels, now and forever.

26. The Rosicrucian-Alchemical Path of Knowledge
    (*Translation from Paul M. Allen, 'A Christian Rosenkreutz Anthology', Rudolf Steiner Publications, New York*)

27. The Rosicrucian-Alchemical Path of Knowledge

trial, hence his deplorable condition after the event. The particular healing he needs is brought about by a wonderful root which the queen places within his mouth.

> Then a root 'twixt his lips she laid there and straightway he fell asleep. (XI: 441)

This root, which in fairy tales is always called the root of life and which is brought by the hare (the imaginative picture of alchemy),[106] is nothing else than man's breath. The breath which enters the mouth and penetrates the windpipe and becomes separated in the lobes of the lungs appears for the imaginative consciousness as the root which the hare Alchemy puts in man's mouth. As soon as this is in the mouth the life processes start again in the body, i.e. the breathing and blood circulation are changed in sleep. Therefore Gawain sleeps as soon as he has the root in his mouth; he wakes as soon as it is taken out again.

> ... The knight slept till even gray,
> Then Arnive the Queen in her wisdom drew the root from his lips away.
> And straightway he woke ... (XI: 451–453)

In fairy tales it often happens, in regard to what has been described here, that a knight is beheaded, has his head stuck on again and that it grows on again through the power of the root. All this is only the imaginative expression for the fact that the digestive process during sleep penetrates into the head while in waking life it only takes place in the rest of the organism. Thus the waking man beheaded, in sleep has his head restored. Numbers of fairy tales or myths will only be understood when we see in them pictures of the organic processes in man which take place in different conditions of consciousness.

Thus in this eleventh chapter, in the adventures of Gawain at Castle Merveil, we have an important piece of Alchemy of the Middle Ages.

Adventure XII

In the twelfth Adventure the poet tells us of hard tests through which Gawain now has to pass. He brings forward examples from the poetry of Knighthood, in order to illustrate from these that the trial through which Gawain must now pass may be regarded as the sum total of these adventures crowded into one. He refers to the adventure[107] which Lancelot endured when standing on the sword bridge, when he fought against Meljakanz. He also quoted Garel, a knight of the Round Table, whose adventure was described later in a poem by Pleier; this adventure is not to be compared with Gawain's. Wolfram tells us how this Garel overthrew a lion in front of the palace of Nantes thus alluding again to a lion fight in connection with the knight Garel. Further, Garel too, used his knife against the lion and had to pay for this deed in a marble pillar.[108] And then, Wolfram quotes an adventure from Hartmann von Aue's 'Ywain'. It is there related how Iwain came to a spring by the side of which lay a great stone. If water were poured over this stone then a mighty tempest arose. As soon as this had exhausted itself, the Lord of the Spring appeared and claimed vengeance. Iwain overcame him and thus withstood the adventure. As Gawain shortly afterwards also comes to a pillar, we may conclude that the meeting with this pillar and the way the accompanying adventure takes place is to be regarded as the continuation of the imperfectly endured fight with the lion. Gawain's relationship with Orgeluse is one of the reasons why he could not fully endure the trial. For this reason the poet reminds us now of Gawain's love and the suffering it is preparing for him. At this point too Wolfram reminds us that Ither also wore Frau Minne's badge. The whole race of Gawain including Ither had faithfully served Frau Minne, and had often been brought under her yoke. Also a sister of Gawain, Sürdamour, the beloved of Alexander the Great, suffered the greatest anguish through love for Alexander. Therefore, says the poet, Frau Minne should now set Gawain free.

Be mighty towards the mighty but here let Gawain go free,
His wounds they so sorely pain him, and the hale should they foemen
   be!   XII: 65–66)

The poet thinks it terrible that Gawain, after having endured so hard an adventure, should now have to be subjected to the billows and tempests of love's passion. We are reminded here of the adventure of Iwain which we have just heard and in which we were told that Iwain had to fight with the Lord of the Spring whose coming is indicated by a great tempest. We are familiar with this Saga in other connections. It is related by Grimmelshausen in *Simplicius Simplicissimus*. This story is also a presentation of the Parzival figure. Simplicius Simplicissimus is the pure fool. The hermit is Trevrezent, the daughter of the Colonel is Kondwiramur. The story here is certainly very decadent in that the Grail appears as a pig's head on a dish and the Grail meal as an officer's mess. But here too it is told that Simplicius Simplicissimus threw stones in Lake Mummel in order to find out whether it was true that it would cause a great tempest. He then descends into a kind of underworld and goes through many adventures. I only mention the story here to show that the tempests thus described are to be understood as the rousing of the Elements caused by human wilfulness.[109] That is what the poet refers to in the lines just quoted.

    Gawain's next adventures are thus entirely due to the fact that his soul-life is not sufficiently purified.

> Quoth the hero, 'Alas, for restless my resting-place shall be,
> One couch did so sorely wound me, and the other hath brought to me
> Sore torment of love and longing! . . .   (XII: 71–73)

The poet tells us that Gawain tossed and turned so that he tore the bandages from his wounds. This means that unpurified desire renewed the wounds caused by his fight with the lion. When the day dawned he was covered with blood. Fortunately he found new clothes laid ready and clothed himself in these. Let us hope that he put on at the same time a new man. At all events, he was for a moment set free from his torments and could now observe the wonders of Chateau Merveil. He found a spacious magnificent chamber. Mounting a staircase he came to a beautiful dome, and here he found a wonderful pillar—Klingsor had had it brought from the country of Feirefis. The window of the dome was adorned with precious stones, diamonds, amethysts, topaz, garnet, chrysolite, ruby, emerald and sardius. The pillar which stood in the middle was a most wondrous pillar. By looking into it one could see reflected all that was going on in one's surroundings:[110]

> And he saw there a greater wonder, and the sight never vexed his eye,
> For he thought him upon the column all the lands of the earth did lie.
> And he saw the countries circle, and the mighty mountains' crest
> Meet, e'en as two hosts in battle, as one vision the other pressed.
> And folk did he see in the pillar, and on horse or afoot they went,
> They ran, and they stood: in a window he sat him on seeing bent.
>   (XII: 113–118)

The pillar is that which in the region of Chateau Merveil corresponds to the Grail. The Grail is hidden and hard to find. It is approached from the circumference and only reached after a journey of sixty miles through the forest.[111] The magic pillar of Chateau Merveil on the contrary is to be found at a place which cannot be left without more ado if a man has once betaken himself to it. Here are imprisoned the four hundred ladies and the four queens. But on gazing into the pillar it is just the surroundings that are revealed.

The poet tells us that this Magic Pillar would be large enough to have provided ample place for the coffin of Camilla. Camilla appears in the Aeneid. She is the daughter of Metabus and Casmilla and is from the Saturn-founded city of Piperno. She helped to conquer the Trojans and fell in battle when Arruns, supported by Apollo of Soracte, attacked her. She is however avenged by Diana to whom she was dedicated as a child. In the eleventh adventure, line 29, the poet has already mentioned her and compared Orgeluse with her. This pillar was meant to bear the coffin of Camilla, i.e. of Orgeluse, for she appears here in the place of Camilla. In these explanations by the poet I see a hint that Gawain should have buried his passion before he came to this pillar. He had not done so and at once sees Orgeluse in the pillar and a knight in attendance on her, with whom he must fight; yet both appear to him on the further side of the river. But first the four queens approached him. The aged Arnive, mother of Arthur, comes with her daughter Sangive and her two young granddaughters, Itonje and Kondrie. Itonje and Kondrie are Gawain's sisters. The aged Arnive reproaches Gawain that he, while still so weak, should have come thither. Gawain however thanks her, calls her Mistress and says her art has sufficiently restored his strength. And now Gawain asks the Mistress concerning this remarkable pillar. Arnive explains to Gawain that the pillar sheds its light for six miles round (compare the sixty mile wood around the Grail with the six miles here) so that everything can be seen which happens within a radius of six miles. This pillar really belonged to the Queen Sekundille and Klingsor had stolen it. Now, as already mentioned, Gawain saw a knight approaching. That he is still tormented with his love for the Duchess is apparent in the following lines:

E'en as hellebore within the nostril pierceth sharp, and a man doth sneeze,
Thro' his eye to his heart came the Duchess, and she robbed him of Joy and ease! (XII: 165-166)

Thus the pillar is a magic mirror in which there appears what is desired and which to begin with leads again to conflict. But this occurs in such a way that a man is thrown back again across the river which he had already crossed. Camilla too, as a child, was bound to a spear and shot across the river when, by invoking the aid of Diana to whom she was thenceforth dedicated, she was saved. In Goethe's fairly tale the pillar does not appear, yet in its place there is the fairy figure of the Green Snake who says to the Will o' the Wisps, 'If you are seeking the Beautiful Lily then you will have to return again over the river which you have just crossed.' The Beautiful Lily lives on the further side of the river. The river with which we are concerned here is the current of passion. If the still unpurified gold of knowledge is thrown into this stream it begins to boil and to rage. The Lord of the river, the Ferryman, appears and is angry.

Gawain must pass through fresh tests whose purpose is the purification of his passion. Only as one purified can he become united with Orgeluse, who here resembles Camilla, the priestess, Diana. The Mistress tells Gawain that he is in no fit state to endure this conflict, he is too badly wounded. Gawain however will not allow himself to be persuaded and dons his armour. He again mounts his steed Gringuljet which the merchant has kept for him. He notes with sorrow how his shield is covered with holes. This shield he had received from his host the ferryman. He now gives Gawain a spear and ferries him back again over the river. And because Gawain is once more seated on a Grail horse his strength is increased and he is able to conquer his foe the Türkowit. At once the ferryman appears and demands the horse of the conquered foe. But Orgeluse still has no word of recognition for Gawain but only asks him if he is prepared to undertake a new task. Orgeluse tells Gawain that she does not really trust him to accomplish it but that if he will undertake the new adventures then he need no longer ride in front of her but can ride by her side. And now she sets him the task of springing across a terrible ravine on his horse. This ravine is called Ligweis Prellius, the Perilous Ford. He must cross this and must there seek for the tree which King Gramoflanz guards. From this he must pluck a bough, weave it into a wreath and bring it to Orgeluse. Klingsor's Forest is the name of this region which he must traverse. When in this way Gawain has been instructed as to the nature of his adventure Orgeluse remains behind. Gawain, with a death-defying courage, springs across the ravine, comes crashing down and falls into the terrible river. He is still not in a condition to endure the test to the end. The torrent of passion has once more seized him.

Fortunately Gringuljet is a very strong swimmer and also Gawain's spear remains unbroken. So, after he has pulled himself out by clutching at the branch of a tree on the further bank, he succeeds in fishing the reins out of the flood with his spear and drawing the horse to a landing place. This water bears the name of Sabin. Thus Gawain got across successfully, found the tree, broke off a branch and won the Garland. Now this Garland was guarded by King Gramoflanz. He himself had a remarkable custom. He sought for combat with each one who broke a branch from this tree, yet he would never fight with a *single* man, this was beneath him. He must fight with at least *two or more* opponents.

> ... he fought not with *one* alone,
> *Two* or more must they be, his foemen! So high beat his gallant heart,
> That whate'er *one* might do to harm him unscathed might he thence depart. (XII: 328–330)

Gawain encountered King Gramoflanz but for his part did not harm him because the King was unarmed. Gramoflanz told him that he had by no means entirely renounced his claim to the Garland, but that he scorned to fight with one man. Gramoflanz bore on his hand a falcon, a present from Gawain's sister Itonje whom he secretly loved. His hat was of peacock's feathers and his mantle of green samite. Gramoflanz then explained to Gawain that he, Gawain, had withstood the adventure which was really intended for himself. And now Gawain realises how everything here is connected up. Gramoflanz had slain Orgeluse's first husband. He then wished to marry Orgeluse but she refused him. And after Gramoflanz has related this he says:

> ... I know that her love to thee
> She hath promised, since here I meet thee, and death wouldst thou bring to me. (XII; 359–360).

Gramoflanz tells him that he has long since renounced Orgeluse and that he, Gawain, must become conscious of what he is now being told, that he is already lord of his wonderland. But Gawain in return must help him to win the hand of Itonje, King Lot's child. He does not guess that Gawain is Itonje's brother. So he entrusts Gawain with a ring and Gawain takes it and agrees to be his messenger. Then Gawain asks him:

> Now tell me, Sir Knight, who may be he who doth conflict with me despise?
> An thou count it me not for dishonour quoth the King 'here my name be told'.
> King Irot he was my father, who was slain by King Lot of old.
> And King Gramoflanz do men call me, and my heart doth much valour know
> That never, for evil done me, will I fight with but one for foe,
> Saving one man alone, hight Gawain, of *him* have I heard such fame
> That to fight with him I am ready . . .   (XII: 386-392)

Gawain now makes himself known to him. Gramoflanz is ready to fight him that he might avenge the death of his father which Gawain's father had brought about. And so they agree on a combat to take place at Bems on the Korka. In sixteen days time they will fight. Upon this they take leave of one another and this time Gawain succeeds with one clear bound of Gringuljet's in reaching Orgeluse's side again without a fall. He hands over to Orgeluse the garland he has won, whereupon she weeps and tells him about her lost husband Cidegast. Now it is particularly important to note the words she uses here.

> . . . his honour aloft he bore
> That none who spake word of treason might reach to it evermore.
> From the root in a true heart planted it waxed and it spread amain,
> Till he rose o'er all men as Saturn doth high o'er the planets reign.   (XII: 467-470)

Thus she compares Cidegast with Saturn. Then she says he was as true as the unicorn that sacrified itself for the purity of the virgin. And now suddenly in Orgeluse the transformation takes place. Gawain has stood the test. He has taken the place of Cidegast-Saturn. His worth has raised him to the outermost planet. As Parzival rode into the Grail Castle with the forces of Saturn so Gawain becomes lord of Chateau Merveil with the force of Saturn. The passion in him is conquered. The death-bringing Saturn has now laid this passion in its tomb.[112] Orgeluse acknowledged this in the following words:

> As gold that is tried in the furnace shineth forth from the flame anew,
> So, methinks, doth it shine, thy courage . . .   (XII: 482-483)

Orgeluse now completely changes her behaviour towards him. He lifts her onto the horse and she is now glad to accompany him. But there is still something she must tell him before she can belong to him entirely. He has heard of Cidegast's love, but another too has won her love, Amfortas. The latter had given her the tent which held the treasures of Tabronit, as love-pledge. First she had endured the death of Cidegast. Cidegast was pure but he could not live. Then Amfortas was wounded so that he too was unable to avenge her. And now she tells him of the magic power of Klingsor, who had planned all the adventures that Gawain had had to endure and with him she had made a pact:

> He that should brave the venture,[112a] and he that should win the prize,
> To *him* I my love should offer; but if so be that in his eyes
> My love were a thing unworthy, the booth should be mine again.
> But now hast thou done my bidding, and in falleth unto us twain,
> And 'twas sworn in the ears of many ...   (XII: 531–535)

We shall presently learn that Parzival, too, had won the garland from Gramoflanz. Therefore Orgeluse had also to belong to Parzival, but he, as we know, had refused her. Thus the tent belonged to her and therefore she can share it with Gawain. We see Gawain, arrived at the end of his journey, at length receiving all through Parzival's renunciation.

Orgeluse now relates how Klingsor's knights by turns both day and night keep guard over this region. Only once did a Knight appear who excelled Klingsor's Knights, and that was Parzival. To him she had offered her love but he had refused it. This too Gawain now learns. Then he asks Orgeluse to keep silent concerning his name and he then rides with her to the Castle. Klingsor's men now greet Gawain as their new lord. Plippalinot too, the ferryman and his daughter greet him. Orgeluse enquiries after the knight whom Gawain had conquered—Lischois Giwellius. The ferryman says he lives and he is prepared to set him free if he receives in his stead a present from the booth sent by Queen Sekundille. The gift he desires is the 'swallow' which is really a harp. Orgeluse then asks Gawain to set free the conquered Türkowit and to exchange Lischois Giwellius for the harp. This is done. Thus ends the chapter in which it is only further related that messengers are sent to Arthur to invite him and all his company to be present at the combat which is about to take place between Gawain and Gramoflanz, so that Lischois Giwellius, i.e. according to our interpretation, Parzival, should be set free. But Parzival is now free of Gawain's spell, for the booth which Gawain has acquired through winning Gramoflanz's crown and through all his other adventures belongs to Parzival also. For, as we shall hear later, the latter makes his appearance, although no mention is made of an encounter with Gramoflanz, decked with his crown. The swallow for which he is exchanged therefore belongs as much to him as to Gawain.

But yet another interpretation suggests itself. Gramoflanz usually only fights with two opponents. Why? Because behind Gawain stands a second, Parzival. That this interpretation is justified, the continuation of the narrative shows.

Adventure XIII

In the thirteenth adventure the poet tells us that Gawain still remains unrecognised at Chateau Merveil. A theme that we meet in the Lohengrin Saga appears also here in the lines:

And she spake not, nor might Arnive learn aught of his name and race. (XIII: 10)

Gawain has sent a message to Arthur inviting him to be present with his knight at his duel with Gramoflanz. He will then have the great satisfaction of leading Arthur again to the mother whom he thought he had lost. Arnive is very curious to know where Gawain has sent the squire, but she is not told this any more than Gawain's name and race. Gawain now sends for the imprisoned knight Lischois Giwellius and *this* Lischois Giwellius is clearly no Parzival, but the real knight Lischois Giwellius, behind whom, as we have explained, Parzival for a while was possibly concealed. Reference has been made to this question in a previous adventure. Gawain now explains to the Türkowit as well as to Lischois that they are henceforth free and released from imprisonment. We are now told that the Türkowit, Lischois and Gawain all wear garments made of a remarkable material. A master named Sarant, after whom the town Sares is called, who hails from Triande, discovered this material. But it is not only called after this Master, but also after the town Thasme in Sekundille's country. This material then, bears the name Sarant-Thasme. Presumably the poet wishes to emphasise the fact that Gawain, as lord of Castle Merveil, now comes into contact with many kinds of Eastern sorcery. After Gawain has set free Lischois and the Türkowit, he seeks out the four queens. First he enquires for Itonje. Softly he asks of Bene the ferryman's daughter which of the four is Itonje. And he receives from her the wished for answer. Bene knew why Gawain asked. So Gawain sat down beside the maiden and asked her if she had never won any man's love. She replies that she has not and says that she has never had more conversation with a knight than she is now having with Gawain. But she does not know who Gawain is and what is his name. Had she known it, she would have recognised in him her brother. But she knows nothing of all that. Then Gawain asks her if she does not know that many knights are enlisted in the service of love. Then the maiden answered that she knew well that the Duchess of Logrois had many knights in her own service. Then he asked the beauteous maiden:
'But tell me, then, who is it that all your knights do battle with.' Then she

answers that it is with King Gramoflanz who wears the wreath of fame. This passage (XIII: 91-92) is perhaps significant in that it explains the wreath of Gramoflanz. We already know that the wreath is something which has to be won from his tree. We are now told what kind of a wreath it is. It is the wreath of Virtue.[113] 'Now', says Gawain, 'Since you talk thus of this knight, you shall learn something more of him, for he aspires to your love, and if you are Lot's daughter, then it is indeed you whom he would win. But I should like to be messenger for both of you.' Thus Gawain wishes to marry his sister to the Guardian of Virtue, so he says to her, 'See this little ring, the worthy hero sends you this and I am his sweet messenger. You need not doubt but that I shall guard your secret.' Then she turned first crimson and then pale. Much agitated she grasped the ring and had to admit that she recognised it. Yes, she told Gawain, she had sent this little ring to Gramoflanz to be used by him as a token should he ever send her a messenger. She had long been well-disposed towards him in thought, though she had never yet seen him. Then said Gawain that he had today made peace with the Türkowit and with Lischois Giwellius, but that he could not forgive them for still being at enmity with King Gramoflanz.

Then Itonje asks Gawain to help her. Gawain could not help seeing that she loved King Gramoflanz and hated Orgeluse. It was a difficult situation for him, but he promised her his help, without betraying that they were children of the same mother. Then they sat down to table. Lischois Giwellius ate with Gawain's mother Sangive. Orgeluse ate with King Arthur's mother Arnive, Gawain's sister sat next to him. The poet says that his skill and his knowledge as a chef does not suffice to enable him to name all the dishes which were served, but that he can say that the squires and the maidservants in serving the dishes did not jostle one another, and that whether they bore food or wine, they conducted themselves with propriety and modesty.

> And a feast they today must look on such as no man before had seen,
> Since vanquished by Klingsor's magic both lady and knight had been.
> Unknown were they yet to each other, tho' one portal it shut them in,
> And never a man and a maiden might speech of each other win;
> And a good thing Gawain he thought it that this folk should each other meet,
> And much he rejoiced in their gladness . . .   (XIII: 163-168)

Thus Gawain succeeded in uniting the men and the women,[114] whilst nevertheless maintaining purity of morals. That he is successful in doing this on the soil of Klingsor's Castle, shows him to be the lord of Castle Merveil. Now follows a description of the joyous feast. There was music and dancing and the knights mingled with the ladies. Gawain, Sangive and Arnive did not dance. Then came the Duchess Orgeluse. Couples sat together and exchanged words of love. At last Arnive said to Gawain that he had been through a difficult time, and asked him whether he would not like to retire. Then Orgeluse says that she will readily undertake to look after him. She committed the care of the Türkowit and Lischois Giwellius to the knights. We are now told how many knights that evening sued for love, and how many were met with a gracious compliance. Thus for many of them the signal for departure came far too soon. Even Gawain felt the power of love. Lischois Giwellius and the Türkowit were escorted with special friendliness. The others departed. Gawain and Orgeluse found two beautifully decked beds ready prepared and placed side by side. The poet says:

> If the twain to their love gave hearing? The tale how should I withhold,
> I would speak, were it not unseemly that love's secrets aloud be told,
> For courtesy doth forbid it; and he who would tell the tale
> Worketh ill to himself; o'er love's dealings true hands ever draw the
>   veil. (XIII: 163-168)

What we are now told is intended to express the power of love that Gawain felt. The poet says that had Gawain not found fulfilment for his longing for love, he would have died. Neither the art of the philosophers, nor the mastery of all the wise men, neither Kankor nor Thebit,[115] the famous physicians, nor Trebuchet the clever smith who fashioned the sword which performed wonders, nor any other kind of art would have helped him. Only that could help him which actually happened. But what took place there remained secret, and the people knew nothing of it.

Why does the poet tell us this? After he has already emphasised that he had succeeded in uniting knights and ladies on the territory of Castle Merveil and in maintaining morality, so that Gawain had won the crown of virtue? And why does he inform us that the same Gawain wished to marry his sister to the Guardian of Virtue? Because he wishes to teach us that the lord of Castle Merveil has learnt to purify the force of the heart.

Meanwhile Gawain's squire has reached Arthur's Court at Bems on the Korka. The squire found the Queen at her usual morning devotions. He handed her the letter and she at once recognised Gawain's writing. The poet tells us in this connection that four and a half years and six weeks had passed since Parzival had left Arthur's Court.[116] The poet makes the Queen say this. She then instructs the squire that he must at once hand the letter to the King himself. To her question as to where Gawain now was the squire replies:

> 'Nay,' quoth the squire, 'I may not, ask not where my lord doth dwell,
> But think, an thou wilt, that good fortune is his, and he fareth
>   well!' (XIII: 327-328)

The squire, following the advice of the Queen, then rode into the courtyard of the castle and asked for the King. To him he gave Gawain's letter. We know that in the letter was the news of the combat about to take place between Gawain and Gramoflanz. Then the content of the letter was communicated to the knights. All of them were at once prepared to start off in order to be present at the combat. Only Kay was of the opinion that Gawain was so slippery and unreliable that if he went to a place to which he summoned one, one could be sure that he would be gone again before one arrived there. After the squire had in this way delivered his message he returned again to Castle Merveil in a few days. The doorkeeper announced the approach of the squire to Arnive. She sent for him and questioned him about his errand. But not even now did the squire betray anything of it. Then the squire sought his lord Gawain and told him that Arthur with all his knights and ladies would come. Gawain was overjoyed to hear this and still told the squire to say nothing of it.

Then one day it happened that Gawain came into conversation with Arnive. They were standing at the window from which one could see the whole landscape, the forest and the river. Then Gawain asked Arnive to tell him what she knew about the story of this remarkable castle and country. Arnive signified her willingness and went on to tell him how this was the land of Klingsor—that it contained countless wonders, that it was called Terra de Labur (Land of Toil). Klingsor's grandfather was Virgil of Naples,[117] who too had been addicted to sorcery. Klingsor had chosen Capua for his capital city. His history however was as follows: at one time there reigned in Sicily King Ibert, who was rich and proud. The name of the King's wife was Iblis. Arnive says that she cannot without more ado reveal Klingsor's secret. She must first ask Gawain's permission to refer to it, for she will have to say something rather unseemly! As Gawain encourages her to speak out, she says that it happened to Klingsor with a stroke to be made a 'capon'. At this Gawain laughed. Arnive however continued. This happened to him at the fortress of Kalot Enbolot. The king had found him sleeping in the arms of his wife; for this he had to yield his manhood to the king in satisfaction.

> Thus was shame wrought upon his body[118]
> So that never more by any woman
> To love's sporting was he chosen.

Much trouble was stirred up through this. In the city of Persida had the art of magic originated. Klingsor had learnt it. He was very powerful, but persecuted men and women with hatred since his own body had been shamed. It gave Klingsor the greatest joy to bring noble men into trouble. Irot who was King of Rosche Sabbins had been afraid of that. He was the father of Gramoflanz. He offered Klingsor the whole of his property if he would only leave him in peace. Thus Klingsor came into possession of the mountains and country for six miles around.[119] From here Klingsor ruled over the realm of the spirits. However many were found between heaven and earth, whether they were good or bad, Klingsor ruled over them all, unless

God protected them from him. Now, says Arnive, it is precisely the land of Klingsor which has fallen into your hands. Klingsor abandons the castle and it is given into your keeping. And those whom Klingsor has made prisoners, they are from henceforth your subjects.

I understand this to mean that Gawain is ruler over those who, through their desire for love, have entered into Klingsor's realm. He to whom that happens is the prisoner of this realm. Parzival too is a prisoner in the realm of Klingsor until he succeeds in showing that he has won for himself the wreath of virtue, the wreath of Gramoflanz, that he is stronger than the lord of the land, stronger than Gawain himself. But we are anticipating the story.

Nobody is in the realm of Klingsor who has not been brought thither by some kind of amatory desire. Arnive tells how even she came to be there. She says:

> Of joy had I once full measure: a crownèd queen was I!   (XIII: 531)

She is in fact the wife of Uther Pendragon. She had never done wrong. Both men and women she had always received in a befitting manner, but, she laments, however true a wife may be and however she may cling to her virtue and chastity, yet she is never immune to the pangs of love-longing which can be awakened in her even by a humble squire. Thus it was that she had already been a very long time in Klingsor's power without anyone coming to free her from this unhappiness. Then Gawain comforts her, knowing that her sorrow would be at an end with Arthur's coming. Even as he spoke he noticed the mighty army approaching, and tears came to his eyes as he saw it.

Arnive observed this and told him that he, on the contrary, ought to be happy, since the army that drew near was that of Orgeluse. But meanwhile the army had approached so near that they could see the coat-of-arms on the banners. They all bore the same device, the arms of Isages (Isaiah) were displayed before their eyes. 'Why,' cried Arnive, 'is not that the coat-of-arms of Uther Pendragon's Marshal?' But it was the Lord Maurin who bore it,[120] the marshal of Queen Guinevere. Arnive did not know that King Uther Pendragon and Isages had long since died and that Maurin had succeeded to his father's office. Of all that she had remained in ignorance, for during her imprisonment no news had penetrated to her. Gawain by giving instruction to the ferryman, saw to it that for today not a single one of Arthur's army should cross the river. Further, Gawain took out of the rich tent at the gate the harp so well known in England, called the Swallow, and gave it to Bene for her father. Thus did the latter receive, in accordance with his wish, what he had demanded for releasing the knight Lischois Giwellius.

When Gawain ordered his army to guard all the outposts he made preparations as if he were encountering a hostile army. No one was yet to know that the army in question was the friendly host of King Arthur. So the knights were ready to defend the castle if necessary. Then the knights asked

Orgeluse if the army was hers. She denied it, and suggested that it might be the army of Gramoflanz since it came from the direction of Logrois. Whoever it was who came, it must be someone who had met with disaster at Logrois. That was true for even Arthur had met with misfortune there. Even Arthur had to suffer that Gaherjet, Garel and Jofreit should be taken prisoners. We are also informed about some other knights and their destiny.

At last Gawain decided to tell his army that he who rode towards them was Arthur. He gave permission to cross the river and presented Arthur to the five ladies. Arthur was very surprised to find among them his own mother. Thus it ended in an exchange of friendly greetings. Whilst now the separate parts of the army took up their positions, and Orgeluse's army too had arrived, Gawain armed himself for the coming fight. He put on his armour to test whether his wounds would still prevent him from fighting. Then he rode out.

> And so had his Fortune willed it, that a knight his bridle drew
> By the side of the river Sabbins, and ye know that knight so true,
> And a rock, men well might call him, for manhood and courage high,
> And no knight might stand before him, and falsehood his heart did fly.
> And yet so 'weak' was his body that no burden it bare of wrong,
> Yea, a hand's-breadth had been too heavy, and a finger length too long!
> And, I ween, of this gallant hero of old time ye oft must hear,
> For my tale hath come to its root-tree, and draweth its goal anear. (XIII: 819–826)

This means that the poet is informing us that Gawain who rides out to encounter Gramoflanz, meets Parzival. The story has come back to its source, the Gawain episode is over. Parzival is once more lord of the adventure. He is freed from what had brought him into dependence upon Gawain. Amorous desire has no more power over him.

Adventure XIV

And now the poet tells us in the fourteenth Adventure how Parzival came galloping up, so strong and powerful, a single man against a whole army, and he came decked with the wreath of Gramoflanz. Thus he too must have passed through Gawain's adventure.

> He too had plucked a sprig from the tree of Gramoflanz,[121]
> A brightly shining garland which Gawain well did know.

Gawain perforce thinks that it is Gramoflanz, for that Parzival has won for himself the crown of virtue he does not suspect. So they ride at full tilt against one another, both riding Grail horses.

> From Monsalväsch they came, the chargers, which each of the knights bestrode. (XIV: 13)

Whilst the two were riding against one another in battle, messengers from King Arthur came to Gramoflanz and his army. Gramoflanz's army had established itself near the sea, between the two rivers Sabin and Poinzaklin, so that between the two rivers and the sea a square was produced of which the town of Roschsabins formed the fourth side. With a flourish of trumpets the army started out from here on its way in order to march against Joflanze. Many ladies rode on magnificent horses whose trappings jingled. Many strange knights and kings had come too—for instance, King Brandelidelein appeared with six hundred ladies. Bernaut de Riviers also was there whose father Narant had bequeathed to him Uckerland. He, too, brought many ladies with him, two hundred maidens and two hundred married ladies. With him were five hundred knights, they had all come to be present at the battle which King Gramoflanz intended to fight. They wished to see for themselves whether Gramoflanz won the victory. When Arthur's messengers arrived, Gramoflanz received them seated upon a high throne. The messenger greeted him, and requested him to abstain from the fight. For Gawain was a child of Arthur's sister, and so he could never agree to the battle taking place. Then, too, he was a member of the Round Table, and thus the Round Table felt itself responsible for the fight. Gramoflanz replied that he would have to go on with the fight. He had already heard that Arthur and his wife had come. He bade the Lady Guinevere welcome, but he could not permit his resolution to be changed because the Duchess Orgeluse had stirred King Arthur to anger against him. This fight with *one* single man could certainly not frighten him; he had never before fought with one man, but only with two or more. For the rest, he was very pleased that the ladies should be freed from their imprisonment; and that she who had won his heart should also witness the fight, this, too, when he thought of it, made him happy.

Meanwhile Bene, the ferryman's daughter, had come to King Gramoflanz and now sat at his right hand. She had brought him a ring, the one that Gawain had given to Itonje as the sign of Gramoflanz's love. The presence of Bene reminded Gramoflanz of his love. That Itonje had sent the ring to him he took as a sign of her love, and rejoiced thereat. The poet does not like it that the King should think with hatred of the brother of his beloved. Now we are told how Gramoflanz arms himself. But meanwhile Arthur's messengers had retired again. On the way home they met Gawain in conflict with a knight. Gawain had taken him for Gramoflanz. We know already that it is Parzival. As the squires approach, the battle has gone so far that Gawain is overcome. When the squires observe this they utter his name in loud lament. Parzival hears this.

> Then he, who erewhile would fight him, of conflict would have no more,

> But he cast from his hand his weapon, and he cried as he wept full sore,
> 'Accursèd am I, and dishonoured, and all blessing from me hath flown,
> Since my luckless hand, unwitting, so sinful a strife hath known.
> Methinks it is too unseemly! Yea, guilty am I alway,
> And born 'neath a star of Ill Fortune, and forced from all bliss to stray.
> And the arms that today I carry are the same that of old I bore,
> For they are of Ill-luck the token, e'en today as they were of yore.
> Alas! that with gallant Gawain I have foughten so fierce a fight,
> 'Tis *myself* whom I here have vanquished, and my joy shall have taken flight.   (XIV: 149–158)

Here the poet says clearly that Parzival's fight with Gawain is a fight with himself. And once again he states it when he makes Gawain say to Parzival:

> Thyself hast thou overthrown, if sincerity is still found in thee.[122]

Thus the two recognise each other. Now we have traversed the whole cycle of the so-called Gawain episode. Let us consider it once more. Parzival has fallen into dependence upon Gawain, into dependence upon him who was destined to be lord of Castle Merveil. This happened because Parzival was not yet above the reach of love's tormenting desire. He whom love compels becomes the servant of the lord of Castle Merveil. In some mysterious way Parzival had shared Gawain's adventure. The two had exchanged both horse and task, yet Parzival's path leads along a different road from Gawain's. Parzival has to practise renunciation with regard to Orgeluse. Gawain has to marry her. That is the difference. Parzival does not become King of Castle Merveil, he is destined to become King of the Grail. Up to the moment when Parzival fights Gawain, he is dependent upon the latter. After he has shown that he is able to conquer Gawain, he is fully and entirely lord of the Adventure. These connections are clearly indicated in the poem, the only debatable point is whether for a while behind the figure of the Knight Lischois Giwellius, Parzival is hidden, later to appear again alongside him.

Whether this hypothesis is permissible or not, it is clear that the Gawain episode is an essential part of the whole poem. Even what has been said as to the equivalence of Gawain and Parzival is not intended to mean that Gawain is only a mask for Parzival. Gawain is quite another person, but a person in whom in a particularly one-sided fashion is expressed what exists too in Parzival, but does not in him come to full development. The full human archetype comes into being if one puts together what individuals experience in their varying shades of character.

Things went very badly with Gawain. Blood-stained and pale, he had sunk onto the grass. Gradually under the care of the squires, he came to himself again. Meanwhile Gramoflanz and intending spectators of the fight drew near. They were all very astonished to have arrived too late and to see that the fight was already over. Meanwhile Gawain had rallied, and was on his feet, although he still could scarcely move. Bene too had arrived, she embraced Gawain and cursed the man who had inflicted on him this suffering. Gramoflanz, too, expressed his regret and said that the fight must be postponed to the morrow. Parzival on the other hand showed no trace of weakness or fatigue. Then he offered to fight on Gawain's behalf. But Gramoflanz refused, saying that he must fight with Gawain, not with Parzival. But Bene turns angrily on Gramoflanz with the words:

> ... 'Fie on thee thou faithless hound,
> Thro' him whom thy false heart hateth thine heart hath its freedom found.
> She to whom thou wouldst do love-service, she liveth at his command,
> Thyself hast renounced the victory which else might have crowned thine hand.
> Thou hast no claim on Love's rewarding, and if ever within thine heart
> Love had for a while her dwelling with falsehood she bare a part!' (XIV: 237–242)

Gramoflanz then drew Bene aside, and assured her that he was pledged to fight, and asked her to tell Itonje that he was faithful to her. But now when Bene learnt that Gawain was Itonje's brother, she cursed Gramoflanz, who rode away. Again the poet emphasises that it is Parzival who has been victorious.

> Wot ye well who hath here been victor? 'Twas Parzival, he alone!
> And so fair was his face to look on none fairer was ever known. (XIV: 261–262)

Parzival then changes his clothes. The invitation to meet the four queens he does not wish to accept. He says that no one will be willing to speak to him, that every man and woman in King Arthur's kingdom had heard the curse that the Grail had pronounced over him. Gawain however persisted, and so Parzival was obliged to go to meet the ladies. It was not altogether pleasant for Orgeluse to be obliged to greet with a kiss the man who had rejected her love, when she had offered him her hand and her lands. And thus it is easily conceivable that she blushed. But once in conversation with him, her embarrassment vanished.

> Then Gawain of right and reason, if Bene his grace would hold,
> Bade her seal her lips to silence, to her lady no word be told
> That King Gramoflanz for his garland doth hatred towards me bear,
> And at the set time tomorrow our strife must be foughten fair,
> Speak no word of this to my sister, and do thou thy tears give o'er, (XIV: 285–289)

Bene, however, weeps and wails, for she says, what will happen tomorrow? For whichever is conquered, whether it be Gawain or Gramoflanz, Itonje will derive nothing but pain, for she will lose either her brother or her lover.

Meanwhile the whole army had returned home and preparations were being made for the midday meal. Parzival was to sit beside the Duchess Orgeluse, in accordance with Gawain's wish. Orgeluse found it rather strange that she should have to sit beside a man who had nothing but scorn for women. But for love of Gawain she was ready to do it. But Parzival said nothing was further from him than scorn. During the course of the meal Itonje noticed that Bene had been crying, and thus she could not eat, for sadness seized her too, and she could not help wondering why Bene was there. She asked herself whether perchance Gramoflanz had given her up. After the meal was over, Arthur received Parzival with the greatest honours. Then said Parzival, it seems that you are ready to admit that a certain measure of praise is due to me, but what does that avail me, unless the Grail Order, too, recognises it.

'Sir, I hear you say, if you are speaking candidly, that I still merit some share of praise. Hard though it is for me to believe, I gladly trust your word. Would that others might also believe it, from whom I parted there in shame!'[123]

Then says the poet, all the knights and ladies assembled around the Round Table. Then Parzival stood up and said to the assembly:

... 'Ye who shall be here
Give counsel, and help me win that which my soul ever holdeth dear;
A strange and a hidden wonder it drove me from out your band,
Ye who brotherhood once have sworn me, and in friendship have clasped my hand,
Now help me by this your knighthood, mine honour to win again. (XIV: 351–355)

Thus the situation is now reversed. Now, all the Knights of King Arthur, through Parzival, are to become seekers of the Grail, Parzival is not to be a Knight of King Arthur. Then Parzival continues and says that he has still another thing to ask. He wants to fight in Gawain's place. He wishes to conquer Gramoflanz, for:

I brake from his tree this morning a bough ere I thence did ride
And for that he of need must fight me—For conflict I sought his land,
And for nothing else came I hither but to fight with his strong right hand. (XIV: 360–362)

Thus we see that Parzival has passed through the Gramoflanz adventure.

Then Parzival tells how he had taken Gawain for Gramoflanz and how he thus came to fight. Now he asks Gawain to yield the fight to him. Gawain however refuses. He says that he must fight himself. Meanwhile, night fell, and Parzival tested his armour and his horse. Gramoflanz passed the night in great impatience. He was very angry that another had fought with Gawain instead of himself, and thus his impatience drove him onto the battlefield. He came alone to the place at which the fight was to take place. Parzival had also made his way thither, and when the two saw each other, they lowered their spears and rode speechlessly at one another. A terrible battle ensued.

It was not until the middle of the morning that Parzival's absence was noticed. Where could he be? Meanwhile a bishop said Mass and Gawain and the knights made their way to the place fixed for the battle.

> King Gramoflanz oft had boasted he would scorn with *one* man to fight,
> He thought here that *six* were his foemen, and each one a valiant knight
> Yet none but Parzival faced him[124] . . .   (XIV: 437–439)

Thus Parzival fought with the force of six fighters. He was penetrated by the might which he had won because longing for love had no more hold over him; steadfastness and fidelity worked in his thinking, feeling and willing. The fight was tending towards a victory for Parzival. And could it be otherwise? For Parzival fought out of friendship, Gramoflanz out of love. Must not friendship be six times stronger than love?

> One for the need of his friend,
> The other slavishly followed the behest of Frau Minne.[125]

The poet is trying to say a great deal to us. He is singing the hymn of praise of selfless fidelity and selfless friendship. Passionate love, egotistic love cannot exist in the presence of the Grail. Now Gawain appeared. By the time he arrived, Parzival had won the victory. Five knights threw themselves between the combatants. Brandelidelein von Punturteis, Bernaut de Riviers, Affinamus de Klitiers approached from one side, Arthur and Gawain from the other. They wanted to end the fight.

> And all the five they thought them 'twas time that the strife should end,
> And Gramoflanz must confess here that no longer he might contend,
> And his own mouth proclaimed him vanquished, and his foeman had won the day—
> And the folk who had seen the combat might never his word gainsay!   (XIV: 463–466)

The poet would say to us, 'Wert thou owner of the orchard from which the crown of all virtues can be plucked, yet thou must suffer defeat. And wert thou so strong as usually to fight with two persons, yet if thou art in the grip of egotistic love, thou art weak.' Ever greater Parzival stands before us—ever more purified from self he emerges. Less and less does he seek something for himself in battle. Ever more does he serve others. That gives him a six-fold power. Thus Gawain arrived just as Gramoflanz had been obliged to acknowledge Parzival the victor. Then he had the satisfaction of being in the same situation as was Gramoflanz the day before. So the combat was once more postponed. It is to take place on the next day. Then Arthur says that he hopes that Gawain will not bear a grudge against Parzival for having undertaken the fight on his behalf. Meanwhile a great council was taking place in Gramoflanz's camp. The knights decided to inform Arthur by letter that he must see to it that tomorrow the right knight came. Gramoflanz gives to his messenger a letter and a ring for Bene. Meanwhile however Itonje had found out that the heroes who were to fight the next day were her lover and her brother. Hence overcoming her maidenly modesty, she came to a decision. She went to Arnive and confessed her love for Gramoflanz and described her pain that her beloved should fight with her brother. Arnive then sent to Arthur to tell him that he must prevent the fight. When Arthur heard the whole story, he cried out, 'Alas, my beloved niece, that thou shouldst so young experience the pains of love, thou willst atone for this in bitterness; it shall be with thee as with thy sister Sürdamur, whose death the Greek Emperor caused' (we know that the Greek Emperor to whom reference is made here is Alexander). And Arthur added that he would willingly stop the fight if he were sure that Itonje and Gramoflanz loved one another. Then Itonje said that she loved Gramoflanz although she had never seen him.

The last sentence is very surprising to the modern reader. He cannot imagine such a situation. But thus it was for a long period of time. There was as yet no personal love. Parzival knew personal love, the others did not yet know it. One loved rather the imaginary picture that one made of a man or a woman from what one heard of them.

The same thing is seen in the Gudrun poem. The girl follows the singer who woos her and he leads her to a king unknown to her. She loves the King merely through the description of the singer. She leaves father and mother and follows the singer to the unknown husband. It was a love the nature of which the modern man has yet to learn to understand. The individual human being of the Middle Ages felt himself as the representative of a certain region of the earth. The other person represented another part of the earth. How the water-spirits sing on the crest of the waves, this is what Hilda heard in the song of Horand—she wished to go to live with the king of the country in which the water-spirits sang so beautifully. One did not love the person for his own sake, but one was oneself a bit of nature, and one loved the nature with which the other person was bound up. Thus it was between Hettel and Hilde. In the Gudrun-song we follow the love through three generations. Not until the third generation, in the love of Gudrun, do we encounter personal love and fidelity. The poems of the Middle Ages mark for us the transition to personal love. It is shown too in Parzival. For when later Itonje and Gramoflanz meet one another, they recognise each other in the midst of a whole host of people, although they had never seen one another.

This parenthesis is interpolated in explanation of a kind of love which has become foreign to us.

Meanwhile Gramoflanz's messengers arrived, and Bene recognised them. She went to meet them and received the letter and the ring. Then she went in search of King Arthur. Itonje received the letter and learned that Gramoflanz still loved her. Arthur too took the letter and read it. In it Gramoflanz declares that his love is unchanging and faithful.

> As the Pole-star doth in the north pole the goal of its gazing find,
> And neither its post forsaketh, e'en so shall our true love be,
> And waver not, one from the other . . .   (XIV: 596–598)

When Arthur read this, he resolved to stop the fight. When immediately after, he received the messengers of Gramoflanz, who bade him see to it that the wrong combatant did not appear on the following morning, he assented to their demands. He then commanded the messengers to invite Gramoflanz to come to him before the fight. One of the squires objected that Orgeluse was still angry with Gramoflanz, but Arthur replied that he would put an end to this quarrel. When Gramoflanz received the message, he came very willingly, for it meant riding to the place where his beloved was. Six princes accompanied him; three princes of the land, his Uncle Brandelidelein, Bernaut de Riviers, and Affinamus de Klitiers. And since each of these took a companion with him, there were twelve persons who accompanied him. Thus, the king came as the thirteenth among twelve. Arthur sent Beaucorps, Gawain's brother, to meet him. He was accompanied by fifty pages, Dukes and Counts and King's sons. Beaucorps was very handsome, and when Gramoflanz saw him he was charmed and thought to himself that Itonje must be like him. Meanwhile Arthur succeeded in making Orgeluse promise not to visit her wrath on Gramoflanz for the death of Cidegast. And thus the way was paved for reconciliation. When Gramoflanz appeared, Arthur said:

> 'Ere thou takest thy seat, bethink thee, if thou dost a maiden love,
> And thou seest her here, thou mayest kiss her . . .   (XIV: 745–746)

Then Gramoflanz recognised Itonje by her likeness to her brother Beaucorps; he kissed her. Thus it happened that the fight was stayed, and that love took the place of hate. The King Gramoflanz was obliged to abandon his hatred which melted like snow in the sunshine. Gawain and Gramoflanz celebrated their reconciliation by a kiss.

> Then Gramoflanz and Sir Gawain with a kiss put an end to strife;
> And Arthur gave maid Itonje to King Gramoflanz to wife ...
> (XIV: 829-830)

That happiness should be complete, Kondrie was given to Lischois Giwellius and the Türkowit, Florant, received Sangive. The Duchess Orgeluse had already long belonged to Gawain. So there were four weddings. But Parzival had no part in the general rejoicing.

> But Parzival, he bethought him of his wife so fair and sweet,
> How pure she was and how gentle—Did he ne'er another greet,
> And offer for fair love service and, wavering, love anew?
> Nay, nay, he was far from such dealings, and naught of such love he knew!
> For a mighty faith so guarded his body alike and heart
> That never a woman living might have in his love a part,
> Save only his queen and lady, Kondwiramur, the flower
> Of women, Love's fairest blossom ... (XIV: 869-876)

Thus Parzival's own love surged up again. He said to himself:

> Of love was I born; how have I thus lost love?

But although he was seized with so strong a longing, yet he knew that love was not for him.

> And he thought, since to me that lacketh with which others are richly blest
> The love in whose sweet fulfilment many sad hearts have found their rest
> Since this sorrow must be my portion I care not what else my lot
> Little reck I what shall befall me, since my joy Heaven willeth not. (XIV: 885-888)

And sorrowfully he gazes upon the joyous company, then he says:

> May God give this folk rejoicing! But I from their joy must flee,
> And wend lonely as of aforetime, since gladness is not for me!'
> Then he stretched out his hand to his harness, and as oft was his wont of yore,
> Unaided he girt it on him, and soon was he armed once more.
> Now sorrow anew he seeketh—When he, who from joy would fly,
> Had armed himself, his charger he saddled right speedily,
> And his shield and spear were ready—O'er his loss did they wail next morn,

For no eye looked on his departing, he rode thence ere the day was born. (XIV: 895–902)

Adventure XV

From the very first lines of the Fifteenth Adventure we receive the impression that we are drawing near to the end and thereby to the beginning of the poem too. We have already drawn attention to the fact that the sixteen Adventures form as it were a sort of circle returning upon itself. The narrative began with the birth of Feirefis, with Belakane's story, with the lines about the black and the white. Now we meet Feirefis. The story told in this fifteenth Adventure belongs to that part of the Grail Saga which was published later than the other parts. It became exoteric at a later date. It is to this Wolfram's opening words refer:

It had grieved many people who were denied this epic[126] that some of them would never get to know about it.
But now I shall no longer withhold it, I will give you the true saga as it is held in my mouth, how the sweet hero Amfortas became whole again.

It is the entry into the Grail Castle which will be described to us in the two following adventures.

If one wishes to prepare one's soul to receive the last two chapters of Wolfram's Grail poem in the right mood, one should read the chapter in Rudolf Steiner's book, *Knowledge of the Higher Worlds* which he has called 'The Second Guardian of the Threshold—Life and Death'. In this chapter a spirit-form is described which Rudolf Steiner calls the Second Guardian. In his *Occult Science*, Rudolf Steiner describes how the Christ Being announces Himself in the Second Guardian of the Threshold. In the former book he makes the Second Guardian say, 'You will some day be able to unite yourself with me, but I cannot find blessedness as long as others are unredeemed! As a liberated individual you might enter this very day into the supersensible world, but then you would be obliged to look down on the still unredeemed beings in the sense-world; you would have separated your destiny from theirs. But you are all linked together; you had all to descend into the sense-world in order to gather from it powers needed for the higher world. Were you to separate yourself from the others, you would be misusing the powers you have been able to develop only in association with them. If they had not descended, you could not have done so; without them the powers needed for your supersensible existence would be lacking. You must now share with the others the powers you acquired in their company. I therefore forbid you admission into the highest regions of the supersensible world as long as you have not applied to the redemption of the world to which you belong all the powers you have acquired. With the powers you have already achieved you may sojourn in the lower regions of the supersensible world; but before the portal of the higher I stand (as the Cherubin with the fiery sword before Paradise), and I forbid your entrance as long as you retain powers that have not been put to use in the sense-world. And if you will not apply your powers in this way, others coming later will apply them. Then a higher supersensible world will receive all the fruits of the sense-world, but the ground in which you were rooted will be withdrawn from you. The purified world will evolve above and beyond you. You will be excluded from it. Then you would be treading the *black* path, while those from whom you have separated yourself would be treading the *white* path.'

It is this which Parzival has to experience in the meeting with his black-and-white brother Feirefis. Now, he has to recall what the poet said at the beginning, in the very first lines of the first Adventure, where he spoke of the black and white magpie, of the Heaven and the Hell, in which the soul can participate, and of the black and white host. There, the poet unfolded what he had to say to us about steadfastness and fidelity. Now Parzival must ponder these opening words in his heart. We might indeed very well take these wonderful opening words as the meditation into which a person has to live, if he wishes pictures of Parzival's life to rise up before him. Through them he will be guided to hold fast what is fleeting, to seize the imaginative pictures which, to use the poet's own simile, scurry through the soul like a scampering hare. But now in the fifteenth Adventure, Parzival meets his human brother, and woe to him who tries to approach the Grail alone, without his human brother. He who wishes to become King of the Grail must remember that it is his duty to redeem all that within himself which is unworthy to become the Guardian of the Grail, and through the light and warmth of his own higher being to lead to the Grail his human brother who cannot behold it (though he can behold the Grail-bearer).

But at first man is hostile towards his human brother whom he must lead with him to the Grail—Parzival, who has not yet recognised Feirefis as his brother, has to fight with him. It was the stiffest fight of his life, but it was also his last. Feirefis is wonderfully armed. His armour is composed of precious stones. Rubies and chalcedons are to be seen in it. Fire-spirits, salamanders, made this suit in the mountains of Agremontin. Above Feirefis's head hovers the Ecidemon. In the poem called the Battle of the Wartburg, the Ecidemon is explained. There we are told that it is man's angel. It is to be seen so united with the human being that, radiant like a shining star, it holds man's higher being above his head in its hands of light. That is why it is popularly said that a man has his good star or his good angel to thank.

Parzival meets his human brother, but he does not yet recognise him as his brother, he is still hostile to him. He does not yet see the streaming rays of the star over the head of the other. He seems to him like a poisonous animal, worse than any poisonous snake. Hence the poet says of Feirefis:

> As reward for his deeds of Knighthood on his helmet a beast he bare
> Ecidemon (daemon), all poisonous serpents they must of its power beware,
> For of life and of strength doth it rob them, if they smell it but from afar. (XV: 39–41)

So it is with human beings. Their attitude to one another is hostile, and if they perceive something of the being of another it does not seem to them like a glittering golden star. Men become poisonous snakes, who cannot endure the smell of the golden star which they take for an Ecidemon. But so long as this is so, men cannot draw near to the Grail. For in the presence of the Grail the Christ-Ego is received, in which all men are united as brothers and sisters. Thus it is a solemn fight to which Parzival is led, a fight the secret of which, as Wolfram von Eschenbach tells us, is only later made exoteric. The army of Feirefis is numerous, how indeed can humanity be otherwise than numerous?

> And his armies were five and twenty, and they knew not each other's speech
> 'Twas a token fair of his riches, and the lands that his power might reach. (XV: 49–50)

Twenty-five women form the retinue of the Grail. The fifth Adventure tells us this. There, before the three burning altars, stood the bearer of the Grail, with twelve women carrying lights on the right, twelve on the left. Twenty-five lights stand before the Grail. The light of the Grail overpowers them all, before its light all self-illumination is as the casting of a shadow. Twenty-five armies follow Feirefis. None can understand the other, each is illumined by the light of its own being. So is the world. In the presence of the Grail all these armies must unite. The Grail-bearer must assemble the twenty-four elders, the thrones of humanity around her. Thus Feirefis, the brother-man, represents the whole host of humanity in all its differentiations, in all its many tongues and many races. The poet tells us that the skins of the men of this army shine in many colours, and Feirefis stands before this army as the expression of the moral being of mankind, as the expression of the will-nature of mankind—black and white, partaking of heaven and hell.

Parzival plunges into battle. The Poet fears he may not be able to withstand, then he consoles himself with the thought that with Parzival is the force of the Grail, and with Parzival is the force of love, both of which will protect him.

> I should sorrow for him whom I brought here, save my heart did this comfort hold,

> That the Grail shall with strength imbue him, and Love shelter the hero bold,
> Since he was of the twain the servant, nor his heart ever wavering knew. (XV: 67–69)

Thus the two combatants confront one another—Parzival a Christian, Feirefis a heathen. The individual is Christian, mankind is still heathen; the individual no longer commits murder, nations still murder one another. When will the individual (Parzival) lead mankind (the human brother Feirefis) into the Grail Castle where the seventy-two nations assemble round the altar of the Holy Ghost, which stands in the middle of the Grail Castle? When will mankind awaken to the knowledge that with the gift of the poem of the Grail, *the age of the Holy Ghost has begun*? When will it recognise that until the time of Christ, every Mystery was a Mystery of the blood, or of the *Father*? After the Mysteries of the Body had been completed, began the Mysteries of the Soul, or of the Son, and in the Ninth Century, in the story of the Grail, faintly dawned the Mysteries of the *Spirit*. When will mankind recognise that the *earth is the Temple of the Grail*, the Body of the Christ? When will mankind recognise this by its actions, and the seventy-two nations of the earth unite through the Spirit? What the last chapters of the Grail story touch upon is still to a great extent a thing of the future.

The poet has awakened in us a certain mood of solemnity before he tells us about this battle. Then he says:

> Nor may I asunder part them, the paynim and Christian knight,
> Hatred they show to each other ... (XV: 77–78)

The poet tries by a picture to show us what he means to indicate by the power of the battle. The frightful din caused by the splintering of the spears against one another reminds him of a fable:

> The lion is brought dead into the world;
> He awakens at the father's call.[127]

Here the poet of the battle of the Wartburg has pointed out how the soul awakens at the call of the Divine Father. Now they fight and the marvellous thing is that the battle takes its course in such a way that it is not Feirefis who is wounded, but Ecidemon. It is the higher man that is injured in this fight.

> And the heathen wrought woe to the Christian, 'Thasme!' was his battle cry,
> And when 'Tabronit' he shouted, he drew ever a step anigh. (XV: 99–100)

'Thasme' is Feirefis's battle cry. It is the name of one of his lands. Tabronit belongs to Sekundille the beloved of Feirefis. In the rhythm of these lines, one experiences the will nature of Feirefis. Feirefis fought with the force of love. What must the Christian meet him with? He too, must turn his thoughts to love. Love must protect him from death, yet not love alone.

> On love let his thoughts be steadfast, else sure he is here undone,
> And he hath from the hand of the heathen in this combat his deathblow won.
> O thou Grail, by thy lofty virtue such fate from thy knight withhold!
> Kondwiramur, thine husband in such deadly stress behold!
> (XV: 111–114)

And now we come to the passage where *the whole mystery of man, his threefold nature*, is revealed. We already know that Parzival and Gawain merely characterise two sides of human nature—now we learn that something similar applies to Feirefis. He too is one with Parzival, for the nature of man is threefold. In the *head* he is Parzival, in the *breast* he is the *Lion Knight*, (Gawain), in the *lower organisation*, in the will nature, he is *Feirefis*.

> Then on high flashed the sword of the heathen, and many such blow had slain,
> To his knee Parzival was beaten—Now see how they fought, the twain,
> If twain ye will still account them, yet in sooth shall they be but one,
> For my brother and I are one body, e'en as husband and wife are one!
> (XV: 117–120)

That is man's Cain nature, that will not be its brother's keeper. He who wishes to approach the Grail must be willing to lead his brother to the Grail. Never ending is this battle which plays itself out between human beings and which is mirrored in the nature of the individual. For the will-nature fights against the man of knowledge. And the man of knowledge fights against the will-nature, and a long path of development is required before the human being reaches the summit of freedom, where he acts out of knowledge, where Parzival and Feirefis stand before the Grail.

And now we learn what it is that protects Feirefis. He had a shield which neither burned nor decayed, the fire of the will could not affect it, it was made of asbestos. This shield had been given to Feirefis by his beloved. She gives him the gift of goodwill. And with it she gives him chrysoprase and turquoise, emerald and ruby, and the carbuncle antrax, and last of all, Ecidemon, the pure animal, the coat of arms of Sekundille.

> And as token of love for his guarding, Sekundille the queen would give
> That wondrous beast Ecidemon—in her favour he fain would live,
> And e'en as she willed he bare it, as his badge did that gallant knight.
> (XV: 127–129)

Thus we see Feirefis equipped with the sub-earthly gifts of the will. Precious stones deck his armour. On the will which penetrates the whole body upwards into the sense organs and beyond depends the magic power of Feirefis. Something quite different protects Parzival.

> Here with purity faith joined issue, and truth with high truth would fight.
> For love's sake upon the issue of this combat each risked his life.
> Each had pledged his hand to the winning of honour and fame in strife;
> And the Christian, in God he trusted since the day that he rode away
> From the hermit ... (XV: 130–134)

Parzival fights out of the force of the super-earthly, out of confidence in God, for since being with Trevrezent, he has conquered doubt. Knowledge fires him. Thus do knowledge and will strive against one another in the human being—out of their union arises true freedom. Once again the poet stresses that he must regard the baptised and the heathen as a single man.

> For I reckon them as one;[128]
> They would think themselves so
> If they knew themselves aright.

The poet is right too in calling the knowledge-man a Christian and the will-man a heathen. How much Christianity there is in our *knowledge*, and how little in our *deeds*! Parzival's battle-cry is Pelrapäre, and as he thinks of his wife and of the Grail new force awakens in him.

But in the fight between knowledge and will, all the uncompensated karma must be revealed, all that for which man has yet to make amends. Parzival once took from the Red Knight his sword. For all his other sins he has atoned but not yet for this. He killed the Red Knight, the Red Knight's sword must now bring death to him, unless grace bestow on him anew his forfeited life. It is only with life *given as a grace* that man can draw near to the Grail to be its King. The *Grail bestows in advance* the life that it claims in the service of humanity.

> ... and the sword so strong and keen
> That Ither of Gahevies bare first brake sheer on the helmet's sheen,
> And the stranger, so rich and valiant, he stumbled, and sought his knee
> —For God, He no longer willed it that Parzival lord should be
> Of this weapon of which in his folly he had robbed a gallant knight. (XV: 173–177)

The next sword thrust of Feirefis must surely kill the defenceless one. But none follows: the enemy does not strike again, but speaks. In the familiar French tongue Feirefis says, 'Keep still and tell me who you are: you would certainly have conquered me if your sword had not broken. Let us make peace.'

So it is with the human being, he fights to the uttermost with his human brother, but shrinks back from the last consequence of his fight. Then they talked to each other, told each other their names and their race, and it transpired that they were *both* of the race of Anjou. A marvellous word this word Anjou [Anschau in German]. Even Cyrus (the anointed of the Lord, as Jeremiah calls him) the Gentle (as the inscription calls him) with whom God had wrestled for twenty-one days (as the Prophet Daniel tells us) without subduing him because the prince *Michael* helped him, even Cyrus, who released the Jews from Babylon and sent them home to build anew the destroyed Temple, is called in the inscription simply the hero of Anschau.

> *Anschau is Michael's land.*
> When he heard these words
> To the heathen quoth Parzival
> How can you be of Anjou?
> Anjou is the name of my land.[129]

And then they recognised one another, although they were born of different mothers. And however different in the different peoples of the earth the earthly mother may be they are nevertheless child of one spirit. How could men fail gradually to recognise each other in their true heritage? Then it dawns on Parzival that this is his brother. He had heard from Eckuba that his brother was black and white. Now he wants to look upon his countenance, now he says to his brother: 'Uncover thy head.' Then he recognises him. But confidence is needed, if this knowledge is to be led to the point of being willing to abandon the armour which protects it, to conclude a real peace. And Feirefis casts away his sword.

> 'Nor mine, nor thine shall this sword be! And straight from his hand it flew,
> Afar in the wood he cast it, and he quoth, "Now methinks Sir Knight,
> The chance for us both shall be equal, if further we think to fight!"'   (XV: 224–226)

And behold, black and white as a magpie was the countenance of the brother. Then their kisses put an end to hatred and wrath. Then we are led back through the poem to the opening lines; then we find ourselves again with the magpie, with doubt, with the black and the white, with steadfastness and unsteadfastness. But now there is a difference, for doubt has at last been conquered, now the *whole human nature* is united, *Parzival, Gawain and Feirefis*. A planetary secret is hidden in what is presented here. Parzival comes with the force of faithfulness, of steadfastness, which, as we know from *Titurel*, is the gift of Saturn. Feirefis calls his god Jupiter. Gawain's god is the god Mars, transformed into healing power. His problem is that of controlling the blood of the heart, of how to subdue the lion. The gods of Feirefis are Juno and Jupiter, but Juno is the feminine form of Jupiter. Thus, in these three heroes are represented the three upper planets. These three knights are the three outer planets when the story is related as starry script. That is perhaps how it appeared to Flegetanis. The whole long epic in starry constellation. Certainly, its original design is only hinted at. Only later did the starry script change into human adventure. Only then did it become true wisdom.

> Then joyful he spake, the heathen, 'Now well shall it be with me,
> And I thank the gods of my people that Gahmuret's son I see.
> Blest be Juno, the queen of heaven, since, methinks, she hath ruled it so,
> And Jupiter, by whose virtue and strength I such bliss may know,
> Gods and goddesses, I will love ye, and worship your strength for aye—
> And blest be those shining planets, 'neath the power of whose guiding ray
> I hither have made my journey—For ventures I here would seek,
> And found *thee*, brother, sweet and awful . . .   (XV: 239-246)

Feirefis has the force of Jupiter, he raises the will-nature to the heights of knowledge of the head. Parzival has the force of Saturn, he carries knowledge into the darkness of death. We have already heard it said of him that his veins and bones poured forth sweat as he lay on his bed in the candlelight. Steadfast fidelity, fidelity through death, that is Parzival's redemption by Saturn. He encounters the dead knight as sun-hero, thus he overcomes death. But Gawain, the Mars man, meets the bleeding knight, knows the secret of the blood on the white snow. Thus they are characterised. Thus the poet teaches us to understand them out of the wondrous wisdom of his planetary knowledge, out of his macrocosmic knowledge of the Grail. And now Feirefis, through Parzival, learns about the death of their father. *He finds the human brother*, but learns of *the death of the father*. But the poet also describes to us a side of human nature in Gahmuret. What we can experience from him is also a side of human nature:

> For myself, and thou, and my father, we three in one bond are bound;
> For tho' men as *three* may hold us, yet I wot well we are but *one*,
> And no wise man he counts that kinship 'twixt father, methinks, and son,
> For in truth for more must he hold it—With *thyself* hast thou fought today,
> To strife with *myself* have I ridden, and I went near myself to slay,

> Thy valour in good stead stood us, from myself hast thou saved my
> life. (XV: 302–307)

Who in the face of this verse can deny that we are interpreting the poet correctly in saying that he wishes in his characters to describe to us the many-sidedness of human nature? Goethe chose the same method in his story of the Green Snake. When the human being has reached the point of experiencing what Feirefis and Parzival experience then he makes the discovery that that out of which he was born, the father-element and mother-element in his nature, that is to say the *earthly* man, is dead. He learns to know the resurrection-force of Jupiter.

> 'Now Jupiter, see this marvel, since thy power so hath ruled the strife
> That from death hast thou here withheld us!' (XV: 308–9)

Now the poet tells us how the two arise, how they both sheathe the sword, how one holds the sheath, the other pushes the sword into it, and how they both feel that they are one with each other. And then they come to the court of King Arthur. And Gawain? Does he experience nothing of this fight? Gawain—so we are told by a Knight of Castle Merveil—has been able to watch the fight in the magic reflecting pillar of Castle Merveil. When knowledge and will do battle, it shows itself in the inner picture-world of memory. There the concept wants to become a picture, and the will draws it down into oblivion. In remembering and forgetting, in seeing imaginations and in their effacement, the two powers of willing and knowing do battle.

> Then from Chateau Merveil rode thither a squire in the selfsame hour,
> And he said in their column mirrored, had they seen in their fair
>   watch-tower
> A mighty fight and a fearful. And where'er men with swords have
>   fought
> I wot well beside this combat their strife shall be held as naught.
> And the tale did they tell to Gawain . . . (XV: 353–357)

Feirefis and Parzival now make their way to Arthur's court. Here they found Gawain who received them in a friendly manner and helped them to disarm. And now the poet describes in detail Feirefis's armour.

It causes universal astonishment among the knights of King Arthur's court, and is admired by men and women. It is decorated all over with precious stones. The sub-earthly forces rendered crystal clear form the armour of Feirefis.

Now we hear in a sort of enumeration the battles both Feirefis and Parzival have fought. Feirefis counts up his captives. Some names we recognise; some are unknown to us, most of them are very remarkable word-pictures which I cannot explain. It is worthy of note that among the prisoners Zoroaster,

King of Arabia, is mentioned. Then Parzival also tells with which knights he has fought. After he has recounted their names, he says:

> 'Were I to name all with whom I fought, I should never reach the end....[130]

Of these fights it is important to note what has already been mentioned and what is based on a statement of Dr Steiner's: that what takes place in the physical world Wolfram describes in detail, whereas what is pure imagination is only enumerated or briefly mentioned. Gawain now has the armour of Feirefis brought. Wonderful precious stones are to be seen in it. The poet says that Hercules (Heracles), Alexander the Great, or Pythagoras, who were still familiar with the starry script, could give information about the science of stones better than he. Now, after all these events, as the heroes sat at Arthur's Round Table the next day, there suddenly appeared the Grail messenger Kondrie. Her face was hidden by a thick veil. She was richly clad. On her dress were woven turtle-doves of Arabian gold, the coat of arms of the Grail. She asked for Arthur and greeted him and the queen. Then she turned to Parzival. She fell at his feet and begged forgiveness. Now she unveiled her face and everyone recognised Kondrie the sorceress. She seemed just the same as ever. Her eyes were yellow at topazes, her teeth were long, her lips violet. Her message came forth from a mouth that was withered. She greeted Feirefis whom she reminded about his Queen Sekundille:

> And to Parzival she spake thus, 'Now rejoice with a humble heart,
> Since the crown of all earthly blessings henceforward shall be thy part,
> For read is the mystic writing—The Grail, It doth hail thee King,
> And Kondwiramur, thy true wife, thou shalt to thy kingdom bring,
> For the Grail, It hath called her thither—Yea, and Lohengrin, thy son,
> For e'en as thou left her kingdom twin babes thou by her had won.
> And Kardeis, he shall have in that kingdom, a heritage rich I trow!' (XV: 767-773)

Amfortas he will redeem by the question that he will ask him. He will prepare joy for the sorrowful, thus he will rise to the stage of 'security of heart'. And now Kondrie describes the Kingdom of the Grail. The Kingdom of the Grail stretches as far as the sphere of the planets—from Saturn to Moon—from the Moon to Saturn.

> Seven stars did she name unto him in Arabic, and their might,
> Right well Feirefis should know it, who sat there, both black and white.
> And she spake, 'Sir Parzival, mark well the names that I tell to thee,
> There is Zwal[131] the highest planet, and the swift star Almustri;[132]

> Almaret[133] and the shining Samsi;[134] great bliss unto thee they bring.
> Alligafir[135] is fifth, and Alkiter[136] stands sixth in the starry ring;
> And the nearest to us is Alkamer,[137] and no dream shall it be, my rede,
> For the bridge of heaven are they, to guide and to check its speed,
> 'Gainst its swiftness, their power, it warreth. Now thy sorrow is passed away,
> For far as shall be their journey, and as far as shall shine their ray,
> So wide is the goal of thy riches, and the glory thine hand shall win,
> And thy sorrow shall wane and vanish, yet this thing it holds for sin,
> The Grail and Its power, It forbids thee unlawful desire to know,
> And the company of sinners henceforth must thou shun, I trow.
> (XV: 779-792)

Thus Parzival as Grail King possessed those forces which the human being gradually unfolds from birth to death. Out of the forces of the moon does the human being form the embryonic life. By the force of Saturn in old age he becomes sclerotic. He is Grail King, who knows that in the human being the Cosmos is active. Amfortas has to learn this through suffering. The return of the stars means pain to him. In Parzival it has become calm knowledge of the connection between macrocosm and microcosm. If he wishes to become Grail King, all his life forces have to be placed at the service of macrocosmic law, and not used for his own purposes. He has to think of the other, of his brother man. Hence Kondrie says to him:

> But *one* knight alone shall ride with thee; choose thou from these warriors here
> And trust to my skill and knowledge to guide thee upon thy way.
> (XV: 812-813)

We already know who Parzival's companion must be.

> ... By his brother sat Parzival,
> And he prayed him to be his comrade, nor his words did unheeded fall,
> For Feirefis spake him ready to Monsalväsch Burg to ride.
> (XV: 827-829)

Whilst they arm themselves for the journey to the Holy Grail, Parzival relates in French what Trevrezent once had told him. No one can come to the Grail through fighting, only if he is called by the spiritual world can a man attain the Grail.

> ... no conflict may win that prize,
> And 'tis vain on that Quest to spend them, since 'tis hidden from mortal eyes.
> (XV: 851-852)

The Fifteenth Adventure closes with the poet telling us how Kondrie, Parzival and Feirefis peacefully set out upon their pilgrimage to the Grail.

Adventure XVI

Meanwhile at the Castle of the Grail—so the poet tells us at the beginning of the sixteenth adventure—Amfortas continues to suffer. How gladly would he have died, but this was not granted him. The Grail gave him ever a continuance of life. Therefore he closed his eyes before it. But he could not do so for more than four days, for then his weakness overcame him, he saw the Grail and was quickened anew. So the suffering continued endlessly till the day when Parzival and Feirefis drew near. There was then a particular constellation of the stars.

> And the time was near when the planet, its course in high heaven run,
> Mars or Jupiter, glowing wrathful, its station had well-nigh won,
> And the spot whence it took its journey—Ah! then was an evil day
> That wrought ill to the wound of Amfortas, and the torment would have its way;
> And maiden and knight must hearken as the palace rang with his cries... (XVI: 37-41)

Pages are occupied with a description of every kind of scent and precious stone that were used for the easing of Amfortas's pain. But the saviour is already approaching. As Parzival is brought before Amfortas, Amfortas says to him:

> 'If e'er men have praised thy valour, then be thou to my woe a friend,
> If *Parzival* men shall call thee, then forbid me the Grail to see
> Seven nights and eight days, and I wot well my wailing shall silenced be!' (XVI: 133-136)

Thus Amfortas prays Parzival to help him remain awake for seven nights, for in sleep man sees the Grail, and to wish not to see the Grail means to wish to remain awake. But something more is involved than the words of Amfortas lead us to expect. The indication is even given that more is implied than what Amfortas has said, for he adds further:

> 'No further I dare to warn thee—Well for thee if thou help canst bring!'

Parzival was deeply moved, and weeping threw himself on his knees. He called on God. Three times he addressed himself to the Trinity and implored the deliverance of Amfortas. What was the suffering of Amfortas? He was given up to the Father-forces, the forces that work in the body: *He could not find the Son*. This was the suffering of Amfortas, that he did not find the way from the Father to the Son. The way from natural necessity, from the compulsion of Nature to freedom of the soul, he did not find. So Parzival was right in addressing the Trinity. And he healed by the words: 'What aileth thee, mine uncle?' What is the answer to this question? What ailed Amfortas? That Parzival on his first visit omitted that which is only born in freedom, in the activity of the soul, viz. the question. This is the *Son* element, this is what Parzival must add, and with this there is brought about the conquest of what is bodily. Therefore the poet here reminds us of the raising of Lazarus by the Son. The Father is death. Concerning this—as Dr Steiner told us—Christ taught the disciples when He spoke of His approaching death with the words: 'I go to the Father.' Going to the Father is going to death. Overcoming death by resurrection is the redemption of the Father-forces by the Son-forces.

> ... He who Lazarus from death did wake,
> And by the mouth of His saint, Sylvester, a dead beast to life did bring,[138]
> Wrought healing and strength on Amfortas—and all men beheld the king,
> And what French folk shall know as '*Florie*' it shone on his face so fair. (XVI: 146–149)

Thus through Parzival's inner soul activity there was added to the *Father* element of the suffering Amfortas, the *Son*. And through the union of the two there followed the resurrection, the renewal of dying Nature. Therein the power of the *Holy Spirit* is revealed. The Grail Saga reveals the *Mystery of the Trinity*. Man and Nature are born from God the Father. Nature in itself is destined to decay. In the Son–God it goes through its death, in order to live again by the power of the Spirit. This is the Mystery of the redemption of Amfortas.

The poet tells us that Amfortas through his healing attained a wondrous beauty. He manifests that radiant transfiguration which the French call *Florie*. So it is with man when he penetrates from the experience of the Father to the experience of the Son. The Sun-force of the Sun shines forth in him and penetrates him. On the Grail a writing appears which names Parzival lord of the Grail. That which had been separated was now united. Kondwiramur is nearing Monsalväsch. In the place where Parzival found the blood drops in the snow he now meets her. Once, on this spot, he fell into a dream overmastered by love's longing, but now he has overcome all this. His love is free from egoism, it has become a healing love which without egotistic desire is a free outraying gift. Like the light of the sun it streams over the world.

Parzival now rides to Trevrizent and tells him that Amfortas is saved by the power of God. It is at this point that Trevrezent confesses that in order to withhold Parzival from the Grail he had deceived him. Trevrezent had told Parzival that the fallen Powers could be redeemed. We have already commented on this passage (Adventure IX, p. 204). Through the Mystery of Golgotha there was given to the fallen powers, to Lucifer himself, the possibility of taking part in the universe once more. The serpent could become the dove. The way in which Parzival had been misled was that Trevrezent had allowed him to believe that the Grail could be won by *strife*. Those who engage in strife, however, can never attain to the Grail, not even those who strive for it. One has to be chosen. Thus Trevrezent now improves on what he had said before, and says:

> ... yet aforetime in sooth I lied,
> For I thought from the Grail to bring thee, and I would hide the truth from thee.
> Do thou for my sin give me pardon, henceforth I thy hand obey,
> O my king, and son of my sister!—Methinks that I once did say
> That the spirits cast forth from Heaven thereafter the Grail did tend
> By God's will, and besought His favour, till their penance at last did end.
> But God to Himself is faithful, and ne'er doth He changing know,
> Nor to them whom I named as forgiven did He ever forgiveness show.
> For they who refuse His service, He Himself will, I ween, refuse,
> And I wot they are lost for ever, and that fate they themselves did choose. (XVI: 185-194)

They are lost because they will continue to strive. But when they *give up striving* then they are redeemed. This is now applied to Parzival, who also desired to strive for the Grail and could not see that the Grail cannot be striven for.

> 'I mourned for thy fruitless labour, for ne'er did the story stand
> That the Grail might by man be conquered, and I fain had withheld thine hand;
> But with *thee* hath the chance been other, and thy prize shall the highest be,
> But since God's Hand doth give It to thee, turn thine heart to humility.' (XVI: 195-198)

The Grail cannot be attained by strife but only by love. That is not true Grail-teaching which says that the fallen Powers are eternally damned. The teaching of eternal damnation is not Christian and is not to be traced back in any way to a Christian source. It should not be rendered 'Eternity' but Aeon. Being shut out from normal world-evolution never holds good for more than definite periods of evolution, and moreover is dependent on the free decision of the being concerned. The true Christian tradition knows that the Holy Ghost is the transformed Lucifer and the Dove is the transformed Serpent; that the Grail was once formed from the precious stone of Lucifer and was filled with the Blood of Christ Who redeems Lucifer himself. This is the real Grail Mystery. Through eating of the tree in Paradise man has fallen. Through partaking of the Grail he is raised again. That is the real meaning of the Lord's Supper.

The following words also in Wolfram's poem hide a riddle:

'Quoth Parzival to his uncle, 'I would see her I ne'er might see
For well-nigh five years (XVI: 199–200)

Dr Steiner once explained this remarkable passage at the Waldorf School in answer to my question. He said: Parzival had not seen Kondwiramur for a long time. More than five years had passed since he had seen her. But it is of no consequence how many months or days have passed beyond five years if once the separation has lasted for that period. *The point is the five years*, for, said Dr Steiner, after a five-year separation love is extinguished. Something still remains, of course, namely the longing for love, but the love is then extinguished. I was astonished at this and replied that I could not understand how love could be extinguished. Nevertheless Dr Steiner said it was so. There is a distinction between love and longing for love. In Dante too we find a similar idea. For the love to have lasted Parzival would have had to see Kondwiramur before five years had elapsed. Thus the poet wishes to tell us that when Parzival met Kondwiramur, his connection with her was over and must again be renewed out of the conscious will.

Kiot of Katalangen recognised the Grail-armour from afar as Parzival now rode towards Kondwiramur. When Parzival reached the Queen's tent, she was sleeping, and the two boys Kardeis and Lohengrin lay by her side. So he found his wife and children in the same place where once he had lost consciousness in gazing on the blood-drops in the snow.

Now if blood and snow had robbed him of his senses and wit of yore,
(In this self-same spot its message the snow to his true heart bore)
For such sorrow she well repaid him, Kondwiramur, his wife—
Nor elsewhere had he sought love's solace in payment for love's fierce strife,
Tho' many their love had proffered—I ween that in bliss he lay,
And converse sweet, till morning drew nigh to the middle day.
(XVI: 249–254)

Then we are told again how the Mass was celebrated and Kardeiss was crowned. He became lord of Parzival's hereditary lands. Parzival now withdrew with Lohengrin and the Templars towards the Grail Castle. Kardeiss was taken to his kingdom by the vassals. On his ascent to the Grail

Castle, Parzival found Sigune dead in her hermitage on Schionatulander's coffin, and now Parzival once more enters the Grail Castle.

Parzival finds the Grail Castle as before. Again he sees the meal, but there is an important difference. On this evening the bloody spear was lacking. This indicates something of importance. Amfortas is now whole. Much is told us by the poet in this picture of the Grail meal without the bloody spear. We know that the spear points to Saturn, and that in representations of the Middle Ages Saturn is connected with the forces which bring old age and death. This time the Grail is comforting and refreshing,[139] it only manifests its upbuilding forces. What otherwise works in human nature to bring about age and death has been entirely spiritualised. We can regard old age as the body becoming frail. But we can also say the life forces raise themselves out of the body, and man becomes more spiritual in old age. Saturn thus brings at one time disintegration, hardening, then however, precisely through the hardening process the spiritual is set free. Parzival as King of the Grail experiences Saturn in a new way, and in a new way also the forces of the Moon.

Only is illicit love unto thee forbidden
(alternative version, closer to German than J. Weston, XV: 791)

This had been said to him. The forces of the Moon, which otherwise serve the body, the bodily upbuilding forces, and the forces of Saturn, which otherwise serve the disintegrating process, are both changed. And the forces of the remaining planets, which play between these poles, are also changed. To this transformation the poet refers when he indicates that this time the bleeding spear is absent. He is King of the Grail who has inwardly entirely transformed his human nature. Alchemy describes this transformation. It describes the attainment of the Grail-Kingship as the attainment of the Kingly Art. This transformation can be spoken of both microcosmically and macrocosmically. In the macrocosm the planetary system undergoes an extraordinary transformation. The sun dies, it has more and more spots. The Sun-Spirit Christ came down to earth in the Mystery of Golgotha and transforms the earth from within. It becomes a new sun. But this process transforms also the other planets. The moon circles around the earth so that it draws ever nearer. One day the earth will again take in the moon. This will happen when the moon through a transformation of her substance, her material substance, will be quite different. There will then be a union of the Sun and Moon forces within the earth. The Sun-Host in the vessel of the Moon will accomplish the transubstantiation within the Earth. The symbol of the Mass points to this future condition of the cosmos, and so also does the whole Alchemy of the Middle Ages. This cosmological process effects a complete transformation of the physiological. It consists in a change in the organisation of the whole human nature. The forces which serve growth and nourishment and which are regulated from the moon will become spiritualised. And the forces of the heart, which form the central point of the inner planetary system, will be laid hold of by the will. Rudolf Steiner has spoken of this transformation and has pointed out that the striped muscles of the heart show that the heart is on the way to becoming a voluntary muscle. These transformations will take place in the course of long periods of time, and they will not only be physiological and cosmological but moral transformations. The Grail King hastening ahead of the evolution of the world, anticipates them. He transforms his whole bodily, psychic and spiritual nature. This transformation has always been known in the mysteries and forms the background of all Cults. It is not by chance that Saturn has the same rhythm in years that the Moon has in days, and that the Moon is connected with birth and Saturn with death. Both the forces of birth and death will disappear in their manner of working today. And this is indicated by Wolfram von Eschenbach when it is said that one day the spear will no longer be visible. When the death forces are changed as a consequence of the previous changes of birth forces, the condition indicated here will be attained. If all that might be described in this connection were described in detail then it would have to take the form of an Apocalypse. Anyone studying the Apocalypse in this light will see how the Sun and Moon are spoken of there and their transformation indicated. To fully expound this mystery the whole human and cosmic nature in its progress would have to be considered.

And now we are told that Repanse de Schoye carries the Grail. Feirefis sees her but not the Grail. He desires her love. She is promised to him if he will be baptised. When this takes place he sees the Grail also. Feirefis comes to the Grail through the bearer of the Grail and through the fact that the one destined for the Grail brings him with him as his companion.

In this picture, much of the future history of humanity is expressed. Feirefis represents the destiny of the East. Feirefis can only receive Christianity by looking to the Western bearer of this Christianity with whom he must unite himself. Then he will accept baptism and be able to see the Grail himself. This is the secret of the Grail history, that the Grail will be carried from the West to the East. In unconscious depths Christianity also is at work in non-Christian confessions, as Dr Steiner taught. But today the East when it looks at the West does not see that which appears to it as worthy of admiration. And so the West misses its task of bringing the Christ Impulse to the East, if it, the West, does not experience a true Christianity. It is furthermore told us that the wife of Feirefis, Sekundille, has died, and that therefore Feirefis can win Repanse de Schoye as his bride. In this, events in the East are indicated which have come to pass there since the Middle Ages. The old wisdom of the East vanishes and dies. The East seeks the Grail in the West, it seeks for the Grail-bearer. Through this Grail-bearer, Christianity reaches the East. But this conclusion of the Grail story points no longer to the history of the 9th, 10th, 11th, 12th, 13th centuries, it is the prophetic history of the age of discovery, and indeed of a still more future history. In this first volume this can only be indicated. If fate allows the addition of a second volume, it will then gradually extend to a presentation of a complete world-history under the aspect of the Grail. Here it must suffice to say that the following verse relates to later times:

> Then first in her distant journey did Repanse de Schoie find joy,
> And in India's realm hereafter did she bear to the king a boy;
> And *Prester John*[140] they called him, and he won to himself such fame
> That henceforward all kings of his country were known by no other name.
> And Feirefis sent a writing thro' the kingdoms whose crown he bore,
> And the Christian faith was honoured as it never had been of yore. (XVI: 587–592)

These are prophetic words and point in an apocalyptic sense to a time later than that of Wolfram von Eschenbach. These things of course, were already preparing themselves in the time that Wolfram could survey. If it proves possible to get as far as a description of the Priest King John all this will become clear. Also as regards the Lohengrin Saga we cannot here go into detail because this volume is chiefly concerned with the 9th century. The Lohengrin Saga, as Dr Steiner showed us, is connected approximately with the history of the year AD 1,000. The culture of the towns under Henry the Fowler forms the background of the Lohengrin Saga. Thus the story of Parzival ends with a brief indication and vision of another period.

The task nevertheless which is to be completed in this volume needs a description of the historical events of the 9th century as a basis for the pictures that have been given. This will be found in the concluding chapter. Here we will close Wolfram's history of the Grail with the words which Wolfram himself uses to conclude it:

> If Chretien of Troyes, the Master, hath done to this tale a wrong,
> Then *Kiot* may well be wrathful, for he taught us aright the song,
> To the end the Provençal told it—How Herzeleide's son the Grail
> Did win, as was fore-ordained when Amfortas thereto did fail.
> And thus from Provence, the story to the German land was brought,
> And aright was it told, and the story doth lack in the ending naught.
> I, Wolfram of Eschenbach, think me that hereof will I speak no more.[141] (XVI: 663–669)

A true initiate, one who has understood his master well, was Wolfram von Eschenbach. He knew that his Master Kiot was concerned to give humanity news of the mighty ruling of the star-world and its reflection in the line of descent of the race of the Grail. Therefore he says:

> Of the hero's children and his race I have told you correctly.
> [literal translation]

6

The Eighth Oecumenical Council and The History of the Holy Grail

Regino of Prüm, the Chronicler from the Monastery founded by the mother of Charibert of Laon, called in the Legend Flos, states that: 'among those raised to the Papal dignity in the city of Rome since the time of Saint Gregory not one proved the equal of Nicholas,' (meaning Nicholas I who was Pope from April 858 until 13 November 867). 'He issued his commands to Kings and Tyrants and his relations with them were as though he were ruler of the whole earth. With Bishops and Priests who observed their Lord's commandments in the right manner he was humble, kind, pious, and gentle, but towards the godless and such as had strayed from the right way he was terrible and fierce in moral denunciation, so that it was justly held that by the will of God a second Elias had arisen again in our time, if not in the body, at any rate in spirit and in power.' (Non corpore, tamen spiritu et virtuti.)

This Nicholas exercised a powerful influence upon the course of events in the world. He acted, as he himself put it, 'in the power of the judgement of the Holy Spirit', which spoke through him. Rudolf Steiner has described[1] the mighty mission of Pope Nicholas in a lecture published by Albert Steffen in the *Goetheanum Weekly* for 8 April, 1923. There Nicholas is described as the representative of the Middle stream between that of East and West. What appears in the historic deeds of Pope Nicholas is the result of a struggle played out on the World Stage more or less behind the scenes. Albert Steffen indicates this in the picture he gives in his drama, *Chef des Generalstabs* (Dornach, Switzerland, 1927) showing Nicholas between two figures: 'A red-robed Prince of the Church with dark countenance presents Nicholas with a Decree for his signature. A dignitary clad in purple tries to withhold him from giving it. He implores Nicholas not to sign. The Pope undergoes an inward struggle, but finally appends his name thereto. Applause resounds throughout the Assembly, and tumult arises. The Prince of the Church triumphantly seizes the paper and waves it aloft. Pope Nicholas with imploring gestures demands it back. Shrill laughter among his opponents.'

The spiritual decision confronting Pope Nicholas was the following: the time had come in the history of the world when it had to be decided whether mankind was ready to guide into earthly evolution that which in earthly

28. Portraits of Pope Nicholas I
    (i) from 'Vitae summorum Pontificum ...' conscriptae a Domenico Tempesta Romano, Rome 1596
    (from a contemporary coin)

    (ii) from 'Ciaconius, A., Vitae et res gestae Pontificum Romanorum ...'. Rome 1677)

29. Portrait of Pope Nicholas I
    (from: 'Bullarium Magnum Romanum', Rome 1739)

realms is the reflection of the Trinity, rightly understood. Ever since Carolingian times the question had become more and more urgent as to how the East and the West could and should think in regard to the relationship of the Holy Spirit to the Father and the Son. This came to expression in the struggle over the 'filioque'. A very good account of the historic progress of the spiritual struggle is to be found in Cardinal Hergenröther's fundamental work on *Photius, the Patriarch of Constantinople, his Life and Work and the Greek Schism* (Regensburg, 1867, Manz, Vol. I, p. 684 seq.).

The West, says Dr Steiner, must by its very nature accept the additional 'filioque', and the East reject it. For the West is more orientated to the event of Whitsuntide and therewith to the problem of the individual spirit-penetration of each single human being by the Holy Spirit, whereby the Holy Spirit proceeds from the Son. The East is more orientated to the John Baptism at which the Holy Spirit brooded over the waters as once the spirit of God at the beginning of Creation. Then the Spirit came down from the Creator, the Father God, even as at the John Baptism it proceeded from the Father God, who there spoke out of the heights about the Son. The 'filioque' conflict thus shows the difference between the psychological constitution of humanity in East and West, how a single truth has to be approached from different angles in East and West. The task assigned to the Middle region is to arrive at such action out of its understanding of the differentiation of humanity over the earth as shall enable the whole of humanity to attain its goal according to its differentiations. The task assigned to Pope Nicholas was that of rightly guiding the Middle. In this task he was confronted with a time in which the first doubts were being expressed with regard to the Trinity. The Grail Legend is a Legend in which is related how the Dove of the Holy Spirit yearly renews its all-revivifying powers; and the message of this resurrection power of the Spirit came to those very men who had fallen into doubt as to the Trinity. It wished to allay these doubts. Thus was it described in the wonderful poem of *Le Grand Saint Graal*,[2] and thus did Wolfram von Eschenbach describe it when he showed how the knight Sir Parzival was led through doubt to bliss (saelde). The doubt here meant relates to the fate of mankind. For in human fate rules the necessity of the World of the Father *and* the freedom of the World of the Son, inasmuch as in destiny necessity and freedom are in a wonderful way mingled. The Spirit which proceeds from the Father *and* from the Son, from the divinely ordained regulating powers, and from humanly-willed purposings, it is this that rules in destiny. THUS, IN THE PROBLEM OF HUMAN FATE IS DEMONSTRATED THE PROBLEM OF THE ALL-RULING SPIRIT IN ITS TWOFOLD RELATION TO FATHER AND SON.

In the time of Pope Nicholas the country now called Lothringen and that called Italy was the Middle Region. In the struggles of the Frankish Lords and Bishops during the period of the ninth century—that is the period of Pope Nicholas—there lived the problems of the Middle.

'How must the Middle be guided with respect to the soul-impulses of the

East?' This question was what ruled in the life of Pope Nicholas I.

In regard to this question Pope Nicholas found a trusty Counsellor in Anastasius, as Hergenröther showed, the same who later, under Hadrian II, the Pope's successor, appears as Anastasius Bibliothecarius. This Anastasius Bibliothecarius is an important personality with whom our knowledge of the Council of 869 is closely connected. For when the legates, on their homeward journey, were overpowered by sea-robbers there survived only the private papers prepared by Anastasius, held to be an authentic report, and Anastasius himself emphatically stated that this alone and no other account of the proceedings of the Council reported the truth. Hergenröther in his work on Photius, Vol. II, p. 64 seq., establishes the credence that must be given to this statement by Anastasius. Thus Anastasius is our witness for the Council of 869. Furthermore he, with Scotus Erigena, is the translator of the works of Dionysius the Areopagite, of which, as he relates in a letter to Charles the Bald, he had already read the Passio as a boy. (Migne Patr. lat. CXXIX. 737). In Anastasius we have to do with a personality who, through his destiny, stands in the stream of esoteric Christianity. He held the Papacy itself for three days but had to yield it up to Benedict III. Yet the counsel of this personality seems to have been indispensable to Nicholas on account of his knowledge of language in intercourse with the Greeks. Ernst Perels also expresses this in his book, *Pope Nicholas I and Anastasius Bibliothecarius* (Berlin, 1920, Weidmann, p. 298 seq.). He says that Anastasius, in knowledge of the sources of Canonical rights, of Church history and Greek history, was 'far superior' to Pope Nicholas. Thus we must adjudge no inconsiderable part to Anastasius in the linking up of the fate of Europe with the East. He stands more in the background of history as one observing its threads while Nicholas stands in the midst of the battle between opposing forces. He who was himself to become Pope assuredly carried out much of that which, through Nicholas, whom he submissively served, he would himself have inaugurated if fate had left him with the tiara. In 869 he stood in history as guardian of the truth. In him I perceive the good counsellor of Pope Nicholas.

Fate took Anastasius on a political mission to Constantinople, to negotiate a marriage in the service of Louis II. Louis II had as wife Engelberga.[3] From her and Louis II, who was the grandson of Hugo of Tours, was born Ermengarde. Thus it was for this Ermengarde, the great-granddaughter of Hugo of Tours, that Anastasius was sent to Constantinople, as marriage envoy, because the Emperor Basilius of Constantinople had sued for the hand of Ermengarde[4] for his son Constantine. That Louis II chose Anastasius is to be understood when we remember that Anastasius was Ermengarde's tutor. (Flodoard, Hist. Rem. eccles 1. III c. 27 M.G. SS. XIII 550). The marriage did not take place. Louis excused himself at the last moment 'on account of unforeseen circumstances.'[5] It was in this way that Anastasius was placed in the position of being able to rescue the statutes of the Council of 869. Gabriel, the Archangel whose office is to be herald to those destined for motherhood, expended upon Anastasius the beneficient powers of his being, and Anastasius put them to the service of the Sun forces of Truth. Fate allowed him and his two companions, Suppo and Eberhard to take part in the last and tenth sitting of the eighth Oecumenical Council on 28 February 870 (Böhmer, *Regesta Imperii Karolinger*, 2nd Ed. p. 509).

Let is now look at the other side from which Nicholas was influenced. This other side is represented by Rothad of Soissons. He it is, apparently, who brought to Rome that remarkable forgery, 'The Pseudo-Isidoric Decretals'. Nicholas at first rejected them and later used them. Professor A. Nissl of the University of Innsbruck (whose early death deprived scholarship all too soon of his services) exposed the secret of these Pseudo-Isidoric Decretals (Nissl's discovery was published from his letters by Prof. Thaner in the reports of the Institute for Austrian Historical Research, Vol. XI Innsbruck 1890, p. 627 seq.). Death prevented Prof. Nissl from working out his discovery. Nissl was evidently rightly convinced that a forger and liar must also be vain[6] so he searched for some sign of vanity in the Pseudo-Isidoric Decretal forgery. He searched to see whether a name could not be found in it by which one could be led to the composer, or to the one who had launched the document.

Two things call for remark: (1) The first sentence of the introduction to the circumlocutory document is a quotation from a writer of the name of Marius Mercator. But instead of naming Marius Mercator, the forged manuscript bears the name of Isidor Mercator. In order to hide the fact that it was something new and to avoid a modern style, the forger had evidently set to work to take single sentences out of innumerable older writings and pieced these together as a mosaic. In this way he had taken the first sentence, of course without naming its source, from Marius Mercator. The quotation is however not a literal one, and in place of the name of Marius appears Isidorus. When we quote the sentence as it really stands in the forgery we come to the second noteworthy thing. (2) The sentence: '*Isidorus Mercator servus Christi lectori conservo suo et parens in domino fidaei salutem*' appeared to Nissl altogether too artificial. The sense of the sentence is 'Isidore Mercator, the servant of Christ, to the kind reader Greeting in loyalty and obedience to the Lord'. Certainly a very fine dedication for the beginning of a book. Nissl rearranged the seventy-six letters of this sentence and the following sentence then appeared: 'Rottadus vero civitatis Suessionensis rector Incmaro Remensi foedo archipresuli dolum', which being translated reads: 'Rothad, the leader of the city of Soissons, to Hincmar of Rheims, the infamous Archbishop, this trick'.

This is an amazing result, as will readily be agreed. For Rothad of Soissons was in fact at strife with Hincmar of Rheims. The phrase is arrived at by a complete exchange of the letters within the sentence as it stood in the writing of Marius Mercator, presuming that the word Marius is replaced by Isidorus. And the whole script is ascribed to Isidorus. But it would be a mistake to take Rothad of Soissons as the author. He is no more than the exponent of a whole school. For the learning contained in the Pseudo-Isidoric Decretals is indeed so great that a comprehensive library is worked into them. In spite of the extraordinarily extensive study of modern learning, so worthy of all respect, it has not been possible to establish convincingly who was the author of the forgery. And a more ingenious aperçu than that of Nissl cannot be discovered by modern investigation. Perhaps however this important matter may be arrived at in the following way: It is not so much a matter of knowing who the falsifier is; the other is really the question: what part the forgery has to play in the course of human events. Let us pursue this further.

The living spirit died when doubts of the Trinity arose. The Council of 869 through which Trichotomy was abolished—the teaching that body, soul and spirit are to be considered as distinct from one another in man—is only the completion of a long series of events. The Council merely expressed what had been accomplished within human evolution. The path to the spirit was no longer accessible in the old way. At the same time Ahriman, the Spirit of Lies, was drawing near. It is all the same whose hand wrote the forgery. Ahriman wrote it; that spirit of Untruth then entering humanity. But upon this fact hangs world history, for how could the modern age come about, the age of the machine, of printing, of the power of the newspaper, without the entry of this Spirit? It had to enter. The question confronting Nicholas was not: Shall this Spirit of Untruth be allowed entrance or not, but only this: As he is entering our life, what direction can be given him into the souls of the mid-European people?[7]

This was the great problem confronting Nicholas and his Counsellor. They solved it as well as they could, but they could not succeed in hindering what had to happen as a world necessity. What was laid upon Nicholas's shoulders was a necessity, before which the question of the guilt or innocence of individuals vanishes. The Pseudo-Isidoric Decretals are the historical document for the entry of the Spirit of Untruth, of which, at the same time, the result must be the expression of the fact that thereafter the spirit, in the sense of later interpretations, was no longer to be spoken of, but only body and soul, the soul being furnished with certain spiritual characteristics.

It was Nicholas of Cusa who, at a much later date, was one of the first fully to see that what then appeared was a forgery, a work of Ahriman. In his work, *De Concordantia Catholica*, in the third book, he expresses his doubts about the genuineness of the endowment of the Church by Constantine (Patrimonium Petri) and in conclusion also about important parts of the Isidoric Decretals (Book III, Chap. II).

It is not the content of the Pseudo-Isidoric Decretals—for example, the elevation of Episcopal power as against worldly power, etc.—which is of first importance, but the morality of being supported by a falsification. And this dependence upon a falsification is no single instance, for the ninth century is full of such falsifications. The Pseudo-Isidoric Decretals are significant only because the place where they were accepted at that time represented the highest spiritual leadership.

This event of world-wide significance was reflected in the Grail Legend. The development of the Western stream is presented in the Parzival Way of Knowledge. Where the Castle of the Grail is actually to be found may be problematical, but one thing is certain, viz. that it is to be sought in the West. Just as clearly is the East represented through Feirefis. He comes from the country of queen Sekundille, which is to be found in the East. The Middle stream is represented by Gawain; his way leads him to Italy and Sicily. Here is Castle Merveil. Thus in the Grail Legend one sees the problem of the time of the ninth century demonstrated by typical representatives and the question arises as to how the Middle stands between East and West. That the story of Gawain has been declared to be an inserted episode not belonging to the whole is a quite special tragedy which appears also elsewhere in Mid-European history. Gawain, the representative of Mid-Europe, the Middle stream, is predestined to become lord of Castle Merveil, to conquer the Klingsor power. When I once asked Dr Steiner whether Klingsor was a real person or merely a figure in the legend he told me that Klingsor was an actual personality; he could not tell me with certainty whether he could be proved to be so from documentary evidence. From spiritual investigation, however, it can be established that Klingsor was Count of Capua. Thence Klingsor sought alliance with the Sicilian Arabians at the Castle of Kalot Bobot.

It is the place which, on the map, for example the atlas of Andrees, is designated as Kalta Bellota, which is to be found in South-West Sicily not very far from the coast where, on the coast the name Sciacca stands. Here, in Kalta Bellota, was the centre to which Klingsor attached himself. Kalath al-Bellut, referred to by Wenrich (*rerum ab Arab gest* . . . comment p. 308) as the *Castle of the Oaks*. Here African Mohammedanism was established. In 840 Kalta Bellota was conquered by the allies of Abu-l'kal-Aghlab ibn Ibrahim who were at the same time the lords of Palermo. In 827 the Arabians came to Sicily. In 831 they conquered Palermo, in 840 Kalta Bellota. Then came the conditions described in the Grail Legend.

Benedict of Soracte says in his Chronicle that the Arabians had come across as soon as they noticed that the Frankish kings were quarrelling amongst themselves.

In 827 a certain Euphemius called the Arabians to Sicily. Being pursued by the brothers of a nun of Syracuse whom he had raped he saw no other way out than to ally himself with the Arabians (cf. Carusius, *History of the Arabs in Sicily*). In 836 the Consul Andreas called in the Arabians to gain their support for Naples in the fight against Sikard of Benevento (Hergenröther, Photius, Vol. II, p. 167). When Sikard died in 839 Radelchis took his place. This again caused Gastalden Pando to call the Arabians to Apulia, where they arrived under the leadership of Kalfun. In 840–41 the Arabians, who had come as friends suddenly overcame Bari, and Pando was tortured and drowned. In spite of this, Radelchis took the Arabians into his pay. The

Arabians thus came into the country because after the death of Count Sikard of Benevento in 839 the inhabitants of the country were divided into two parties of which the Benventians chose Sikard's Chancellor Radelchis, and the Salernians Sikenult, Sikard's brother (Erchempertus, *History of the Langobards*). Pando, who had invited the Arabians, was the son of Landulf I cf. the genealogical tree in Peregrinus's *Historia principum Langobardorum*[8] (Naples, 1749. Vol. I, p. 65).

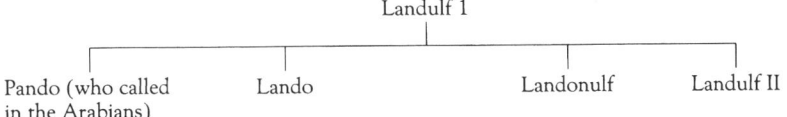

In 862, after the death of his brothers, Landulf II became sole Count of Capua. He is a remarkable personality. (I have to thank my friend Dr Eugen Kolisko for directing me to the personality of Landulf in this whole connection. He drew my attention to the significance of the only writer who speaks of these matters, Erchempertus). In Chapter 21 on Landulf II Erchempertus writes (the citation here given is a translation kindly made for me by Herrn Joachim Schultz):

> He was the youngest son and, as was later revealed, his mother, while still bearing him (Landulf II) in her womb, giving rein to sorrowful thoughts, had a vision. It appeared to her that she had given birth to a flaming torch. Falling to earth, this spread fire over a wide region and appeared to burn up the whole of Benevento. Then the dream or vision vanished. Deeply distressed she hastened to impart the dreadful tidings to her husband. Hearing the conclusion of the vision the father foretold the future in verse:
>   Alas, sweet wife, what a fate pursues us!
>   Thy terrified countenance portends a frightful prophesy.
>   It is overshadowed by the birth as yet in thy body.
>   It shall love not, it shall separate those bound by blood bonds
>   And finally shall drive apart the citizens by poisonous speeches,
>   And rage like burning fire in the hearts of the righteous.
> What he uttered in spiritual ecstasy we have had to see with our own eyes, for by his deed—and by the sword rather than by fire—innumerable innocent people have perished. Yet that fire which was later kindled at his instigation, (to speak in the symbols of this picture), took hold of the blood of the human race. That this did not seem inconceivable to anyone or to have been an invention of the imagination I have almost as many witnesses as there are dwellers in the town.

Further, in chapter 31 we read, 'It was that Landulf, clever in character, but habitually sly, all too greedy and assiduous, ambitious beyond the ordinary, vain beyond measure, a violater of monks, a robber of humanity . . . he was a despiser of his own princes, a forswearer and traitor to his own grandchild. He knew nothing beyond the desires of his own flesh. He got no peace, not even at his death. Wherever he saw alliances being welded he set his will against them, sowing the seeds of disruption. Should that appear inconceivable to anyone, let him pay regard to the many troubles he heaped upon Guaiferius. Thrice he swore to him that he acknowledged him as chief. He much preferred to capture the souls of innocent men than to regard anyone as equal in worth, let alone more worthy of honour. . . He only liked always the half-men and gave them preference. In spite of this he fulfilled the words of the prophet Isaiah (III. 4), "Effeminate men shall rule over them." If I were to try to relate the deed of this man in sufficient detail, time would pass I think more quickly than the words could shape themselves to speech. But should any wish to hear more he can read it in my verses.' (It is not quite certain whether by these verses Erchempertus meant the prophecy quoted above, or others which have not come down to us).

This Landulf II now met the Emperor Louis II in Montecassino and won so great an influence over him that he (the Emperor) made him 'a third man in the realm'. In Chapter 36 Erchempertus writes: 'By reason of this elevation in rank he strove with ardent desire for the Archbishopric of the whole of Benevento, and tried to make Capua a metropolis. But the Lord did not allow this to happen and he did not win the high position.' It was further perceived by the Emperor Louis II that he wished to be united with his daughter Winigis. But the Emperor's wife Engelberga assisted her husband and daughter in preventing this (p. 518 Böhmer, *Regesta Imperii I*, Karolinger 751–918, 2nd ed., Innsbruck, 1908).

From these quotations there is certainly enough to show that what is described in the Grail Legend as the neighbourhood of Castle Merveil is in full accord with the moral tone of the picture given us in the facts and character-sketches we have quoted from history. Here as elsewhere legend and history agree most wonderfully.

Thus in what has been just described there also comes to expression that immorality which finally materialised in the fact of the Pseudo-Isidoric Decretals. *The description of Klingsor's character* given by Wolfram von Eschenbach has its *historic archetype in Landulf II, Duke of Capua*. And what the legend relates of the alliance with the Arabians can be referred to Landulf's brother Pando. It becomes more and more clear that the period round about 869 provides the historic background for what appears in Wolfram von Eschenbach's Parzival as artistic creation.

7

The Grail Lineage

In working through the Chronicles of the European countries, Kiot found in those of Anjou the right karmic setting to make him believe that he had discovered the Grail lineage.

Kiot, as we know, took his start from the prophecies of the Astrologer (of Flegetanis). In the starry script (1200 BC) he read that after the end of twelve hundred years the Sun Spirit Christ would make himself manifest in a chosen human being, in Jesus. The Sun-Host would rest in the Moon-Chalice. As a fruit of one of the tribes led by the Moon God Jehovah that perfect body was to appear which should be worthy to receive the Sun Spirit. The history of the Jewish race is an earthly reflection of the starry script. Abraham came from Ur of the Chaldees (from the land of the star wisdom). In his blood was imprinted what the Babylonians observed in the heavens. The twelve tribes reflected on the earth the twelve signs of the Zodiac ruling in the heavens. That has long since been a matter of knowledge. Rudolf Steiner has shown us how the wanderings of the Jewish people are the wanderings from one planetary force to another. In Egypt the Jewish people, who were under the guidance of the Moon God Jehovah, met with the Hermes or Mercury cult. In Babylon during the Babylonian captivity the Jewish people came into contact with the Ishtar-Venus worship. In Jerusalem the Jewish people became a vessel for the Sun Spirit. This had been prepared, stage by stage.

In 1200 BC the Jews prophetically foreshadowed their Sun leadership. In Joshua we have the personality who, through everything known about him, is to be seen as the prophetic anticipation of the figure of Jesus. Joshua was first called Hosea, and both words are identical with the word Jesus. Joshua is moreover he who, when the manna (bread) failed, brought grapes, i.e. wine, as prophecy of the glories of the Promised Land. At this point of the Jewish people's evolution occur the prophecies of Flegetanis.

Now Kiot asks himself in what way was there anything analogous in the time of Parzival. Where was there to be found in his time a people worthy of serving the Grail?

In the ninth century the Christ Impulse must quite clearly have had a different form and manner of working from that which it had in the Old Testament times. At that time the Sun Spirit, the Christ, the Light of the

World, had not yet descended into a human ego. The Logos had not yet become Flesh. In the ninth century AD the earthly life of Christ had been already for a long time a fact of history. The risen, living Christ, who had permeated the individual human ego, strove to lay hold of this ego-nature from within. He began to work from ego to ego, i.e. socially. To my mind there is no doubt that since the ninth century we have passed a still further stage of our evolution, in that in these times the Christ Impulse wishes to lay hold of the peoples. Individually we are Christians; as members of racial or national groups we still struggle on, as it were, unbaptised.

A whole people that, as a people, would fain live the Christian life, does not exist. The Christian State is still a Utopia.

In the ninth century this problem was still at an early stage. The 'State' was not yet born. Blood bonds and the ties of family relationships were closely bound up together with great landed properties, and were the foundations of the evolution of that time. During the time that had elapsed since the Folk Wanderings, a mingling of blood among the European peoples was taking place. The same period saw the beginnings of Christianity. The Irish monks brought in a Christianity which, as a continuation of the Druid cult so closely connected with agriculture, had a tendency to associate itself with the economic life. Roman Christianity allied itself with the progressive powers of State politics. Grail Christianity remained the way for purely human development. Its objective was the individual. But at the same time in the Grail Temple, as a vision of the future in the seventy-two choirs, the union of the seventy-two peoples of the earth was to be seen.

This was now the question for the ninth century; can Europe as the Middle country find its evolution apart from the East and West in such a way as to lead the East to the Grail, by showing it how worthy of love is the Grail bearer? That was the experience of Feirefis, the representative of the East.

Thus arose the task assigned to the Middle, say round about the region of Lothringen (Lorraine)—to cause a light to ray forth to illumine the East.

What stood out as an historic impulse at that time within a wide field of activity was expressed as though in symbolic history in the fate of St Odilie.

Odilie was born of a house the head of which, Adalrich, or Eticho, her father, had inherited the dukedom of Alsace in 666. He is a personality to whom all that rests upon the individual, through the fact that his indwelling forces come by physical inheritance, is a grave burden of responsibility.

Therefore when a child who was blind, Odilie, was born to him, he said to himself: now people will ask, 'Who has sinned, the child or its parents?' He therefore wished to kill the child to escape the suggestion that it was his fault that Odilie was born lacking the sight of her eyes. Thus thought the father. Not so the mother. To rescue the child she, with the help of the child's nurse, brought her to her own family at Beaume les Dames. There the child grew up.

In Regensburg, to the East of Palma (Beaume les Dames), there then lived

30. Duke Eticho and his daughter St Odilie
   (from Silbermann, P.A., 'Beschreibung von Hohenburg oder dem St. Odilienberg', 1781)
   (Early portrait of the sculpture on St Odilienberg)

31. Duke Eticho and his daughter St Odilie
    (From Eccard, J.G., 'Origines Familiae Habsburgo-Austriacae', 1721)

32. Duke Eticho and his daughter St Odilie
   (Original sculpture in its present state of preservation)
   (For the acquisition of this picture, as well as for manifold literary references and all kinds of other help, I have to thank Herrn Camille Schneider.)

33. *The bell from Arlesheim Church with the portrait of St. Odilie, the Patron Saint of Arlesheim. The inscription reads:* 'Domine Acclude in nobis Lumen Veritatis.'

Erhard, Bishop of Regensburg. By grace a divine vision was granted him. He received the command to go to Palma, with his brother Hydulfus, to baptise the blind maiden. At the baptism she would receive her sight. And so it befell. The cosmic power which, as the light of the world, opened the eyes of him who had been born blind, gave light to the eyes of Odilie also at the touch of Bishop Erhard's baptismal water. He named the child St Odile, Sol Dei, Sun of God.

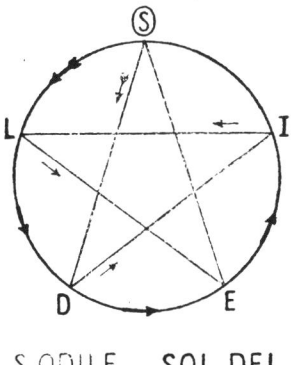

S ODILE   SOL DEI

The above can be read by either following the arms of the pentagram or the circumference of the circle.

Thus in the legend St Odile is described as the Sun of God. Father and daughter face each other as light and darkness. It was a gloomy thought to the father that it was through him that the light was darkened for Odilie. Notwithstanding that, she came to the light.

At Eticho's court lived Odilie's younger brother whose heart was drawn to her. He sent her horses and a carriage and she returned home. For this however his father whipped him soundly. When Odilie became old enough her father demanded of her that she should marry. She however did not wish to do so. Driven from home in consequence she fled to the hill near Adalrichsheim (Arlesheim near Basel) which, interpenetrated as it is with caverns, was regarded from old as a hermitage. What she here met with and what influences she felt history does not relate. It was at least a place where Odilie experienced that there she could find refuge from the forces pursuing her. Rudolf Steiner has told us about this flight. We refer our readers to the accompanying letters, also reproduced in facsimile on pp. 288, 289:

Berlin Friedenau,
26 November 1927

Dear Dr Stein,

I willingly accede to your wish to have a copy for use in your book

34. Facsimilie of letter from Eliza von Moltke, 26 November 1927

Arlesheim 27.12.27.

Sehr geehrter Hr. Stein!

Ich freue mich sehr in der Lage zu sein, Ihnen konkrete Antwort auf Ihre Frage geben zu können. Sie fragen, ob ich weiss welchen Berg Herr Dr. Steiner in seiner Mitteilung vom 31. August 1915 mit den Worten bezeichnet: "der Berg, der vis à vis unserem Dornacher Bau steht." — Ich kann auf diese Frage sehr genaue Antwort geben, da Dr. Steiner gelegentlich meiner ersten Anwesenheit in Dornach im Spätherbst 1915 mich zu einem Gang mit ihm nach der Ermitage aufforderte und dort an Ort und Stelle wo man vom Theater aus den Dornacher Bau liegen sieht mir sagte: "Hier dieser Berg ist die Stelle zu der Odilie geflohen ist."

Mit freundlichem Gruss Ihre sehr ergebene

Eliza von Moltke
geb: Gräfin Moltke Huitfeldt

35. Facsimilie of letter from Eliza von Moltke, 27 December 1927

of what Dr Rudolf Steiner told me on 31 August, 1917, about the Odilienberg in Alsace.

'The Odilien Cloister on the Odilienberg was originally a seat of pagan Mysteries, later christianised by the saintly Odilie. One hundred and fifty years before Nicholas I, the German Duke Eticho lived at the Odilienburg. He had a daughter Odilie, who was blind, and whose father wished to kill her on that account; she was blind so that she might receive her sight at baptism. More than once she was most wonderfully rescued, thus at one time fleeing before her father's pursuit but under her younger brother's protection, she sought refuge in the hill facing our building at Dornach, and was again rescued in a miraculous way on the return journey, and at that time there happened the transformation of the old Mystery Centre into a Christian Cloister. Thence proceeded that Christian stream which Pope Nicholas was concerned to propagate, the stream which was to be in complete opposition to the Byzantine. Later there was a continuous interchange of letters between the Odilienberg and Pope Nicholas. This stream Duke Eticho wished to destroy; he stood in the service of the Merovingians.

This Cloister was a source whence the substance of Christianity spread through the West; hence Odilienberg was the centre of so many fights with Alsace'.

With friendly greetings, Yours faithfully

(signed) Eliza von Moltke
geb. Gräfin Moltke Huitfeldt.

Arlesheim 27.12.27

Dear Dr Stein,

I am very glad to be in a position to give you a concrete answer to your question. You ask whether I know which hill Dr Steiner meant by the words, 'The hill standing opposite our building at Dornach': words which he used to me on 31 August 1917. I can answer precisely that on my first visit to Dornach in the late autumn of 1917 Dr Steiner invited me to a walk with him to the Hermitage, and there at a spot from which one can see the Dornach Building from a fissure in the cliff face he said to me: 'Here, this hill is the place to which Odilie fled.'

With friendly greetings, Yours faithfully

(signed) Eliza von Moltke
geb. Gräfin Moltke Huitfeldt.

Thence, Odilie, as it appears and as the legend relates,[1] fled to Freiburg. On her return her father's opposition was broken down. One of the centres of heathen Mysteries from olden times, existing in the stronghold, was now transformed into a Christian Cloister through Odilie. It is more than likely that Irish Christianity found entrance there. Odilie herself deeply experienced her connection with John the Baptist. Up on the hill she prayed. Down in the valley, she healed the sick. Thus the Niedermünster arose down in the valley on the Pilgrims' Way, a centre of the Mysteries and a centre of healing, side by side. Near Niedermünster Odilie herself planted three lime trees. An unknown spiritual guide gave her the three branches to plant and cherish. She planted them as the outer sign that Niedermünster was dedicated to the Holy Trinity.[1a] To this Niedermünster in the valley under the stronghold, by the guidance of fate, a wise destiny brought the relic of the first blood-outpouring of Jesus. Hugo of Tours followed a divine command in bringing it thither. Thus through him Tours, whence Charlemagne set out on his great cultural mission into the world, is closely connected by destiny with the Odilienberg.

Near the stronghold stands the cloister and the Church of Andlau. Richardis, wife of Charles III, had charge of it. Here honour was done to the head of Lazarus which they believed they possessed, and so in this we have a link with early Christianity. And here were guarded relics from Cyprus where later the Order of the Templars set up its centre. We know that the Red Knight came to Andlau. The Grail and Parzival Legends lead us to this neighbourhood in the time of the ninth century.

What Charlemagne inaugurated through the 'filioque', what Pope Nicholas I continued—the formulation of the mission of Middle Europe—was brought to an end by a descendant of the line of Odilie—Leo IX. He finally (1054) separated the Greek and Roman Churches.

As the ninth century is the subject of this volume, these later events can only be touched upon. But Odilie's biographer, Dionysius Albrecht, in his *History von Hohenburg, oder St. Odilienberg*, 1751, shows quite clearly that he was conscious of the mission of the line of Odilie.

He writes (p. 56): 'This ducal line became widespread, as once was the line of Jacob, viz.: from the centre of Alsace towards the evening in France, towards the morning in the Roman and Austrian realms, towards midday in Spain, and towards midnight in Saxony and Brandenburg'. Just as Jacob's seed, according to the stars in their order, spread to all points of the compass, so also did the race of Odilie. And Rudolf von Habsburg is a direct descendant of Saint Odilie's brother. Maximilian boasted with pride of this descent. The House of Baden, too, derived thence, and by his marriage with Giselbert, daughter of Lothar I, the Count of Maassgau also was united with the House of Brabant (Hessen). So, too, the House of the Dukes of Lothringen were descended through the male line from Eticho. By the marriage of Maria Theresa with Francis I, the House of Habsburg united with that of Lothringen to form what was later the Austrian Empire. Through the female descent there were naturally more and more of the ruling families united with the House of Eticho. The older genealogies show that, for example, the daughter of Hugo von Tours, Adelheid, married as her second husband Count Robert the Strong, Duke of the Franks, and so became the female ancestor of the Capet Kings. Certainly after quite a short time the Capet Kings became connected through the female line with the descendants of Eticho. Thus the son of Hugh Capet, King Robert II of France, married Bertha of Burgundy (vide table to illustrate the relationships of the personalities connected with the Grail Legend at the end of the book). From this marriage were descended the remaining kings of France and of Portugal. Whether the old Carolingians and Merovingians can be closely connected genealogically with the family of Odilie must remain undecided, as the old genealogies, which make the ancestral father of the Carolingians, Arnulf of Metz, into a grandson of Ansbert and Blithilde, daughter of Chlotar I, are not to be relied upon as sources.[2]

As a matter of fact most of the ruling families of Europe were of the race of Odilie. And an old tradition emphasises this. The mission of these family connections was not so much to form a powerful House, i.e. turning a family spirit into a spirit of the times (as happened for example with the Hapsburgs of Odilien descent); its task was to expand what is bound up with the family into what is Cosmopolitan. A Gabriel blood-connection, which, indeed in some of its branches, bore on its coat of arms the Gabriel Lily,[3] was to become the vessel of the world-irradiating Sun-Impulse. Thus was the Kingdom of God to arise. In the time however during which this should have been accomplished it was neglected.

In this book (dealing as it does only with the ninth century) we cannot undertake to show in what form that problem can be solved today. It must suffice here to mention Rudolf Steiner's *Kernpunkte der Sozialen Frage* (*Towards Social Renewal*—see Bibl.).

Here, however, I should like to point out that those who are connected with the Grail story are members of one family. The genealogical table at the end of the book may be regarded as a little summary given by way of example, to illustrate the relationships of the personalities bound up with the Grail Saga. It illustrates how those connected with the history of the Grail are linked together in a family relationship.

One sees, for instance, that Godfrey of Bouillon, whose companions in arms founded the Order of the Knights Templar, stands in a relationship with the family of Odilie. Charibert of Laon, Charlemagne, Hugo of Tours, Charles III, Richardis, Dietrich of Alsace, Philip of Alsace are all within this connection. Philip of Alsace was the Master of Chrétien of Troyes. His father was the recipient of a blood relic.

Thus, in summing up I might say: The Grail race has the mission of expanding to cosmopolitan proportions all that belongs to the narrow group, of enlarging separate interests to world interests. In our time this mission lies no longer with the family group. How the present day faces this impulse will only become clear as, through our consideration of the ensuing centuries, we step by step draw nearer to the problem.

Afterword

We are at the end of the exposition which the contents of the first volume aim to provide. They embody the attempt, following a suggestion by Rudolf Steiner, to view the historical events of the Ninth Century in the light of the Parzival and Grail Stories. The author of them puts forward a first attempt in this direction. It goes without saying that such a first endeavour must be incomplete in very many directions. Although I am quite well aware of this myself, nevertheless I have decided to make my working material publicly available; for only through the co-operation of many is it possible to do justice to such difficult matter. When I consider the sizeable army of every research worker who has sought to clarify the sagas, legends and historic background of the Grail narrative in connection with other centuries, I can quite well imagine that plenty of new facts are still to come to light when once the Ninth Century is worked over also by many co-workers with a like love for the Grail research.

Here in this place, I must thank all the people who have helped me in the execution of this work. It is a quite extraordinarily large number. I have been assisted to be able to make journeys to many of the historic sites that come into consideration, to visit them for myself.[1] I have been equipped with the means to be able to take photographs—some of which could be included in the book as illustrations. I was also able to procure literature hard to come by. Numerous friends have collected so much material for me in German libraries and abroad, that it could only be partly used here, and will be published as the further work progresses.

Essential help was also given in certain respects by those who either supplied me with the translations, or, where my knowledge of the language was lacking, as with Hebrew, supplied me with their knowledge.

To all these persons and above all to those who have given me suggestions through their ideas, may I here once more express my heart-felt thanks; and finally also to the management and all the individual members of the Landesbibliothek (National Library), Stuttgart, for so much friendly assistance, and to Orient/Occident Publishing Company, who have so magnanimously made the printing of this book possible.

Stuttgart, Easter 1928
Dr Walter Johannes Stein.

Appendix I

From the Collected Works of Saint Gregory the Great
(Migne, Patrologia latina Vol. 77)
Translated by Joachim Schulz

The following passage is printed here because it gives an explanation of the mysterious 'Nonnosus' of the Waldo Legend.

'I will now relate something from a neighbouring locality which came to me as reported by the Reverend Bishop Maximian (of Syracuse) and the old monk Laurio whom you know, who are both still alive. This Laurio was brought up by St. Anastasius in the Monastery called Suppentonia, near the town Nepesia. Anastasius again was in constant touch with Nonnosus, a man of estimable life, and head of the Monastery of Mount Sorakte, this both on account of the nearness of the Monastery and because of the high character and aims of its head (Martyrology, 2nd September). Nonnosus, on his part, lived under a very severe Prior, whose behaviour he bore with wonderful serenity. Among the brothers he was distinguished for his gentleness and the Prior's anger had often been mitigated by his meekness. Since the monastery lay on a mountain-top there was no level land for cultivation even for a small garden for the brothers. But a narrow ledge jutted out of the side of the hill. It was quite covered by a natural outcrop of rock. One day while the Reverend Nonnosus was considering it, it struck him that the spot could at least be made fit for growing cabbages if it were not covered with that mass of rock. But it was clear that fifty (or according to another account, five hundred) span of oxen could hardly remove such a mass. Since reliance upon human labour must be a doubtful matter, he addressed himself to divine aid and concentrated on prayer throughout the stillness of the night. Next morning the brothers, coming to the spot, found the mighty mass of rock had withdrawn to the extent of one hundred and eighty paces, so that the brothers found themselves presented with a wide space.

Another time, a glass lamp, which the reverend man was cleaning in the oratorium, fell from his hand and was broken into innumerable pieces. Fearing the weight of the Prior's anger, he swiftly gathered together all the pieces and laid them before the altar, and sighing deeply sank down in prayer. Raising his head from his prayer he found the lamp intact, the broken pieces of which he had gathered together in such fear. By two such miracles he imitated the Fathers: in the case of the rocky mass, the deed of Gregory (called the wonder-worker) who removed a mountain; in the case of the restoration of the lamp, the miraculous deed of Donatus, who made a broken bowl whole again.

Peter: As I see it we have here new miracles after the manner of old.
Gregory: Would you like to hear too of how Nonnosus imitated the deeds of Elisha?
Peter: Yes indeed, I ardently wish it.
Gregory: Once in the Monastery, when the oil was giving out, and it was time to gather in the olives, but no fruit was to be seen on the olive trees, it seemed good to the Prior that the brethren should go to work outside, in the neighbourhood, to gather olives in order that they might bring oil to the monastery as wages for their labour. The godly Nonnosus, however, with the greatest humility prevented this, in order that the brethren who were to go out should not suffer harm in their souls by seeking to earn the oil. And because some olives appeared hanging on the trees of the monastery, he had them gathered in and brought into the oil-press, so that the oil, however little, might be squeezed out. So it was done and the brethren brought the oil thus obtained in a little vessel to Nonnosus, the servant of the Lord. He immediately placed it upon the altar, and when everyone had departed he remained in prayer. After a while the brethren were recalled and he charged them that the oil which they had brought should be taken and divided amongst all the vessels in the monastery, pouring a very little in each, so that all, as it were, should partake by the grace of that same oil. The oil being poured in, the vessels were immediately stoppered. On the following day they were opened and all were found full.
Peter: Let us declare daily that the words of truth are fulfilled which say: 'My father worketh hitherto, and I also work'.

(John V.27) p. 467.

Letter 22

He (Gregory) says that he will hear Maurentius with regard to the property he was trying to secure.

Gregory to Nonnosus
May God Almighty tell your heart with what honour and love I am bound to you. And being unable to express this by letter, I shall, as fit opportunity offers, take care to demonstrate it to you in deeds. As further guarantee of

the good faith of this benificence I assure you that when your humble Maurentius comes about the property which your honour desires, we will comply with his wishes in every way (p. 646).

Letter 51: To the Bishop Maximian

When he (Gregory) thought of writing of the miracles of the Fathers which had taken place in Italy, he prayed Maximian to impart to him all he remembered.

Gregory to the Bishop Maximian in Syracuse
My brethren who live in intimacy with me urge me, by all means, to write a brief account of the miracles of the Fathers, which, as we have heard, have taken place in Italy. Thereto I urgently desire the support of your love (in another edition: wisdom) so that you may briefly write me what you have in your memory and what you have been fortunate enough to experience. For I remember that you related something that I have forgotten about the Lord and Abbot Nonnosus who lived with the Reverend Anastasius of Pentomi. I beg of you to write down this and anything else—in case there is anything else—in a letter, and send it to me speedily, unless you yourself can come to me.

He (Nonnosus) was Provost of the Monastery on Mt. Sorakte, under a very stern Prior. Later he was Abbot of the same Monastery. 'Lord', St. Gregory called him in accordance with the Rule of St. Benedict, Ch. 63; but 'Abbot' because, as was believed, he carried on the battle of Christ. So he could be named Lord and Abbot.

Appendix II

Introduction and Preface to the Edition of the Book of Jashar
Printed in Venice 1625
The Printer's Preface

The following is from an Hebraic source which contains certain traditions similar to those we find in Wolfram von Eschenbach's poem. For the translation from the Hebrew I have to thank Dr Paul Rieger of Stuttgart.

Thus speaks one of no account: My witness in the Heavens and my Fortress in the heights, the God of the World knows, and Israel will know, how much suffering I have gone through and how much trouble I have taken to bring out this book. From the day I was banished from my home country, the city which is a Mother to Israel, the city of the wise and the learned, the famous town Fes, God has cast me out homeless and, for my heavy sins, has broken my strength with suffering upon suffering, until the time when I came to the Italian harbour-town, Livorno, which is under the leadership of our lord and master, His Serene Highness the Grand Duke, Don Ferdinand di Medici. Day and night I find no solace. Sleep flees from my eyes while I must continually think and ponder in my heart how heavy has been the labour of my blessed father, the crown of my head, physically and financially, to have this book printed. May God reward him for all this. Only now has one been found to make me a copy of this book, the learned scholar and theologian Rabbi Jacob ben Atiah. He made the copy from an original old manuscript of which the letters were almost obliterated. Without his great learning it would not have been possible for the copy to have been made on account of its age and its worn lettering. My late father, being a friend of his, lent him this manuscript so that he might make a copy. In the year 5373 [Jewish calendar] (1613) I unfortunately had to leave my home and family on account of the famine, the plague and the war. There was fighting at that time between the sons of the old King of Morocco who had died. Each of his sons wanted to be king and lived at the expense of the Jews until only the smallest remnant of them was left. Many Jewish families were quite blotted out, and innumerable books, old and new, printed and in manuscript, were burnt, torn up and destroyed. Woe to the eyes that had to look upon it. For the evil and the good may God be praised. Because I now feared that this book too would share the fate of others, I worked incessantly, writing begging letters to my exiled brethren in the faith, in the towns of Argel, Tetuan and Fes, where the book might be found. After a lengthy search it proved to be in the keeping of a respected member of the Community, R. Mose Chassan. When he found that I had the intention to have the book printed, that it might be circulated everywhere, he did not hesitate to send me the book as a gift. May God reward him for this deed.

In all humility I had prepared the book *Kethoneth Josef* (Joseph's Coat) that falls into two parts. The first part contains explanations of certain passages of the Bible which I expounded according to my ability. The second part contains sermons which I had delivered to the Community. I have also composed a third work in explanation of individual writings and words of our wise men. If God spares my life I shall have these works printed. But in spite of all this I have decided to print this book first because the printing of this *Sepher-Hajaschar* is calculated to arouse reverence for God and to bind human hearts to God, that they may experience through it the wonders of God and His beneficent deeds towards our fathers of old, and how He chose us from amongst all peoples. All this can be fully gathered from the preface to the book, in which are indicated the thirteen excellences which are adapted to lead men to trust in God and to have faith. I personally found the clues to the explanations of difficult parts of the Pentateuch in many places in this book. Through this book they are explained without any trouble, because here facts are circumstantially described which are only briefly given in the Pentateuch. Likewise circumstantial statements are to be found in this book which our teacher has only touched upon in the Talmud. For this reason I did not give precedence to the printing of my above-mentioned book but will publish this book first, and I am sure that in doing so I shall give all Israel cause for great joy. I trust to God to strengthen and support me in the coming years that I may print my own books. I pray to God that for the sake of His Holy Name and His Holy teaching, He will ever keep me in His love and faith, and lead me in peace and in the paths of justice. Amen.

Introduction

This is the book that is called *Sepher-Hajaschar*.

Tradition tells us that when Jerusalem, the Holy City, was destroyed by Titus, all the leaders of the Roman army sought ingress for the sake of booty. Among them there was one of the officers of Titus, Cedrus by name, who made his way in and found a large, roomy house, and seized as booty all that he found there. As he was leaving the house he observed the wall and noticed that there was a room hidden in it. Breaking up the wall and the building he found there an earthen vessel full of books, namely, the Pentateuch, the Prophets, lives of Saints, books of the kings of Israel and the kings of the Gentiles, and also many other Israelitish books. Among these were books of the really authentic Mischah (i.e. the Jewish tradition) and also many scrolls lay there. He discovered further all kinds of food and wine and an old man who sat there reading the books.[1] The officer, seeing this surprising picture, was overcome with astonishment, and said to the old man: 'Why are you sitting here alone with no one by?' The old man replied, 'For many days and years and ages have I known that Jerusalem would be destroyed. Therefore did I build this home and arranged this chamber in the wall and took these books with me for my reading. So also vessels of food did I bring here, for I said to myself, "Perhaps one day that will serve as rescue."'

Then, as God ordained, did the old man find pity in the eyes of the officer. With all honour did he bring him away thence, with all his books. They went from city to city, from country to country, until they came to the province of Seville (Asbilia). The officer found the old man ripe in wisdom, science and knowledge of all kinds. He was well acquainted with every kind of wisdom, and seeing this, the officer raised him to still greater honour, so that he was entertained in his household for good, and became his teacher in all wisdom. In their wisdom they built a large house outside Seville into which they put all their books. The house stands there until this day. There they wrote down all those things which would happen to the kings of the world until the arrival of our Saviour.

It came to pass that after we[2] had undergone many things at the hands of the kings of Edom, we had to wander from city to city, from country to country, in bitter suffering. Then there came into our hands this book, called Tholedoth Adam (the Geneology of Adam, that is, of humanity) with many books which originally came from this house outside Seville. These books had come later to the city of Naples, now under the rule of the noble kings of Spain. Seeing that the books were rich in wisdom, we conceived a plan to get them printed like many other books that had fallen into our hands. *For this book is especially valuable* and has many points of excellence, more than all others. Twelve copies of it came into our hands. We have studied them throughout and see that they agree the one with the other, without the slightest variation or addition or lack, with no difference of word or letter.

They are absolutely identical and form *one* version. And because we now saw all kinds of excellences in this book, our hearts were moved to form the decision to have them printed. We found therein written that this book is called Sepher-Hajaschar, and it appears that the reason for this name was that in the arrangement of all its words all things were in order, as they happened in world history, nothing earlier or later. For in this book you find nothing related later that had happened earlier, or anything anticipated which only occurred later. Rather is everything written down in its own place and time.[3] In addition you find it announced in all its words that someone has died in such and such a year of life of another, etc. Hence its name Sepher-Hajaschar, but it is usually called *Sepher Tholedoth Adam* (the book of the genealogy of man). The reason for this is that it goes by the name of its opening words. (Genesis 5,1.) The true name however is Sepher-

Hajaschar for the reason already mentioned. Today the book is found translated in the handwriting of the Greeks. They call it *Libros de los diritos*; it is also to be found among the Romans who call it *Libro de las palabras, de los dias, di pitos, de los grandes, de los niras, di pwis (Difaûtes) murir Joshua*. It is found today also in the handwriting of the kings of Edom who call it *losti libro napiniiznas de Adam*. It is written in the book of the Hasmonites, which has come into our hands, that in the days of King Ptolemy of Egypt he commanded his servants to collect all the books of religion and world-history to be found anywhere in the world, in order thereby to become wise, and to search in them concerning the things of the world. Furthermore, in order fully to practise what is right and just, he commanded that they should compile from all these books a single book containing the laws of the kings, of law and religion (faith) and all the needs of the world. They went forth and collected 965 books[4] and brought them to him. Then he sent them out anew in order to complete the thousand books. This they did; thereupon princes of Israel appeared before him and said to him, 'Our Lord and King, why are you taking all this trouble? Send to Jerusalem to the Jews that they should bring the book of their Thora to you, which was written by the hand of the prophet at the command of God. In that book you will find the last words of wisdom and a judgement concerning everything you desire. Then the King hearkened to their words. They sent him this book, for they could not give him the book of God. For they said, 'We cannot give the divine book of Thora into the hands of a heathen.' When the book came into Ptolemy's hands he read it. It pleased him greatly; he sought therein according to his wisdom and found what he sought, and willingly forsook all the books collected for him, and honoured those who had advised him in this matter.

After some time the princes of Israel brought to his notice that the Jews had not sent the king the book of Thora. They came and said to him: 'Our Lord and King, the Jews made a mock of you[5] for they have not sent you the book of the Thora about which we spoke to you but have sent you another book which was in their hands; therefore send again to them to deliver you the book of Thora, for in it you will find far better what you seek than in the book they sent you.' When the King heard this he was overcome with anger towards the Jews, and was in a rage until he sent a second time to them that they should hand over the book Thora to him. Fearing however that they would again make a mock of him he was cleverer than they, and sent for the seventy aged men who were amongst them and set them in seventy separate houses so that each individual should write out the book of Thora so that no variation between them could be found. And behold, the spirit of holiness rested upon them and the seventy old men wrote him seventy books, all the seventy old men, and all had the same text without lack or addition of a sentence. Then he rejoiced greatly, honoured the old men and all Jews, and sent gifts to Jerusalem as it is there written. But when he died the Jews conceived a wise plan against his son. They took the book Thora out of his treasure-chamber but left the other book and did not take it with them, so that every king who should rule after him should come to know the wonderful deeds of the God they honoured, and that He had chosen Israel out of all the people, and that there was no God beside Him. The book is thus to be found in Egypt to this day. And from this time onwards the book spread to all countries until it came into our hands, living here as we do today in banishment in the city of Naples which is under the rule of the King of Spain, and behold, in this book are to be found most of the names of the Kings of Edom, and of Rome (Kittim), and of Africa, who lived in those days, although all this has nothing to do with the main object and content of this book.

There is a special reason why it is necessary to make known to everyone who publishes this book what is the difference between the wars of Israel and the wars of the heathen. A conquest among heathen kings is chance. Not so however in the case of a Jewish conquest over the heathen, for then the victory is through divine miracle as long as Israel puts his faith in the divine name.[6] This book has many excellent points, which all have the one effect of strengthening trust in God, and of confirming surrender to God and His Will. The first excellence of this book is that it exactly describes the creation of man and the occurrence of the Flood, the years of the twenty generations and their transgressions, and in what epoch they were born and died. And thereby it strengthens our hearts so that we have confidence in the *name of God* when we see the great wonders He achieved in the days of old. The second excellence is that it relates the birth of Abraham in detail and how far his surrender to the *name of God* went, the fate that befell him with Nimrod; then the history of the generations of the time of the Flood, how God scattered them to the far ends of the earth, and how they built for themselves all the countries and towns which have kept their name to this day; and thereby we approach to a knowledge of the Creator.

The third excellence is that it retails in particular the fidelity of the three progenitors of the race to God, and the content of their fate, who preached to us the fear of God. The fourth is that the book tells us the history of Sodom and recounts its sins and the causes of its destruction, thereby estranging us inwardly from all evil. The fifth is the dependence of Isaac and Jacob on God, Sarah's prayer and her grief at the sacrifice of Isaac, which is a quite special excellence inclining our hearts to serve God. The sixth is that it represents the wars of the sons of Jacob with the men of Sichem and the seven towns of the Amorites. These fill our hearts with true confidence in God, because they trusted in God, for example, in the case where ten men destroyed seven towns, which would not have been possible if it were not for the trust in God that ruled their hearts. The seventh excellence is that it represents the fate of Joseph in Egypt with Potiphar, his wife and the King of Egypt. All this fills our hearts with the fear of God, and keeps us back from all sins, so that finally God shall lead us to the good. The eighth excellence is what happened to Moses our teacher—the peace of God be with him—in Ethiopia and Midian. From these stories we experience the powerful Deeds of God, which He did to the Just, and this confirms us in our trust in God. The ninth excellence is that it relates everything that happened to Israel in Egypt, the beginning of their servitude, how they had to endure slave labour under the King of Egypt, and what their fate was in all this. God rescued them because they trusted in Him, and there is no doubt that whoever reads the history of Egypt during the nights of the Easter Festival will derive great benefit therefrom as it says, 'Whoever relates much of the Exodus from Egypt is especially praiseworthy' (The Haggada). Before all things we ought to notice that this narration is literally true if it is learnt and read according to the Haggada, and I am sure that great benefit is to be derived therefrom. So do we in the present time in the country belonging to Spain, in exile; after reading out the whole Haggada we begin to read this book as far as it concerns the history of Egypt, from the wanderings to the description of their departure as given in this book. The eleventh excellence is that one finds there part of the exposition of our sages, and exponents of the Bible have explained the Thora with a commentary; as, e.g., in regard to the angels who met Jacob as he came from Aram, as they were going to Esau. Further, the chapter about Gabriel who taught Joseph seventy tongues, and likewise how he relates that he punished Midian on the field of Moab, and so forth. The twelfth, that every preacher who preaches before the Community can, from this book, obtain matter of his preaching which the Bible exponents have not otherwise explained; thereby they will win the hearts of their hearers. The thirteenth is that all merchants and travellers who otherwise have no time to study the Thora can read in this book and derive benefit therefrom for their souls, and joy for their bodies, when they hear of things which are quite new and are to be found in no other book, for thereby must man think on God and trust in Him. And seeing that the book has such power and so many excellent points, we find therein reason for printing it without adding or omitting anything, and so we began to print the fifty books that they might be in the hands of our brethren, those who hope with us, so that the book may be distributed to all generations, through every town, every family, every country, that they may all see the wonders of God and the benefits which He bestowed upon our fathers since the beginning, and how He chose us out of the peoples. Thereby will the thoughtful have the benefit of taking the fear of God into their hearts, for we trust in the Lord, in Him do we find our support, and from Him do we pray for help and salvation, that He may support us in this work, for it is a pious work. May He grant us happiness and keep us in the right paths, delivering us from error and trespasses, as it was said by the Prophets: 'Who knoweth all trespasses? Cleanse us from our hidden sins.' May God bring us a successful issue, may He lead us in the path of blessedness for His Mercy's sake. May He fulfil the prayer of our hearts for good! Amen. May it please him.'

Appendix III
St Lawrence and the Grail Tradition of St Juan de la Peña in Spain

The mention of the cup of Valentia is the reason for the reference to the following legend.

At the time of the Holy Father Sixtus II (Pope, 257–8), there lived St Lawrence, a devoted pupil to the Pope. Because of his purity and modesty the Pope held him specially dear. So Sixtus made him one of the seven deacons of Rome. In this capacity it was Lawrence's duty on the one side to administer the Church property, and on the other to care for the poor. His deepest satisfaction however lay in the fact that he was permitted to assist the Pope whenever he read the Mass.

When, during the persecutions of the Christians in the years 257–8 by the Emperor Valerian, Sixtus also was brought to martyrdom, Lawrence full of sorrow, broke out with the words, 'O my Father, whither goest thou without thy son? Whither dost thou haste, O Priest, without thy Deacon, thou who hast never before raised the Host without thy servitor?'

Sixtus hearing these words turned back and said to Lawrence, 'In truth thou art destined for still greater deeds, and in three days thou too shalt taste of death.'

And so it happened as he had prophesied. For Lawrence was persecuted and asked to deliver up the Church property of which he was guardian.

At this point a later legend inserts something into the story. It is said that amongst these Church properties was to be found that cup which Christ had used at the Last Supper. Thus the significance of his refusal was that he was unwilling to deliver up the Grail vessel to the Romans. Instead he begged for time for reflection and when the poor were gathered together for the gifts which they were accustomed to receive, Lawrence said to the Judge, pointing out the great crowd, 'These are the Church's goods.' The Judge however had no mercy on him. Lawrence was condemned and, as had been prophesied, was laid upon the gridiron upon the third day. As he lay, still alive, on the fire, he said to the Judge, 'See, the one side is roasted enough; turn me now upon the other side and eat.'

This happened upon Mount Viminal, and on the Via Tiburtina was Lawrence buried. But the cup, so it was said, was brought to Spain to the

36. The Cup which is preserved in Valencia Cathedral, Spain
   It came there from the monastery of S. Juan-de la Peña, and according to a later legend
   it is supposed to have been guarded from the Romans by Saint Laurence.

Monastery St Juan de la Peña. Thence, through King Martin, it was brought to Valencia, where it is still to be seen to this day. But what is the meaning of this tale? For what reason did the writer of the legend insert this Grail tradition into the story of St Lawrence at a later time? He wished clearly to awaken us to a search as to whether a connection could not be found between St Lawrence and the Grail-stream, on the one hand, and the Monastery St Juan de la Peña on the other hand.

This is still to be investigated further.[1]

Appendix IV
The Chronology in Wolfram's Parzival

An excellent study of the chronology of Wolfram's Parzival was published by Rührmund. This treatise is to be found in: 'Zeitschrift für Deutsches Altertum', Moriz Haupt, Vol. VI, Leipzig, 1848 (Weidmann) pp. 465–478.

Therein is shown how in spring, at the time of sowing, Parzival left his mother and departed on his first journey. On the first day he came to the forest Brizljan, on the second he met Jeschute, on the third he defeated Ither and came in the evening to Gurnemanz. He remained with him fourteen days and on the eighteenth day of his journey reaches Pelrapär. Here on the twentieth and twenty-first days he celebrates his marriage with Kondwiramur. At Michaelmas Parzival left Pelrapär and came to the Grail Castle. On the next day after reaching the Grail Castle, Parzival reconciled Count Orilus with Jeschute and took the many-coloured spear of the Knight Taurian. Four and a half years and three days after this, Parzival arrived on Good Friday at Trevrezent's abode.

From this statement we can now reckon backwards. Rührmund places Easter on the first of April and calculating backwards he reckons that Parzival rode from Pelrapär to the Grail Castle for Michaelmas. But the assumption that Easter was on April the first is quite arbitrary.

The reckoning is different if one takes into consideration that the decisive experiences of Parzival always happen at the special festival seasons. Therefore it is easy to conclude that it was not *about* Michaelmas but *at* Michaelmas that the Grail Castle was reached for the first time. For this and the following calculation I am indebted to the suggestion given me by Fräulein Dr E. Vreede, leader of the Mathematical–Astronomical Section at the Goetheanum. In accordance with this, if we now reckon that Parzival arrived at the Grail Castle on 29 September, i.e. on Michaelmas Day, then the taking of the spear falls on the 30 September. Four and a half years and three days later Parzival comes to Trevrezent, i.e. on 3 April. This day is a Good Friday.

Through a fine work of Frederick Westberg: *Die biblische Chronologie nach Flavius Josephus und das Todesjahr Jesu*, Leipzig, 1910 (successor of A. Deichart), 3 April is proved to be the date of Christ's death and Rudolf Steiner has given us this date as a result of spiritual–scientific research. In his *Soul-Calendar* for the year 1912/13, under the date 3 April, Rudolf Steiner makes the statement: 'The third of April is the death-day of Jesus Christ, according to spiritual investigation.'

Thus Parzival was with Trevrezent on a special Good Friday, 3 April, the date of Christ's death. Four and a half years and three days earlier he was at the Grail Castle at Michaelmas. Now one understands the statement concerning the three days. They are the three days of April. The experiences of Parzival at the Castle of the Grail also appear in a new light. For it is on St Michael's Day that Parzival receives the Grail Sword, that is the Michael Sword. But the saying engraved upon it he was not able to read; for he lived without regarding the mystery of the progress of time.

Rührmund notices besides that Parzival, after he had conquered Gawain, on the first day of Whitsuntide, was called to the Grail. Again it was a special Whitsuntide, for this Whitsuntide fell on the day of the first outpouring of the Spirit.

Starting from these considerations we may ask: When in the ninth century did Good Friday fall on the 3 April? By reckoning we find that it was so in the years 823, 828, and 834.

[Another candidate for an Easter Sunday falling on 5 April is the year 845—tranl.]

Appendix V

Text and Facsimile of two letters by Her Excellency Eliza von Moltke-Huitfelt

Friedenau, 10 Dec. 1927

Dear Dr Stein!

I will also gladly oblige you in making the following note available to you for your book:

A conversation between Pope Nicholas and his counsellor, the Cardinal, which Dr Rudolf Steiner conveyed to Eliza von Moltke on 17 June 1924.

Pope:	Must we lose what spirituality has brought us by the descent of heaven to earth in the tidings of the Crucified One?
Counsellor:	What is outmoded must fade; death is merely renewed life. I see the life of Europe rising out of Asia's decline.
Pope:	It is a difficult decision.
Counsellor:	Nevertheless, it is required by higher powers so that Ahriman is given proper direction into soul-life which shall shine forth from Franconia to the East. 'Twas told me by the Northern Lights, which also possess a soul, as I lay in my own country one bright summer evening and listened to the voice of Gabriel, who wishes to bring a New Europe to birth.
Pope:	Are you sure?
Counsellor:	There can only be certainty where higher powers are speaking, and I am sure that their message is clear.
Pope:	Maybe they speak clearly enough, but I also know that the centuries to come will weigh heavily upon our souls.

Eliza von Moltke
née Countess Moltke Huitfeldt.

Friedenau 3 Dec. 1927

Friedenau 10 Dezember 1927.

Sehr geehrter Dr Stein!

Auch die folgende Notiz stelle ich Ihnen gerne für Ihr Buch zur Verfügung:

Ein Gespräch zwischen dem Papst Nikolaus und einem Pater, dem Kardinal, von Dr. Rudolf Steiner am 1ten Juni 1924 an Eliza von Moltke mitgeteilt:

Der Papst: Sollen wir verlieren, was uns Spirituelles brachte, nachdem die Hände von dem Gekreuzigten den Himmel auf die Erde senkte.

Der Pater: Was alt geworden, soll verwelken, es ist der Tod nur neues Leben. Ich sehe Europas Leben entsteigen aus Asiens Niedergang. —

Der Papst: Es wird der Entschluss schwer.

Der Pater: Doch höhere Geister wollen ihr, um Ahriman die rechte Richtung zu weisen, im Seelenleben, das von Franken nach dem Osten leuchten soll. Das Nordlicht, das auch eine Seele hat, das hat es mir gesagt, als ich in heller Sommernacht auf heimatlichen Steinen der Stimme lauschte, die von Gabriel kommt, der uns neues Europa gebären will.

Der Papst: Bist du sicher?

Der Pater: Aber es gibt nur Sicherheit, wo die höheren Geister sprechen, und ich bin sicher, dass sie deutlich sprechen.

Der Papst: Deutlich mögen sie sprechen; aber ich weiss auch, dass die Jahrhunderte, die da folgen auf unseren Seelen lasten. —

Eliza von Moltke
geb: Gräfin Moltke Huitfeldt.

37. Facsimilie of letter from Eliza von Moltke, 10 December 1927

Dear Dr Stein!

I will also gladly put the following note at your disposal for your book: Letter from Dr Rudolf Steiner to Eliza von Moltke from 28 July 1918 concerning Pope Nicholas and his counsellor:

'During the Ninth Century the Counsellor stood at the side of Nicholas with an overall view of the map of Europe. It was the task of Nicholas at that time to comprehend the ideas which were to separate East and West. Many were the people involved in this separation. It was this on which the Counsellor with his wide perspective was to pass judgement. But in those days people were much closer to the spiritual world. They were conscious of the approach and withdrawal of Spirit-beings. But the inhabitants of Central and Western Europe wanted to distance themselves from the Spirit-beings. Even at that time they had to make preparations for the coming of materialism. In the 9th Century Nicholas and his adviser possessed a great deal of direct spiritual awareness. The Adviser often used to say: "The Spirits will withdraw from Europe, but later on the Europeans will long for them to return. Without the Spirits the Europeans will create machines and other contrivancies. Therein will be their greatness. But through that they will develop in their own souls the archetype of 'Western Man', which will lead Ahrimanic culture to its highest pinnacle and will set it in place of themselves."'

Yours faithfully
Eliza von Moltke
née Countess Moltke Huitfeldt.

38. Facsimilie of letter from Eliza von Moltke, 3 December 1927

Notes

Chapter 1

1. The name 'Perceval' denotes one who strives in a certain way for higher knowledge and inner development. From this point of view, Perceval is not the name of an individual, but of a type. There are many Percevals, but these are not spoken of here. We are dealing with a definite personality, whose destiny has been described by Wolfram von Eschenbach.
2. A complete edition in German of the *Perceval* of Chrétien de Troyes and his continuators has been published by the Orient-Occident Publishing Company—Stuttgart, The Hague, London. This translation of the Old French verse is the work of Dr Konrad Sandkühler. Through him this most important poem has thus been made available to a large number of German readers, thereby assuring a rightful place to Chrétien's microcosmic description of the Grail alongside the macrocosmic aspect portrayed by Wolfram. I consider it to be an important historical event in German cultural life that this significant aspect of the Grail has been made available.

Chapter 2

1. The characteristic differences between these two descriptions will be dealt with later.
2. Isaiah LXIII, 1-3: 'He comes from Edom, with dyed garments from Bozrah; glorious in his apparel, marching in the greatness of his strength—Wherefore art thou red in thine apparel, and thy garments like him that treadeth in the winefat? I have trodden the winepress alone and of the peoples there was no man with me: yea I trod them in mine anger, and trampled them in my fury: and their life-blood is sprinkled on my garments and I have stained all my raiment.'
3. K. Beyerle, p. 434, *Kultur der Abtei Reichenau*, 1925, (Verlag der Münchner Drucke) says: '"Der Pater Nonnoso" in chap. 2, changed more correctly into the vocative "Nonnose" by a younger hand, is obviously thought to be a proper name. It is different in Chap. 6, where Abbot Waldo is called by the original writer, "Nonnoso Waldo", "Nonnosus" here being used as an adjective. In this second passage a writer of the 15th century has written the word Waldo over "Pater Nonnoso" in chap. 2, and therewith indicates that Abbot Waldo himself, to whom the writing is dedicated, is intended.' But we must ask, why is Waldo spoken of as Nonnosus? Nonnosus became administrator in the Monastery of St Silvester on Mount Soracte, which was

founded by Karlmann in 748. Gregory the Great relates of him a miracle concerning the increase of oil, which he compares with the deed of Elisha (2 Kings, IV). Compare Migne, *Patrologia latina* vol. 77. The writer of the blood-legend of Reichenau feels himself as an empty vessel in which is no oil. He calls upon Nonnosus-Waldo that he might fill him as Elijah did Elisha. He appeals to his power over the increase of oil. He wishes to work as a true pupil of the stream which Waldo also serves. His own forces are not sufficient. The text of this is given in Appendix 1.

Azan is really Prefect of the city of Osca (Huesca in the Spanish Mark). He sent the key of his city to Charles the Great and declared himself willing to surrender. Our author confuses him with the Monk from the East who, by order of the Patriarch of Jerusalem, brought relics from the holy grave of Christ to Charles the Great at Aachen, and from there, accompanied by the saintly Zacharias, by order of Charles, took back presents in return to Jerusalem. The confusion is groundless but is probably caused by the Chronicles mentioning both men close together. Cf. Annals of Lorscher, and Einhard, to the year 799. (K. Beyerle, pp. 368–9, vol. I, *Die Kultur der Abtei Reichenau*). According to Lembke in his history of Spain, the name Azan should be Hassan. The mention of the Spanish Mark is perhaps important. In the legend concerning Hugo of Tours given later in this chapter we meet it again. Fra Gaetano, in his work, *Il Catino di Smeraldo Orientale gemma Consagrata*, Genoa 1726, mentions a Chalice of Huesca. This Chalice is kept at Valentia. Cf. *Acta Sanctorum*, August, Vol. II, p. 504 ff. See Also Appendix III.

5. It is Leo III.
6. It is scarcely credible that a hero of the courage of Charles the Great should be afraid of so short a journey on the sea. Rather is it clear from the whole content of the story that *the journey over the sea to Corsica is the picture of a soul-spiritual undertaking* to which Charles the Great did not feel equal. Brave in outer deeds he was nevertheless afraid when it was a question of travelling on the sea of the soul-spiritual world. That he occasionally did so is shown by the legends which have been handed down.
7. Einhard could not have been called a priest before 819, since his marriage was not annulled until 819. Cf. the interesting book by Max Buchner, *Einhard als Künstler* (Einhard as Artist), p. 105. This book praises Einhard in a beautiful way and gives a very living picture of his nature and work. It appeared as No 210 of: *Studien zur deutschen Kunstgeschichte*, Strasburg (J.H. Ed. Heitz) 1919.
8. Thus the author of the 'Translatio' characterises Einhard and his friend. In the Court of Charles the Great they form the 'Latin Stream'. This was little inclined to venture on the uncertain sea of spiritual experience.
9. This Waldo belongs to the other stream at the Court of Charles the Great. In the course of our studies we shall learn to know him more exactly. It is the Grail Stream. The friends of Waldo concern themselves with the spread of Christianity in the national language and seek to further esoteric Christianity.
10. Thus we have in Azan a kind of Amfortas figure before us, a Guardian of the Grail to whom, however, it is not granted to find a truly kingly successor. For it is not Charles himself, but Waldo and Hunfrid who call forth in

themselves the courage to travel as pilgrims across the ocean of the spiritual world to the island where the Grail is guarded. This island need not be defined geographically.

11. Similar relics are to be found, e.g. in the list of relics at S. Pietro Montorio on the Janiculum in Rome, e.g. 'Wood of the Holy Cross', 'A thorn from Christ's Crown of Thorns'. Cf Terribilini, Descripti Templorum urbis Romae, Book IX (Bibliotheca Casanata).

12. The author wishes to emphasise that it is precisely Waldo and Hunfrid who are able to fetch the Grail but not Charles the Great or the other Counsellors, e.g. Einhard.

13. The author of the 'Translatio' says this in refutation of Einhard's biography of Charles the Great in which the Grail Stream is silent. Ph. Heber is the first to have remarked about this. Cf. his interesting work, *Waldo, Kaiser Karls des Grossen geistlicher Rat und die älteren Waldenser* (The Spiritual Counsellor of Charles the Great and the older Waldensers), Vol. VI, Nos 4 and 5 of *der Wahre Protestant*, ed. Mariot, Basel 1857. I owe it to my friend Wilhelm Rath and to Dr Maria Röschl, leader of the Youth Section at the Goetheanum, for having my attention drawn to this work.

14. At this point Ph. Heber remarks, loc. cit. p. 328: 'The records of the monastery, however, show us how on the contrary from the 12th Century onwards, everything was done to obliterate the memory of him and to hide the fame of his name under a bushel.'

15. This light on the grave of Waldo was extinguished after 1144. Ph Heber says, loc. cit. p. 329, 'In order to bring him into complete forgetfulness his name from now onwards is omitted from the list of Abbots without allowing the numerical succession to appear to be broken.'

16. Cf. K. Beyerle, p. 370, Vol. I, *Die Kultur der Abtei Reichenau*. The monastery of Schännis lay between the Zürcher and Wallenstatter Lake. (Note by Mone.)

17. Eichhorn on p. 332 of his *Episcopatus Curiensis in Rhaetia* mentions a cross-fragment decorated with gold and precious stones.

18. Zizers is on the Rhine, three hours north of Chur. (Note by Mone.)

19. Swanahild's name is entered in the book of the community of Reichenau. She lived in the time of the Emperor Henry I.

19a. Adalricus von Lenzburg. Cf. p. 333. Episcopatus Curiensis in Rhaetia sub metropoli Moguntina chronologice et diplomatice illustratus opera et studio, P. Ambrosii Eichhorn, 1797.

20. loc. cit. Eichhorn: 'S. Crucis particulum sponsae parentibus donavit, eo circiter tempore, quo anno 919 Burchhardus dux arcem Kyburgicam obsedit.' Here Walther is characterised as Walther of Kyburg. With regard to this cf. T.E. Pipitz: 'Die Grafen von Kyburg', Leipzig (Weidmann) 1839. According to Spangenberg's Saxon Chronicle a Wilhelm von Kyberg fought against the Hungarians at Merseburg in 933.

21. Burkhard I (917–926) Duke of Swabia. His wife is Reginlinde. His daughter is Bertha, the wife of Rudolf II of Burgundy who possessed the 'Holy Lance'. (Geschichtsschriften der deutschen Vorzeit. Vol. 29, p. 44.)

22. Mone remarks here: 'Thus Swanhild came from Linzgau and wished to pass through Reichenau to Zurzach which was considered a holy place because the relics of the holy Verena were kept there and were celebrated in the 10th

Century' (cf. Miracula S. Verense by Pertz). Karl Beyerle says, (p. 370, Vol. I of *Kultur der Abtei Reichenau*: 'Before the year 881 a nunnery had been founded in Zurzach, whose centre-point lay in devotion to the holy Verena; Charles III made over this cloister in the aforesaid year to his wife Richardis.' (This is the holy Richardis, the founder of the cloister at Andlau, which received possession of the relics of the holy Lazarus) Cf. Jos. Rietsch: 'Die nachevangelischen Geschichte der bethanischen Geschwister und die Lazarusreliquien in Andlau (Strasburger Diözesanblatt 1902-1904).

23. Mindersdorf.
24. Udalrich, Swanahilde's brother, No 637 of the professed list of monks from Carolingian times, p. 1177, Vol. 2: 'Die Kultur der Abtei Reichenau'.
25. Tongolf is entered in the register of brethren under names inserted later.
26. Vergil's *Aenead*, 6, 535.
27. St Kilian † 689, Apostle of the Frankish lands of the Main. Acta Sanctorum, apud Bolandus. 8 July.
28. Erchingen is the present Langdorf near Frauenfeld in Thurgau which belonged to the Abbey of Reichenau through the gift of Charles III (p. 371, K. Beyerle: 'Die Kultur des Klosters Reichenau'). In Dümmlers *Geschichte des Ostfränkischen Reiches* it is said that Langdorf belonged to Chadolt the brother of Liutward the beloved Chancellor of Charles III.
29. † 741.
30. The manuscript of 1434 is meant.
31. The author of the legend in the MS. of 1434.
32. That this was actually so is shown by the report of Ermoldus Nigellus. Behind Lothar, Hugo and his friend Matfrid stand as Judith's companions, who both also bore crowns, as Ermoldus Nigellus describes at the Baptism of the Danish King. They were thus highly revered. Cf. Jahrbücher der deutschen Geschichte 814-830, Ludwig der Fromme von Simson, Leipzig, 1847.
33. 'Desramè (Terramer) leads the Saracens. Undoubtedly reference is here made to Abderhaman who, after the downfall in 720 suffered by the Saracens at the hands of the then Duke of Aquitaine, made a fresh invasion in France in 730 with a terrible army augmented by a number of Africans and Arabs.'
34. It is clear that the legend here attributes to Charlemagne what occurred in the time of his co-regent and, after his death, sole ruler, Louis the Pious.
35. This refers to the fact that Pippin, recalled by the leaders of the rebellion, marched on Orleans, drove out Odo (who had been installed there by Bernard of Barcelona in place of Matfrid) and reinstated Matfrid. Cf. p. 345, Böhmer, Regesta imperii, Vol. I. *The Carolingians 751-918*, 2nd Ed. Innsbruck 1908.
35a. p. 288 et seq. Simson, Ludwig der Fromme, Vol. I. of 'Jahrbücher der deutschen Geschichte, 814-830'. 'Matfrid apparently lost the Monastery of Meuny on the Loire, which was his benefice, Hugo lost the Nunnery of St Julian near Auxerre. No doubt they were allowed to keep their inheritances.'
36. A single source tells that Hugo was sentenced to death: the court astronomer. Cf. p. 288, Simson, *Ludwig der Fromme*, Vol. I, Jahrbücher der deutschen Geschichte 814-830.
37. Michael holds the scales and it is to him that Hugo is turning.

38. This is not a historical fact. The motif is the same as in the legend of Flore and Blancheflur.
39. Aio of Friaul also belonged to the embassy. Spatarius Leo, who ten years previously had fled from Sicily to the Emperor in Rome, as well as the Doge Willeri, accompanied the embassy.
40. There is no reason to doubt the authenticity of this journey merely because it is recorded in a single document.
41. It is clear that such records of relics are misunderstandings. Originally the term 'Virgin's milk' signified the illumination bestowed by the divine Sophia. Goethe speaks in *Faust*, Part I, verse 455 of the breast of the Goddess of Wisdom (Diana of Ephesus) and Mephistopheles speaks of it in verse 1892.
42. Such a relic came into the possession of the Werden Monastery in Upper Bavaria, founded by St Ratho, general of the Emperor Henry I (*Acta Sanctorum*, June, Vol. III, p. 899).
43. In the Bible, the narrative about the Circumcision, which marks the covenant of the children of Israel with the Lord, Genesis XVII, 10, is followed by the story of Gabriel and Michael appearing with the Lord (the three men mentioned in Genesis XVIII, 2). In Joshua V.2, the second circumcision is recorded. Then it is stated that the people went short of Manna and in verse 13 Michael appears again. Joshua asks him: 'Art thou for us or our adversaries?' Michael replies: 'Nay, but as a captain of the hosts of the Lord am I now come.' Then Joshua prays and Michael says, 'The place whereon thou standest is holy.' The third circumcision is that of Jesus. It corresponds to baptism, to the giving of the name. 'And when eight days were accomplished for the circumcising of the child his name was called Jesus, which was so named of the angel (Gabriel) before he was conceived in the womb' (Luke II, 21). And once again Michael approaches, which is testified by Simeon when he says to Mary, 'Yea, a sword shall pierce through my own soul also.' After the circumcision, after the receiving of the name, man finds his help in Michael. The receiving of the relic was, therefore, a symbol of the approach of a divine aid and guidance.
44. Fortunatus was in reality the Patriarch of Grado. Charlemagne conferred on him the Abbey of Moyenmoutier and Fortunatus gave it relics from the East. In his critique of J. Rietsch's disquisition (*Die nachevangelischen Geschichte der bethanischen Geschwister und die Lazarusreliquien zu Andlau* (see Note 22), L. Pfleger points out that Fortunatus sent there a relic of Lazarus and relics of Stephen the Martyr. Fortunatus came to the court of Charlemagne approximately in the year 803.
45. In *Der Heiligen Leben und Leiden*, Vol. I. Leipzig 1913, p. 331 f., we read in the chapter entitled 'Von Sankt Carolus dem grossen Kaiser', Charlemagne received flowers which, springing from the Cross, turned into marble, then a nail from the Cross, Christ's loin cloth, Mary's shift, the swaddling clothes of Jesus.
46. Jacobus Wimphelingus writes in 1651 in his: *Katalog der Strassburger Bischöfe* under the section dealing with the 58th Bishop:
LVIII Conradus.
'Cognomento Wentzeslai, Eligitur anno Domini millesimo centesimo septuagesimo nono, vicesima dei decembris. Sub eo monasterium in

Nidder-Münster primo fuit dedicatum in honorem sanctae Dei genitricis Mariae, ab Episcopo Mantuano sedis apostolicae legato. Est ibidem crux ex laminis Argenteis non parva; in qua haec est inscriptio antiquis caracteribus facta, 'Anno ab incarnatione Domini millesimo centesimo nonagesimo septimo reparata est haec crux ab Edelinda Abbatissa, Abbatiae suae vicesimo secundo anno, sub Henrico Imperatore Romanorum et Rege Siciliae, anno regni sui sexto, in qua reconditum est praepucium Domini, de ligno Domini, de veste Mariae virginis, brachium sancti Basilii, brachium sancti Dyonisii caeterorumque sanctorum reliquiae. Item septimo Idus Julii haec crux sacratissima de Parisio, ductu angelorum sanctorum, camelo directa est ad hunc locum, ab inclyto Hugone et conjuge sua Abba et infra. Herzog Hug von Burgund und Aba.'

47. This is also mentioned by Eichhorn.
48. The 'Gate of Death' was attained on the path of initiation. Compare, for example, Job XXXVIII, 17. The man who passes through it recognises the rock from which Christ's water of life comes forth. Compare Matthew XVI, 18. 'On this rock I will build my church (a community of men confessing the Christ Impulse) and the gates of hell (death) shall not prevail against it'.
49. Gebwiler relates that Hugo kept the relic in a chapel standing in his bedroom. Often by night he and Dame Aba would hear the angels sing at the shrine. Then he said it was not right that the sacred thing should remain with them and he wanted to encase it in a silver cross, place this on a camel and let it go wherever it chose, and where it stopped the relic was to stay.
50. Reproduced in Johannes Andreas Silbermann, *Beschreibung von Hohenberg oder dem St Odilienberg*, Strassburg (Lorenz und Schuler), 1781, p. 53. This picture was made after an older copy that was in an old Psalmbook, kept in the old Chartreuse in Strasbourg. It became a prey to the flames together with the Strasbourg library on 24 August 1870 (Gass, J., *Chartreuse de Molsheim*, p. 34) where it was probably kept after the Revolution together with the other books of the Chartreuse. (Compare Schmidt, *Zur Geschichte der ältesten Bibliotheken*, Strassburg, 1882, p. 20).
51. The Cross resembles the State Cross in the Vienna Treasury which likewise is 'ein Prankenkreuz' with the representation of the four Evangelists.
52. The figure of Christ shows the feet placed in juxtaposition.
53. Genesis XXII. When Abraham desires to sacrifice his son Isaac, this son is given back by God and the mission for the whole Jewish race is laid on him. And now God sacrifices His Son, which is symbolically expressed in the sacrifice of the ram. Mankind is to enter into communion with God in the earthly sphere through this divine sacrifice. The picture shows this scene, which appears as an Old Testament prototype of Hugo's story.
54. Hosea-Joshua is sent by Moses to the place where he is no more able to go. As a token of having found the land he brings back the cluster of grapes (Numbers XIII, 17 et seq.).
55. 'Who is it that cometh from Edom with dyed garments from Bozrah?... Wherefore art thou red in thine apparel, and thy garments like him that treadeth in the winefat?' (Isaiah LXIII, 1-2). Compare the beginning of the Reichenau legend, (Chapter II).
56. Compare also John III, 14, 15. Here it is mentioned that to the heavenly bread, Manna, the heavenly water, Budhi, must be added.

57. Psalm XL, 7, 8.
58. While the Cross was being made, Dame Aba, the Duchess, had two books written with gold and silver letters on parchment dyed with presil. One of them contained the Gospels and Epistles of the year, while the other had on it the Collects, exorcisms and blessings, used throughout the year. Both these books she ordered to be provided with silver covers. She likewise ordered a beautiful Bible to be copied and, when the Cross was completely ready, she laid the Cross on one side of the camel's back and the three books were placed on the other side, in order that the burden might be equal. Hieron, Gebwiler, p. 67, *St Ottiliens Fürstlichen Herkommens, Heiligen Lebens und Wandels Histori*, Strasbourg, 1521.
59. It can therefore not be a physical object, but can only be a cult or piece of knowledge.
60. A feature reminiscent of Hertha's chariot.
61. According to an ancient tradition this spot is shown (even now) to the visitor to Niedermünster, situated so beautifully and peacefully. The imprint of the camel's foot is visible on a rock standing half upright in the middle of the walled square of the ruin that is considered to have been the chapel of the Knights of St Jakob, near the great curve of the road where the Hotel of St James originally stood, before it was burned down. If you go towards Niedermünster you will find the walled square after having turned a few steps to the right.
62. Thegan certifies Hugo's descent from this race in his memorandum of the year 821.
63. My attention was drawn to the existence of this book on the occasion of a visit to Odilienberg. Frau Dr Ita Wegman, recorder for the High School of Spiritual Science at the Goetheanum, in Dornach, has told me that a study of the historical figure of St Odilie would furnish many clues in the investigation of the spiritual history of humanity. To this hint I owe the fact that in my Grail investigations I have been led to sure and certain historical foundations.
64. 'It is the diplomatic Histoire de l'Abbaye royale de St Denys in France . . . by M. Félibien, Benedictine monk of the Congregation of St Maur, Paris, 1706, which is here used. In this are extracts from the book: *Miraculi Sancti Dionysii*, written by a monk of St Denys at the time of Charles the Bald. Le Comte quotes from this book in his annals T. VII, p. 78 in order to denounce the fact that Waldo's name is lacking in this official list of Abbots and, on the contrary, appears by an error as a private man in the monastery.' (Heber op cit. p. 347, Note 19.)
65. See Chapter III.
66. Einhard writes, 'It was at that time that he received the name of Emperor and Augustus, which at the beginning was so repugnant to him that he assured us if he could have known the Pope's purpose he would not have entered the Church that day in spite of its being a high festival day of the Church'.

Chapter 3

1. *Berte as grans piés.*
2. The Amiral is the Eastern ruler.

3. Basil Valentine writes e.g. in the treatise, 'Of the Great Stone of the primeval Wise Ones' in the 6th key: 'Therefore in seeking to attain the desired end, a certain measure must be absolutely regarded in thy mixing of the philosophic liquors in order that the greater part shall not overcome the lesser and thereby annul it' etc.
4. Thus there are altogether seventy-two ladies.
5. The Amiral.
6. Basil Valentine writes:
   A stone was found, not costly,
   From which might be drawn a volatile fire,
   Of which the stone itself is made
   Of *white* and *red* united.
7. See p. 63.
8. See p. 86.
9. Something similar is related in the legend of St Brandan, which is likewise a kind of Grail-legend. Cf. Carl Schröder, *Sankt Brandan*, obtainable in a Latin and three German texts. Erlangen (E. Besold) 1871.
10. Alchemy is the doctrine of the transformation of man to a higher stage. At the higher stage he has to learn to unite the clear consciousness of his human nature with the pure nature of the plant. What it does unconsciously he must do consciously. Alchemy describes how this may be attained in stages and also what kind of transformation the human organisation goes through in this inner development. It first teaches the cleansing of the individual soul by clear thought. Then the bringing of the quickened ensouled spiritualised human being to a condition which is neither waking nor sleeping nor living nor dead, but a fifth condition. In this condition he experiences illumination. If he succeeds in bringing this illumination down into his everyday consciousness then he has completed the whole path. He has then transmuted the darkness of earth-life (the coal) into the radiant diamond. Through illumination he acts intuitively.

Chapter 4

1. Cf. Rudolf Steiner, *Christmas*, Single lecture: Berlin 13.12.1907 (Anthroposophical Publishing Co. 1923).
2. In the legend of Charlemagne's Crusade, he finds King Hugo ploughing the earth with a golden plough, a proof that Hugo is connected with the Persian legend. The Book of Jasher calls Cain's weapon the plough.
3. Dr Steiner speaks about this in the cycle, *Christ and the Spiritual World*, Leipzig, 1913/14.
4. So says Sopranis in his biography of William Embriacus the conqueror of Caesarea in the year 1101. At that time this William Embriacus acquired an emerald vessel which was revered as the Grail. Cf. Fra Gaëtano in his *Sacra Catino*, Genoa 1726. Sopranis refers to Herodotus Book II, Chap. 44, where an emerald is spoken of in the Temple of Hercules, an emerald *that shone by night*. However the shining emerald mentioned by Herodotus is indeed no physical object but an experience in the Mysteries.
5. Cf. Rudolf Steiner, *Mystery Centres*, Lecture 10, Dornach 14.12.1923, 'The

Chthonic and Eleusinian Mysteries—the transition from Plato to Aristotle.
6. [Cf. W.J. Stein: 'The Categories of Aristotle' in *The Present Age*, Nov./Dec. 1938, Vol. III, no. 11/12, and 'Alexander in Search of a Conquest', *Modern Mystic* and *Monthly Science Review*, Oct. 1937.]
7. This is a free rendering of what Kessler describes in his book about Mani, *Mani, Forschungen über die manichäische Religion*, Konrad Kessler, Vol. I, p. 306. Berlin 1889, together with indications Rudolf Steiner has made on this subject.
8. Cf. Kessler: *Mani*.
9. *The East in the Light of the West*. Berlin 1909.
10. That Thomas Aquinas wrote against Manichaeism does not alter the fact that he may be taken as a representative of the *true* Manichaeism. What he fought against was already a travesty.
11. I am indebted to Dr Günther Schubert for this reference to Huart.
12. Cf. Rudolf Steiner, *Building Stones for an Understanding of the Mystery of Golgotha*, 7th Lecture (London, Rudolf Steiner Press, 1972).

Chapter 5

1. It is presumably superfluous to mention that this aspect cannot be introduced into education. Anthroposophy is there for adults. The teacher applies its impulse to himself, but he only brings to the pupil what is pedagogically justified. In this book, however, the pedagogical point of view is not the only one which counts.
2. Cf. Rudolf Steiner, *Riddle of Man* (New York, Mercury Press, 1991). The quote from Fichte comes in his introduction to his lectures concerning 'The Self-education of the Scholar'—*Die Bestimmung des Gelehrten*, 1794.
3. The Light of the World that descends into the darkness.
4. In the writings of Basil Valentine the 'Pelican' is the name of the fourth degree of initiation. First degree, the black Raven; second degree (that of the many-coloured Imaginations) the brightly-coloured Peacock; third degree (where Inspiration as the Divine Word, the harmony of the spheres, sounds forth) the Swan; fourth degree (when the fire of Knowledge gives the strength to ray out the Spiritual Light into the darkness) the self-sacrificing Pelican. The disciple who still wanders in darkness is compared to the black Raven; he knows the Spiritual Light only through his studies. When he reaches the second stage, that of the Peacock, he must beware of pride. In the third degree he meets death and must sing the Swan's song. He then dies to everything earthly.
5. According to Albrecht von Scharfenberg.
6. For Wolfram's contemporaries, 'Panther' and 'Anchor' were perhaps still the heraldic figures of distinct families, so that there is a historical indication in his presentation of them, as well as a symbolic meaning. (See note 98a)
7. Cf. chapter VI.
7a. This part of the verse shows that Wolfram did not consider the anchor to be merely a realistic representation, but that it also had a symbolic meaning.
8. i.e. Herzeleide.

9. The capital of the country.
10. Clerk here is the equivalent of teacher or savant.
11. This view was really current among the Shiites (cf. Weil's *Geschichte der Kalifen*. Vol. II, p. 201.
11a. Cf. Ludwig Emil Iselin: *Der morgenländische Ursprung der Grallegende*, Halle a.S. (Niemeyer), 1909, who indicates Wolfram's probable sources for this statement.
12. Translator's note: In Styria.
13. In breaking the commandment: 'Thou shalt not kill'.
14. See last paragraph of Adventure III, where Parzival's experiences are linked to the sign Leo.
14a. Actually, she is the daughter of the Alsatian Count Erchanger (see: History of the Kingdom of the East Franks by Ernst Dümmler in the Jahrbücher der deutschen Geschichte 860–876, 2nd Ed., Vol. 2, p. 36, Note 4). Richardis married Charles III in the summer of 862 (see: p. 614, Böhmer, Regesta imperii, I., Carolingians 751–918, 2nd Ed. Innsbruck 1908).
14b. Son of Donald V. Cf. Arnold Wion 1554–1605, who was the first to give this date; quoted by E. Bécourt: *Andlau, son Abbaye—son Hopital ses Bienfaiteurs*, Strasbourg (Fischbach) 1914–1921. An excellent source-book.
15. Anchaius, King of the Scots.
16. Of Nazianz.
17. The date of the foundation has been rendered approximately certain through a deed of gift on behalf of the Church of the Redeemer at Eleon (the old name for Andlau) of 10 July 880. (Cf. p. 677, Böhmer, op cit.)
18. In Tongern or Lüttich. This church was founded by St Maturnus, of whom the legend runs that he is the youth of Nain raised from the dead by Christ. The legend of his life and its relation to Alsace is narrated by L.G. Glöckler, vicar of Stotzheim (who died unfortunately at an early date) in his remarkable work *Sanct Maternus or The Origin of Christianity in Alsace and the Rhineland*, Rixheim (A. Sutter) 1884. According to the legend Maternus was repeatedly raised from the dead and Glöckler points out how these renewed resurrections are connected with the renewal of the church at Tongern (op. cit. p. 354). The endowment of this church in token of gratitude for the imperial coronation is therefore significant.
19. Bishop of Mastricht.
20. Op. cit. Böhmer, p. 700. The endowment is dated 26 June 884.
21. Maidiers, Meurthe, arr. Nancy cant. Pont-a-Mousson.
22. Arnals of Fulda.
23. (Underlined by the author.) This information is said to be drawn from *Pictura Andelacensis antiqua*. 'Between the grilled window and the narrow open window leading into the sanctuary where presumably the pious parents of St Richardis were laid at rest, one perceives at the top the *Red Knight*, accusing St Richardis before the emperor who is on horseback.' (Bécourt, p. 118, Vol. 1). Compare a file of papers in the Library of Strasburg, 'Life of the Holy Maiden and Empress Richardis', printed in 1660.
24. Ancient picture in Andlau: 'One sees St Richardis lifting up her hands, standing next to the Bishop, who raises his right hand over her, in the left hand he holds a cross, next to him stands the clerk holding the Bishop's staff. The image shows how St Richardis sought the counsel of the Bishop

Liutuuardus and how she had given him the cross.
25. Böhmer, *Regesta Imperii*, 2nd ed. Carolingians 751–918 p. 721. The reasons for the banishment were: the charge of adultery with the Empress (Regino 887) and 'fidem catholicam pervertere et redemptori nostro detrahere laborabat dicens eum unum esse unitate substantiae, non personae, cum s. ecclesia credat et confiteatur eum in duabus substantiis unam habere personam.' (Ann. Fulda IV.)
25a. An old picture in Andlau bears the inscription: 'Here St Richardis followed the coffin of her friend from the Hochenburg to its burial in the Minister of Andlau'. (Bécourt, op. cit. p. 119.)
26. Ann. Fulda IV. 'Cum eo machinari studuit, qualiter imperatorem regno privaret.'
27. The denial of the authenticity of this journey in later writings can be traced back to the Bollandist Stilting, who wrote *The Life of St Richardis* (Act. SS. Boll. Sept. tom. 5). Yet he merely says, 'this journey is only mentioned in the Strassburg Breviary and not in other sources,' (op. cit. p. 799: apud alios non reperio, ideoque incertum videtur').
28. Rietsch, op. cit. p. 306.
28a. Publ. Orient–Occident–Verlag Stuttgart–den Haag–London 1927. Part I The Templars in Cyprus. Part II the Crusaders.
29. Cyprus was conquered very early by the Phoenicians (under King Hiram I of Tyre) but the Grail legend names the Hercules temple of Tyre as the first place where the Grail vessel was preserved. Thus Cyprus belongs to Grail territory from very ancient times.
29a. The annals of Fulda (Part IV) call Liutward 'ex infimo genere natum'. But the syllable 'Liut' occurring in his name points to his relationship with the race of Etich, in which names such as Liutfrid, for example, occur frequently. He was of Swabian descent and it was just the important people of Swabia who were his enemies, perhaps just for the reason that he had a better claim to the throne (as also did Arnulf of Carinthia) than Charles III was prepared to admit. Arnulf's mother also had the syllable 'Liut' in her name. She was called Liutswinda and was called a 'nobilis femina'. Arnulf was also deposed by Charles III, although he was next in succession.
30. Who later becomes Parzival's wife.
30a. The derivation of this name is given by Iselin in *The Oriental Origin of the Grail Legend*, (Halle a.S. 1909, p. 44) as 'Agareni', i.e. The Sons of Hagar, an Arabic designation.
31. San Marte, *Titurel*, by Albrecht von Scharfenberg, Magdeburg 1841, p. 64.
32. 'Wilhelm von Orange und Titurel', Wolfram von Eschenbach, *Der jüngere Titurel*, A. von Scharfenberg, Magdeburg 1841, Vol. II.
33. These colours refer to stages in the alchemistic process. Konrad Fleck describes the horse of Flore in a similar way. Earthly senses are bearers of the starry script.
34. Cf. GA. 149 'Christ and the Spiritual World and the Search for the Holy Grail' lecture 5 and GA 144 'The Mysteries of the East and of Christianity'.
35. A detailed account of Wolfram will be found in *Deutsche Forschungen*, published by Fr. Panzer and J. Petersen, H. 7. Frankfurt (Diesterweg) 1922: Albert Schreiber, *Neue Bausteine zu einer Lebensgeschichte Wolframs von*

Eschenbach. I am indebted to Herrn Ammerschläger for referring me to this work.
36. The German text enumerates the five senses: hearing, sight, smell, taste and touch. (Translator.)
37. White and red are the colours of Kondwiramur. Parzival recognises them later in the snow upon which lie the red drops of blood.
38. Literally: 'I bowed to his hand in gratitude'—the gesture of humility. (Translator.)
38a. The Duke of *Arscoth* cannot be further identified. Alan Macquarrie writes ('Scotland and the Crusades', published by John Donald Ltd, Edinburgh 1985):
'The fleet was divided into three parts when it left Dartmouth; the Germans and Flemings travelled under their own commanders, while the remainder was further divided under the command of four constables. The Scots probably accompanied *Saher de Archelle*, one of the constables from England'.
39. At the same time Alfonso VII of Castille (known also as Raimond) conquered the town of Almeria near Granada; then Raimond of Barcelona, Count William of Montpelier and, by the sea, the Genoese and inhabitants of Pisa were his helpers. In Almeria the treasures of the West Goths were kept. Among these was found a vessel of green glass with which Grail legends were connected. The Genoese kept it as booty (cf. Pasqual y Orbaneia [Gabriel], *Almeria Illustrada*, 1699 and Fra Gaëtano da S. Teresa, *Il Catino*, Genova 1726. Here it is related that the 'Sacro Catino' came from Tyre. King Hiram gave the vessel which was preserved in the temple of Hercules to the Queen of Sheba, who brought it to Solomon. From Jerusalem it came into Caesarea in 1101 along with the army of the Crusader King Baldwin I, and fell to the Genoese. Both works are referred to by Th. Sterzenbach in his important *Ursprung und Entwickelung der Saga vom heiligen Gral* (1908). In the work *Almeria Illustrada*, (Berlin Library: Qu 104), in Part 3, p. 92 is to be found a copy of the emerald shining plate or vessel, an oval, covering two intersecting triangles. This picture is symbolic. Fra Gaetano gives a realistic copy. The oval bears the inscription: 'Forma de el Plato de esmeralda en que Christo ceno que esta en Genova' (The shape of the emerald plate in Genova from which Christ ate and drank).
40. This can be seen from Chrétien's presentation of the Saga taken as a whole, in spite of the fact that in the text he calls the vessel a precious stone, and not a vessel to contain blood.
41. This extinguishing of imagination comes to pass through an inner act which is consummated when the human being, seeing the imagination, asks himself, 'Am I not myself that which appears in the picture?' Through thus using imagination for the purpose of self-knowledge, through this relation of the pictures to the features of his own character, the imaginations are incorporated, they are 'eaten', i.e. they are extinguished.
42. The judgement of one's personal characteristics by the Cosmos.
43. The models of what we ought to be.
44. By the ruby is meant the organ for the highest—for intuitive knowledge.
45. The lance, here portrayed as an imaginative picture within Parzival's vision,

is also an historical and physical object. The centurion Longinus who pierced the side of Christ on the Cross and who gave rise to the legend which comes from Zöbingen near Ellwangen, first used it (cf. Steichele, Bisthum Augsburg III, p. 549). The Syrian Ephraem in the 39th Hymn of his so-called Nisibinian Hymns brings this lance into connection with the lance of Phinehas. He says the lance guarded the Tree of Life. Adam, who had fallen, returned through it to Paradise. According to a saga, Constantine the Great, mentioned by Liutprand in his *Book of Recompense*, had possessed this lance. Count Samson, who is mentioned in Migne, *Patrologia Latina*, as the counsellor of King Hugo of Italy, gave it to Rudolf II of Burgundy. Henry I received it from him in connection with the cession of a much contested strip of territory in Alemannia. This 'Imperial Lance' played a great role in the mythological history of the Emperor. Liutprand describes the lance and A. Weixlgärtner has given a penetrating criticism and translation of this passage from Liutprand. He has carefully investigated the lance that is now in the Vienna Treasure Chamber (cf. *Die weltliche Schatzkammer in Wien*. A Schroll, Jahrbuch der Kunsthistorischen Sammlungen in Wien). This lance is also known as the Maurice Lance because the Abbot of St Maurice in Valois had the guardianship of it for a time (cf. F. de Mély, *Les Dieux ne sont pas morts*, E. Leroux, Paris, p. 125 et seq.; also R. Berg, *Der Heilige Mauricius und die thebaische Legion*, Halle a.S. 1895). Charles Martel used it in the battle of Tours (P. Giry, *Vie des Saints*, 22 Sept. acta St Mauricii). Charlemagne conquered Spain with it as far as the Ebro (Lelièvre). Widukind reports that Konrad I delivered the lance to Eberhard to give to Henry I, etc: We must distinguish between (1) this lance, and (2) the one found in Antioch on 14 June 1098. Raimund de Aguilers, Chaplain to Count Raimund de St Aegidio, writes about it. Peter Bartholomew, through a vision, found it in the Church of Peter of Antioch (cf. Röhricht, *Geschichte des ersten Kreuzzuges*, Innsbruck 1901 and the literature which is mentioned there, especially Romania IX, 34 Note 1 and XIX, 564 Note 1). With this lance Julian the Apostate was killed by St Merkur. De Mély relates the fate of this lance. Vartad († 1271) says this lance is the same as the one with which the Jews pierced an image of Christ (cf. Mansi, Conc. XIII, 23 et seq.). Mély says that this lance is now in Eschmiatzim.

Yet another holy lance (3) is mentioned in the Chronicles of Tabari. This lance had been dug up by Chosroes and its fate is related by De Mély. It resides in Rome and its point is in Paris. The 'Chronicon Pascale' says that a General of Chosroes sent the point to Nicetas—Louis the Saint won it from Constantinople in 1248. [See: Life of St Louis, Golden Legend, Vol. VII, p. 210.]

A fourth lance (4) is in Cracow. It is a copy of the imperial lance of Otto III given to Boleslaw the Brave on the occasion of his pilgrimage to the grave of the holy Adalbert.

For the whole connection which we are following up here their authenticity need not concern us. The lance is an object which appears in inner vision for Parzival. For the symbolism of the Empire what was inner vision has become externalised.

46. Cf. L.E. Iselin, *Der Morgenländische Ursprung der Grallegende* (The Eastern Origin of the Grail Legend) Halle a.S. 1909, p. 111. 'The Antioch–Constan-

tinople liturgy which goes by the name of St Chrysostom and which appeared in the second half of the first millenium is a proof of the fact that in the Greek Church the holy lance had its place alongside the Eucharistic vessels in the form of a lance-shaped knife which was used for breaking the sacred bread and which was also carried around in procession with the Chalice and paten (cf. R. Storf, *Die griechischen Liturgien*, etc. 1877, p. 129 et seq.). According to the Liturgy of St Chrysostom, in the preparation of the Sacrament a square piece of the holy bread was cut out with the holy lance and deeply engraved with the form of a cross'. (See also: p. 61, F.C.J. Los, *Das Keltentum in Wolfram's Parzival*, Amsterdam, R. Los 1927.)

47. Probably carbuncle. [Translator.]
48. Concerning this knife cf. Miss J. Weston's *The Legend of Sir Percival*. For the use of knives at the time of the Jewish Passover, cf. Joshua v. 2.
49. Jessie Weston translates this 'gold inwoven silk'. [Translator.]
50. Trevrezent had once received it as a gift from Parzival's father. It was cut out of green stone.
51. Cf. Rudolf Steiner—The Soul's Awakening, Scene V, p. 82. Philia says: 'When Saturn soon will shed its rays on you of many-coloured light, use well the hour . . .' (Transl. H. and R. Pusch, Toronto 1973.)
52. Cf. Basil Valentine, 'My spirit is sweet, cold as ice', he makes Saturn say.
53. Miss Jessie Weston evades the translation of this word—her lines run: 'For the best of their hawks flew from them nor stooped to the lure again, But all night in the dusky shadows of the woodland it did remain (VI, 35) Trans: 'His crop so full that no dainty tempted him further. He passed the night with Parzival'.
54. Literal translation: 'These colours resemble the body of the queen of Pelrapär. They wrought a spell on his senses, and he remained as if asleep'.
55. Symbols of the union with divine love, the love from above.
56. Literal translation: 'Thy joy's goal and thy pain's guarantee.
57. Parzival had slain Ither, the husband of Lammire, a sister of Gahmuret. Gawain was blamed for having killed Kingrisin, the husband of Fleurdamur, who is also a sister of Gahmuret. Gawain's deed was therefore similar to Parzival's.
58. 'Gamely letter' (wildliche Brief): This 'wild' refers to game taken in hunting.
59. Gahmuret—m. 1. Belakane, who has a sister (name unknown)

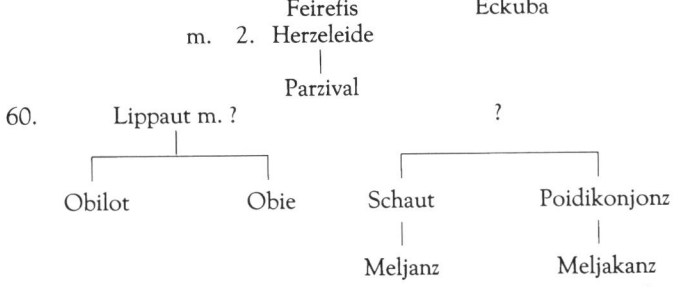

61. The poet purposely coins this word in analogy to 'Perce-val'.
62. Wolfram has five years.

63.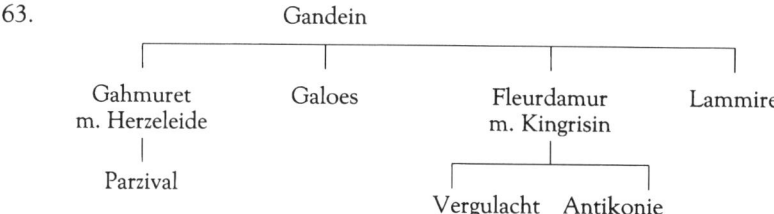

64. Thegan says (cf. his writings of the year 821) about Hugo of Tours that he came of the race of Eticho (the father of St Odilie) and was among all men the most fearful.
65. We have seen that *the archetype of Orilus is Charles III*, about whom the records of the monastery St Vaast, near Arras, say 'but, after he had lost the kingdom, Charles is said to have been strangled by his own people: certain it is that he soon left this life, we hope, to possess the heavenly one.' He was buried in the Monastery Pirmins (Prurin), that is to say, in Reichenau. His wife Richardis had already taken the veil.
66. Basil Valentine says in his lines upon Saturn that the garnet is Saturn's stone.
67. Or more literally: 'If today be his Helping Day, let him help me if he can.'
68. In the introduction to the Book of Jaschar in the edition of Petrus Aloysius and Laurentius Bragadinus, which was printed in Venice in 1625, it says, 'It is on record that the name of the book is Sepher Hajaschar. And it has been established that the reason for his name lies in the fact that all its sayings are arranged just as they have happened in the history of the world. None earlier and none later. For thou wilt find in the book nothing that took place earlier, recounted later, or things recounted in advance that took place at a later date. Rather each thing is described in its time and place.' (See Appendix II.)
69. Seville is referred to as Asbilia in the introduction to the Book of Jaschar. Thither an old man carried and guarded the ancient sacred wisdom he learnt as to the total destruction of Jerusalem by Titus. One of Titus' officers named Sidrus took pity on this old man and brought him to Seville, where he became the old man's pupil. According to this story, then, Seville possessed a tradition of ancient wisdom.

    See H.P. Blavatsky, *Isis Unveiled*, Vol. I, p. 637 English facsimile edition, where reference is made to the significance of the Book of Jasher. Here we use not the English and American editions, but the Hebrew edition in the original, because it contains much that is not to be found in the other editions.
70. August Koberstein speaks of this poem in his *Über das wahscheinliche Alter und die Bedeutung der Geschichte vom Wartburger Krieg*, Naumburg 1823; Lucas, C.T.L. *Über den Krieg von Wartburg*, Abhandlungen, Historische und literarische, der Königlichen deutschen Gesellschaft zu Königsbert 1838; Hermann v. Plötz, *Über den Sängerkrieg auf der Wartburg*, Weimar 1851; J.C. Rinne, *Schulprogramm*, Zeitz 1842.
71. *Wartburgkrieg*, edited, arranged, translated and annotated by Carl Simrock, Stuttgart and Augsburg, Cotta 1858, p. 194.
72. In 1. Kings VII, 14, it is said of King Hiram, 'He was a widow's son of the tribe of Naphtali, and his father was a man of Tyre'.

73. See *Die Drei*, Vol. VI, No 1, April 1926, Stuttgart, p. 68.
74. Gen. XLIX, 10: 'The sceptre (or staff) shall not leave Judah, nor a staffbearer as descendant, until the Messiah comes, and the obedience of the people is his'. The authorised English version reads as follows, 'The sceptre shall not depart from Judah, nor a lawgiver from between his feet until Shiloh come; and unto him shall the gathering of the people be'.
75. This is according to the authorised English version. The Luther Bible from which Stein quotes gives: 'but Cain shall be burnt'.
76. Ephraim the Syrian writes about the Lance of Phinehas in the 39th hymn of his so-called 'Nisibenic Hymns'. This passage is rendered into German by Iselia in his book: 'Der morgenländische Ursprung der Grallegende' [Oriental Origin of the Grail Legend] p. 114.

    English translation: 'I have been frightened (says Death) by the Lance of Phinehas which, by having slain, has overcome Death. The Lance has preserved the Tree of Life. I have been pleased, but also worried, that it keeps men away from Life, but also that it keeps the ordinary folk from Death. Now, because of the Spear which pierced Jesus, I have also been hit. He is the Pierced One and I must lament. From Him spurted forth blood and water. Washed and alive Adam returns to Paradise'. This took place in Lazarus. Through his awakening Adam returned to Paradise.
77. Ernst Uehli: *Eine neue Gralsuche*, Der Kommende Tag Verlag, Stuttgart 1921, says in his chapter entitled, 'The Grail as a Mystery of the Ego', 'In reincarnation the true interrelationship of the physical and the spiritual worlds can be perceived. Without the knowledge of repeated earth lives the true connection between the two worlds is lost'. Uehli was the first courageously to lead Anthroposophy to comprehend the starry writing of Flegetanis Kiot.
78. The Legend of Barlaam and Josaphat, ascribed to St John of Damascus (Theatiner Verlag, Munich). Translated from the Greek by Ludwig Burchard, p. 171.
79. Jessie Weston's translation gives Anjou, but the German is Anschau.
80. Cf. *Forschungen zur Verfassungs-und Verwaltungsgeschichte der Steiermark*, Vol. 3, Graz 1900, p. 207: *Geschichte der Landeswappens der Steiermark* by A. Siegenfeld.
81. There are 72 tongues which fell into confusion at the building of the Tower of Babel. In the Book Jaschar it is related that Gabriel (who as the messenger of birth taught the mysteries of genealogy) taught Joseph seventy languages. He who learns them from Gabriel is able to find the lost word, i.e. to attain to the altar of the Holy Ghost.
82. Rufolf Steiner writes in his *Occult Science—an Outline*, Rudolf Steiner Press, 1969, p. 305: 'The hidden knowledge which is gradually taking hold of mankind, and will increasingly be doing so, may in the language of a well-known symbol be called the Knowledge of the Grail. We read of the Holy Grail in old-time narratives and legends, and as we learn to understand its deeper meaning we discover that it most significantly pictures the heart and essence of the new Initiation-knowledge, centering in the Mystery of Christ. The Initiates of the new age may therefore be described as the "Initiates of the Grail". The pathway into spiritual worlds, the first stages of which were set forth in the preceding chapter, culminates in the "Science of the Grail".'

83. Literally, 'Thoughts of my wife stole my senses from me'.
84. This emphasis on the earth is found in the Book of Jaschar. There we are told that Cain killed Abel with the plough. And God says, 'A curse upon thee, who hast swept thyself from the earth, which opened her mouth to receive thy brother's blood shed by thy hand. In the earth thou hast buried him. So it shall come to pass that the earth, when thou cultivatest it, shall henceforth not give to thee her force as heretofore.' The editor of the Book of Jaschar adds in explanation, 'the earth herself has sinned, in drinking Abel's blood. She ought not to have received him, but to have rejected him.' (ed. Venice 1625)
85. We here translate direct from Stein who follows Pannier's version at this point, and not Simrock as does Jessie Weston at IX, 558–560.
86. Jowett's translation.
87. I have to thank my friend Dr Karl Schubert for the reference to this passage of Jung-Stilling's.
88. J.H. Friedlieb, *Die Sibyllinischen Weissagungen*, Leipzig, 1852.
89. Corresponds to Miss Weston's translation IX, 634–6.
90. This is not Miss Weston's translation, which is rather too free at this point.
91. Miss Weston translates it, 'sweat streamed from every limb'. V, 341.
92. Better: 'how is their name known?'
93. It has already been said that the Grail-experience is anticipated in the experiences of childhood.
94. Cf. Wolfram von Eschenbach's Parzival II, 128. (Jessie Weston: III, 283, omits mention of the eleven generations but merely says: 'Woe worth us! that none of her children should live still...' Wolfram says: 'Woe unto the world, that we do not have descendants of hers unto the eleventh generation'.
95. Miss Weston's translation of these lines is not sufficiently literal for our use here.
95a. Miss Grove's translation substitutes 'Cumberland' for 'Kukumerland'. The latter has nothing to do with Cumberland in England. Viktor Stracke who has made a special study of the district where the Grail Saga of Wolfram is located, has identified 'Cucumber' land with the region around the river Gurk in Kärnten and a small river of the same name flowing into the Save south of the Drau. 'Gurke' is the German for cucumber.
96. Stein correlates Mazadan with MacAdam. Miss Weston translates 'son of Adam', as in the original German.
97. We know that the lance and Saturn are connected.
97a. Rührmund, who has written a remarkable book about the chronology of the Grail (Zeitschrift für deutsches Altertum, Vol. VI, Leipzig 1848) says that Simrock is wrong to say that this scene took place in the spring. The Medieval text gives: 'Summerlichen Schnee' [Summer Snow].
98. Hence the lance.
98a. James Douglas Bruce in *The Evolution of Arthurian Romance from the Beginnings Down to the Year 1300*, Vol. I, Göttingen 1928, says on p. 321, note 16, about the Panther Coat of Arms as the emblem of Styria. 'The Lord of the Castle of Steyer was connected by marriage with the family Antschau. Ulrich von Stubenberg lived in their neighbourhood in 1216. He had the other emblem of Parzival, the Anchor. Cf. A. v. Siegenfeld, *'Das Landes-*

wappen Steiermarks', Graz 1901, in 'Forschungen' zur Verfassungs—und Verwaltungsgeschichte der Steiermark', Graz 1900, Vol. III. In this the mythological history of the Panther is given in detail. It is the fire-breathing animal which sleeps for three days in a death-like sleep and the scent of which is pleasant. The bearers of this coat of arms have been investigated genealogically with regard to their family relationship. For Stubenberg's Anchor emblem cf. A. Schönbach, 'Anzeiger für deutsches Altertum', XXVII, 149 et. seq. 1901. [Zeitschrift für Deutsches Altertum 45.]

99. In this region it is a question of developing heart forces. One of these forces which is necessary to the mood which is here unfolded is the acquisition of a certain sense of balance in life.

100. In the region of the ferryman what Gawain wins becomes loss. He conquers but loses his horse.

101. The narrative here stands in the constellation of the Waterman.

102. See my Dissertation: *Die moderne naturwissenschaftliche Vorstellungsart und die Weltanschauung Goethes, wie sie Rudolf Steiner vertritt*; 1921, Der Kommende Tag A–G, Verlag Stuttgart, p. 82. ('The modern scientific way of forming concepts and Goethe's view of life as interpreted by Rudolf Steiner'.)

103. The path of knowledge set forth by Goethe in his fairy tale is presented in my thesis in conscious dependence on the fairy tale but in scientific terminology. The connection will be found if it is sought. I speak, e.g. on p. 12, of the river; p. 41 of the two ways across the river. The world of the lily which kills what is living and brings to life what is dead is explained on p. 75, etc.

104. This riding on the lion occurs when one learns to transpose the excessively strong pulsation within the upper vessels to the lower part of the organisation. There are two illustrations of this (see pages 226–27).

105. In the German: 'gedoppelt Gampilon', a kind of heraldic dragon.

106. This hare is depicted in the picture of the 'Mons Philosophorum' (see pages 230–31).

107. Noted by Karl Simrock in his translation of Parzival.

108. Gärel ouchz mezzer holte, dâ von er Kumber dolte in der marmelînen sûl.

109. Goethe describes something similar in his fairy tale, how the river surges and boils when the will o' the wisps laughingly shake into it the gold of their still unpurified wisdom. This event is described by Rudolf Steiner in his Mystery drama *The Portal of Initiation*, in the scene where Capesius and Strader appear with the Spirit of the Elements.

110. When a man rises to the Sphere which is above desire, then the world of the senses in which the surrounding world is reflected appears in the imagination as composed of precious stones. Gawain enters this sphere, but cannot as yet remain in it.

111. A German mile is about $4\frac{1}{2}$ English miles.

112. Henceforth desire will become for him a formative force which he will no longer misuse.

112a. I.e. the overcoming of passion.

113. The Middle High German text says 'der werdekeite kranz' [the crown of worthiness]. What virtues form the wreath we have already indicated in speaking of calmness and equanimity. They are the virtues which cause the heart to beat quietly and evenly. Through them is opened the city of twelve

gates, built of precious stones.
114. The inward occurrence here described causes what has been achieved by the soul to become permanent, unquestioned habit.
115. Thebita Th'âbit ... el Harrani the Sabean (826–901). Regarding him see: Paul Hagen, *Der Gral*, Strassburg, Trübner 1900, in 'Quellen und Forschungen zur Sprach- und Kulturgeschichte der germanischen Völker; ed. by Brandl, E. Martin, E. Schmidt, No. LXXXV. Also D. Chwolsons Die Ssabier und der Ssabismus. St Petersburg 1856, I, p. 546.
116. Zeitschrift für Deutsches Alter'tum, edited by H. Haupt, Vol. VI, Leipzig 1848, p. 470, Rührmund, 'Chronologie im Parzival'.
117. There is a vast literature on this subject. Several works should be mentioned: Konrad von Querfurt, published by G.W. Leibnitz in *Scriptores rerum Brunsvicensium*, Tome 2, pp. 695–698 (Konrad was Chancellor to Henry VI and his regent in Naples and Sicily). Then there was the Englishman, Gervase of Tilbury (Professor in Bologna, later in the service of Otto IV, Otia imperialia I p. 881 et seq. Both tell of Virgil's magic. About 1150 a Frenchman, a vassal of the English King, came to Naples and wanted to take away Virgil's corpse. From that time onwards people's attention was drawn to him (cf. K.L. Roth concerning the magician Virgil in Franz Pfeiffer's 'Germania', Quarterly for German Antiquarian Research, 1859).

John of Salisbury tells of the man who wanted to acquire Virgil's corpse in order to learn his art. He met this man 'Ludovicus' in Apulia. [Dr Stein gives many other references to books and documents—Trans.]
118. Taken from Karl Pannier's German translation. Jessie Weston's version at XIII 488–9 follows Simrock.
119. A German mile is about $4\frac{1}{2}$ English miles.
120. The name Maurin was borne by the father of Suppo II, of Salic descent, who from 871–5 was Duke of Spoleto, and therefore merely Count of Turin. He was a cousin of Engelburga, the wife of Louis II, cf. Dummler: *Geschichte des Ostfränkischen Reiches*, Vol. III, 2nd Ed., p. 20.
121. Miss Weston's translation (XIV, 8–9) fails to emphasise the 'He too'. We here give an alternative [Trans.].
122. Miss Jessie Weston's translation (XIV, 175–6) is not quite literal.
123. Corresponds to Jessie Weston (XIV, 328–334) which, however, is unsatisfactory and we substitute the prose translation by Mustard and Passage, Vintage Books 1961.
124. The force of six virtues works in him.
125. This is a more literal translation than that of Miss Weston.
126. This corresponds to Jessie Weston's version XV, 1–5 [trans.].
127. Literal translation (ed.).
128. XV, 146 in Jessie Weston is too free [trans.].
129. Jessie Weston translates it as 'Angevin', XV, 201–2.
130. This corresponds to Jessie Weston's translation: XV, 628–30.
131. Saturn.
132. Jupiter.
133. Mars.
134. Sun.
135. Venus.
136. Mercury.

137. Moon.
138. Related in *The Golden Legend*, J.M. Dent, Temple Classics 1900. Vol. II, pp. 202–3. St Sylvester conquers twelve masters. As the twelfth killed a bull by uttering the unspeakable name of Jehovah, Sylvester brought it to life again in the name of Jesus Christ.
139. Referring back to Parzival's first visit to the Grail Castle the story says: 'That evening when they were all devoid of joy because of the bloody spear, the Grail had been brought forth for help, because they had hoped for consolation from it; but Parzival had left them in their plight.' [Translation by Mustard and Passage, Vintage Books, 1961.]
140. In the German he is named John and the title only *later* becomes 'Prester John' which is then borne by the succeeding kings [transl.].
141. In the German follows the line 'except what the master has spoken about it.'

Chapter 6

1. *Supersensible influences in the History of Mankind*, lecture VI, Dornach, October 1922.
2. P. 86, Wolfram von Eschenbach, Part I, Introduction by P. Piper in Kürschners Deutsche National literatur, Vol. 5, Section I, Stuttgart (Union). The full text is to be found in *The Vulgate Version of the Arthurian Romances* published by Oscar Sommer, Vol. I, *L'estoire del St Graal*, Washington 1909.
3. Engelberga is often mistakenly shown in genealogical tables as daughter of Louis II of Germany. The origin of this error is the description given of her by Charles III as 'dilectissima soror'. But Louis the German is only the *godparent* of Engelberga and therefore refers to her as 'dilecta ac spiritalis filia nostra'. This points to no physical relationship. (Cf. Dümmler, *Geschichte des Ostfränkischen Reiches*, 2nd Ed. Leipzig 1887, Vol. III, p. 65 and note, p. 278. Also Vol. II, p. 402). This explanation is due to Dr Ernst Müller, Leipzig.
4. Hugo v. Tours m. Bava   Louis the Pious.
   | |
   Ermengarde m. Lothar I   Louis the German   Charles the Bald
   |
   Louis II m. Engelberga
   |
   Ermengarde
   (whose tutor was Anastasius.)
5. Later Ermengarde married Boso, the Provençal count. Their son Louis was king of Italy. In 903 he was taken by Berengar and blinded.
6. E. Seckel writes in his article, 'Pseudoisidor' Realenzyklopädie für protestantische Theologie, Vol. XVI, 1905, p. 285:
   'He who credits the great imposter with the human weakness of vanity side

by side with his cleverness, will be inclined to expect from him (in an anagram or the like) a hint as to his own personality which, though concealed as far as possible, may yet be decipherable.
7. This information is conveyed in a letter from Rudolf Steiner to her Excellency Eliza von Moltke, which is reproduced in facsimile with a translation in Appendix V.
8. On p. 431 seq. of this work Vol. II an interesting essay is to be found concerning the family tree of St Thomas Aquinas and his descent from the Count of Capua. (I am indebted to Dr Eugen Kolisko for this reference.) One need not be surprised about this kinship of St Thomas. The Grail Saga also shows us kindred of Parzival in Klingsor's domain. Not in the blood, but in soul and spirit, the noble and ignoble show their difference.

Chapter 7

1. Cf. Barth, M. '*Der Heiligen Odilia Flucht nach Freiburg, oder St Ottilien in Baden* (Bulletin Ecclésiastique du Diocèse de Strasbourg', XLIII Anné, Strasbourg 1924, Nos 12/13).
1a. Dionysius Albrecht, *History of Hohenburg*, p. 118.
2. In connection with this and other genealogical points I owe the warmest thanks to Herrn Dr Ernst Müller, Leipzig. Through the wealth of his specialist knowledge he has been able to explain many connections, and was of assistance in finding documentary proof.
3. Odilie's father bore the lily in his crown (Dionysius Albrecht, p. 44). Clovis I received the lily from a Waldbruder, to whom the Angel (Gabriel) had brought it in a vision for the king (ibid. p. 45). The 'Floovant' saga says of this Clovis: King Flos of Alsace was his confederate.

Afterword

1. In this connection I owe a particular debt of gratitude to Mrs Julietta Leroi (Stuttgart), as well as to her son Mr (later Dr) Alex Leroi.

Appendix II

1. In the *Vulgate Version of the Arthurian Romances*, published by H. Sommer, Vol. I, *L'estoire del St Graal*, Washington 1909, p. 161, it is told in a similar way how Vespasian (son of Titus) found Joseph of Arimathea in prison and set him free. He possessed a book composed by Christ, in which was described the history of the Holy Grail and the lineage of the people connected with it.
2. The printer now speaks again and refers also, presumably, to his father who collaborated in his work.
3. The same idea is found in the Parzival poem of Wolfram von Eschenbach, cf. p. 183, 1.1. 10-15:
    And he, who hath asked me, and since silence my lips must seal

> Was wroth with me as his foeman, his anger might naught avail,
> Since I did but as Kiot bade me, for he would I should hide the tale,
> And tell unto none the secret, till the venture so far were sped
> That the hidden should be made open, and the marvel of men be read.
> (IX: 346–350)

4. This is obviously a mistake and should be 995. Yet the text gives 965.
5. A play upon the name of King Ptolemy is seen here. King Ptolemaus Lagi. Arnebeth, the hare means in Greek lagos (coward). In order not to offend the king, the Jews translated the word *lagos* (Hare) by rabbit. In holy script it reads 'the hare is an unclean beast. The Jews' play upon the words Ptolemaus Lagus referred to this name. (Dr Rieger is my authority for this.) For the rest, the text treats of the Greek translation, the so-called Septuagint.
6. Thus Israel also conquered when Baalam wished to curse it, for the curse became a blessing in his mouth through the inspiring Divine Power which saved Israel.

Appendix III

1. See literature on this subject: Johan Briz Martinez (already mentioned by Fra Gaëtano) *Historia y antiguedades de San Juan de la Peña*, Saragossa 1620, and the *Escolanus*, which he likewise mentions.

Select Bibliography

Books and lectures by Dr Rudolf Steiner referred to by Dr Stein—in order of mention in the book:

'Christmas'. See *The Festivals and their Meaning* (London, Rudolf Steiner Press, 1981).
Christ and the Spiritual World (London, Rudolf Steiner Press, 1963).
The East in the Light of the West (London, Rudolf Steiner Publishing Co., 1940).
Building Stones for an Understanding of the Mystery of Golgotha (London, Rudolf Steiner Press, 1972).
The Mysteries of the East and Christianity (London, Rudolf Steiner Press, 1972).
The Mysteries [Die Geheimnisse] (New York, Mercury Press, 1987).
The Gospel of St Matthew (London, Rudolf Steiner Press, 1965).
Occult Science: An Outline (London, Rudolf Steiner Press, 1969).
Knowledge of the Higher Worlds (London, Rudolf Steiner Press, 1976).
Towards Social Renewal (London, Rudolf Steiner Press, 1977).

Other Relevant Works

Eileen Hutchins, *Parzival* (London, Temple Lodge Press, reprinting 1992).
E. Jung and M.L. von Franz, *The Grail Legend* (London, Hodder and Stoughton, 1971).
John Matthews, *Grail and the Quest for Eternal Life* (London, Thames and Hudson, 1981).
Jessie L. Weston, *The Quest of the Holy Grail* (London, Frank Cass, 1964).

Index

Aaron = Hârûn ar-Rašid (786–809), Caliph, called King of Persia (c.f. p. 85) 46
Aba = Bava, wife of Hugo of Tours 30, p. 47 note 46, p. 48 note 49, orders two books to be written p. 53 & note 58, 54, 61
Abbaye de Charroux 44
Abbey of St Denis (St Dionysius) 53
Abdallâh, son of Harun al-Raschid and a Persian woman with surname al-Ma'mûn (q.v.) 88
Abderhaman, Arabian General ('Abd-ar-Rahmân Ibn Abdallâh) called Terramer in the legend (q.v. or Desramè, dies 7.10.732 in Battle of Tours and Poitiers p. 33 & note 33
Abderhaman II ('Abd-ar-Rahmân al Modhaffar), Caliph of Cordoba (822–852), son of al-Hakams, fights against Bernard of Barcelona 32
Abel 193, killed with a plough p. 194 & note 84
Abraham, sacrifices his son (legend of Hugo) p. 53 & note 53, had his son restored to him by God (Hugo Legend) came from Chaldea, the land of star-wisdom 281, mentioned in Book of Jaschar 301
Absalom, revolted against his father David (c.f.2 Sam. 13–14, 85–88) 34
Abû, Arabic for 'father'
Abû-Ga'far al Mansûr, Caliph (754–775) 85
Abû-l'kal-Aghlab ibn Ibrahim 278
Abû Marvan, warlord of Abderhaman II 32
Adalbert, Saint, b. 955, befriended Otto III, killed 997, his corpse ransomed by Duke Boleslaw p. 143 note 45 (fourth lance), buried in Gnesen
Adalbert, son of Hunfrid, inherits Azan's blood-relic (later blood-relic of Reichenau) 20, driven from Churrätien by Ruodpert, vassal of Emperor Louis 20, flees to his brother in Istria and reconquers Churrätien with his brother's help 21
Adalrich (Eticho) father of St Odilie 282
Adalrichsheim = Arlesheim near Basel 287
Adalricus of Lenzburg, vide Udalrich (2)
Adam, p. 143 note 45 (lance 1), p. 186 note 79a, 187 et seq., 189, 193 et seq., 217, 223, 299
Adam, MacAdam 191
Adamant (diamond) 101
Adela, Abbess of the Royal House of the Merovingians, Head of Pfalzel Abbey near Trier 63
Adelheid, Head of Convent of Andlau 108
Adelheid, daughter of Hugo of Tours, alleged ancestress of the Capets 291
Aeneas 208
Aeneid 234
Affinamus de Klitiers 249
Aghlabites, rulers in Africa in 9th c. 98
Agimbert, accompanies Lothair 1 to Italy 54
Aglai = Aquileia 183
Agremontin 213, 254
Ahasver 116, 120
Ahkarin, name of Baruch (q.v.) derived from 'Agareni' 120
Ahriman 277
Aio of Friaul, member of Hugo's legation to Constantinople p. 42 note 39
Aix-la-Chapelle, relics brought there 12, 44,

relics of the first shedding of blood brought by Charlemagne

Albaflore 180

Albinus, mentioned in Hugo Legend as one of Charlemagne's sages 30

Alchemy in connection with Wolfram's Parzival. What it is p. 99 note 10,
basic substance of the alchemical process is black in colour and gives birth to the black and white son, the degrees of alchemical initiation p. 96 note 4,
the architectural structure of alchemical writings 98,
Gahmuret's grave 100,
the soft diamond, cause of Gahmuret's death 101,
colours of alchemical process p. 121 note 33, 142, 143, 156,
starry script on earth 123,
influence of stars on earthly substance 131,
blood of Christ as substance of inspiration 137,
Granatjachant (carbuncle ?) as table top 143,
heavenly bread 145,
experience portrayed in fourth key of Basil Valentine 148, illustr. p. 198, 196 et seq.,
Basil Valentine's teaching about the many colours of Saturn and about its coldness 155,
about the garnet p. 181 and note 66,
the earth's transformation through spilling of Abel's blood 194 and note 84,
the phoenix 196, 197,
Saturn and moon operative within man 209 et seq, alchemy in Castle Merveil 225 et seq., riding on the lion p. 229 and note 104, illustr. pp. 226, 227,
the hare as symbol of alchemy 232, illustr. pp. 230 and 231,
alchemy during sleep 232,
refinement of gold (first key of Basil Valentine) 237,
the science of stones 262,
planetary influences pp. 262 and 263 and notes 131–137,
alchemy in cosmos 268,
alchemy in Saga of Flor and Blanscheflur, what it is p. 77 note 10,
reduction of stone into its four elements, the work of fire 69,
rose and lily 70,
four types of wind 70,
colours in alchemical process 70, 71, concerning the proper weight (sixth key) p. 71 and note 3

Alcuin, sage and friend of Charlemagne 30

Alexander the Great 1, 120, 233, 250, referred to as an expert on stones 262

Alfons I, King of Portugal (1128–1157), during his reign Portugal became free of Castille under whose suzerainty it had been p. 136 note 39

Al-Mamun, Caliph to whom Aristotle appeared in a dream 88

Al-Mansur, Abbasidian Caliph (757–775), c.f. Abû-Ga'far al Mansur 85

Almeria, where treasure of West-Goths, containing green Chalice was found p. 136 note 39

Alsace 55, 282

Altars, three 139

Aluin (see Alcuin)

Amfortas 2, 119, 137 et seq., 205 et seq., 238, 264 et seq.

Amiral, name of Oriental potentate 69 and note 2

Amor 219

Anastasia, Saint 18

Anastasius, Saint 294

Anastasius Bibliothecarius 275

Anchor, coat of arms 96 and 98, 120, p. 214 note 98a

Andlau 42, 291 (see illustr. pp. 106/7 and 114/5)

Andreas, Consul 278

Anflise, legendary Queen of France 118, 119, 175

Angelic Being, Christ-Angel, jewel in Lucifer's crown 79, 205

Anjou (see Anschau)

Ansbert 291

Anschan, land of Kyros 191, 362

Anschau, Parzival's country (c.f. Anschan and Antschau) 98, 99, 191, 362

Antanor 125

Antikonie 175

Antioch p. 143 note 45

Antschau, a Styrian family p. 214 note 98a

Antwerp, where a relic of the first shedding of blood is said to have been brought 44

Apocalypse 269
Apollo of Socrate 234
Apulia 278
Aquileia 183
Aquitania, Duke of (Eudes) p. 33 note 33
Arabism 77
Arabs 81, 278 et seq.
Archetypal man 82
Archetypal plant 228
Archetypal wisdom, preserved by
  Charibert of Laon 77,
  comes to expression in mythical pictures
    of Plato's philosophy 80,
  further diffusion through Aristotle 80
Archetype of man 246
Aristotle (384 B.C. – 322 B.C.) founder of
  logic 2,
  first 'Western' man 80,
  Arabisation of Aristotle's teaching 88,
  importance of Aristotle's views on
    transubstantiation 88 and 89
Arlesheim near Basel 287, illustr. pp. 286,
  288, 289 and 304
Arnebeth, the hare p. 300 note 5
Arnive, mother of Arthur 99, 229, 235
Arnulf of Carinthia 102/3, 113, 214
Arnulf of Metz 292
Arruns 234
Arscoth see note 38a. p. 136
Arthur (name of Guardian of Round
  Table), every century has its Arthur 99,
  125 et seq., 154, 158, 248,
  his lineage 206
Arthurian race 176
Arthur's knights = knights of the sword 6,
  154,
  representatives of forces of starry
    heavens 158
Asbestos 211, 257
Ashes 197
Asia 180
Askalon 164, 174
Ass, she-ass of Bileam (Balaam) 186
Attila 178
Austria, descent of Imperial House from St
  Odilie 291/2
Avendroyn, King of 172
Azan (Hassan), alleged Prefect of City of
  Jerusalem p. 12 and note 4, illustr.
    pp. 16 and 17,
  Grail Guardian, a kind of Amfortas
    figure 14, p. 15 & note 10

Babylon 2, 99, 191, 281
Baghdad, meaning of name 86
Balaam (Bileam) 185, p. 301 note 6,
  killed by spear of Phinehas 186 and note
    76,
  higher wisdom spoke through him 190,
  his inspirer 185, 186,
  his Christ prophesy 186
Balch, fire-temple in Baghdad 85
Baldag (Baghdad) 71, 100
Baldebert, Bishop of Basel 64
Baldur, originally a God, earthly
  counterpart Siegfried I
Baldwin I, King of Jerusalem, brother to
  Godfried of Bouillon († 2.4.1118)
    p. 136 note 39
Baldwin III 136
Barbigöl 178
Barcelona 136 note 39
Bari 278
Barlaam 190, p. 191 note 78
Barmacides, their family and their history
  85 et seq.
Baruch, Caliph 96, 99,
  his coat of arms the anchor, also
    adopted by Gahmuret 96,
  Baruch Ahkarin p. 119 and note 30a,
    120
Basara 85
Basel (Basle) 14, 19
Basil, the Holy, the Great († 379) p. 47
  note 46
Basil I, Emperor of Constantinople
  (867–886) 275
Basil Valentine, his works preserved for
  posterity by J. Thölde, part-owner of
  Frankenhausen salt-mines and Secretary
  of Rosicrucian Order p. 71 note 3, p. 73
  note 6, p. 96 note 4, p. 98, 196, 199,
  203 and illustr. p. 97, 198 and 227
Bava (see Aba)
Beaucorps 251
Beaume les Dames, place where St Odilie
  gained her sight 282
Beauroche 168
Belekane, meaning of name 'Pelican', first
  wife of Gahmuret, mother of Feirefis,
  black-skinned 92, 96, 253
Bellefontaine, Imäne of Bellefontaine 103
Bems on R. Korka 237
Bene, ferryman's daughter 221, 239, 245
  et seq.
Benedict III, Pope (855–858) 275

339

Benedict of Soracte 278
Benevento, Sikard of 278
Bernaut de Reviers 245, 249
Bernhard of Barcelona, son of William of Orange, Spanish Margrave, said to have beguiled Emperor Louis the Pious by magical arts 33,
pseudonym Naso (see Nasion) 33
Bernhard of Clairvaux (b. 1090, † 20.8.1153) 136
Bertha, wife of Rudolf II of Burgundy, daughter of Burkhard I and Regelinda p. 21 note 21
Bertha of Burgundy 292
Bertha (Bertrada junior) wife of Pippin, daughter of Charibert, mother of Charlemagne 63,
descended from Flos and Blancheflos 68, 76, 86
Bertrada junior (see Bertha, wife of Pippin)
Bertrada senior, grandmother of Bertrada junior 63/4
Bileam (see Balaam)
Birminga in Allemania, chapel belonging to Liutward 116
Black and white, black and white Feirefis 84, 127, 206, 254,
black and white armies 92, 95,
black and white dog, Gardevias, on one side black and white 121,
black and white magpie 94, 98, 127, 254,
black and white path to higher knowledge 254
Blankenheim 63
Blavatsky, Helena Petrovna, née Hahn (b. 1831, † 8.5.1891) 1875 founded Theosophical Society with Colonel Olcott († 1907) 186, 206
Blithilde 292
Bloie Bretagne 9
Blood legend (of Reichenau) 10 et seq., points to presence of Grail Knights in company of Charlemagne (e.g. Waldo), first appeared in writing c. 950 28, p. 53 note 55, illustr. pp. 16 & 17
Blood relics, several kinds symbolic of different ways of experiencing the spirit 44, illustr. pp. 60, 134, 135
Blood-forces, Parzival has to overcome wildness of blood-forces 6
Blood drops p. 129 note 37, 156/7, 267
Blood-shedding of Christ, at circumcision, at the agony, at the scourging, at Crucifixion, at piercing of His side 44 and 45
Bodhisattva 190
Böhme, Jakob, (b. 1575, † 17.11.1624) 138
Boleslaw I, the Brave (992–1025) p. 143 note 45 (4th spear)
Book of Kiot 202
Boso, Count of Vienne (after 871) and King of Cisalpine Burgundy (Arelat), married Ermengarde, daughter of Louis II, reigned 880–887, p. 275 note 5
Bosra (Isaiah 63, 1–3) 10 and note 2, p. 53 note 55
Brandan, Saint, legend of his voyage a Grail legend p. 76 note 9
Brandelidelein of Punturteis 245, 249
Brandigan 127, 131, 167
Bread and wine 281
Brescia 53
Brikus, descendant of Mazadan from whom Ither, Arthur and Gawain are also descended 206
Brizljan Appendix IV, p. 306
Brobarz 127
Brother man 84, 164, 254, 255
Bruges 44, 136, illustr. p. 134 and 135
Brumbane 168, 205, 211
Brunhilde, in the Nordic account a divine Walkyrie, in the Song of the Nibelungs an earthly woman 1
Buddha 93, 191, 195
Budhi, oriental term for 'Water of Life', i.e. the power not only to *know* what is good (Manas), but to *do* what is good as a matter of course p. 53 note 56
Bull, constellation of Bull 79
Burgarit, accompanied Lothair I to Italy 54
Burgundy 30, 42, p. 47 note 46
Burkhard I, Duke of Swabia (917–926), husband of Regelinde, father of Bertha, the wife of Rudolf II of Burgundy, owner of Holy Spear p. 21 and note 21

Caesar, Julius 100
Caesarea p. 136 note 39
Cain (the Kenite) 186, 191, 193, 194, 200, 206
Cain's nature within man 257
Caliphs and their Viziers compared to Merovingians and Carolingians 86

Camel p. 47 note 46, p. 53 note 58, p. 54 et seq.
Canaan 185
Capadocia 180
Capesius in Rudolf Steiner's Mystery Drama 'The Portal of Initiation' p. 233 note 109
Capet kings 291/2
Capua 278/9
Carbuncle 208
Carl Martell (see also Charles Martel) † 741, 29
Casmilla 234
Chadolt, brother of Liutward, owner of Langdorf p. 25 note 28
Chaironeia, battle of 1
Chalon 44
Charibert, Count of Laon, son of Bertrada senior, father of Bertrada junior (mother of Charlemagne), the 'Red Knight' in 'Flore and Blanscheflur' 64, 76,
inspirer of legation to the East in 765 76, 86,
his connection to Monastery of Prüm 271
Charlemagne 10, 12, p. 14 note 6 et seq., rival streams at his court, the Latin stream of Einhard and the Grail stream which Waldo served p. 14 notes 8 & 9, 28,
Charlemagne unable to fetch Grail himself p. 19 note 12,
mentioned in blood-legend of Reichenau 28,
according to this he brings the relic of the blood-shedding to Aix-la-Chapelle 44,
forms a treaty with Roman Church through his coronation as West Roman Emperor by Pope Leo III, thus combining esoteric Grail-Christianity with exoteric Roman Catholicism 65,
conquers Spain through the might of the Holy Spear p. 143 note 45,
emphasis on line of descent from his mother pp. 212/3, illustr. pp. 13, 16, 17 and 60
Charles Martel, son of Pippin (Pepin III) b. ca. 688, † 22.10.741, buried at St Denis in Paris, bore spear of St Maurice in Battle near Tours p. 143 note 45
Charles II, the Bald, (b. 823, † 6.10.877), only son of Louis the Pious through his second marriage to Judith, brings relic of first shedding of blood from Aix-la-Chapelle to the Church of Our Saviour near Carosium 44, 46, p. 64 note 64
Charles III, the Fat, (b. 839 † 13.1.888) husband of Richardis, to whom he bequeathed the Convent of Zurzach p. 22 note 22,
gave Erchingen to the Monastery of Reichenau p. 25 note 28, 42,
appears in legend of Charlemagne's Crusade under the name Charlemagne 42,
his lands 103, p. 105 note 14a
archetype of Orilus p. 180 note 65, illustr. p. 104
Charroux 44
Chlotar I 292
Chosroes p. 143 note 45 (spear 3)
Chrestien de Troyes, poet of Conte du Graal 7,
microcosmic version of Grail legend p. 8 note 2, 132, 201, 203, illustr. p. 134
Chrétien de Troyes (see Chrestien de Troyes)
Christ p. 53 note 52, 185, 188, 203, 256, p. 265 note 138, 268, 281, 307
Christ-Angel 205
Christ Ego, received by sight of Grail 255
Christianity 203,
Christianity in West and East 269
Christ impulse, how it can only be one-sidedly interpreted by the peoples of the world 80,
Kiot searches for the bearers of Christ impulse in his day 191,
Christ impulse comes to the people 192, 282,
will be renewed in our time 192
Christ prophesy of Balaam 186,
and of Flegetanis 189
Chronology of Parzival poem p. 241 and note 116, Appendix IV, 306
Chrysostomos, Saint (b. 344, † 17.9.407), litany ascribed to him p. 143 note 46
Chur p. 20 note 18
Churrätien 20
Cidegast, first husband of Orgeluse, compared with saturn 237
Cidrus = Cedrus = Sidrus p. 183 note 69, 189, 298
Circumcision of Jesus 44, p. 46 note 43
Claris, friend of Blanscheflur 72 et seq.

Clarisse 119
Clasp and girdle 224
Clauditte, daughter of Burgrave Scherules 171
Clement, mentioned in Hugo legend as sage of Charlemagne's court 30
Coal 84
Colours in alchemistic process 70/71, pp. 72/73, and note 6, p. 121 and note 33, 139 et seq., 156/7,
   colours in Grail procession 143
Compostella 136
Conrad, 58th Bishop of Strasbourg 47
Constantine, son of Emperor Basil of Constantinople 275
Constantine the Great (323–337) son of Helena, according to Luitprand he owned the Spear of the Empire p. 143 note 45
Convent of St Anastasia 18
Convent of Andlau 42, 44, 291
Convent of St Julian near Auxerre p. 36 note 35a
Convent of Pfalzel near Trier, a royal Merovingian foundation 63
Coronation of Charlemagne as Emperor 65
Corsica, sea journey denoting spiritual mission p. 14 note 6
Cosmos, its future transformation 84/5, 268
Coulomb, near Nogent-le-Roi 44
Council, 8th Ecumenical 203, 275 et seq.
Cracow p. 143 note 45 (spear IV)
Creation (see Genesis)
Cross of Niedermünster, reference to Isaiah 63 10,
   inscription on Niedermünster Cross p. 47 note 46, illustr. frontispiece, and pp. 49, 50, 51, 56 and 57
Cross of the Empire, preserved with Spear of the Empire in Secular Treasure Chamber of Vienna p. 53 note 51, illustr. p. 52
Crown of Lucifer 79, 205
Cupid 219
Cusanus, Nikolaus, real name Chrypffs (crab) b. 1401, † 11/12 Aug. 1464, Cusanus and pseudo-Isidoric forgery 277
Cyprus, conquered by Hiram, Lazarus buried there, Templars had their centre there p. 116 & note 29,
   relics from Cyprus 291
Cyrus 259

Dame Adventure 179
Daniel the Prophet, concerning Cyrus 259
Dante (b. 1265, † 14.9.1321)
   Construction of Divine Comedy 91,
   panther encountered by Dante 96,
   Dante's Paradiso and Goethe's Fairy Tale 221
David as precursor of Christ 191
Death experience 148, 196/7
Degrees of inner development p. 96 note 4
Denis, Saint, of Paris 53, 64, caption to illustr. p. 13
Descent of Sun Spirit to earth 78, 268, 281
Destiny, insight into the sway of destiny 93, 195,
   Grail-Seeker celebrates his destiny 151,
   it inexorably demands compensation 152,
   unconscious leadership of destiny 153,
   problem of destiny 274,
   blow of fate, how it should be met 162
Diamond, same material as black coal 84,
   Gahmuret's diamond-studded helmet 100, 101,
   diamond armour of Grail King 167
Diana, portrayed as Goddess of Wisdom at Ephesus p. 44 note 41,
   Diana in Saga of Piperno 234
Dietrich II of Alsace 136,
   recipient of blood-relic which came to Bruges illustr. p. 134
Dionysius the Areopagite 19, p. 47 note 46, 64, 66, 275
Diotima as bringer of love 80
Discoveries, Age of 269
Dodine 154
Dog, constellation of 123,
   dog's leash 120
Dornach near Basel letter pp. 287, 290
Dove 94,
   from heaven 201, 274,
   dove as transformed serpent 266
Dragon, above fountain of Kunneware as picture of wild forces of blood 6, 154,
   above helmet of Orilus 152
Drave, Drau, river in Carinthia 102, 214
Dream of Caliph al-Mamun 88
Dream of Herzeleide 101/2

Dschemschid, fabulous king who received golden dagger (plough) 2

Dullness–Doubt–Blessedness, stages of inner development of single individual as well as man in general 5, 94, 166

Earth as Grail Temple 256,
   Earth in Grail story p. 194 & note 84,
   earth-citizen must become citizen of cosmos 3

Easter 200, Appendix IV p. 306

Eberhard of Franconia, brother of Konrad I (911–918) conveys Imperial Sword to Henry I, the Fowler, (919–936) p. 143 note 45

Eberhard, companion of Anastasius Bibliothecarius on his legation journey to Constantinople 276

Echardus, of Hugo legend, mentioned as belonging to Court of Charlemagne 30

Ecidemon, Angel of human being 208, 254,
   daemon of man, man's higher self 256

Eckuba of Janfuse 165, 259

Eckunat (Ehkunat) brother of Mahoute 118,
   possessor of Grail-Sword and Dog's leash 120, 180,
   killed Kingrisin 165, 177,
   killed Orilus 180
   his importance in Grail story 180

Edelinda, Abbess of Niedermünster 47 note 47

Edom p. 53 note 54

Eginarddus (see Einhard)

Egypt, gift of Nile 2,
   mentioned in Book of Jaschar 301

Ehkunat (see Eckunat)

Einhard (Eginardus) not a priest before 819 p. 14 note 7,
   Einhard and his friends formed the 'Latin' stream at Court of Charlemagne p. 14 note 9, p. 19 note 12, 28, 62,
   biographer of Charlemagne p. 19 note 13, 65,
   advisor to Charlemagne 30, 41, illustr. p. 13

Eisenhart, knight in service of Belekane, possessor of wonderful suit of armour, loses his life whilst riding without it 92

Elders, twenty-four 144

Elements, involved in alchemical process and thus play a role in Saga of Flore and Blancheflur 69, 76, p. 203 & note 109

Eleon, old name of Andlau p. 108 note 17

Elias, Bishop, accompanied Lothair I to Italy 54

Elijah 186,
   fills Elisha with his strength as Nonnosus-Waldo fills the writer of the Legend of Reichenau with his (strength) p. 10 note 3,
   Nicolaus I likened to him 271

Elisabeth 120

Elisabeth of Hennegau 137

Elisha 295

Ellwangen, place in Swabia p. 143 note 45

Emerald, term indicating inner experience of solar plexus which appears green in imagination p. 80 note 4

Era of Holy Ghost 256

Erchanger, father of Richardis p. 105 note 14a

Erchempertus, Chronicler 279

Erchingen in Thurgau (present day Langdorf), gift to Monastery of Reichenau by Charles III p. 25 note 28

Erchinobaldus (see Eschinobaldus)

Eremitage 183

Erhard, Bishop of Regensburg, baptised St Odilie 287

Ermengarde, daughter of Louis II and Engelberga p. 275 & note 4

Eschinobaldus, advisor to Charlemagne, mentioned in Hugo Saga 30

Eschmiatzim [Edjmiadsin] p. 143 note 45

Ethnise 207

Eticho (Adalrich, Eutiychs) father of St Odilie p. 178 note 64, 282, illustr. pp. 283, 284, 285, letter 290,
   race of Eticho p. 117 note 29a, 291

Europe, its spiritual mission 89

European soul must find its soul-bride at the Caliph's Court 76

Eve 193

Evil and evil-doers, their redemption 81, 89

Fairytale of Green Snake and Beautiful Lily 220, 225, 261

Falcon 155, 175

Family tree and Grail 188, 213,
   family tree of those connected with Grail p. 275 and note 4, p. 279 note 8, Appendix I, 294,

family tree of Grail race Appendix II, 297 et seq., 119, 124, p. 166 note 59, p. 168 note 60, p. 174 note 63, 207
Faust of Goethe, a Manichaean document 83, 210/11
Faust of Lessing 88, 89
Faustus, Manichaen Bishop 89
Faymorgan 174, 213
Feirefis, black and white human brother who cannot see Grail 84, 164, 206, 253, born in Africa where European and Arabic streams meet 66,
half-brother of Parzival, son of Gahmuret and Belekane 96,
Feirefis, Gawain and Parzival form a unity which together makes complete human being 165,
Klingsor's pillar comes from land of Feirefis 234,
Feirefis, representative of East 278, 282
Fenix, legendary King of Spain, mentioned in Saga of Flore and Blanscheflur 68, 76
Ferdinand of Medici, mentioned in foreword to Book of Jaschar 297
Ferryman 220, (see also Plippalinot)
Fes, town mentioned in Book of Jaschar 297
Fichte, Johann Gottlieb, makes sport of those who live in dullness of soul 95
Filioque, subject of dispute 271 et seq.
Fisherman 132, 139, 220
Five years 267
Fleck, Konrad, wrote Saga of Flore and Blanscheflur 67
Flegetanis, Kiot's source 184, 281, heathen 184,
first to write about Grail 184,
Persian word 184,
inherited clairvoyance 184,
could read destiny in stars 93, 137, 202,
spoke through mouth of Balaam 185,
his relationship to Hiram and Hosea-Joshua 185
Fleurdamur 124, p. 174 and note 63
Floramie 180
Florant (see Türkowite)
Flordibale 180
Flordiprintze 180
Flore and Blanscheflur, nucleus of story comes from East 67,
greatest world-historical impulse of 8th/9th centuries contained in form of charming story 68,

origin of name French for Palm Sunday, which is day on which both were born 69,
grandparents of Charlemagne 213
Flore, Saga identifies him with Greek Emperor Heraclius 68
Flore's horse, its colour sequence symbolises stages of alchemistic process 70/71
Folkmission of Jews p. 53 note 53, 80, 281
Fontaine Sauvage, spring beside which Trevrizent dwells 183
Fortunatus, Patriarch of Grado (in legend of the Knight Hugo called Patriarch of Jerusalem). Charlemagne lent him Abbey of Moyen Moutier, arrived ca. 803 at Charlemagne's Court and sent relics of Lazarus and Stephen the Martyr to the Abbey p. 46 and note 44
France, Kings of, their descent from and connection with Grail Saga 291
Freedom, consists of uniting Will and Knowledge 257
Freiburg, Odilie's flight thither 290
Friaul (Friuli) 183
Friedebrand, opponent of Eisenhart 92
Frimutel 119, 149, 180, 207

Gabriel, Archangel, succeeded by Michael p. 46 note 43,
Gabriel as announcer of genealogical secrets and the lost word p. 192 note 81,
as announcer of birth 201,
way from Gabriel to Michael must be sought 203,
Gabriel puts his forces at disposal of Anastasius and the latter dedicates what he thus receives to the sun-forces of truth 275/6
Gabriel, doctor at Court of Harun-al-Raschid 86
Gafar, Vizier of Harun-al-Raschid, his decapitation 86
Gaherjet 244
Gahmuret, Parzival's father 96 et seq., 175, 213
Galoes, Gahmuret's brother 96, killed by Orilus 98
Gandein, Gahmuret's father 96, 102, 176, 183, 213
Gandilus 118

Gardevias, mysterious dog which guards the ways of the earthly world, which leads the way to the starry script 120
Garel 232/3, 244
Garnet, stone belonging to Saturn, p. 181 and note 66
Gateway of death, reached in experiencing path of initiation p. 48 and note 48
Gaurivon 213
Gautier de Doulens, continuator of Chrestien's Conte du Graal 7
Gawain 160, 161 et seq. 261, 214 et seq., his ancestry 206,
representative of middle realm 278
'Gawain episode' 161, 167, 214, 244, 246
Gawain's horses, their significance a) Gringuljet (q.v.) b) Ingliart (q.v.), Grail horse, later Parzival's horse 168
Genesis, creation story is cosmology as well as a description of the path of knowledge 187
Gentleness, its power 83
Gerbert, continuator of Chrestien's Conte du Graal, 7, 8,
writes an interpolation between the continuation of Gautier and that of Manessier 7
Gerolt (Gerald) mentioned in Hugo Saga as one of Charlemagne's heroes 30
Gervase of Tilbury, historian (b. ca. 1150, † ca. 1235) p. 242 note 117
Giselbert, Count from Maasgau 291
Goblet, given by merchants in exchange for Blanscheflur 69
Gods, erstwhile rulers of human destiny, later projected on earth as human individualities 1
Goethe's fairytale 220, p. 228 note 103, p. 233 note 109, 261
Golden star 255
Golgotha, what happened in cosmos at moment of Golgotha 78, 266, 268
Gondishapur 87, 88
Good and evil, teaching of Mani about it 81 et seq.
Good Friday 182, 200, 306/7
Goose 148, 155/6, 216/7
Gorgegris = Gurzgri, Schionatulander's father 118
Gottfried (IV) of Bouillon, Duke of Lower Lorraine, King of Jerusalem († 1100). his ancestry 292

Gottfried, accompanies Lothair I to Italy 54
Gradalis = step by step (gradual) 5, 79, 188
Grail, '... there was a thing ... called Grail' 143,
name derived from 'gradalis' (q.v.), man passes step by step through planetary spheres in time between death and rebirth 5,
Grail cannot be striven for 179,
name 'Grail' written in stars 137, 190,
what Rudolf Steiner says about it, p. 192 note 82,
outshines all other lights 255,
morality of members of Grail race 174
Grail bearer 164, 269
Grail Castle 132 et seq.
Grail Christianity 62, 65, 282
Grail experience of Trevrizent 199
Grail experience in 8th/9th centuries 9 et seq.,
Grail experience of different types of people 199
Grail horse 181, 182
Grail knight = knight of 'word' 6, 154, 212
Grail lineage (see tables at end of book)
Grail procession 143 et seq.
Grail story, made exoteric c.a. 1180 (vide R. Steiner) 9,
refers to events of 8th/9th centuries 9
Grail sword, shattered and restored 180,
meaning of Grail sword (see 'Word')
Grail temple 192
Grajanabach (see Greian River)
Gramoflanz 236 et seq.
Granada p. 136 note 39
Granatjachant (carbuncle ?) stone through which sun is visible 143,
described by Rudolf Steiner as 'seeing midnight sun' (lecture cycle XXII, lecture VII)
Grand St Graal p. 274 and note 2
Grapes, brought by Joshua and Caleb from promised land p. 53 and note 55, 185, 281
Greeks had capacity to understand Spirit 80
Green snake of Goethe's fairytale 235
Gregory the Great (590-604) p. 10 note 3, 271, Appendix I, 294
Greia (Grajan Bach = Greia brook) small

river flowing into Drau or Drave in Carinthia 213
Grimald 63
Grimmelshausen 233
Gringuljet, Gawain's horse 168, 179, 181, 219
Guaiferius 280
Guardian of the Threshold 253
Gudrun poem 1, 250
Guinevere 125, 158, 243
Gunther 178
Gurass, husband of Sibylle (1) 69
Gurnemanz of Graharz, Parzival's teacher, grandfather of Schionatulander 118, 126, 127 et seq., 306, Appendix IV,
Gurnemanz a kind of Mephisto 128, 149

Habsburgs, their relationship to family of Odilie 291,
their mission 292
Hadrian (Adrian) I, Pope (772-795) 30
Hadrian II, Pope (862-872) 275
Hagen, projection on earth of God Hödur (q.v.)
Haido, (vide Heito), Bishop of Basel (805-823)
Haman 116
Harun-al-Raŝchid (Hârûn ar-Rasid) (786-809) 86 et seq.
Hassan (vide Azan)
Head, bleeding head in dish, true imagination of anti-Grail impulse 87
Healing 146
Heavenly bread 145
Heito (Haido) Bishop of Basel (805-823) 42, 64
Henry I, the Fowler (919-936) p. 44 note 42, p. 143 note 45, 270
Henry, Count of Burgundy († 1112) father of Alfons I, King of Portugal († 1185) 136
Henry VI (1190-1197) p. 47 note 46
'Henry', poem of 'Poor Henry' 2
Heraclius, Greek Emperor, according to Saga he was father of Bertha, Charlemagne's mother 68
Hercules, Plutonic Sun-hero 80, 262
Herder, 'Die Erde als Stern unter Sternen' (the earth as a star among stars) 3
Heredity 212
Heribert (vide Charibert)
Hermit, has doubts about the Trinity, sees in a vision the history of the Holy Grail ca. 750 A.D. 9
Hermolaus 88
Hertha p. 54 note 60
Herzeleide 91, 98 et seq., 207, 212
Hettel 250
Hetti, Archbishop of Trier (814-847), uncle to his successor Tietgaud (847-863) 63
Hilde 250
Hildesheim 44
Hilduin, Waldo's successor as Abbot of St Denis 66
Hidulph, Saint (vide Hydulfus)
Hincmar, Archbishop of Rheims (b. ca. 806, † 882) 276
Hiram 80, p. 136 note 39, p. 185 and note 72, 186,
son of widow of the tribe of Naphtali p. 185 note 72,
son of a man from Tyre, p. 185 note 72
History, Oriental, Greek 1,
history lessons in Class Twelve 1
Hochburg (stronghold), Odilienberg 290/1, illustr. p. 60
Hödur, originally a God, projected on earth in Hagen 1
Holy Spear, object of inner vision for Parzival 142 et seq., 208/9, 268,
in symbolism of Empire this inner thing is externalised see p. 143 note 45
Horand 250
Hosea (vide Joshua)
'How if God might send what should bring to my woe an end?' Parzival's cry for help 182
Huesca, prehistoric Mystery Centre in Spain = Osca p. 12 note 4
Hugh Capet, named after clerical robe 'cappa' which he wore as lay Abbot of St Martin of Tours, founder of Capet dynasty (b. 938, † 24.10.995) 292
Hugo of Tours, brought Cross and relics to Niedermünster, 10, 291, see also illustr. frontispiece and pp. 49-50 and p. 60,
Grail-seeker at Charlemagne's Court 28,
husband of Aba 30,
advisor to Charlemagne 30,
born of princely family 30,
owned Convent of St Julian near Auxerre p. 36 note 35a,

condemned to death by Charlemagne p. 38 et seq.,
legate to Constantinople 811 42, 44, 46,
connected with relic of first shedding of blood 44/5,
his daughter married Lothair I 46,
accompanied Lothair I to Italy 53,
descended from race of Eticho p. 178 note 64, illustr. p. 43,
his descendants p. 275 note 3,
his connection with Liddamus p. 178 note 64
Hugo, King of Italy, son of Count Thietbald of Provence and Bertha, daughter of Lothair II of Lorraine († 10.4.947) p. 143 note 45
Hugo Cross (see Cross of Niedermünster)
Hugo legend (Hugo of Tours) p. 12 note 4, 29 et seq.
written down 1434, its contents to be found in historical records 29
Hulindis, nun from convent near Trier in the Pfalz 63
Humanity, its origin according to Manichaean philosophy 82
Hunfrid, friend of Waldo, enfeoffed with land in Istria 14,
recipient of blood-relic of Azan given him by Charlemagne (later owned by Reichenau) p. 15 note 10, 20, illustr. pp. 16/17, pp. 18/19 and note 12
Hydulphus (Hidulphus) brother of Erhard, Bishop of Regensburg 46, 287

Ibert, King of Sicily 242
Iblis, Mohammedan Lucifer in female form 242
Imagination 137, 138 and note 41, 179, 196, 225
Illumination 187
Imäne of Bellefontaine 103
India, settled by nomadic shepherd folk 2
Ingliart, Gawain's horse 168,
comes into Parzival's possession 172, 174,
dies 181, 206
Initiation, third degree, 'third work' of Basil Valentine 199
Inspiration 138 et seq., 151, 208
Ipomidon 99
Irmina, Mother Superior at Royal Merovingian Benefice at Oehren near Trier, sister of Adela 63

Irot, father of Gramoflanz 237
Isaac 53,
mentioned in Book of Jaschar 301
Isages = Isaiah 243
Ishtar-Venus cult in Babylon 281
Isidor Mercator 276
Isis 123
Israel, position of Israelites 1200 B.C. 185
Istria 14, 20
Italy 274, 278
Ither von Gahevies, Red Knight encountered by Parzival 105, 124 et seq., 152, 206, 214, 223, 233, 306,
his ancestry 206
Itonje 235, 239
Ivory stool at Grail banquet upon which the table-top of Granatjachant was placed 143
Iwan of Nonel 143
Iwanet 125

Jacob Ben Atiah, Rabbi mentioned in Book of Jaschar 297
James, Saint, his burial 136
Jaschar, Book of p. 183, note 68,
mentioned by Blavatsky p. 183, n. 69, 408 et seq.
Je-hoschua = Joshua 185
Jehovah p. 46 note 43, 185, 281
Jeremiah 259
Jernis of Reile 143
Jeroboam 32
Jerusalem 12, p. 136 note 39, p. 183 note 69, 189, 298, illustr. pp. 134/5
Jeschute, wife of Duke Orilus 7, 105, 151, 180, 306
Jesse, accompanied Lothair I to Italy 54
Jesus p. 46, note 43, 78, 281,
Child of Luke Gospel, the Grail 185, 204,
name Jesus = Joshua 185
Joflanze 245
Jofreit 244
Johanna (Jeanne), Countess in Flanders to whom Manessier dedicates his addition to Conte du Graal 8
John VIII, Pope (872–882) 108
John, Prester 207, 270
John the Baptist 291
Jonah, representative of a certain kind of clairvoyance 184
Josaphat p. 191 note 78

Joseph, husband of Mary of the Gospels p. 192 note 81
Joseph of Arimathea 80, 136, 189, p. 299 note 1
Joshua p. 46 note 43, p. 53 note 54, 185/6, 281
Juan, San Juan de la Peña in Spain 303, illustr. p. 304
Judith, wife of Emperor Louis the Pious p. 32 note 32, 33
Julian Apostate (b. 332, † 26.6.363) nephew of Constantine the Great, his way of destiny from Strasbourg to Gondishapur, his connection with the Grail 87,
said to have been killed by the spear of St Merkur (St Mercury) p. 143 note 45 (spear 2)
Julien, Saint, Convent near Auxerre p. 36 note 35a
Juno 260
Jupiter 259/60

Kahenis 181, 193
Kalath-al-Bellut 278
Kalfun 278
Kaltabellota = Kalot Bobot, Kalot Enbolot, Kalath al-Bellut (Castle of the Oak-trees) 242, 278
Kankor 241
Kanvoleis 124
Kardeiss 131, 267
Karidöl 155, 167
Karlmann, founder of Monastery of St Silvester on Mount Soracte 748 p. 10 note 3
Karma (see also Destiny) 258
Karnachkarnanz 103
Karnant 150, 180
Kärnten (Carinthia) 180
Kastis, Herzeleide's first husband who dies before the marriage has been consumated 99, 212
Kay 122, 125, 159, 242
his rehabilitation through Wolfram 160
Keller, Jakob, bell founder of Zürich illustr. p. 286
Kilian, Apostle of Franconian lands of the Main p. 24 note 27, 25, 27
Kingdom of God 292
Kingrimursel 164, 168, 174, 176
Kingrisin 164, 174
Kingron 130

Kings, seven represent stages of development in evolution 71
Kiot of Catalonia (Katalangen) 119, 129, 267
Kiot, Wolfram's mysterious source 137, 177, 183,
has studied Grail lineage 178, 281,
points to connection between Franconia, Styria and Seville 183,
he was a Christian 184,
found a book in Toledo 184,
what the book is 202
Klamide 127, 130, 165
Klauditte of Kanedig 120
Klauditte, daughter of Burgrave Scherules 171
Klias 167
Klingsor 33, 99, 215, 238, 242, 278, 280
Knife (see Silver knives)
Knights of St James p. 59 note 61
Knowledge, path of Parzival to the Grail 161
Kolisko, Dr Eugen 279
Kondrie (Kundry) Grail messenger 7, 181, 262,
her appearance 162,
sister of Malkreatur 217,
her curse 163/4
Kondrie, Gawain's sister 235
Kondwiramur 119, 127, 147, 156, 172, 216, 233, 257, 306
Konrad I of the Franks (911–918) p. 143 note 45
Konrad III, the Hohenstaufen (1138–1152) takes part in 2nd Crusade (1147–1149) 136
Konrad, Chancellor of Henry VI p. 242 note 117
Kronos (see Saturn)
Kufa 112
Kundry (see Kondrie)
Kyburg p. 21 note 20

Lac (also Lach) King, father of Jeschute 150,
also name for the spring where the Grail-sword can be mended 151, 180
Lächtamreis 178
Lähelein 103, 105, 153, 205
Lalande, kingdom of Duke Orilus 105
Lambert, accompanies Lothair I to Italy 54
Lambertus, Bishop of Maastricht p. 109 note 19

Lambro 53
Lammire 124
Lance (see Holy Spear)
Lance of the Imperial Treasure in Vienna p. 143 note 45, illustr. 140/1
Lance of Phinehas p. 143 note 45, p. 186 note 76
Lancelot 232
Lapis Exillis 196, 199,
 the literature on this subject can be referred to in Gustav Ehrismann (Zeitschrift für deutsches Altertum and Literatur, ed. Edward Schröder, LXV, Vols. 1 & 2, Berlin 1928)
Laskoit 118
Lassalies, descendant of Mazadan, from whom Parzival is also descended 206
Laurence, Saint, Deacon of Rome 258, roasted alive 303, see illustr. p. 304
Laurio, Monk 294
Lazarus 111, p. 186 note 76, 192, 265, his skull p. 22 note 22, 42, p. 46 note 44, p. 113 and note 27, 291, illustr. 114 & 115
Leo III, Pope (795-816) p. 12 note 5, 30, 65
Leo VI († 911) the Wise, or the Philosopher, Emperor of Constantinople, gave Lazarus-relics to Richardis 111, 113, 116
Leo IX, Pope (1049-1054) 291
Leroi, Alex p. 293 note 1
Leroi, Julietta p. 293 note 1
Lessing's Faust 88
Letter with written blessing sent by Klauditte to Eckunat 120
Liasse 118, 127, 128
Libbeals 206
Liddamus 177,
 knight who will not fight 178,
 his connection with Hugo of Tours p. 178 note 64,
 sets Gawain task of searching for Grail 179
Ligweis Prellius, the Perilous Ford 236
Lily 76,
 as coat of arms 203,
 of Gabriel p. 292 and note 3
Lindau 21
Lion, born dead, awakened by father's call 256,
 fight with lion 225, 228 et seq.,
 rider on lion's back 229,

knight of the lion 257
Lippaut p. 168 note 60
Lisbon 136
Lischois Giwellius 216, 252
Literature main-lesson, Class Ten 1
Lit Merveil (magic bed) 222, 225, 228
Liutswinda, mother of Liutward p. 117 note 29a
Liutward, Lord High Chancellor to Charles III, mentioned in Richardis legend p. 25 note 28, 214, (see also Luitward).
Livorno (Leghorn) 297
Logos 78, 79, 188
Lohengrin 131, 212, 239, 267, 270
Longinus p. 143 note 45
Lorraine (Lothringen) 274
Loss and gain 169, p. 220 note 100, 221
Lot 237
Lothair (Lothar) I 46, p. 32 note 32,
 called Oliver in legend of Charlemagne's Crusade to Constantinople 46,
 married to daughter of Hugo of Tours 46, 53
Lothringen (see Lorraine)
Louis the German (843-876) 46, p. 275 note 4
Louis the Pious (814-840) 20, 28, p. 34 note 34, 46, 54, p. 275 note 4, supposedly snared by enchantment of Bernard of Barcelona 33
Louis II p. 275 note 4, 280
Louis III (b. 888, † 928) son of Count Boso and Ermengard, later King of Italy (Arelat) p. 275 note 5
Louis VII 136
Louis IX, Saint (1226-1270) 1248 acquired lance-point disinterred by Chosroes p. 143 note 45 (lance 3)
Lucifer, his fall 79, 193, 203,
 (see also Crown of Lucifer) possibility of his reinstatement in Universe 266
Luitward, mentioned in Richardis legend 109
 (see also Liutward) – various ways to spell his name
Lunquit, place mentioned in Saga of Flore and Blanscheflur 69

MacAdam = Son of Adam = Cain 191
Macrocosmic picture of Grail given by Wolfram p. 8 note 2, 137, 201

Macrocosmic and microcosmic aspects and correspondence between them 199
Magic fountain in tower where Blanscheflur was imprisoned, symbolic of alchemistic process in respect of circulation 72, 77
Magpie, enchanted bird, half dove, half raven in appearance 94, 127, 254
Mahaute, mother of Schionatulander 118
Malkreatur 217 et seq.
Manes (see also Mani) his importance 84
Manessier, continuator of Chrestien's Conte du Graal 7, 8
Manetho 185
Manfilot 119
Mani, founder of Manichaeism, his conception of evil, his unity with Christ's deeds 81 et seq.
Manichaean principle working through Parzival 163, 173
Manichaeism, titles of Manichaean works 84,
Manichaeism and alchemy 84
Manna p. 53 note 56
Mansur, Abu Gafar Al-Mansur, Abbasidian Caliph (754-775) 85
Mantua p. 47 note 46
Marangliss of Brevigariess 172
Maria Theresa (1740-1780) 291
Marius Mercator († after 451) 276
Mars 260
Martin, King, allegedly brought Chalice to Valencia 305
Mary, mother of Jesus 44, p. 47 note 45
Mass 89, 268
Matfrid of Orleans, friend of Hugo of Tours p. 32 & note 32,
put in charge of Franconian troops by Charlemagne on expedition to Spanish Mark 32/3,
driven from his lands by Bernard of Barcelona, reinstated by Pippin p. 35, note 35,
owned Priory of Meuny on the Loire p. 36, note 35a,
receives Veltlin estates of St Denis 53,
accompanies Lothair I to Italy 54
Maturnus, Saint, identified in legend with Young Man of Nain p. 109 note 18
Maurentius 295
Mauricius (St Maurice) p. 143 note 45
Maurin, Guinevere's Field Marshal p. 243 note 120

Maximilian (1493-1519) 291
Mazadan 174, 191, 206
Meljakanz 103, p. 168 and note 60, 232
Meljanz, King of Li 168 and note 60, 178
Mensur, technical term in Alchemy (see Weight & Measure)
Mephistopheles 128, 149
Merkur, Saint (Saint Mercury) killed Julian Apostate p. 143 note 45
Merovingians 292
Merseburg p. 21 note 20
Metabus 234
Metamorphosis, Goethe's teaching about it 1
Meuny, Priory on the Loire p. 36 note 35a
Meyer, Priest in Andlau illustr. pp. 106/7 and 114/15
Michael, Archangel p. 38 note 37, p. 46 note 43, 79, 186, 187, 201, 203, 259
Michael the Stammerer of Byzantium, sends writings of Dionysius the Areopagite to Louis the Pious, 827 66
Michaelmas 306
Michael's sword = Grail sword 307
Microcosmic portrayal of Grail by Chrestien de Troyes p. 8 note 2, 137, 201
Microcosmic aspect of Grail as experienced by Trevrizent 199
Microcosmic and macrocosmic aspects and their correspondence to one another 199
Mindersdorf (Muneheresdorf) p. 22 note 23
Miracle of Nonnosus 294/5
Mithras 79, 157
Moab 186
Molsheim 29,
Georg's Church illustr. p. 57
Molt, Emil, founder of Waldorf School in Stuttgart 1
Moltke-Huitfeldt, Countess Eliza von, Excellency, letters from Eliza von Moltke pp. 287, 290, 308 and 310
Monasteries, Chalon 44,
Lindau 21,
Niedermünster p. 47 note 46, illustr. p. 57,
Reichenau (Pirmins) 14, p. 180 note 65,
San Juan de la Peña p. 303, illustr. p. 304,
Silvester p. 10 note 3
Monks, Irish 282

Monsalväsch 149
Moon, is to Cosmos what skeleton is within man 199
Moon forces 201, 209, 268
Moon God 185
Moon religions among nomadic shepherd folk 2
Moon sickle 190
Montecassino 280
Moses = Osarsiph 185,
mentioned in Book of Jaschar 301
Moyenmoutier p. 46 note 44
Muhammed with surname al-Amin, son of Hârûn-al-Rašid 88
Müller, Dr Ernst, Leipzig, p. 275 note 3, p. 291 note 2
Muneheresdorf (see Mindersdorf)
Muntore in Andulasia, where Flore went to school 69
Mysteries 79, 189, 256

Nabor, Saint 55
Nabor, St Nabor, Alsation village 55, 58, illustr. p. 56
Name and race, kept secret 239
Nantes 125, 233
Naples 68, 242, 278, 299
Narant 245
Nasion, portrayed as devil in poem 'Wartburgkrieg' (see Naso) 33
Naso, pseudonym for Bernard of Barcelona (see Nasion) 33
Nebuchadnezzar 100
Nepesia, site of Suppentonia Monastery, mentioned by Gregory the Great 294
Nibelungen (see Twilight of the Gods)
Nibelungenlied 1, 178
Nicephorus I, Emperor (802–811) 42
Nicetas p. 143 note 45 (lance 3)
Nicolaus I, Pope 63, 271 et seq., letters pp. 290, 308, 310
Nicolaus of Cusa 277
Nicolaus Chapel illustr. p. 60
Niedermünster 10, p. 47 note 46, 54, 58, 59, 290, illustr. pp. 56/7 & 60
Nineveh 100
Ninth Century, Herzeleide lived in 9th Century 91,
Spirit of Untruth entered into world-history in 9th century 277
Ninus 100
Noah 186/7
Nogent-le-Roi 44

Nonnosus, pseudonym for Waldo in the legend in which he is also named as Abbot of St Silvester Monastery long before his own time p. 10 note 3, 294
Norgals, Parzival's country 99
Northern France (and England), centres of Arthurian knights 6
Novalis 90

Obie p. 168 and note 60, 169 et seq.
Obilot p. 168 note 60, 169 et seq.
Odilie, Saint 58, p. 62 and note 63, 108, p. 178 note 64, 282 et seq. illustr. pp. 283–285
Odilienberg 54, 108, 290/1 (see Hochburg) illustr. pp. 49–51, p. 60, pp. 106/7 and 114/5
Odilie's descendants 291/2
Odo, enfeoffed with Orleans in place of Matfrid by Bernard of Barcelona p. 35 note 35
Oil, miracle of oil increase by Nonnosus 294
Oliver (see Lothair I)
Organ for perceiving destiny developed by studying Grail story 93
Orgeluse of Logrois 207, 216, 234
Orient and Occident 78 et seq.
Orilus, Duke, husband of Jeschute 7, 98, 103, 105, 152, 306,
killed by Eckunat 180,
Charles III, his prototype p. 180 note 65
Orleans 32, p. 35 note 35
Ormuzd, gives golden dagger (plough) to Dschemjid (Djemjdid) 2,
surrounded by twelve Amschaspands 81
Osarsiph = Moses 185
Osca (see Huesca)
Otto III (983–1002) p. 143 note 45 (lance 4)
Otto IV (1198–1215) p. 242 note 117

Palermo 278
Palma = Beaume les Dames 282
Pando, called Arabs to his assistance 278/9
Panther, in coat of arms 96, 103, 117, 214 & note 98a
Paradise rivers 188, 207
Paris, in Saga of Flore and Blanscheflur, who gave accolade to Helen, Goddess of Beauty 69

Paris, city p. 20, note 15, p. 47 note 46, 55, 137, p. 143 note 45 (lance 3)
Parzival (see also Perceval) pure simpleton who nevertheless is guilt-laden and must atone for it 2,
gains knowledge through pity 2,
keeps connection to his spiritual source by sending conquered knights to lady who guards fountain 7,
Parzival poem of Wolfram von Eschenbach 91 et seq.,
Parzival once more hero of story 161, 179, 244, 246.
Parzival possesses strength of six knights, i.e. six virtues 249
Parzival and Gawain, two sides of human nature 165, 166
Parzival, Gawain, Feirefis, three aspects of human nature 165
Patelamunt, Belekane's city 92, 98
Pater Lyra 42
Patriarchs, their great age 186, 187
Paul, Saint 66, 111
Pavia 14, 19
Peacock p. 96 note 4, illustr. p. 97
Pelican, depicted on Niedermünster Cross 53,
symbol of Christ 96,
blood of Pelican 208, illustr. pp. 49 & 97
Pelrapäre 127, 211, 306
Pepin (Pippin) II of Héristal († 714) 63
Pepin the Short III (b. 714, † 768 – [Stein says † 783]) King of Franks, father of Charlemagne 29, 35, 86
'Perce-Val' in star-writing 124 p. 169 note 61, 190
Perceval (Parzival) generic name for all who search for higher knowledge in the way of a Parzival p. 7 note 1
Peri Mergiana 206
Persians, discoverers of agriculture 2,
announcement of Christ to Persians 80, inventor of calendar 200
Persian element in Grail story p. 80 note 4,
Grail first kept in Hercules temple p. 80 note 4,
Persian element of Hugo legend p. 79 note 2
Persian influence at Caliph's Court 89 (see also Barmacides)
Persian King, Caliph's title in Franconian documents 85

Persian woman, subsidiary wife of Harun-al-Raschid 88
Persida 242
Peter, Apostle 44, 53, 111
Peter Bartholomew p. 143 note 45 (lance 2)
Peter's Church in Antioch p. 143 note 45 (lance 2)
Peter's Church in Rome 65
Pettau 102, 214
Pfalzel near Trier 63
Philipp of Alsace († 1191) inherited blood-relic of Christ from his father 136
Philipp II of Macedonia (b. 383 B.C., † 336) 120
Philipp II, Augustus, King of France (b. 21.8.1165, † 14.7.1223) son of Louis VII and Adela of Champagne 137
Philosophy, combines wisdom and love in its name 2
Phinehas, his lance p. 143 note 45,
kills Balaam p. 186 note 76,
his later incarnation 254
Phoenix, a being-free-of-the-body, whether never incarnated or the part of man free of body 196, 197
Picimont de Kluse 122
Pictures in Parzival poem appear twice because modern consciousness demands renewal of Mysteries 7
Pilate 80
Pillar in Castle Merveil 233 et seq., 261
Piperno 234
Pippin II (see Pepin II)
Pippin III (see Pepin III)
Planetary secrets 260
Planetary world 161
Planets 154/5,
their names in Arabic 262/3,
the wanderings of the Israelites from one planetary dominion to the next 281,
upper planets represented by Parzival, Gawain and Feirefis 260
Plato, incorporated Grail secrets into his 'Symposium', the last of the Orientals 80, 194, 210
Plimizöl 155
Plippalinot (see Ferryman)
Plough 2,
in Mithras tradition, p. 79 note 2
Poidikonjons 103, p. 168 and note 60
Points of view of present work, author indebted to Rudolf Steiner 1

Poinzaklin 245
Poitou 44
Pompey 99
Portugal, kings of Portugal, their ancestry and connection with family of St Odilie 291
Praeputium Domini (see relic of first shedding of blood)
Precious stones, Chalice from Huesca p. 12 note 4,
  Azan's onyx vessel 15,
  jewels from Blanscheflur's grave 70,
  karfunkel (carbuncle) 71,
  carbuncle of unicorn 208,
  Grail as jewel in Lucifer's crown 79,
  Gahmuret's diamond helmet, emerald cross on 100,
  Gahmuret's grave 100,
  jewels on dog-leash 120,
  granatjachant 143,
  Sigune's garnet p. 181 and note 66,
  Grail a precious stone 204, 79,
  jewelled floor at Castle Merveil 224,
  jewels on windows at Castle Merveil 234,
  jewels on windows at Castle Merveil 234,
  jewels of Feirefis 254, 257, 261,
  Alexander the Great's knowledge of stones, knowledge of Hercules and Pythagoras concerning same 262
Prienlaskoss 206
Prüm in the Eifel 63, 271
Prurin p. 180 and note 65
Pseudo-Dionysos 66
Pseudoisidor p. 276 note 6
Pseudoisidoric decretals 276
Ptolemy I, founder of Ptolemaic dynasty, ruled in Egypt 305–285 B.C., son of Lagos p. 300 and note 5
Punturteis 193
Pythagoras 262

Radelchis 278
Raimund, Count of St Aegidio, p. 143 note 45 (lance 2)
Raimund of Barcelona p. 136 note 39
Ram, sun stood in sign of ram when Mani appeared (vide Mani) 81
Rath, Wilhelm p. 19 note 13
Ratho, Saint, General of Henry I (the Fowler), founded Monastery of Werden in Upper Bavaria p. 44 note 42

Raven 94, p. 96 note 3, illustr. p. 97
Ravenna 18
Red Knight, in Saga of Flore and Blanscheflur 64, 72,
  in Parzival Saga 105 et seq., 166, 171/2, 291,
  in legend of Richardis p. 109 note 23
Regelinde, wife of Burkhard I, Duke of Swabia, p. 21 note 21
Regensburg 136, 282
Regino of Prüm 271
Reichenau 9 et seq., 111, 116, illustr. pp. 16 and 17,
  library at Reichenau 62
Reincarnation 189
Relics, mentioned in the book as symbols of man's spiritual striving, not in order to renew worship of them, a tangible point of departure for historian (relics of the Holy Cross p. 18 note 11), relics received by Charlemagne from Azan (later relics of Reichenau) 15 and 18,
  relics received by Charlemagne as related in legend of his Crusade to Constantinople 44,
  relics received by Charlemagne from the Patriarch Fortunatus p. 46 note 44, 53,
  relics received by Charlemagne according to 'Holy legend' p. 47 note 45,
  relics of St Lazarus 111, illustr. pp. 114/5,
  relic of sacred blood of Bruges 136, illustr. pp. 134/5,
  relic of first shedding of blood incorporated into Cross of Niedermünster (Hugo Cross) 10, 44, 53, 290, illustr. pp. 49–51, 56/7
  relics of Sacred Tomb p. 12 note 4
Repanse de Schoye, Grail bearer 119, 138, 207, 269
Retracing of experiences after having seen Grail 146, 149, 151
Rheinbach near Bonn 63
Rhythms, cosmic rhythms and human development 209
Richard, accompanied Lothair I to Italy 54
Richardis, Saint, wife of Charles III, the Fat, was given Convent of Zurzach p. 22 note 22,
  founded Convent of Andlau (Alsace),
  inherited relics of St Lazarus 291,

353

fetches head of Lazarus from Constantinople 42,
takes place of Empress in Saga of Charlemagne's Crusade 42, illustr. pp. 104, 106/7, 114/15
Richardis legend 105 et seq.
Rieger, Dr Paul, translator of Appendix II p. 300 note 5
Ring and clasp 105, 122
River in Goethe's fairytale of Green Snake and Beautiful Lily p. 233 note 109
Robert the Bold (or Strong) Duke of Frankish kingdom († 923) 292
Rohas 183, 213
Rohitscherberg (Rohitscher Mountain) 183, 213
Roland, hero mentioned in Hugo Saga 30
Romans, had power to spread Christianity 80
Rome p. 18 note 11, 44, p. 143 note 45 (lance 3)
Root 232
Röschl, Maria, Dr, leader of Youth Section at Goetheanum, Dornach p. 19 note 13
Roschsabins 242, 245
Rose and Lily, mentioned in Saga of Flore and Blanscheflur, picture of Flore's higher self and his soul-bride 70
Roses 72, 77, 126
Rosicrucians 77, illustr. pp. 226/7
Rothad of Soissons 276
Roumania 180
Ruby, organ of intuitive cognition appears as shining ruby p. 142 note 44
Rudolf II of Burgundy († 937), married Bertha, owner of sacred lance p. 21 note 21
Rudolf of Hapsburg, descendant of St Odilie's brother 291
Rudolf, mentioned in Hugo Saga as one of Charlemagne's heroes 30
Rumold 178
Ruodpert, vassal of Emperor Louis, supplanted Adalbert in Churrätien 20

Saangau 214
Sabin 236, 245
Saelde (blessedness, certainty) – dullness – doubt – Saelde, connected with word 'soul' = certainty of soul 5, 94/5, 205
Salamander 254
Salisbury (salebieres) place where an important document concerning Parzival was found in sealed parchment 8
Samson, Count p. 143 note 45 (lance 1)
Samson (Judges 14–16) 228
Sangive 235, 252
Santiago de Compostella 68, 136
Saragossa 32
Sarant-Thasme, kind of cloth 239
Sares, name of town 239
Satan, in Mani's teaching 82
Saturn 95, 142, 145, 153, p. 155 and note 52, 156, p. 181 note 66, 181, 193, 209, 210, 212, 234, 237, 259, 268, 269
Satur(n)day 181
Schampfanzon 164, 174
Scharfenberg, Albrecht von 118, 119
Schatelmerveil (Castle Merveil), Klingsor's Castle 99, 161, 165, 167/9, 214, 278, counterpart of Grail Castle 167
'Terramerveil' 221
Schaut, father of Meljanz p. 168 note 60
Schenteflur 118
Scherules, Burgrave's daughter 170/1
Schiites, religious sect p. 100 note 11
Schionatulander, comrade at arms to Gahmuret 100,
killed by Orilus 118,
his destiny 118 et seq., 180
Schirniel of Lirivoyn 172
Schoisiane 119, 207
Schröer, Karl Julius 211
Schubert, Günther p. 85 note 11
Schubert, Dr Karl p. 194 note 87
Schultz, Joachim, translator of Reichenau legend and legend of Nonnosus 10, translator of quotations from Echempertus 279,
Appendix I 294
Schwanhilde (see Swanahild)
Sciacca 278
Scotus Erigina 275
Secrets of the Grail 183
Segramors 157/8
Sekundilla, first wife of Feirefis 120, 218, 235, 257/8, 269, 278
Seneca 35
Sepher Hajaschar, Book of Jaschar p. 183 note 68, 297 et seq.
Seth (sheth) 186
Seventy, interchanges with 72 in occult writings, c.f. account in Numbers 11, 24–27, where it is shown that 70 is

really 72, seventy (seventy-two) languages, p. 192 note 81, 30, seventy-two choirs in Grail temple p. 192 note 81, 256, 282,
seventy rooms in tower where Blanscheflur is imprisoned 71/2,
the earth is Grail temple of future – 72 nations will gather round the altar of Grail 256
Seville p. 183 note 69, 213, 299
Shapur, King 81
Sheba, Queen of, brings star-wisdom to Solomon 80
Shedding of Christ's blood, circumcision, agony in the garden, scourging, crucifixion, spear wound 44
Sibawaiha 85
Sibyline books 194
Sibylla (1) sister of Flore's mother, wife of Gurass 69
Sibylla (2) seeress 194, 208
Sibylla (3) wife of Dietrich of Alsace 136
Sicily 18, p. 183 note 69, 213, 242, 278
Sickness of Amfortas 209 et seq.
Sidrus (see Cidrus)
Siegfried (see Baldur)
Sigune 7, 117, 149, 180 et seq., 268
Sikard of Benevento 278
Sikenulf, brother of Sikard 279
Silenus, God of Wisdom 80
Silken cloth of Gawain, what it is 160, 174
Silver knives in Grail procession p. 143 and note 48, 164
Silvester, Saint 194, p. 265 note 138
Simeon, Saint 42, p. 46 note 43
Simplicius Simplicissimus 233
Sirius 123
Sixtus II, Pope 303
Skeleton 148, 196, 199, illustr. p. 198
Slander, a goad to self-knowledge 175, 176
Snake (see Green Snake)
Snake poison 208
Socrates 31, 123
Sohar 187
Soissons 276
Sol dei 287
Solomon 80, p. 136 note 39, descent from him denotes a particular type of clairvoyance 184
Soltane 102, 126
Soma Cult of India 2
Son of widow p. 185 note 72
Soracte, Apollo of 234

Sorakte, Monastery of Saint Silvester on hill of Sorakte, the Prior (and later Abbot) of which was Nonnosus p. 10 note 3, 294 et seq.
Spartarius, Leo, member of Hugo's legation to Constantinople p. 42 note 39
Spear 142, (see also Lance) Spear of the Empire p. 143 note 45, illustr. pp. 52, 140/1,
Spear of Ither of Gahevies 152,
Spear of Troyes, of Taurian 154, 157, 193, 306
Spell required to mend broken Grail-sword 151
Speyer 136
Spiritual science of Rudolf Steiner, named by him 'Science of the Grail' p. 192 note 82
Staff-bearer p. 185 note 74
Stages of inner development p. 96 note 4
Star, good star = angel of human being 254
Star forces, represented in Arthur and Round Table 158
Starry spaces 161
Starry script 20, 121, 137, imaginations spread out in heavens 151, 165, 180, 186, 188, 189, 190, 202, 215, 260, 281,
star wisdom, starry script as genealogy 185/6
Steadfastness, a virtue which must be attained by Grail King, Parzival first to acquire it, loaned by Saturn 95, 259, opposite to this in Castle Merveil 214
Steffen, Albert 271
Steiner, Rudolf, Dr, founder of anthroposophical movement, Chairman of General Anthroposophical Society after Christmas 1923, architect of first and second Goetheanum buildings in Dornach, † 30.3.1925. Director of Independent Waldorf School in Stuttgart, in which capacity he planned its curriculum. The latter is founded on anthroposophical knowledge of man 1, 293,
all important ideas of this present volume derive from him 3,
his visit to 11th Class of Waldorf School, 16.1.1923 5.
Literary references:
Grail story made exoteric ca. 1180 9,

Flos and Blancheflos wished to preserve esoteric Christianity in its purity, Charlemagne combined it with exoteric Christianity 65,
the teachings of Dionysius Areopagita, mentioned in Gospels, are reflected in writings of so-called Pseudo-Dionysius 66,
concerning the Saga of Flore and Blancheflur 76,
concerning relationship of Plato to Aristotle 80,
the capacity of different nations to accept Christianity 80/1,
about Mani 84,
Chrestien's Grail poem 137, 201,
Jakob Böhme 138,
about the leaders of humanity 144,
Goethe's Secret Revelation ('The Mysteries') and the Grail 144,
connection of Arthurian knights with the stars 158,
of different kinds of clairvoyance 184,
concerning age of Patriarchs 186,
origin of imaginative insight 187,
about the true path of occult development 188,
of Perceval and the heavenly script 190,
Barlaam and Josaphat 190,
about Grail experiences 199,
how Richard Wagner was inspired to compose his Parsifal 200,
Chrestien de Troyes' view of the Grail from microcosmic aspect 201,
Michael as inspirer of cosmopolitan movement 201,
importance of 8th Ecumenical Council 203,
concerning hereditary forces 212,
Goethe's fairytale of Green Snake and Beautiful Lily 220,
Genesis 4.1 (Adam knew his wife) 223,
explanation of medieval portrayal of rider on the lion 229,
concerning John 14, 12 (awakening of Lazarus) 265,
heart as voluntary muscle 269,
how Christianity works secretly to embrace non-Christian confessions 269,
about Lohengrin Saga 270,
mission of Pope Nicolaus I 271,
about Filioque dispute 274,
concerning wanderings of Israelites 281,
of Christ's death day 306.
Oral transmissions:
'Grail' derives from 'gradalis' (gradual) 5,
'Saelde' connected with 'Seele' (Soul) 5,
date in history of events described by Wolfram von Eschenbach is 8th/9th centuries 5/6,
Arthurian knight = knight of sword, Grail Knight = knight of word 6,
Grail sword shatters when it is old, renewed at its spiritual source 6,
dragon above Kunneware's spring is picture of wild forces of blood 6,
why pictures appear more than once in Parzival poem 7,
counterpart of pure Grail forces (head in dish) 87,
character of Gurnemanz 128,
imaginations in Wolfram's Parzival 179, 262,
imaginative picture of skeleton when one becomes free of body 196/7,
prophetic experience of initiation during childhood 197,
Grail experienced in head 199,
constellation by which Easter is fixed 200,
importance of five years for separation of loved ones 267,
Klingsor 278.
Written communications in letters from her Excellency Eliza von Moltke:
Pope Nicolaus I 308, 310,
Odilie's flight 287, 290
Stephen I, Saint (997–1038) 42, p. 46 note 44
Stephen II, Pope (752–757) 76
Stilting, Bollandist p. 113 note 27
'St Jakob', Spa hotel near Niedermünster p. 59 note 61
Strader in Rudolf Steiner's Mystery Drama: 'Portal of Initiation' p. 233 note 109
Strasbourg 27
Structure of Parzival poem 91, 154, 166
Styria 117, 180, p. 191 and note 80, 213
Sub-earthly experiences of Parzival 161, 201
Sun, spiritual, sun-forces and those active in sun's shadow 199, 201,
change taking place in sun 268
Sun God = Christ 185

Sun hero 126, 154, 212
Sun 'host' in moon sickle 190
Sun religion, characteristic for agrarian peoples 2
Suppo 276
Suppo II, Duke of Spoleto (871–875) Count of Turin after 875 p. 243 note 120
Sürdamour, Gawain's sister 233, 250
'Swallow', name of harp from Queen Sekundilla's booth 238, 243
Swan p. 96 note 4
Swanahild (Schwanhilde), wife of Walther, lived at time of Emperor Henry I (the Fowler) 21,
entered in Book of the Community of Reichenau p. 21 note 19,
received blood-relic of Azan (later of Reichenau) from Udalrich (2) 21,
sister of Monk Udalrich (3) p. 23 note 24,
gave Azan blood-relic to Monastery of Reichenau 7.11.925 27, 117
Sword, threat of sword averted in like manner through divine intervention in both Hugo Saga and in Saga of Flore and Blancheflur 76,
sword of Ither of Gahevies 148, 180,
sword is shattered 206, 258,
sword = word issuing from man's mouth 6,
Grail sword shattered when it grows old, restored at spiritual source 6,
shattered sword = poem itself in fragments 8,
Grail sword = Michael's sword 307
Sword bridge 232
Synthesis of ancient Mystery wisdom collected together in Aristotelianism and Manichaeism, significance of latter 85
Syracuse 278

Tabronit 164, 174, 238, 256
Tampaneis Gahmuret's page 100
Tampentaire (Tampentäre) 119
Tartarus 196
Taurian 154, 157, 193, 306
Teanglis of Texag and Tamilone, king 122
Templars, Manichaeic in their outlook 83
Temple of the body, temple of God 192
Tenabrock, Countess 143
Terdelaschoye, fairy in Feimurgan 206
Terra de Labur 242
Terramer, name of Abderhaman's General (q.v.), name of Wolfram in poem of Wartburg contest 33
Terre de Salväsch 149
Thasme 239, 256
Thebit p. 241 and note 115
Theodoric, one of Charlemagne's heroes mentioned in Hugo Saga 30
Theodulus, Bishop of Vaudois 111
Thomas Aquinas 44,
concerning Antichrist and future of the world 85,
his attitude towards Manichaeism p. 85 note 10,
his descent from Count of Capua p. 279 note 8
Thora 300
Threefold human nature 145, 257
Tietgaud, brother of Grimald, Archbishop of Trier, plays part in story of Pope Nicolaus I 63
Time, secrets of time 182,
when the time is ripe 146
Titurel, old man on couch in Grail Castle 146/7,
built covering for Grail 147,
his descendants 149,
his significance for human evolution 147, 192, 207, 214
Titus p. 183 note 69, 189, 298
Toledo 184, 190
Tongolf (Tougolf) entered in Book of Community of Reichenau p. 23 note 25, 26
Tours p. 143 note 45 (lance 1)
Trachonte, herb which is supposed to grow from blood of dragons which have been slain 208
Transfiguration 265
Translatio sanguinis Domini (legend of Holy Blood of Reichenau) 9
Transubstantiation 88, 268
Trebüschet (Trebuchet) 150, 152, 210, 241
Tree of Life p. 143 note 45, 188
Trevrezent, Trevrizent 119, 181, 183, 233, 265/6, 306,
the 'Quick-Doer' 149,
his mission 149/50
Triande 239
Tribalibot 217
Trichotomy, doctrine that body, soul and spirit are separate entities 203, 277

Trier 63
Trinity 188, 203 et seq., 265, 274, 290
Trojans 234
Tougolf (see Tongolf)
Turkentals 105
Türkowite (Florant) 235, 238, 252
Turon (see Tours)
Turtledove, Grail symbol 206
Twilight of the Gods, reflected on earth in battle of Nibelungs with Huns 1
Tyre p. 80 and note 4, p. 116 note 29, p. 136 note 39, p. 185 & note 72

Uckerland 245
Udalrich (1) son of Adalbert of Churrätien, inherits blood-relic of Azan (later of Reichenau) 21
Udalrich (2) (Adalricus of Lenzburg) son of Emma (q.v.), inherits blood-relic of Azan (later of Reichenau), marries Walther's and Swanahild's daughter, whereby Swanahild comes into possession of blood-relic p. 21 and note 19a
Udalrich (3), gate-keeper at Monastery of Reichenau, p. 21 and note 19a, brother of Swanahild 23 and note 24
Ulfilas 66
Ulrich of Stubenberg, for some time wore anchor like that of Gahmuret, Parzival's father p. 214 note 98a
Ur of the Chaldees, native town of Abraham 281
Urian 215 et seq., 218
Uther Pendragon, King Arthur's father 99, 229

Valencia p. 12 note 4, 303, illustr. p. 304
Valerian, Emperor 303
Venus 219
Verene, Saint, her relics famous in 12th century, preserved in Zurzach p. 22 note 22
Vergil, Magician 242
Vergulacht 174, 215
Vespasian (69-79 A.D.) 189, p. 299 note 1
Virgin's milk, symbol of the light of enlightenment, dispensed by the divine Sophia 44
Vogelsberg 58
Volraudus (Volrautus) court official of Charlemagne 30

Volrautus (see Volraudus)
Voyages of discovery, Age of discovery (see discovery)
Vreede, Dr Elisabeth, leader of Mathematical–Astronomical section at Goetheanum 306
Vulcan, God 69

Wagner, Richard 200
Wala, accompanied Lothair 1 to Italy 54
Waldo, Abbot of Monastery of Reichenau (also called Nonnosus q.v.), Grail-seeker and bearer of almost totally ignored historical current of 8th/9th centuries at Carolingian Court 10, p. 14 note 9, p. 15 note 10, p. 19 note 12, 28, 62, enfeoffed with Bishoprics of Pavia and Basel 14, 64,
father confessor to Charlemagne 14, Abbot of St Denis 19, 64,
mediator between Charlemagne and his young son Pippin in the affairs of the Langobardic Empire 64,
his memory erased in 12th century (1144) p. 20 and note 15, p. 64 and note 64, 202, illustr. pp. 16/17
Waldo legend (see blood-legend of Reichenau)
Waldorf School, time-table 1 et seq., 91
Waleis, land of Parzival 99,
Queen of Waleis = Herzeloide 99
Walther, husband of Swanahild 21, 27
Walther of Kyburg p. 21 note 20
Warentrudis, Abbess of Convent of Pfalzel near Trier 63
Wartburg contest 33, p. 184 and notes 70/71, 256
Wegman, Dr Ita, minute-keeper for School of Spiritual Science at Goetheanum, Dornach p. 62 note 62
Weight and measure in alchemy p. 71 note 3
Werden, Monastery in Upper Bavaria p. 44 note 42
Wertheim, Count of, Wolfram's overlord p. 127 note 35
Wetti of Reichenau 63
White garment of Redeemer 164
White knight, Parzival became such, but only for a while 166
White and red p. 73 note 6, p. 129 note 37
Whitsuntide 307

Wilhelm, Count of Montpellier p. 136 note 39
Willeri, Doge, attendant of Hugo on legation to Constantinople p. 42 note 39
'William of Orange', poem by Wolfram 120
Will o' Wisps in Goethe's fairytale p. 233 note 109
Winigris 280
Wisdom which must become a vessel to contain love 80,
(see also Angelic Being), transmutation of love into wisdom 144,
harmony of wisdom 145
'Woe, what is God?', Parzival's cry of anguish 166
Wolfhart 178
Wolfram von Eschenbach, poet of Parzival poem 5,
records macrocosmic aspect of Grail p. 8 note 2,
Wolfram, a thoroughly initiated person 270
Word, primeval, cosmic 79,
lost 146
Word of blessing inscribed on Grail sword 149
Word-sword, Grail-sword 145, 151, 180
World of stars 2
'Work of nature' is how alchemistic process is described, because man is too ignorant to build up his own body consciously 71
Wound of Amfortas 207/208

'Ywain', by Hartmann of Aue 233

Zabuloni's book 184
Zacharias, priest at Court of Charlemagne p. 12 note 4
Zarathustra 78
Zizers on the Rhine p. 20 note 18
Zöbingen, place in Swabia, where Saga of Longinus had its origin p. 143 note 45
Zodiacal pictures 79, 126, 132, 154, 166, 186, p. 221 note 101, 281
Zoroaster, king of Arabia, mentioned as being one of prisoners of Feirefis 261
Zurzach, locus reverentissimus, a Nunnery, centre of worship of St Verene, bequeathed by Charles III to St Richardis 881 p. 22 note 22, 25, 27

Genealogical Tables

Genealogical table to make clear the relations

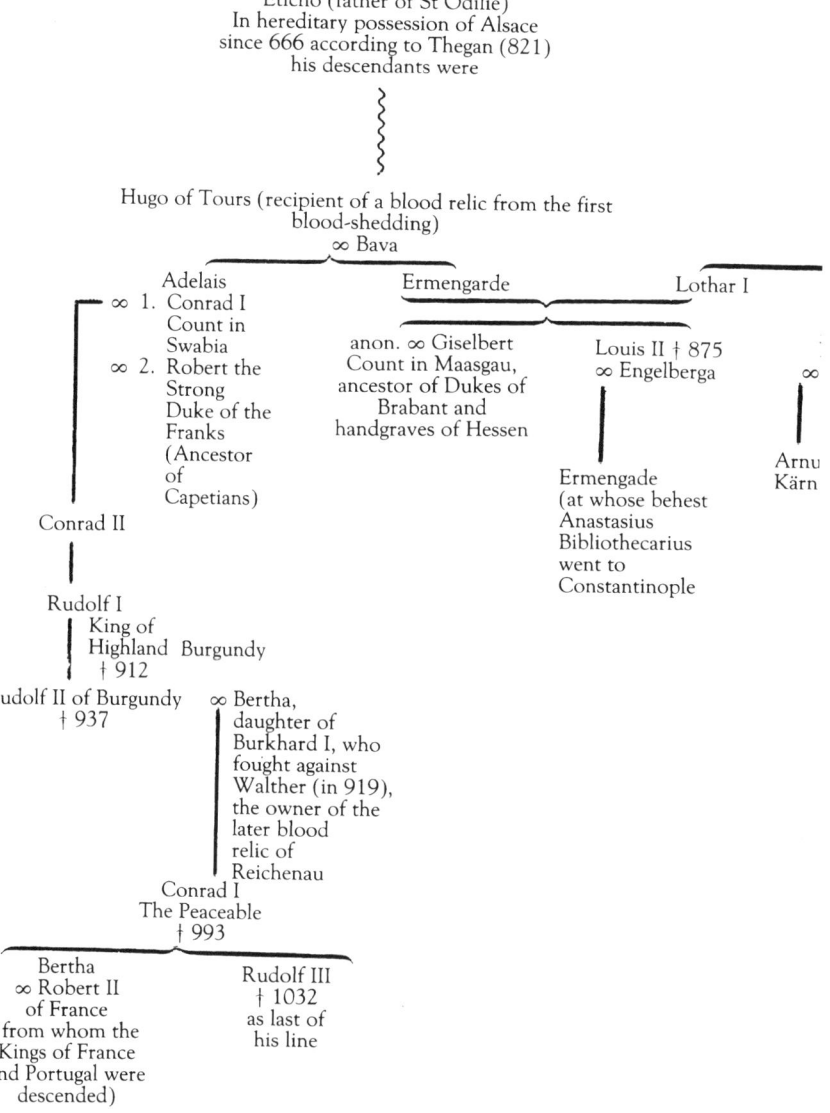

I am indebted to Dr Ernst Müller of Leipzig for much of the content of this table.

# of persons connected with the Grail Saga

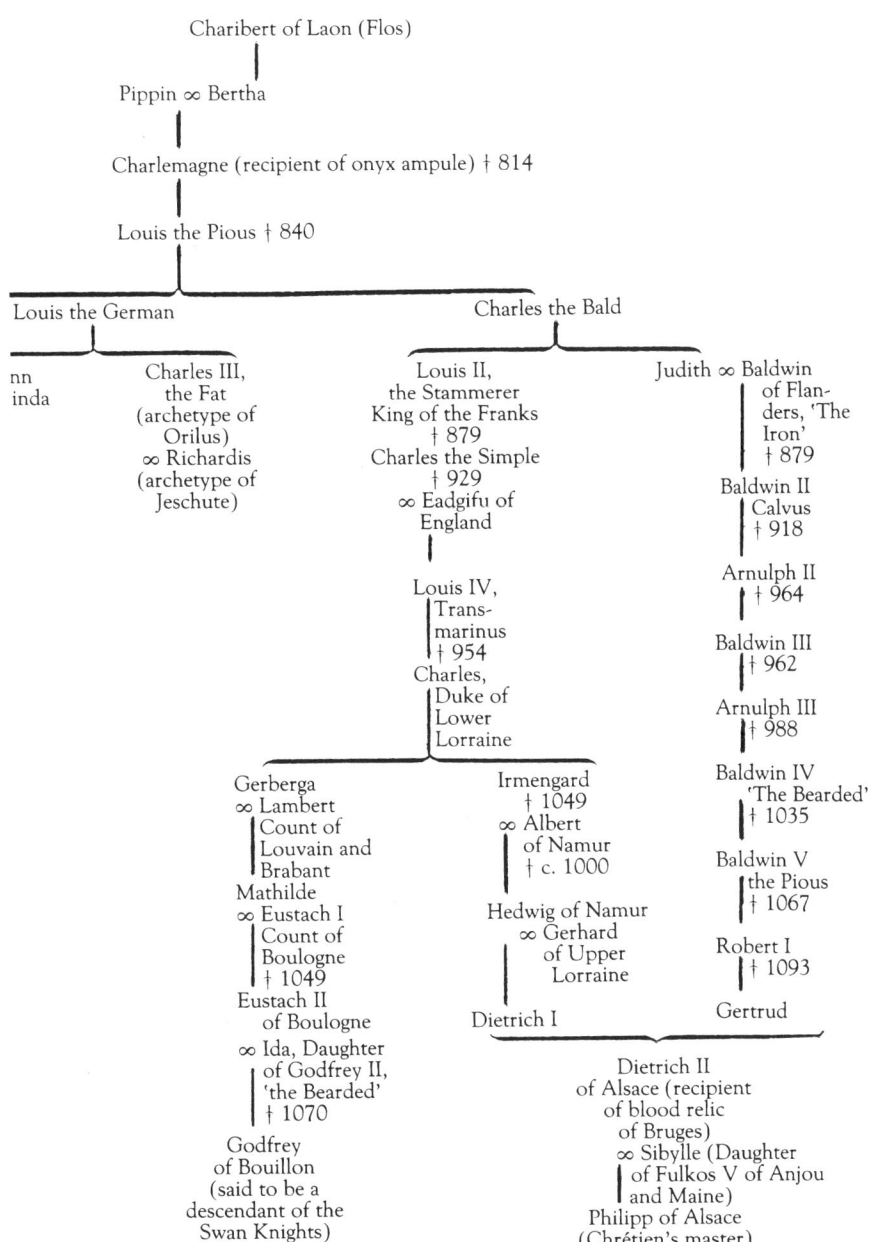

Genealogical table showing relationship o

Parzival's descent from the Grail Guardian fr

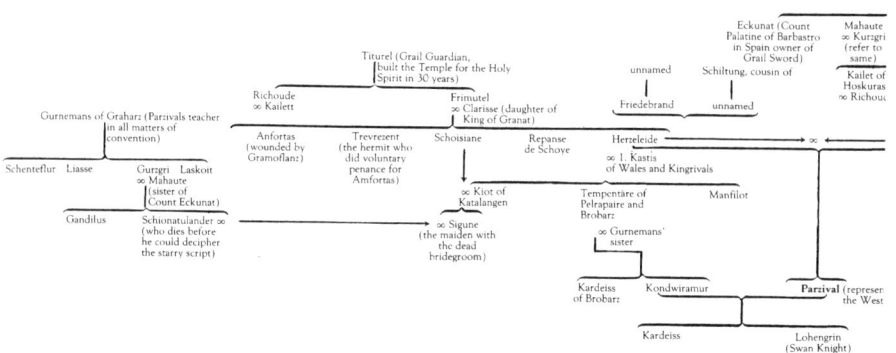

(In the preparation of this table Paul Otto Oldendorff has rendered essential help).

·sonalities from Wolfram's Grail poem.

mother and from Cain from his father

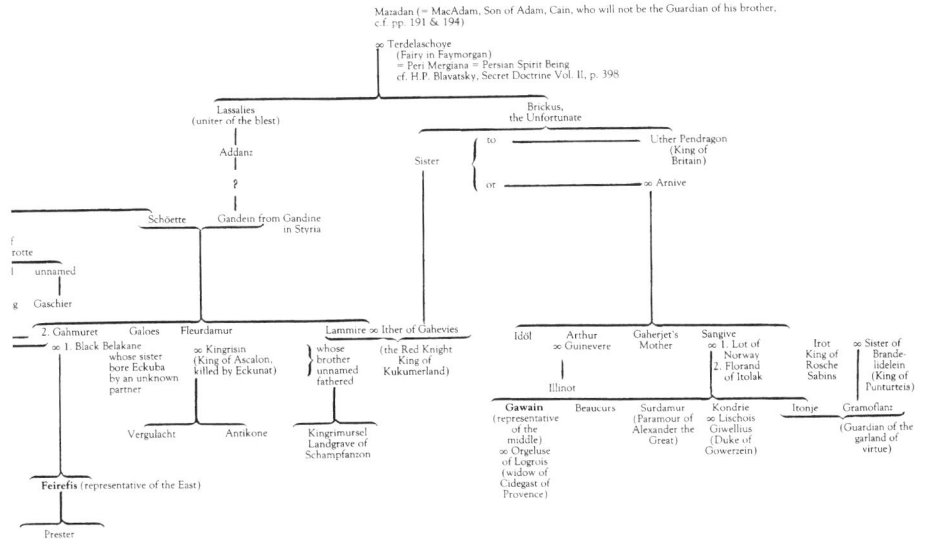